The Politics of Information in Early Modern Europe

The invention and spread of newspapers in the seventeenth century had a profound effect on early modern European culture and politics. The European pattern for the delivery and consumption of political information provided the model for the rest of the world. However, the transition to printed news was neither rapid nor easy and a greater circulation of news had widely varying effects.

Recent research has revealed much about the origins and development of news publishing in each of its European settings. This book is the first to bring this research together in a comprehensive survey. The international contributors to this volume study all of the most important information markets in Europe. Topics covered include:

- the relation between printed and manuscript news
- the role of censorship mechanisms
- effects of politics on reading and publishing
- effects of reading on contemporary politics.

What emerges from this research is a new view of political information as an enterprise, and of the products of information as commodities circulating far and wide.

Brendan Dooley, Research Coordinator at the Medici Archive Project, has taught Cultural History and Media History at Harvard University and the University of Chicago. His most recent book is *The Social History of Skepticism: Experience and Doubt in Early Modern Culture*. **Sabrina A. Baron** is Visiting Associate Professor of History in the Department of History at the University of Maryland, Baltimore County. She was previously Visiting Associate Professor in History at George Washington University and a Fulbright Lecturer in World History at Tirana University in Albania.

Routledge Studies in Cultural History

1. **The Politics of Information in Early Modern Europe**
   Edited by Brendan Dooley and Sabrina A. Baron

The Politics of Information in Early Modern Europe

Edited by Brendan Dooley and Sabrina A. Baron

London and New York

First published 2001
by Routledge
2 Park Square, Milton Park, Abingdon, Oxon, OX14 4RN

Simultaneously published in the USA and Canada
by Routledge
270 Madison Ave, New York NY 10016

Routledge is an imprint of the Taylor & Francis Group

Transferred to Digital Printing 2006

Typeset in Baskerville by Taylor & Francis Books Ltd

British Library Cataloguing in Publication Data
A catalogue record for this book is available from the British Library

Library of Congress Cataloging in Publication Data
The politics of information in early modern Europe/edited by Brendan Dooley and Sabrina A. Baron.
Includes bibliographical references and index.
Contents: Eyes, ears, news, and plays/Stuart Sherman – Manuscript news/printed news : the two faces of dissemination in early seventeenth-century England/Sabrina A. Baron – News and pamphlet culture of mid-seventeenth-century England/Michael Mendle – News, history, and the construction of the present in early modern England/Daniel Woolf – The origins of the German press/Thomas Schröder – Newspapers in the Netherlands/Otto Lankhorst – Instruments of political information in France/Jean-Pierre Vittu – Policy and publishing in the Habsburg Netherlands/Paul Arblaster – Politics and press in Spain/Henry Ettinghausen – The war, the news, and the curious : Italian Military gazettes during the Holy League/Mario Infelise – The politics of information in seventeenth-century Scandinavia/Paul Ries – News and doubt in early modern culture/Brendan Dooley.
1. Press and politics–Europe–History–17th century. I. Dooley, Brendan Maurice, 1953– II. Baron, Sabrina A., 1959–.
PN4751 .P62 2001
070.4'449324'09409032–dc21 00-059231

ISBN 0–415–20310–4

Printed and bound by CPI Antony Rowe, Eastbourne

Contents

Contributors

Paul Arblaster teaches in the Literature Department of the Katholiek Universiteit, Leuven, Belgium and recently finished his Ph.D. at Oxford University wth a thesis on the newspapers of the Low Countries. Forthcoming publications include contributions to *A European Court in Brussels: Albert and Isabella, 1599–1621.*

Sabrina A. Baron teaches in the History Department at University of Maryland, Baltimore County. She has published essays on seventeenth-century English history and is completing a book on licensing for the press in early seventeenth-century England.

Brendan Dooley, Research Coordinator at the Medici Archive Project, has taught in the History Department at Harvard University. His publications include *Science, Politics and Society: The 'Giornale de' letterati d'Italia' and its World* (Garland, 1991), *Italy in the Baroque: Selected Readings* (Garland, 1995), and articles in numerous journals, including *Annales. Histoire, Sciences Sociales, Rivista storica italiana, Journal of Modern History, European History Quarterly, Journal of the History of Ideas, Società e storia* and *Révue d'histoire moderne et contemporaine.*

Henry Ettinghausen teaches in the Department of Spanish, Portuguese and Latin American Studies at the University of Southampton. He is the editor of *La Guerra dels Segadors a través de la premsa de l'epoca* (Curial, 1993) and *Noticias del siglo XVII: relaciones de sucesos naturales y sobrenaturales* (Puvill, 1995). In addition, he has published articles in *European History Quarterly, Etad de Oro* and *Anthropos.*

Mario Infelise teaches at the University of Venice. He is the author of *L'Editoria veneziana nel Settecento* (Angeli, 1989); *I Remondini di Bassano: stampa e industria nel Veneto del Settecento* (Tassotti, 1980). He has also edited, with Paola Marini, *L'Editoria del '700 e i Remondini: atti del Convegno, Bassano, 28–29 settembre 1990* (Ghedina & Tassotti, 1992) and *Remondini, un editore del Settecento* (Electa, 1990).

Otto Lankhorst works for the University Library of Nijmegen (the Netherlands). His publications include *Reinier Leers, 1654–1714, uitgever & boekverkoper te Rotterdam: een Europees 'libraire' en zijn fonds* (APA-Holland Universiteits Pers, 1983); with H.H.M. van Lieshout, *Eleven Catalogues by Reiner Leers, 1692–1709:*

a Reproduction (HES Publishers, 1992); with Jan Roes, *De Gezegende pers: aspecten van de katholieke persgeschiedenis in Nederland tijdens de 19de en 20ste eeuw onder redactie van Mechteld de Coo-Wijgerinck* (Kerckebosch, 1989); and, with P.G. Hoftijzer, *Drukkers, boekverkopers en lezers in Nederland tijdens de Republiek: een historiografische en bibliografische handleiding* (Sdu Uitgevers, 1995).

Michael Mendle teaches at the University of Alabama. His books include *Dangerous Positions: Mixed Government, the Estates of the Realm, and the Making of the Answer to the XIX Propositions* (University of Alabama Press, 1985) and *Henry Parker and the English Civil War: The Political Thought of the Public's Privado* (Cambridge University Press, 1995).

Paul Ries is a fellow of Darwin College, Cambridge, and has held a lectureship in the faculty of Modern and Medieval Languages at Cambridge. He is currently working on an edition of *Den Danske Mercurius, 1666–77.*

Thomas Schröder teaches in the Neuphilologische Fakultät of the University of Tübingen. He is the author of *Die ersten Zeitungen: Textgestaltung und Nachrichtenauswahl* (G. Narr, 1995).

Stuart Sherman teaches at Fordham University. His publications include *Telling Time: Clocks, Diaries, and English Diurnal Form, 1660–1785* (University of Chicago Press, 1996).

Jean-Pierre Vittu teaches at the University of Orleans, France. He is the editor, with Henriette Asséo, of *Problèmes socio-culturels en France au XVIIème siècle* (Paris, 1974), and has published articles in *Révue d'histoire moderne et contemporaine, Dix-huitième siècle, Studies on Voltaire and the Eighteenth Century, Les Cahiers de Tunisie, IBLA (Tunis)*, as well as in many collections of essays.

Daniel Woolf teaches in the Faculty of Humanities at McMaster University, Canada. He is the author of *The Idea of History in Early Stuart England: Erudition, Ideology, and 'The Light of Truth' from the Accession of James I to the Civil War* (University of Toronto Press, 1990). He has also edited, with John Morrill and Paul Slack, *Public Duty and Private Conscience in Seventeenth-Century England: Essays Presented to G.E. Aylmer* (Clarendon Press, 1993); and, with Thomas Mayer, *The Rhetorics of Life-Writing in Early Modern Europe: Forms of Biography from Cassandra Fedele to Louis XIV* (University of Michigan Press, 1995)

Introduction

Brendan Dooley

Information: the very term itself seems to suggest electronic blips on a computer screen rather than quill pens; or the soft click of fingers on a keyboard rather than the heavy pounding of the hand press. Instead of renouncing the term in this book, however, we surround it with qualifications. And we call political information whatever may be thought or said about events connected with the government of states and with cities and their peoples. The fresher it was, the more it deserved to be called 'news.' Can opinion be information? It can, no less than information may be opinion. The interchangeability of the terms is part of politics. And information concerning politics, politics concerning information: these expressions, in brief, define our subject matter. In bringing together a kaleidoscopic sampling of what recent scholarship has discovered about the first century of news, we hope to make a unique interdisciplinary contribution to a growing field.

The contributors to this book reflect the culmination of twenty years of media studies that have finally begun investigating seventeenth-century political information from a historical point of view. We recognize our debt to the many scholars on both sides of the Atlantic who have made our work possible. As historians of the book, we are riding the crest of the wave first made by Henri-Jean Martin, Elizabeth Eisenstein, Roger Chartier and Robert Darnton, among others.[1] As media historians we have benefited from the efforts of Jeremy Popkin, C. John Sommerville, Joad Raymond, Michael Harris, Jean Sgard, Pierre Retat and many more.[2] What both of these disciplines can offer in a broad comparative context we hope our readers will discover in this volume.

Indeed, the seventeenth century has been called many things: an age of genius, an age of gold, an age of Galileo; a century of revolution, a century of challenge, a century of change. Our book in no way seeks to steal from it any of the glory accruing from the accomplishments that have earned it such striking characterizations. Rather than subtracting from the current picture of the age, if anything, we hope to add to it one more feature. By bringing the creation of a political information business closer to the centre of early modern urban life, where it was experienced at the time, we hope to illuminate an aspect that only blunted hindsight has been able to obscure – an age of nascent information media, a century of emerging public opinion.

We have attempted to join investigations of the commercial aspects of the diffusion of information with its political ramifications in a way that reflects the perceptions of people in the period. Samuel Butler was not the only writer to notice that news writing had become a business, although perhaps he said it most pithily. 'A news-monger,' he claimed,

> is a retailer of rumour, that takes upon trust and sells as cheap as he buys. He deals in a perishable commodity, that will not keep; for if it be not fresh it lies upon his hands, and will yield nothing. True or false is all one to him; for novelty being the grace of both, a truth goes stale as soon as a lie. ... He is little concerned whether it be good or bad, for that does not make it more or less news; and, if there be any difference, he loves the bad best, because it is said to come soonest; for he would willingly bear his share in any public calamity, to have the pleasure of hearing and telling it.[3]

To what Butler noticed about the venality of news writers, the libertine earl of Rochester, John Wilmot, added this concerning the monotony of their accounts: 'The world, ever since I can remember, has been still so insupportably the same, that 'twere vain to hope for any alterations. Therefore I can have no curiosity for news.'[4] However, the press and popular criticism in the seventeenth century did little to dampen the enthusiasm of readers for what was fast becoming one of the most widely read written genres. The politics-obsessed upholsterer described by Joseph Addison in a famous number of *The Tatler*, recalled below by Daniel Woolf, was no doubt only one of many tradesmen who, by the early eighteenth century, wasted life and livelihood in the anxious pursuit of world-class ephemera. [5]

Nor was England the only place where the avalanche of material available to excite the interest of the curious concerning the political realities of the time, by the turn of the seventeenth century, was viewed with considerable diffidence. Wailed a Paduan pamphleteer:

> You who after silly tales are lusting,
> Anxious to hear rumours and reports,
> Quickly run and look at the gazettes,
> And see if the news is good, fine, or disgusting. [6]

In Germany, meanwhile, Johann Ludwig Hartmann complained about: 'The pleasure which many people derive / from relishing to hear something new.' [7] And in Rotterdam, Pierre Bayle inveighed against what he took to be the deliberate inaccuracies in the Continental press. In Italy, as Brendan Dooley suggests in Chapter 12, at least some observers wondered whether there was any likelihood of getting a secure grip on political reality at all.

Of course, political information had existed long before the seventeenth century. Few were the Renaissance princes who did not seek to establish diplomatic ties with other princes by way of the written word – the substance of which, indeed, was just as likely to leak into the public forum then as it was later on.[8] Few again were the prominent merchants who did not communicate regularly by letters to their representatives, their dealers and their customers; and these communications were just as likely to contain the latest political news as the latest economic news.[9] Regular newsletters already began to circulate in Europe by the second half of the sixteenth century. And political information, in one form or another, was one of the earliest products of the printing press.

The development of states and economies across the seventeenth century put the political information business on an entirely new footing. Writers and distributors were more and more often connected, either as employees or as clients, with the mechanisms being used by rulers in the struggle to achieve some measure of central control – from diplomatic corps to postal bureaux to notarial and judicial colleges. Episodes connected with the building of the new state structures made more and more news: wars, rebellions, changes of rule and the day-to-day exercise of authority.[10] Commercial considerations were at least as important as political ones in the creation of the first public mail routes in the late sixteenth century by a fruitful collaboration between private firms and the governments of Europe.[11] These routes were essential to the propagation of regular newsletters that were often the bases for printed newspapers.

Wherever they emerged, the products of the new political information business were as unprecedented in quantity as they were various in kind.[12] Manuscript newsletters and printed handbills, occasional newsbooks and printed newspapers, poetry and prose; there seems to be no reason not to refer to this material as the journalism of the time. Whatever we may call it, from accounts of the works and days of powerful rulers to portrayals of this or that authority in this or that embarrassing situation; from descriptions of battles and sieges to descriptions of weddings and funerals; from comments on the latest grain prices to comments on the latest plague regulations, the business of political information diffused the stories that obsessed early modern minds.

Among officials more or less close to governments, the widening sphere of political discussion occasioned by the circulation of information excited not amazement but fear. According to Paolo Sarpi, adviser to the Venetian senate, secrecy was the best policy.[13] And if information got out, the Bolognese printmaker Giuseppe Mitelli illustrated what might happen. In his famous 1690 print dedicated 'To the War-Obsessed,' a man in spectacles sits on a stump in a city street reading aloud from a newspaper. Around him characters from different social levels and occupations listen in. One cries, 'It cannot be!' another insists, 'Yes it is!' In a corner of the print, a Frenchman and a Spaniard exchange blows, obviously the subject of the story. As they fight and tear at each other's hair, yet another bystander comments, 'Oh what folly!' as if to reprove the folly of governments that drag their peoples into useless warfare.[14]

According to the notorious Milanese adventurer and heretic Gregorio Leti, discussion and contention ought to be encouraged, and it was only a matter of time before it began to focus on the authorities themselves. In fact, only fifteen years after John Milton's plea for freedom of the press in *Areopagitica*, Leti noted that the very texture of politics was about to change:

> Tyrants used to do evil with the assurance that their actions would be recognized, or, indeed, revered by the people as being good perforce. Another system is now in place. And however bad princes are, even if inclined to evil by their nature, they never dare to perform tyrannical actions, because they see their peoples ready with their tongues wagging to inseminate throughout the streets and squares the poison of discord that can turn monarchies into republics. [15]

This was a frightening prospect for most rulers. Indeed, in order to 'diminish the usual reverence expected from the obedience of a people,' Leti concluded, just 'talking about their actions from dawn to dusk' was sufficient.

Among governments and entrepreneurs alike, a powerful reminder of what might become an extraordinarily effective way of stirring passions and steering interests was the use of the printed word in times of civil unrest. The case of England, analysed here by Michael Mendle, was emblematic. There, the calling of the Long Parliament was followed by a season of political publishing unmatched anywhere else. From reports on speeches made by major figures during the parliamentary debates to reports on sermons by important dissident preachers, to advertisements for petitioning drives, the press provided a relentless account of the points of contention as they began to mount. For the principal grievances against the monarchy, the printed version of the *Grand Remonstrance* served as powerful propaganda. A war of words accompanied the war on persons in press accounts on both sides and in the lurid descriptions of every show trial and execution before the Commonwealth was born.

Yet the revolutionary potential of the press was felt elsewhere as well – and not only in France, where a 'Fronde of words,' many of them printed on clandestine presses, accompanied the Fronde of the parlements. In Naples, Masaniello and his followers were reputedly inspired, in their protest against the Spanish government's fiscal policies, by the circulation of information about a previous rebellion in Palermo. Once they achieved mastery of the city, they turned to news about Holland for examples of a new form of republican government. While they debated about the organization of the government, their supporters stoked the passions of Neapolitans by printed pronouncements and pamphlets, which were duly refuted by similar productions by Spanish sympathizers.[16]

Generator of fear and incitement to enthusiasm, the political information business was hard for contemporaries to ignore; and it has become increasingly hard for modern historians to ignore. We have attempted to join investigations of the commercial aspects of the diffusion of information with the political ramifications in a way that reflects the perceptions of people in the period. However, no simple approach to understanding it seems ready at hand. A dry listing of titles simply will not do, however well-accoutred with bibliographical descriptions, variations by copy and edition, and locations where examples may be found. Of such tools we now have many.[17] We recognize their indispensability and encourage their proliferation. But they offer no clearer insights into the day to day making and use of political information now than they did when they were first begun. An analysis of the contents of the products of the press alone will not suffice either, no matter how detailed, how well informed by the criteria of modern literary criticism, or how large the database. For all the precious insights such studies may offer concerning the structure of texts, by themselves they provide no clear indications concerning the structures of production and reception.[18] And in order to see how the political information business affected early modern society, a deeper knowledge of production and reception is absolutely indispensable. For similar reasons, biographical anecdotes of the early heroes of the political information business will not suffice either, however well-founded in archival documentation.[19] Although such research must lie at the basis of any history of the information business, we also need to know exactly how these individuals were situated in their political, cultural and economic worlds. However much we may learn about the publishing history of political information, or its legal history,[20] these are also not enough. Indeed, some combination of all these approaches is clearly appropriate, and the contributors to this book utilize each of them in various ways.

For in situating our monographic research into a wider context, many grand narratives are there for us to choose. None of the ones that have recently come in or out of vogue seems entirely adequate. Searching for the genesis of the modern information industry makes no more sense than judging the accuracy of reporting according to modern criteria – for better or for worse.[21] Such an approach runs the risk of missing the uniqueness of what Thomas Schröder, in chapter 5, calls the 'media landscape' of the seventeenth century, and focusing only on the features that would later achieve importance rather than on all the features that were there. Viewing this history in terms of the formation of modern methods of behaviour modification makes no more sense than viewing seventeenth-century absolute monarchies as versions of modern police states. Such an approach fails to account for the significant differences between technological capacities then and now, just as it fails to account for significant gaps between the theory of absolutism and its actual practice.[22]

Viewing this history exclusively in terms of the emancipatory potential of the press makes no more sense than viewing the seventeenth-century revolts and revolutions as in some way precursors to the French Revolution.[23] Such an approach runs the risk of attributing purposes that our protagonists could never have had; and even supposing the operation of a law of unintended consequences over the long term, such an approach runs counter to a number of current social sciences assumptions about what political information can do in any age. Outside the realms of media historiography and journalism education *per se*, any statements about the formation of an enlightened public opinion are customarily taken with a healthy dose of scepticism. Those theorists who have not altogether given up on the possibility of forming a workable model for the relationship between information, opinion, political institutions and the psyche, have suggested that genetics and family life must be given equal weight with anything communicated by the media.[24] And those who do not reject outright the notion that a truly free press is possible in a democracy – whatever we might mean by these terms – have suggested that diffidence concerning public opinion has driven modern governments into practices of secrecy so carefully guarded that they differ from their old regime counterparts only in degree.

Some recent press historians searching for an antidote to the emancipatory view of the press have looked to general systems theory.[25] The connection with our subject may seem somewhat remote. But like the biological systems that are the models for this theory, all societies, we must agree, need ties binding individuals to one another and to the past and future. Furthermore, societies must continue to modify their responses to stimuli on the basis of new information. And new information is constantly incorporated into the society and made part of its self-reproduction. Journalism and the press might play an obvious role here, not necessarily an emancipatory one. Liberal outcomes are by no means guaranteed; nor are peaceful ones. Taking the longest possible view, whatever to us may appear violent, destructive or irrational may from society's standpoint merely be a passing phase or even a means of self-adjustment or of collecting forces to reinforce network ties within the system. As the society develops there is no telling what institutions might come and go. Nor is there any telling in advance which may be more adapted for the ever-increasing complexity that seems to the systems theorists to be the society's real goal.

An advantage of this approach is that it promises to take account of more of the contents of the products of political information than ever before. Since virtually anything could be construed as providing the social process with the basis for new reactions to environmental stimuli, all aspects of the media are equally important. Furthermore, it treats all kinds of information in the same way, as playing the same role, so it promises to avoid socioculturally-determined preferences for a particular type of political discourse.[26]

Combining an emancipatory view with a systems view in the light of modern psychology, at least in his later work, Jürgen Habermas has suggested that improved communication dissolves the bars of the iron cage of social structures that imprisons the human personality. As the social world in which individuals live becomes more and more complex, he argues, things get done in a more and more bureaucratized and impersonal fashion. Social actions that used to be steered by personal negotiation and contestation of validity claims by actors are now steered by non-linguistic forms of communication in terms of money and power. When verbal communication drops out in this way, irrational results are possible. However, Habermas' contention that the free flow of communication in an unregulated public sphere can bring rationality back has not gone without opposition. According to John Rawls, discussions regarding the public realm, as distinguished from the private realm of the family and civil society, must be subjected to the limitations imposed by the accepted beliefs and criteria of evidence generally accepted as the 'public reason' of the given society.[27]

As relevant to the press in the seventeenth century is some earlier work by Habermas tracing the historical development of the public sphere.[28] In his view, public discourse at first served mainly to represent and reinforce the position of the ruling classes. The validity of assertions was determined by status, not by argument. With the consolidation of commercial capitalism and the formation of a bourgeoisie, family life came to be differentiated and recognized as an independent world. Eventually, the sphere belonging to private individuals and their families began to take on public characteristics of its own. New channels of communication opened up, at first in England and later elsewhere. In private gathering places – coffee houses, salons – private individuals came together to form an alternative public sphere where validity claims could be discussed without reference to status. Meanwhile, a public conscience in opposition to public authority began to emerge, as literary figures began to appeal to the tastes of wider audiences and to criticize the courts. Literary journals were formed, and so also eventually were journals concerned with private life. While a new sphere began to open up to private individuals, the ruling classes began to treat their subjects as a 'public' by publicizing decrees and actions in newspapers and propaganda pamphlets. Finally, state power came to be seen and contended for, in print and everywhere else, as a means for economic advancement, and the bourgeois public sphere came into its own. Although evidence for the full emergence of a new public sphere is difficult to find in any of the countries examined by our contributors, we can scarcely avoid concluding, with Schröder here, that the invention of new mechanisms for the diffusion of information everywhere provided the basis on which a new public sphere could be constructed in the future.[29]

The contributors to this book are well aware that modern theories of communication can only be applied to the press in our period while keeping in mind the difference between a mass medium and a medium widely differentiated for consumption by specific social groups; between modern literacy rates and early modern ones.[30] Except where written information was accompanied by word of mouth, 'all Rome' was never any more saturated with a story than was 'all Paris.' A veritable 'public opinion' in the sense enshrined in early twentieth-century sociology is nowhere to be found. What people knew about affairs within the corridors of power depended upon who they were. A lawyer or a doctor was likely to be better informed than a butcher or a baker. What they knew also depended on where they were; and not all cities were alike. Paris was better served by information than was, for example, Strasbourg. The strands of urban Europe reached thinly from centre to centre across vast stretches of landscape, where the political environment seemed far less crucial than the natural environment to the daily practices of existence. And even though the passage of troops from one battle to the next, just as the movement of prices between boom and bust, could intrude profoundly into an otherwise self-contained and autarchic village culture, nevertheless, political knowledge and intelligence extended unevenly and with great difficulty beyond the great demographic concentrations.

We are also aware of the many other roles the political information business of the seventeenth century may have played besides its emancipatory one. In Venice, for instance, as Mario Infelise shows in chapter 10, it played a powerful role in reinforcing a European, Christian, indeed, Venetian identity, in contrast to the military enemy, the Ottoman Turks. Victories were viewed as successes by a Christian people; defeats as victories by an alien assailant. The enthusiasm of Venetian crowds for the cause could be measured by the celebrations and festivities mounted on the occasion of the arrival of every piece of good news. And their indignation against those who did not share their religion, their country or their views, could be measured in their attacks on the Jewish ghetto when Christianity's fortunes seemed to be on the rise.

In this period, political information came to be bought and sold in appreciable quantities for the first time. The distribution of such knowledge and intelligence became a definite trade, while the mechanisms for this distribution slowly evolved. Our contributors trace the way in which the information business created networks between one part of Western Europe and another. The earliest Dutch corantos were quickly translated and circulated in England, while manuscript pamphlets originating in England were subsequently printed in Holland, as Sabrina Baron shows in chapter 2. Some Dutch newspapers were printed expressly for distribution in France (see Otto Lankhorst, chapter 6). Danish and Swedish newspapers relied heavily for information on their German counterparts (see Paul Ries, chapter 11). The war journals of Venice drew upon manuscript and printed sources originating in Vienna (see Infelise). Stories, retold and embellished, could eventually travel the length and breadth of the Continent, as information unified the capitals of Europe for the first time.

The results of this commerce now appear to have been as far removed from easy assumptions about the role of information in society as the structures for its production were from later and more familiar ones. Our contributors, while paying due attention to the history of the spread of information and its repercussions, have considered ways in which their results add to our knowledge of the history of everyday life, the history of commodities and the history of mentalities. Information sharpened conflicts; it furnished new venues for symbolic interaction of every type. It even inspired a category of thought about itself, in terms of the earliest what we might call media theory. And last but not least, as Daniel Woolf notes in chapter 4, it helped form a modern conception of time.

Although this book makes no attempt to provide a synthetic narrative of seventeenth-century political information, some of the basic structures that could be put at the service of such a narrative clearly come into view. Everywhere in Europe, in the late sixteenth century, the 'media landscape' bears certain similar features. In each country, a well-developed network of semi-private newsletters was accompanied by printed publications devoted to single events, political handbills, political poetry, commentary and engravings. Everywhere in Europe, in the first decades of the seventeenth century, the number and variety of journalistic publications experienced a notable increase.

And again, everywhere in Europe, printed newspapers emerged. With varying intensity and regularity from place to place, by the end of the seventeenth century, newspapers had become the method *par excellence* for conveying political information.

The chapters here, read chronologically, give an overview of all the stages during the period of the seventeenth century. After Schröder's account of the first newspapers in Germany, we move to England, where manuscript and printed news, as analysed by Sabrina Baron, was giving the first accounts of the reign of James VI and I and the early reign of Charles I. This is followed by France, by Jean-Pierre Vittu, where Théophraste Renaudot's much-imitated gazette took off in the 1630s. In the same period, the press in the Spanish Netherlands began a period of considerable independence from Spain, Paul Arblaster shows, as control over censorship mechanisms passed from Spanish authorities to local ones. And just when the pro-government press in Spain itself, illustrated by Henry Ettinghausen, was moving into full swing, in England, the Civil War introduced one of the liveliest periods of press experience in any country, as described by Michael Mendle. Newspapers in German existed from an early date in Scandinavia, as Paul Ries shows; but the first Swedish-language example began in 1643, followed over two decades later by the first one in Danish – in verse. Finally, in the 1680s in Venice, described by Infelise, a veritable news frenzy began, fed by popular enthusiasm about the Turkish Wars following the liberation of Vienna.

Our contributors place us on the scene of reporting in a host of extraordinary circumstances. We may thus better imagine what contemporaries might have learned about the succession crisis of Jülich and Cleves or the struggle between the Emperor Matthias and the Viennese Estates on the eve of the Thirty Years' War (Schröder). We hear the echoes in the Spanish Netherlands press of the Spanish military losses of the 1630s (Arblaster), in the English newsletters of the war in the Palatinate in the same period (Baron), and in the Venetian press of the military victories in Greece in the 1680s (Infelise). We too become witnesses to the verbal battles between king and Parliament in the English Civil War, and to General Monck's 'press releases' (as Mendle calls them) in 1660. And our credulity, too, is tested by reports of the thirty-five demons who apparently descended upon the town of Castro in the summer of 1613, and to the monster with thirty-three eyes who spoke to a crowd in Latin in Bayonne in the same year to warn of upcoming disasters (Ettinghausen).

We show how a story became news – from the first recording of an event by an eyewitness to its eventual distribution in a newsletter or printed work (Baron, Mendle, Infelise). Postmasters often played an important role, not only as retailers of rumour, in a very literal sense, but as licensed importers of printed news – as Paul Ries shows. What reports a writer or entrepreneur chose to transform into news for the benefit of his customers depended upon his own inclinations, or, in many cases, upon the authorities involved. Also in Ries' contribution, we find our way into an early modern press room, to consider the physical limitations placed on the reproduction of news by what Roger Chartier has called the Typographical Old Regime.

Along the way, our contributors reveal a veritable gallery of news entrepreneurs, set in their appropriate contexts. One would be hard put to invent a better example than Marchamont Nedham in London, who, as Mendle shows, started out his news-writing career as a fiercely pro-Parliament writer at the beginning of the Civil War, only to switch to the king's side in 1647, and again to Cromwell's side during the Protectorate, managing, like the Vicar of Bray, to hold on to his living through the political vicissitudes of his time. In shrewdness he was only equalled by Andreas de Amansar y Mendoza (Ettinghausen), who provided deliberately negative accounts of the reign of Philip III in order to make the next reign seem all the more glorious. The rambunctious side of journalism is typified by John Pory, whose fondness for gossip was almost as legendary as his fondness for drink – as Sabrina Baron shows. The respectable side is typified by the Widow Graet in Antwerp, described by Arblaster, who took over her husband's business and became the first successful publisher of a Flemish-language newspaper in her city.

The portrait gallery extends to an equally remarkable collection of news readers. For Richard Davies, dean of Ross, who visited the English coffee houses in the late seventeenth century, was by no means the only reader who wrote down his impressions about what he heard being read. There was also the country physician Claver Morris, who hearkened to news about France in the early eighteenth century. And if any reader came close to the obsessive compulsiveness of Addison's famous upholstery maker, this was certainly Henry Prescott in the same period, who read everything he could about foreign affairs and recorded it in his voluminous diary. Of course, not all readers came away from their readings with the sensation of having been instructed or even entertained. Daniel Defoe's dismay about the untruthfulness of news was exactly matched by Sarah Cowper. Nor was England (as shown in these examples from Woolf) the only place where the reproduction of news was viewed with a jaundiced eye. And besides Pierre Bayle, who criticized the French-language newspapers that arrived in Rotterdam, we meet Lorenzo Magalotti, who (Dooley shows) criticized any news publications at all that arrived in Florence.

In the course of the century, news created new categories of thought about itself. Not only were the new media (according to Dooley) among the most constant topics of discussion in the new media. Early on, the newsmonger became a recognizable figure in literature; and the figure in Ben Jonson's play, *The Staple of News*, discussed by Stuart Sherman, was matched later in the century in the drama of Ludwig Holberg noted by Paul Ries. Myths about the sale and use of news began to develop, as opinions about its usefulness or uselessness began to form. At the same time, news contributed (argues Woolf) to the emergence of an on-going sense of the present, of contemporaneity, of many people living the same moment, as distinguished from a sense of history, entombed in the past. Such a conceptualization helped form the basis for the novelist's notion of time.

Our contributors reveal important variations from place to place. In Germany, for instance, single edition political reports emerged at a very early date: 1488, according to Schröder's account. Here, too, a monthly format emerged as early as 1598, providing the model for the weekly papers that were soon to appear. In Spain, Ettinghausen points out, gazettes appeared very late, but the single edition press was voluminous quite early on. And while monarchical absolutism in France very nearly succeeded in limiting the production of printed news to a few privileged suppliers in the capital, as Vittu shows, monarchical absolutism in the Spanish Netherlands, Arblaster suggests, never really imposed effective central control.

Particularly significant differences can be detected between England and the Continent. With over 350 titles of news publications of all kinds appearing in the period from 1641 to 1659 alone, the unparalleled vitality of the English media landscape is impossible to ignore. Here, twenty years of interregnum threw censorship into such utter disarray that certain periods seemed to be entirely free from it. Political information and commentary could therefore circulate almost without limitation. Again, with the lapse of the 1662 Licensing Act in 1679, there began a period of relative press liberty, checked only by the libel laws. In England, furthermore, literacy rates were perhaps the highest in Europe. So the possibilities of abundant production opened up by the peculiar censorship situation were matched by a wide potential market; and the press was able to wield a political power far greater than in any other place. In France, by contrast, censorship mechanisms operated almost without interruption throughout the seventeenth century, and royal control over the book industry actually increased. Here writers and entrepreneurs depended much more on the patronage of the king and nobility than upon a growing public. Here monopolies on certain kinds of information regulated the flow. And here an officially sponsored gazette was the major source of information.

However, the argument about English exceptionalism should not be carried too far. London, where the book industry was almost entirely centred, was not England; nor was Londoners' passion for the printed word matched in other cities, if we consider that printers in Norwich were occasionally reduced to selling groceries.[31] Furthermore, literacy rates akin to English ones were reached in some Dutch, German and Italian cities as well. As far as publications critical of the regime were concerned, England was obviously not alone. Even in France, where central control was particularly effective, there flourished a lively clandestine market – both manuscript and printed; and the same went for other areas where absolutism was the reigning theory of government.

Another polarity that emerges from these chapters is between the centralization of the rest of Europe and the relative decentralization of Germany and Italy. In the latter places, the diffusion of new publications, including manuscripts, reflected the same patterns as the widely scattered diffusion of every other sort of publications. These patterns in turn reflected political divisions within these countries. Italy was a crazy quilt of eighteen very different states, from the over-large Kingdom of Naples to the tiny dukedom of Garfagnana. In

Germany, political differences, which included the dichotomy between free Imperial cities like Emden and cities belonging to one or the other of the larger states, such as Munich, were accompanied by further divisions along religious lines. In France, by contrast, publication was unquestionably centred in Paris, and provincial presses often merely produced reprints of the Paris gazette.

A final polarity was observable between the states at the core of Europe and those at the periphery. None of our contributors has considered, say, the Polish information press or that of Hungary – for good reasons. In the seventeenth century there was little to speak of in terms of news publication in these areas. Printing had gone on in Hungary since the beginning; and some scholarship (surely with exaggeration) claims King Mathias' *Dracola Waida* (1485) as the first newspaper.[32] However, by the seventeenth century, no such initiatives existed, or, if they did, not a trace has survived. In Poland, too, printing emerged very early on, and continued, especially in Krakow, throughout our period.[33] But the *Polish Mercury* begun in Krakow and Warsaw in 1661 was an isolated venture of its kind and failed to find an audience. And if the disastrous depredations of Turk, Cossack and Tatar invasions of Poland, followed by those of the Swedes – the so-called 'Swedish Deluge' – were not sufficient to supply fuel to a political information business, the reason is not hard to find. Here, as in Hungary, the economic boom of the sixteenth century failed to result in urban development comparable to what had been essential to a political information business elsewhere.[34] As late as 1700, only one city, Warsaw, had over 10,000 inhabitants, compared with 22 cities in Spain and 51 in Italy in the same period. The privileged nobility succeeded in restricting the wealth and authority of the towns, while the predominant system of feudal landholding in the countryside retarded the emergence of middling groups of readers.

The Ottoman lands were a case apart. Not only was literacy generally much lower than elsewhere but printing was introduced much later.[35] Even in the larger towns and cities on the borderlands with Europe, where the population was more or less sedentary, impediments to the development of European-style communications networks came from ingrained habits induced by the peculiar form of domination exercised in these countries. A coercion-intensive state and a capillary system of surveillance discouraged the circulation even of handwritten information beyond the inner circles of power. Word of mouth communications therefore continued as the medium of choice, exchanged in the marketplace or perhaps in the many coffee houses that became a fixture of Ottoman life from the late sixteenth century onward.[36]

More than pieces in a larger geographical puzzle, however, the chapters here offer variations on a theme. Each writer has taken the political information business in a special time and place as an opportunity to apply diverse approaches and research methods. Naturally their conclusions differ significantly. Woolf, focusing on the history of mentalities, sees political information as contributing to a common sense of the present. Schröder, by contrast, using predominantly a content-analysis method for the first two German newspapers, notes that, at the beginning of the seventeenth century, the creation of a political present was a long way off. What is more, at least in Germany, he says, the emancipatory potential contained in the structure of the growing industry was far from being realized. Mendle, particularly sensitive to the political problems to which information responded during a period of civil unrest in England, and which it raised in turn, emphasizes its emancipatory effect. Infelise, scouring the archives to unearth the urban micro-structures of an international communications network, finds more importance in the aspects of production than in the effects on its readers. Ettinghausen, impressed with the newspapers' coverage of everyday life, insists on their role in reinforcing the existing political and social situation. Dooley, focusing on intellectual developments, sees it as contributing, in some circles, to a sense of bewilderment.

Rather than pointing to a single conclusion, this book above all shows that the closer we get to the workings of the political information business, in terms of content, production, distribution, and consumption, the more complex our object becomes. We hope these essays will encourage at least as much further reflection on these problems among our colleagues and their students, as the opportunity to present them has given us. If we succeed in demonstrating the usefulness of an interdisciplinary and comparative perspective, we will have attained one of our major goals in this book. And if we succeed in proving that journalism history is an important part of seventeenth-century history, with a specific contribution to make in the areas of politics, social structures and economies, we will have made our main point. We invite the next generation of studies on the early modern world to integrate these insights into the newly emerging picture of the period.

Notes

1 Henri-Jean Martin, *Livre, pouvoirs et société à Paris au 17e siècle*, tr. as *Print, Power, and People in 17th-Century France* (Metuchen, NJ, 1993) by David Gerard; Elizabeth L. Eisenstein, *The Printing Press as an Agent of Change: Communications and Cultural Transformations in Early Modern Europe* (Cambridge, 1979); Roger Chartier, *The Cultural Uses of Print in Early Modern France* (Princeton, 1987), tr. Lydia G. Cochrane; Robert Darnton, *The Literary Underground of the Old Regime* (Cambridge, MA, 1982).

2 Jeremy D. Popkin, *News and Politics in the Age of Revolution: Jean Luzac's Gazette de Leyde* (Ithaca, 1989); C. John Sommerville, *The News Revolution in England: Cultural Dynamics of Daily Information* (Oxford, 1996); Joad Raymond, *The Invention of the Newspaper: English Newsbooks, 1641–1649* (Oxford, 1996); Michael Harris, *London Newspapers in the Age of Walpole: A Study of the Origins of the Modern English Press* (Rutherford, 1987); Jean Sgard, ed., *Dictionnaire des journalistes, 1600–1789* (Grenoble, 1976); Pierre Retat, ed., *L'Attentat de Damiens: discours sur l'événement au XVIIIe siècle* (Paris, 1979).

3 A. R. Waller, ed., *Characters and Passages from Notebooks* (Cambridge, 1908), p. 126.

4 Jeremy Treglown, ed., *The Letters of John Wilmot, Earl of Rochester* (Oxford, 1980), p. 117.

5 *The Tatler*, no. 155.

6 The anonymous Paduan pamphleteer published *Istoria graziosa e piacevole, la quale contiene un bellissimo contrasto, che fà la città di Napoli con la città di Venezia, dove si vede la grandezza e la magnificenza di queste due gran città d'Italia* (Padua, n.d.).

7 Ahasver Fritsch's comments were in his *De Novellarum, quae vocant Neue Zeitungen, hodierno usu et abusu* (Jena: Bielckianis, 1676), n.p.

8 Garrett Mattingly, *Renaissance Diplomacy* (London, 1955), chaps. 10–11.

9 In general, John J. McCusker, *The Beginnings of Commercial and Financial Journalism* (Amsterdam, 1991) and Viktor Klarwill, *The Fugger News-Letters* (New York, 1925–6), 2 vols, tr. Paulina De Chary and Lionel S. R. Byrne.

10 An overview of statebuilding might start with: Charles Tilly, *Coercion, Capital and European States, 900–1990* (Oxford, 1990), as well as Perez Zagorin, *Rebels and Rulers, 1500–1600* (Cambridge, 1982), 2 vols; and Geoffrey Parker, *The Military Revolution. Military Innovation and the Rise of the West* (Cambridge, 1989).

11 Bruno Caizzi, *Dalla posta dei re alla posta di tutti. Territorio e comunicazioni in Italia dal XVI secolo all'Unità* (Milan, 1993), chap. 1.

12 Quantitative data are in Sandro Bulgarelli, *Il giornalismo a Roma nel Seicento* (Rome: Bulzoni, 1988), p. vi; Thomas Schröder, *Die ersten Zeitungen. Textgestaltung und Nachrichtenauswahl* (Tübingen, 1995), p. 1; G. A. Cranfield, *The Press and Society, from Caxton to Northcliffe* (New York, 1978), p. 19. Compare David L. Paisey, 'Literatur, die nicht in den Messkatalogen steht,' in *Bücher und Bibliotheken im 17 Jahrhundert in Deutschland* (Hamburg, 1979), Wolfenbüttler Arbeitskreise für Geschichte des Buchwesens, 4 Jahrestreffen, ed. Paul Raabe, p. 124; Helmut W. Lang, 'Österreiche Zeitungsverlagsgeschichte im 17 Jahrhundert,' in *ibid.*, p. 135.

13 *Scritti giurisdizionalistici* (Bari, 1958), ed. Giovanni Gambarin, p. 221.

14 Entitled 'Il venditore di stampe e d'avvisi,' the engraving is reproduced in Francesco Novati, 'La storia e la stampa nella produzione popolare italiana,' *Emporium* 24, no. 141 (1906): 181–209.

15 *Dialoghi politici, ovvero la politica che usano in questo tempo i principi e repubbliche italiani per conservare i loro stati e signorie* (Geneva, 1666), 1: 250.

16 Some are reproduced in Vittorio Conti, *Le leggi di una rivoluzione. I bandi della repubblica napoletana dall'ottobre 1647 all'aprile 1648* (Naples, 1983). The pamphlet by Alejandro del Ros, *Catalogna disingannato. Discorsi politici* (Naples: Egidio Longo, 1647), was published in Naples in both Italian and Spanish. The pamphlet entitled, *Il cittadino fedele, discorso breve della giusta generosa e prudente risolutione del valoroso e fedelissimo popolo di Napoli, per liberarsi dall'insoportabili gravezze impostegli da Spagnuoli* (Naples: 1647) is edited in Rosario Villari, *Per il re o per la patria. La fedeltà nel Seicento* (Bari, 1994), pp. 41–58. In addition, there was Don John's brief but controversial pardon, declaring the people could hold their own fort but neglecting most of their other demands. In addition, Pier Luigi Rovito, 'La rivolta costituzionale di Napoli (1647–48),' *Rivista storica italiana* 98 (1986): 367–462; Salvo Mastellone, 'Holland as a Political Model in Italy in the Seventeenth Century,' *Bijdragen en Mededelingen betreffende de Geschiednis der Nederlandedn* 98 (1983): 568–82.

17 A few examples: Jean Sgard, ed., *Bibliographie de la presse classique* (Geneva, 1984); Alberto Bertone Pannain, Sandro Bulgarelli, and Ludovica Mazzoli, *Il giornalismo romano delle origini: secoli 16–17: Mostra bibliografica* (Rome, 1979); U. Bulgarelli, *Gli avvisi a stampa in Roma nel Cinquecento* (Rome, 1967); Folke Dahl, *A Bibliography of English Corantos and Periodical Newsbooks, 1620–42* (London, 1952); Carolyn Nelson and Matthew Seccombe, *British Newspapers and Periodicals, 1641–1700: A Short Title Catalogue* (New York, 1987); Holger Boning, ed., *Deutsche Presse: biobibliographische Handbucher zur Geschichte der deutschsprachigen Presse von den Anfangen bis 1815: kommentierte Bibliographie der Zeitungen, Zeitschriften* (Stuttgart-Bad Cannstatt, 1996), vol. 1.

18 This is by no means to disparage contributions by Rétat and Sgard (eds), *Presse et histoire au 18e siècle: l'année 1734* (Paris, 1978); Jean Varloot *et al.*, *L'annee 1768 à travers la presse traitée par ordinateur* (Paris, 1981); P. Jansen *et al.*, *L'année 1778 à travers la presse traitée par ordinateur* (Paris, 1982); as well as anthologies such as Martino Capucci, Renzo Cremante, and Giovanna Gronda, eds, *La biblioteca periodica. Repertorio dei giornali letterari del Sei-Settecento in Emilia e in Romagna* (Bologna, 1985–87), 2 vols; and Joad Raymond, *Making the News: An Anthology of the Newsbooks of Revolutionary England, 1641–1660* (Moreton-in-Marsh, 1993). Enrico Stumpo presents and explicates a continuous series of Roman manuscript newsletters in *La gazzetta de l'anno 1588* (Florence, 1988).

19 A few examples: Howard M. Solomon, *Public Welfare, Science and Propaganda in Seventeenth-Century France: The Innovations of Théophraste Renaudot* (Princeton, 1972); Paula McDowell, *The Women of Grub Street* (Oxford, 1998).
20 Examples: Nevio Matteini, *Il 'Rimino', una delle prime gazzette d'Italia* (Bologna, 1967); Maria Augusta Timpanaro Morelli, *Delle prime gazzette fiorentine* (Florence, 1963); Joseph Frank, *The Beginnings of the English Newspaper, 1620–1660* (Cambridge, MA, 1961); James Sutherland, *The Restoration Newspaper and its Development* (Cambridge, 1986); Robin Myers and Michael Harris, eds, *Censorship and the Control of Print in England and France 1600–1910* (Winchester, 1992); A. C. Duke and C. A. Tamse, eds, *Too Mighty to Be Free: Censorship and the Press in Britain and the Netherlands* (Zutphen, 1987).
21 Some perspective of the sort is obviously inevitable in works such as G. A. Cranfield, *The Press and Society From Caxton to Northcliffe* (London, 1978); Claude Bellanger, Jacques Godechot, Pierre Guiral, and Fernand Terrou *et al.*, *Histoire générale de la presse française* (Paris, 1969), 5 vols, I: vii, xv, 38; José Sanchez Aranda, *Historia del periodismo Español desde sus origenes hasta 1975* (Pamplona, 1992).
22 This is not to disparage contributions such as Mark Knights, *Politics and Opinion in Crisis, 1678–81* (Cambridge, 1994) and Thomas Cogswell, 'The Politics of Propaganda: Charles I and the People in the 1620s,' *Journal of British Studies* 29 (1990): 187–215; as well as Jeffrey K. Sawyer, *Printed Poison. Pamphlet Propaganda, Faction Politics and the Public Sphere in Early Seventeenth-Century France* (Berkeley, 1990), which utilize the concept of propaganda in a critical way.
23 Godechot *et al.*, *Histoire* I: vii, xv, 38; Richmond P. Bond, 'Introduction,' *Studies in the Early English Periodical* (Chapel Hill, 1957), p. 6; William Rivers, *The Mass Media* (New York, 1975). For an excellent critique of ideas of objectivity in journalism, see Michael Schudson, *Discovering the News. A Social History of American Newspapers* (New York, 1978).
24 Jacques Ellul, *Propaganda* (Paris, 1962; English tr., New York, 1973). In addition, Ferdinand Tönnies, *Kritik der Öffentlichen Meinung* (Heidelberg, 1922); Elizabeth Noelle-Neumann, *Die Schweigespirale* (Munich, 1980), Eng. tr., *The Spiral of Silence: Public Opinion – Our Social Skin* (Chicago, 1984); Terence H. Qualiter, *Opinion Control in the Democracies* (New York, 1985).
25 For what follows, see Brendan Dooley, 'From Literary Criticism to Systems Theory: Twenty Years of Journalism History,' *Journal of the History of Ideas* 51 (1990): 461–86. A good guide to early systems theorists' critique of social theory is Walter Buckley, *Sociology and Modern Systems Theory* (Englewood Cliffs, N.J., 1967). Most recently, Niklas Luhmann, *Social Systems* (Stanford, 1995, orig. publ. Frankfurt, 1984), on which I followed the critique by Danilo Zolo, 'L'ultimo Luhmann: La sociologia come teoria generale dei sistemi autoreferenziali,' *Rassegna italiana di sociologia* (1986): 533–50.
26 Edgar Morin, *Rumour in Orléans* (New York, 1971, orig. publ. Paris, 1969), pp. 269–71. Morin has since produced a kind of *summa* of systems theory in relation to communications in three volumes: *La méthode* (Paris, 1977–1980). For the application to journalism history, see Claude Labrosse, 'Introduction,' in Labrosse, Pierre Rétat, and Henri Duranton, *L'Instrument périodique: la fonction de la presse au 18e siècle* (Lyon, 1985), p. 10.
27 A useful overview is Evan Charney, 'Political Liberalism, Deliberative Democracy and the Public Sphere,' *American Political Science Review* 92 (1998): 97–111, detailing the Benhabib–Rawls debate. Compare Jürgen Habermas, *The Theory of Communicative Action* (Boston, 1984–87), 2 vols, tr. Thomas McCarthy.
28 Jürgen Habermas, *The Structural Transformation of the Public Sphere* (Cambridge, MA, 1989; orig. publ. *Strukturwandel der Öffentlichkeit* [Neuwied and Berlin, 1962)]), tr. Thomas Burger. Concerning Habermas' work and the public sphere, see Craig Calhoun, ed., *Habermas and the Public Sphere* (Cambridge, MA, 1992), which includes a critical introduction by Calhoun, pp. 1–50; and 'Further Reflections' by Habermas, pp. 421–61.

29 Compare David Zaret, 'Religion, Science and Printing in the Public Sphere in Seventeenth-Century England,' in Craig Calhoun, ed., *Habermas and the Public Sphere*, pp. 212–35; Sarah Hanley, 'Social Sites of Political Practice in France: Lawsuits, Civil Rights and the Separation of Powers in Domestic and State Government, 1500–1700,' *American Historical Review* 102 (1997): 27–52; Craig Harline, *Pamphlets, Printing and Political Culture in the Early Dutch Republic* (Boston, 1987).

30 Concerning this last problem, interesting perspectives are offered by the papers collected from the conferences at Göttingen, 1990, and Paris, 1993, in, respectively, Hans Erich Bödeker, ed., *Histoires du livre: nouvelles orientations* (Paris, 1995); and Roger Chartier, ed., *Histoires de la lecture: un bilan des recherches* (Paris, 1995).

31 David Stoker, 'The Regulation of the Book Trade in Norwich, 1500–1800,' *Publishing History* 5 (1979): 127. For what follows, Henri-Jean Martin, *Livre, pouvoir et société a Paris au dix-septième siècle* (Geneva, 1969), 2 vols, Appendix. In addition, *idem*, 'Renouvellements et concurrences,' in H.-J. Martin, R. Chartier *et al.*, *Histoire de l'Édition française, vol. 1: Le livre conquérant du Moyen Age au milieu du 17e siècle* (Paris, 1982), p 385; Aniello Fratta, 'L'attività degli Anisson di Lione nel carteggio con Antonio Magliabechi, 1669–1708,' *Sociologia della letteratura*, 3 (1979): 115–30.

32 R. A. Houston, *Literacy in Early Modern Europe: Culture and Education, 1500–1800* (London, 1988), p. 178, reporting such scholarship. For the rest, István Barta *et al.*, *Histoire de la Hongrie des origines à nos jours* (Budapest, 1974), pp. 179, 181–6.

33 Barbara Bienkowska and Halina Chamerska, *Books in Poland, Past and Present* (Wiesbaden, 1990), eds and tr. Wojciech Zalewski and Eleanor R. Payne, pp. 11–19.

34 For what follows, Jan de Vries, *European Urbanization, 1500–1800* (Cambridge, MA, 1984), pp. 28–31; Norman Davies, *God's Playground. A History of Poland, vol. 1: The Origins to 1795* (Oxford, 1981), p. 451; Zsigmond Pál Pach, *Hungary and the European Economy in Early Modern Times* (London, 1994), chap. 10; F. W. Carter, *Trade and Development in Poland. An Economic Geography of Cracow, From its Origins to 1795* (Cambridge, 1994), pp. 173–7, 195.

35 Ira M. Lapidus, *A History of Islamic Societies* (Cambridge, 1988), pp. 333–43, 592; Serif Mardin, 'The Modernization of Social Communication,' in Harold D. Lasswell, Daniel Lerner, and Hans Speier, eds, *Propaganda and Communication in World History* (Honolulu, 1979), vol. 1, pp. 381–443; and Bruce McGowan, 'Ottoman Political Communication,' *ibid.*, pp. 444–93.

36 Ralph S. Hatto, *Coffee and Coffeehouses. The Origins of a Social Beverage in the Medieval Near East* (Seattle, 1985); Karen Barkey, *Bandits and Bureaucrats. The Ottoman Route to State Centralization* (Ithaca, 1994), pp. 127–8.

Part 1

The English model

Early modern English men – and women – exhibited an innate thirst for information of all sorts, and perhaps especially for information about current events, better known as news. This thirst consumed information and news from across the spectrum of availability – from the most trivial to the most earth-shattering, whether rumour, personal experience, gossip, official report, slander, eye-witness account, royal proclamation, stage portrayal, or fantasy. The thirst for news was slaked from a variety of fountainheads, among them conversation, official communication, eavesdropping, public debate, acting, private correspondence, social gatherings, observation, and the printed and written word. All human faculties were involved in the absorption and digestion of news.

News, then as now, was the 'common currency of social exchange.'[1] From slanderers and libellers to gossipmongers, from prostitutes who traded sexual favours for news to polite dinner conversation at high noble tables and in the queen's withdrawing chamber, from broadside ballads to politically partisan newsbooks, news fuelled the interactions of most if not all early modern communities. Indeed, our own early twenty-first century greeting, inveterate ice-breaker, and accepted avenue of approach 'What's new with you?' is not far removed from the common hailing of the early seventeenth century: 'What news?' Dissemination of news was a direct route to social contact, intellectual stimulation, and political ferment. The thirst for news was innate and enduring – a craving never fully satisfied over either time or geographic location.

In early seventeenth-century England, one particular current event served to focus this natural English thirst for information in a new and different way, and in so doing, elevated social and political awareness to unprecedented levels. As was also the case on the Continent, this pivotal event was the Thirty Years' War, and it was intense interest in the progress of the war that originally fostered the emergence of a printed news publication industry in England.

Printed news reports of the war in the form of gazettes, or corantos (often rendered as 'currents' by contemporaries) began to be imported into England from the Low Countries from the outset of hostilities in 1618. The corantos were single-sheet broadsides printed in Dutch. Readers with no competency in that language soon began to get translations of the corantos' contents reported in manuscript newsletters. However, by 1620 it was clear that there was a growing market for information about the war among English readers, and that there was money to be made in larger, vernacular editions. London Stationers set out the first English translations in 1620–21, and by the end of 1621, Nathaniel Butter and Nicholas Bourne had established a regularly weekly quarto newsbook, selling for 1–2p. per issue, which appeared in numbered instalments. Soon, Butter employed editors who compiled unique English news publications from the accounts available in a variety of imported Continental corantos and letters of intelligence.

The English corantos printed only foreign news, fluctuated in popularity and success, were closely monitored by the Privy Council, and were suspended completely between 1632 and 1638. Nevertheless, they provided the first regular quencher of the English thirst for news, and *pace* Joad Raymond, they also provided a model for the printed books of domestic news that quickly emerged out of the chaotic domestic political situation which enveloped England in the 1640s, and prefigured the modern newspaper.

The regular and plentiful dissemination of information about current events which first emerged in the 1620s had an effect also on the English political psyche. News publication provided information upon which opinions about political events and the actions of governors and their administrations might be founded and developed. Being presented with a variety of information from a variety of sources allowed for fellow-feeling and comparative analysis. News contributed to the formation of partisan political opinion, designed to further a particular point of view and accomplish a particular goal. This is less obvious in early news publications, except perhaps for Butter's 1620s newsbooks which carried the Elector Palatine's coat of arms on the title page – but by the 1640s, the intent of newsbooks was no mystery at all. Every political perspective had its own, often multiple, newsbooks to support and promote it. Ben Jonson and other early critics of printed news publication were proven prescient – printed news was recognized to be malleable and manipulatable for whatever purposes its creators or its consumers wanted it to serve. It could be dangerous enemy or powerful ally, or both. The provision and analysis of news became over time a necessary, forward-looking need of the political process in shaping public opinion as a means of garnering popular support. What had once been fresh and immediate and inspiring news, would, through the agency of print publication, endure to become backward-looking, fixed and permanent, history, and equally necessary to modern conceptions of acceptable foundations for politicized public opinion.

The chapters in this section offer three 'present time' glimpses into the nature of news and its dissemination in early- and mid-seventeenth century England; the general impact of news upon early modern readers and their actions; and the interaction between information and politics in early modern contexts.

Stuart Sherman explores the relationship between theatre and contemporary reality – the 'two-way' transfer of information from 'page to stage' – laid out in dramatic works of Ben Jonson, a contemporary observer and satirist of the rise of the corantos and the accompanying all-consuming, incautious thirst for news. Sherman calls attention to the necessity of using multiple human faculties to absorb news – eyes, ears, mouth especially – in a world where oral transmission, manuscript transmission, and print dissemination were interdependent and equally vital. Sherman's analysis addresses the tangle of early modern 'convergent media' and the need for the contemporary consumer to sort through information, to throw out rumour, gossip, and fabrication while holding on to the more substantive news – if possible. Jonson set out to argue that what is seen and heard is closest to reality and truth, more fixed and less ephemeral, freely offered and freely absorbed, but what he actually illustrated was that print provided fixity and endurance, as well as accuracy, in transmission of information – and that information in the form of news could be successfully 'commodified.' In other words, it was possible to achieve both profit and reliability in the early modern English printed news industry, a situation belied by contemporary commentary. Sherman details a 'competition between modes of authority' in early seventeenth-century England, a competition from which, in his view, print – in particular, the printed news – emerges a clear winner.

Sabrina Baron also addresses the relationship between different modes of dissemination of information in early seventeenth-century England through an examination of the forms and texts of news publications. She argues that if print was coming into its own and attitudes toward printed news were becoming more positive during that period, manuscript newsletters simultaneously continued to satisfy a crucial need in dissemination and consumption – namely providing information about domestic current events. In contrast to Sherman's view, Baron sees manuscript newsletters and oral transmission of news as just as vital as, if not more important than, printed news publications in the formation of popular opinions which inspired political stances and actions. She focuses on the organizational and informational connections between news published in print and news published in manuscript before 1641, alluded to by Jonson, and, as Baron emphasizes, in fact central to understanding the motivations of the news industry. Because the state recognized those qualities of print that Jonson came to recognize – enunciated by Sherman as permanence, uniformity, and pervasiveness – the state exercised close supervision of the printed news industry which, paradoxically, caused manuscript publication rather than the burgeoning pre-Civil War print culture to function as the conduit for disseminating politically inflammatory information. Had Jonson lived longer, he, like the duke of Newcastle, would have recognized as well the political impact, and therefore the danger, that was more inherent in oral and manuscript transmission of news than in printed news.

Michael Mendle contributes to this examination of the development of the seventeenth-century English news industry, and its role in disseminating information crucial to political opinions, an analysis of the ultimate maturation of printed news within the 'anything would sell' print market of mid-century when state restrictions on print publication disappeared. Mendle describes a 'news-driven pamphlet culture' from which arose two other intimately connected developments that once again transformed the dissemination of news – the use of shorthand and the emergence of the reporter. Shorthand writing empowered reporters through real-time, verbatim coverage to perform events immediately and freshly for readers of printed news, in the manner advocated by Jonson for hearers of his plays as well as for hearers of news. In Mendle's analysis, the fixity and pervasiveness of print had come full circle, obtaining the most valuable qualities of oral transmission and manuscript newsletters, and exceeding their advantage as modes of dissemination. But if printed news was less retrospective recollection and reconstruction of past events in this era, it was also increasingly recognized 'as the raw material for history.' Mendle writes that news was both 'momentary scoop and enduring record.' The cheap little long-despised ephemeral pamphlets of news were collected in great assemblages which have, as the original collectors intended and Mendle illustrates here, shaped posterity's perceptions of mid-seventeenth-century events, perhaps more than any other source. It was also out of the rapidly changing attitudes of mid-century that the printing press evolved into a means for conducting state business as well as challenging state authority. Ultimately, in Mendle's analysis, printed news and its malleability were crucial to both the overthrow and the restoration of the Stuart dynasty between 1640 and 1660.

The final chapter in this section, by Daniel Woolf, is an overview of the social and political constructs of news and history from the mid-sixteenth to the early-eighteenth century. Woolf argues that the forward-looking view of seventeenth-century news as a product of oral transmission and the backward-looking view of early modern news as the precursor of modern print media must be synthesized into a more appropriate 'present time' view of news as a pivotal element in the emergence (for the first time) of something resembling a 'public sphere' in late Stuart England. Woolf's long-view analysis tempers some of the claims made for the achievements of printed news in the other chapters which concentrate more intensively on the early and mid-seventeenth century. He argues that printed news could not have had too significant an impact on the formulation of public opinion, in the Habermasian sense, until technological and transportation advances of the late seventeenth and early eighteenth centuries were achieved. Prior to those developments, the superiority of print dissemination resided only in its capacity for 'mass-reproduction.' He places news further outside the realm of history than does Mendle, although Woolf sees conceptions of the role of news in history going back to the corantos. Echoing Baron's conceptions of the vitality of manuscript newsletters and the enduring centrality of oral transmission, Woolf describes manuscript and oral dissemination surviving the Civil War to keep the mouth and ears engaged in consuming and dispersing information well into the later period. He sees no collision, such as Sherman searched for, between traditional transmission of news and the mediation of print.

Woolf concludes, however, as do the other authors in this section, that there was a discernible 'collective response of readers to the news' in early modern

England; in other words, some formulation of public opinion based on dissemination of information – information in the form of news, which elicited 'possible resolutions' to situations that varied greatly, but which were all, in the final analysis, political.

Notes

1 Joad Raymond, *The Invention of the Newspaper: English Newsbooks 1641–1649* (Oxford, 1996), p. 1.

1 Eyes and ears, news and plays

The argument of Ben Jonson's *Staple*

Stuart Sherman

At Drury Lane Theatre one evening in late October 1779, the curtain fell on a performance of *Hamlet* only to rise again some minutes later, as the playbill had foretold, on the debut of a new afterpiece by the playhouse's manager/proprietor, Richard Brinsley Sheridan. Here, in the words of the text published two years after, is what greeted the audience's eyes and ears:

> *Mr. and Mrs. Dangle at breakfast, and reading newspapers.*
> *Dangle* (reading headlines): *Brutus to Lord North. – Letter the second on the State of the Army.* – Pshaw! *To the first L–dash D of the A–dash Y.*[1]

The play was *The Critic*, and those spoken *dashes* are worth pondering. In reading the day's headlines aloud, Mr Dangle might easily fill the blanks with their obvious content ('first Lord of the Admiralty'); he adheres to the orthography by way of expressing his distaste for this kind of news (he will make his own preferences clear in a moment). But he also accomplishes for the playwright a little layering of perceptions on the part of the audience. The eye beholds the breakfast table and its occupants; the ear absorbs Dangle's disdainfully scrupulous rendition of the news text, dashes and all. The mind's eye, in consequence, conjures up the text as Dangle sees it, close up: a line of print, not speech. Sheridan has arranged things so that merely by looking at the stage and hearing the voice, the audience must almost perforce imagine a product of the press.

An ephemeral product – mere newsprint – deployed here for an ephemeral but pointed effect: it ushers in a satire on the news business that will culminate in the arrival of Mr Puff, arch-publicist and aspiring playwright. At the same time, *The Critic*'s opening stages a striking moment in the long history of an intricate relationship – between stage and page, between play and print. The reconstruction of that history has produced extraordinary scholarship, most of it mapping the route by which the evanescence of live performance moves towards the comparative permanence of the printed play text. That story begins with the intricate, often piratical work of Elizabethan compositors, producing texts without the collaboration of the author, and advances to a second stage with Ben Jonson's decision, in 1616, to publish his own plays as *Works*, a move that excited surprise and some scorn. The alternate route, along which plays interact with *im*permanent modes of print, with the evanescences of the daily news, has been less studied by scholars, even though the materials for mapping are many: newspaper items, pamphlets, commentaries (proto-reviews) in literary magazines and periodical essays, and, finally, in the mid-eighteenth century, in periodicals devoted entirely to the theatre. Along this route, the traffic is notably two-way. Over the decades dividing Jonson and Sheridan, plays increasingly *represent* news that has first appeared in print, as when Dangle reads simulacra of recent headlines. At the same time, plays increasingly *become* news, providing the papers with much needed copy. At the beginning of *The Critic*, Dangle seizes upon this second phenomenon as a source of respite:

> *Dangle:* Pshaw! – Nothing but about the fleet and the nation! – and I hate all politics but theatrical politics. – Where's the *Morning Chronicle*?
> *Mrs Dangle:* Yes, that's your gazette.
> *Dangle:* So here we have it. – *Theatrical intelligence extraordinary* …
>
> (10–13)

Sheridan sketches the two-way traffic in less than a minute; having read the news on stage, Dangle now delights to find an account of the stage upon the page. *His* gazette, the *Morning Chronicle*, had made its reputation by the unprecedented proportion of space and attention it devoted to the theatre, not only its copy, where *theatrical intelligence* and criticism abounded, but in its advertising format, which accorded the playhouses pride of place: the largest ads, situated in the first column on the first page (in which spot that very morning, many members of the audience at Drury Lane would have seen *The Critic* blazoned).[2] The *Chronicle* thus furthered a process long in development, in which plays had begun to establish a second kind of record, not as text preserved within the fixed bindings of splendid folios, but as report and review marketed in folio half-sheets, bought and discarded daily. The two-way traffic between the venues entailed both collaboration and competition. Each sought sustenance from the other; and at the same time vied with the other for the attention and authority accorded by a paying audience.

I'd like here to look at the moment of the traffic's inception. Jonson stands at the start of this story too. In 1620, the year in which English-language corantos first appeared in London, Jonson produced a mocking court masque called *News from the New World.*[3] In 1626, after a nine-year absence, he resumed his mockery in a new play performed at Blackfriars and at Court, *The Staple of News* (i.e., the storehouse or emporium of news), in which he displays with dripping scorn a syndicate of newsmongers bent on achieving a monopoly over the distribution of fresh intelligence. Taken together, the masque and the play frame the first theatrical response to the new phenomenon of periodically printed news. Like Sheridan 150 years later, Jonson sets out to satirize the news business, but the difference in design between the satires indexes their difference in historical position: Sheridan shows his audience the page of news, the line of print, on the incontrovertible assumption that they have read something like it within the last twenty-four hours, and will again within the next forty-eight hours (the play premiered on a Saturday, and there were as yet no Sunday papers). Jonson shows his audience the operations of the syndicate out of a manifest desire that they never purchase its products again. He intends that the two-way traffic between news and plays should begin with a collision; I propose to trace some of the trajectories and some of the consequences.

Let me linger a moment, though, at Drury Lane, as a means of getting back to these beginnings. Members of the audience on *The Critic*'s opening night may have been at least subliminally aware that they had compassed within a single evening not only the history but even the pre-history of the long encounter between plays and newsprint. About two hours before hearing Dangle's dashes, they had been listening to Hamlet adjuring Polonius to take care of the visiting players, in words that had served for nearly two centuries as the *locus classicus* for the relationship between theatre and contemporary reality: 'Do you hear, let them be well used, for they are the abstract and brief chronicles of the time.'[4] The line is cutomarily invoked for its loftier resonances, its suggestion that these performers manage when on stage to epitomize their epoch (Hamlet will elaborate this notion later, when he instructs the players 'to hold as 'twere the mirror up to nature; to show ... the very age and body of the time his form and pressure' [3.2.21–4]). But the line possesses a plainer meaning too: that the players, moving rapidly around the country, are able to carry abundant, fresh gossip from place to place.[5] (Hence Hamlet's warning to Polonius that 'After your death you were better have a bad epitaph than their ill report while you live' [2.2.521–2]).

In *The Critic*, Sheridan conspicuously takes up this touchstone. Both Mr Dangle and Mr Puff quote Hamlet's line (1.1.18–19, 2.1.6–7) and give it their idiosyncratic gloss. In so doing they are transposing the text into a new world where the prince's metaphor appears to attach itself to a familiar and concrete referent. This world (as Sheridan has taken pains to show from the first) possesses 'brief chronicles' in plenty and at hand: the *Morning Chronicle*, the *St. James Chronicle*, and all those other four- and six-page papers which had gradually displaced the earlier notion of a chronicle, as cumulative, weighty, and voluminous, with a new print model: concise, continuous, portable, and disposable.

When Burbage first spoke these words at the Globe, ca. 1600, they possessed no such referent. Hamlet appends the adjective 'brief' in order to distinguish his figure from the long, sustained documents that the noun names, and to bend it to the transience of the actors' craft. The kind of text he conjures up to make his metaphor does not yet quite exist in Elizabethan culture. Pamphlets, newsbooks, and ballads, keyed to sensational stories and special occasions, had purveyed the news abundantly, albeit sporadically, during the preceding decades, but the combination of concision and continuum that the prince conjures in a phrase had not yet found embodiment in print.[6] Dubbing the actors '*the* ... brief chronicles' of the time, Hamlet implies even by the definite article that there are no others; his point is partly that theatrical action is like no kind of writing at all. Throughout his encounters with the actors, Hamlet remains preoccupied with those elements of their craft which distinguish it from writing: the necessity of bodily presence to make transmission possible; the consequent, ineluctable evanescence of the transaction (the touring players are just passing through); the meshed activity of the performers' bodies and voices and of the audience's responses. In his later pronouncements on 'the purpose of playing,' Hamlet continues his emphasis on the immediate and the corporeal: Nature stands before the players' 'Mirror,' and in that moment 'the age and body of the time' takes in the data of its 'form and pressure.' He envies the actors' capacity not merely to reflect bodies but also to affect them, to 'amaze indeed / the very faculties of eyes and ears' (3.2.20–4). And so his final figure for the actor as news-medium modulates accordingly, from writing to live performance: 'If you mouth [the speech] as many of your players do, I had as lief the town-crier spoke my lines' (3.2.2–4). The comparison of course is negative. 'My lines,' are those 'dozen or sixteen' concerning royal murder which Hamlet has inserted into the old play to make it news, and he is insisting that the actor deliver this news more deftly than the crier. But in shifting the metaphor from 'chronicle' to 'crier' Hamlet is moving to ground more familiar to his initial audience, in whose world the distribution of news, like the performance of plays, rests heavily on human presence. The body of the crier, like that of the actor (and unlike that of the chronicler), must occupy the same space and time with those of the audience, if communication is to take effect.

There is this difference, however, between the crafts: the crier deals emphatically in the auditory – the operations of mouth and ears are essential, of eyes less so. (It is possible to absorb the crier's data from within the confines of one's home, for example, as Samuel Pepys demonstrates in a diary entry: 'I sat up till the bell-man came by with his bell, just under my window as I was writing of this very line, and cried, "Past one of the clock, and a cold, frosty, windy morning".'[7]) What makes the crier repellent to Hamlet is partly his specialization, in the working of the mouth; the actors, by contrast, must attend as well to the workings of the visual ('Nor do not saw the air too much with your hand' [3.2.4–5]), in order to amaze the very faculties of eyes *and* ears. For the crier's auditors and Hamlet's first audience, the rendition of news, unlike the performance of plays, often privileged sound over sight. But this priority, already in flux thanks to the sporadic advent of printed news in the late 1500s, underwent an emphatic shift during the 1620s, with the debut of the corantos and periodical newsbooks in English. Through the enterprise of a few energetic booksellers, Hamlet's metaphorical 'brief chronicles' now actually existed – palpable, purchasable, pitched to the eye rather than the ear, yet patently ephemeral: further news would come along in the next 'continuation.'

Jonson, who lived to witness the innovation as Shakespeare did not, lived also to mount the first theatrical counter-attacks. Having sought in 1616 the sanctuary of print permanence for his *Works*, he proceeded in the following decade to decry the cultural consequences of print impermanence. In *News from the New World*, and in *The Staple of News*, the casual likeness that Hamlet proposes between actors and chronicles splits and hardens into a commercial competition, as to whether the theatre or the printed sheet might lay the stronger claim to serve as the time's 'abstract.' In both the masque and the play Jonson maps the contest onto the human body, as a competition among those 'very faculties' that interest Hamlet: eyes, ears, mouths. But where Hamlet posits collaboration among those faculties, Jonson, goaded by the innovations and the competition, posits emulation: Which faculty should take precedence? To what medium should it attend? And what should be the form of its attention? Johnson's interest in this kind of sensory contestation is familiar from his long-running quarrel with Inigo Jones as to the relative importance of the visual and the auditory in the court masques on which they had collaborated.[8] But critics have not seen or shown how the same struggle informs his attacks on the new enterprise of news – and complicates it with intimations of his own complicity.

In *The Staple of News*, Jonson declares his priorities early. Here are the first lines of the play's Prologue, delivered, conventionally enough, by an actor speaking as proxy for the absent playwright:

> For your own sakes, not his, he bade me say,
> Would you were come to hear, not see, a play.[9]

He wishes, that is, for a sundering of the senses, with sound in the ascendant and sight discarded from the reckoning, though he does not quite explain how this process might work within the theatre. Still, by the time the Prologue speaks these lines, Jonson has already infused the wish with a local, circumstantial, comic urgency. For though these are the first lines of the Prologue, they are not the first of the play. They come at the end of a long induction, which began with this actor's hapless first attempt to deliver this same speech. There he gets no further than six words in – three iambs of his five beat line – before he is interrupted by the arrival of 'four gentlewomen ladylike attired,' who introduce themselves as Gossip Mirth, Gossip Expectation, Gossip Tattle, and Gossip Censure, and demand seating in the chairs on stage customarily reserved (as the Prologue-speaker anxiously reminds them) for noble *men*: 'We ... come,' proclaims their leader in a formulation plucked from Ovid, 'to see and to be seen' (Induction 8–10). Their loquacity as well as their sobriquets soon manifest a third intent as well: to talk and talk and talk some more. Their gossip will fill four 'Intermeans,' following each of the play's acts except the last. In them, the energies of sight and conversation delay the 'hearing' that the playwright has in mind. His hierarchy of faculties is toppled even before it is pronounced.

So, when the gossips at last permit the Prologue to resume his speech, he dilates in detail, as though chastened by this fresh experience, on the threat to theatre incarnate in the audience's indulgence of eager eye and active tongue.

> Though we his actors must provide for those
> Who are our guests here in the way of shows,
> The maker hath not so. He'd have you wise
> Much rather by your ears than by your eyes,

And prays you'll not prejudge his play for ill
Because you mark it not and sit not still,
But have a longing to salute or talk
With such a female, and from her to walk
With your discourse, to what is done, and where,
How and by whom, in all the town but here.
(Prologue for the Stage 3–12)

Jonson here expands his earlier allusion to Ovid. In *Ars Amatoria*, the women who attend the Roman games 'to see and to be seen,' come in hope of seeing not the spectacle but the audience. Jonson's variant consists in his tracing the collaboration of eye with tongue to produce a compound distraction, a 'walk with … discourse' that occludes present perception, leading the talkers over 'all the town but here.' In the next few lines, Jonson maps the walk and also laments it:

Alas, what is it to his scene to know
How many coaches in Hyde Park did show
Last spring, what fare today at Medley's was,
If Dunstan or the Phoenix best wine has?
(13–16)

Listing the names of London's taverns, Jonson's lines enhance the dangerous agency of the mouth, as conduit not merely of talk but voracious appetite, and again link it with the eye in the seamless transition from the 'show' in Hyde Park to the fare at Medley's.

When, however, in the next line, the speaker continues to decry such trivia, he suddenly stops himself short, implicitly resolving to enumerate and discuss them no more.

They are things – But yet the stage might stand as well
If it did neither hear these things nor tell.
(17–18)

The self-interruption suggests a possible instability in the satire, whereby the speaker may become absorbed in the processes he is denouncing, as though simply to list 'these things' is to talk the talk and walk the walk of discourse. Having had his first sentence cut short by the gossips, the Prologue now cuts short his own discourse as an *incipient* gossip, whose tongue is in peril of being subdued to what it works against. That peril infuses the proportions of the prologue. Though Jonson repeatedly but inexplicitly urges the primacy of the ear, he devotes most of his attention and his lines to the iniquities of the eye and tongue: in his eagerness to defeat them, they dominate the argument. His anxiety manifests itself also in a tiny alteration of the Prologue's opening line. In the first version, at the start of the Induction, the line begins: 'For your [i.e. the audience's] sake, and not *ours*' [i.e. the players' and the playwright's]. When the

Prologue resumes after the Gossips' interruption, the second possessive shifts position: 'For your sake and not *his*' [i.e. the playwright's alone]. The Gossips, then, have already made a difference. After their arrival, Jonson quietly cuts himself off from the collective that is putting on the play, leaving the actors to face the audience alone. The Induction posits the theatre as the site of an uneven struggle between a masculine poet (a maker) arguing for the priority of the ear, and a feminized audience energetically committed to the primacy of the eye and mouth. *The Staple of News* starts out not as a competition between the theatre and the print news syndicate, but as a combat within the theatre itself, conducted against the appetites of the audiences' eyes and mouths which the playwright's medium foredooms him to feed.

Yet from the start, Jonson has taken pains to link the war he wages within his own medium with the attack he proposes to launch against the upstart news. The words with which Gossip Mirth first interrupts the Prologue establish this connection:

> Come, Gossip [Tattle], be not ashamed. The play is *The Staple of News*, and you are the mistress and lady of Tattle; let's ha' your opinion of it.
>
> (Induction 2–4)

Tattling, in other words, is the forerunner of the 'new' news, the fluid, costless, cottage version of the impulse and the industry that the Staple syndicate will seek to technologize, commercialize, and monopolize. Attacking both the gossips in his theatre and the journalists outside it, Jonson implies that he is fighting the same war on two fronts.

At the same time, the play sustains a nuanced differentiation between the two, marking and warily dissecting the present cultural moment of transition, when talk – the mode of the gossips and the criers – is beginning to be displaced by text. The plot takes place on the twenty-first birthday of Pennyboy Junior, a Prodigal Son in costly modern dress, who just a week earlier learned from a virtuous beggar the news of his father's death and hence of his own new wealth. By the end of the day and the play, Pennyboy will invest both his inheritance and his enthusiasm in the glamorous news-syndicate newly installed in the building where he lives; he will then discover and repent this error, woo and win the fair Pecunia ('lady wealth'), and reconcile with his father who, as it turns out, has only feigned death and then dogged his offspring (*disguised* as the virtuous beggar) in order to test and observe his handling of his sudden prosperity. In the opening scenes, set in the prodigal's new apartment, Jonson modulates from the realm of the Gossips just established in the Induction, to that of the Staple down the hall, whose moment in the play as in the culture is fast approaching (the audience will witness the Staple in action for the whole of Act 3). Within this modulation, the appetites of eyes and mouths function as the chords common to both keys. Like the Gossips, Pennyboy, attended by his shoemaker, tailor, linener, haberdasher, and barber, evinces a keen desire 'to see and to be seen,' as he makes abundantly clear in his opening monologue to the audience:

...[L]ook on me, and with all thine eyes,
Male, female, yea hermaphroditic eyes,
And those bring all your helps and perspicils [optical glasses]
To see me at best advantage, and augment
My form as I come forth, for I do feel
I will be one worth looking after shortly.

(1.1.4–9)

Pennyboy not only caters to the visual appetite that Jonson has decried in his spectators; he feels it too, as when he confesses to Pecunia that

I cannot satisfy
My curious eyes, by which alone I'm happy,
In beholding you.

(2.5.59–61)

Elsewhere in the sensorium, Jonson encapsulates the cultural transition from talk to text in the person of Pennyboy's barber, Tom, whose present profession is proverbial for its purveyance of gossip. Appropriately, he is both the first to tell Pennyboy of the new syndicate, and the first to see in it an opportunity for self-advancement: he persuades his master to buy him a clerkship, thus turning himself from amateur gossip into professional.

That Pennyboy is in effect also already involved in the enterprise, Jonson signals by a small pun: 'Rascal,' says the heir to his linener, 'sits my ruff well?' 'In print,' answers the tradesman. The phrase, proverbial, meant just 'perfectly,' but with the Staple setting up nearby it means something more: it specifies where this obsession with the visual will end. In just such punning terms the interrupted Prologuist earlier chided Gossip Censure: 'O ... You come to see who wears the new suit today, whose clothes are best *penned*' (Induction 40–1), that is, both 'feathered' (by the costume-maker) and 'described' (by the playwright); within the sentence structure, the designer's visual effect again takes precedence over the poet's language. Here, as later with the phrase 'in print,' Jonson makes plain that 'fashion' and 'news' are the same contemptible and evanescent thing.

In 1626, though, the modes of evanescence are multiple – news is disseminated concurrently as something spoken (tattle), something 'penned' (manuscript newsletters), and something 'in print' (corantos, newsbooks). Jonson's play is remarkable for its attention to all three modes – and to their interaction. The chief real-life objects of his satire are the pioneers of periodical print journalism – Thomas Gainsford, Nicholas Bourne, and above all Nathaniel Butter, whose name, endlessly metamorphosed, provides the play with its most recurrent running gag. But as both a theatrical strategy and a representational gambit, Jonson depicts his staple of news not as a print shop but as a newsletter scriptorium, in which mouths and pens move abundantly, and print hovers to one side as a known reality and a commercial possibility, much on the managers' minds but not yet on their own premises.[10] At one point the Staple's 'Register' (i.e. editor in chief) compares his workplace to Chaucer's 'house of fame' (3.2.115), but Chaucer's echo-chambered rumour mill is purely auditory, 'ful of rounynges and jangles' [whispers and outbursts] – the sounds, according to Chaucer's source in Ovid, of 'each new teller add[ing] something to what he has heard'[11] Jonson's, by contrast, is a site of convergent media, visible and audible, newly mixed.

This convergence distinguishes *The Staple* as the second instalment in what amounts to Jonson's two-part satiric theatrical history of the news business. In *News from the New World*, produced six years earlier, the means of transmitting news are clearly categorized and set apart. Jonson incarnates each in the person of a different kind of practitioner: two heralds, who deliver the news by word of mouth; a chronicler, who specializes in sustained manuscript and boasts that 'my great book' will 'fill up ... three ream of paper at least';[12] a factor of news, who runs a scriptorium and writes 'my thousand letters a week ordinary, sometime twelve hundred, and maintain the business at some charge' (32–4); and a printer so visually and commercially obsessed that he assumes the heralds' news is something that can be seen and bought. 'What's the price of 'em?,' he asks; to which one herald retorts, 'Price, cocks-comb! what price, but the price o' your ears? As if any man used to pay for any thing here.' *Here*, of course, is James's court, and as the herald's reply suggests, in this region there is no doubt as to which medium is the superior. The heralds, who demand nothing but the attention 'o' your ears,' are the only ones who possess the news and deliver it; the chronicler, the factor, and the printer only hunger after it, hoping to commodify it by one means or another. In the masque they can be held at bay.

But not in the later play. There, the media are more muddled, as a sample transaction will suggest. A 'she Anabaptist' enters the shop in search of intelligence (Jonson continues to mock the female taste for news, and hence the feminizing influence the news exerts over those like Pennyboy, who is now watching the operation with an eye towards further investment):

> *Anabaptist:* Ha' you in your profane shop any news
> O' the saints at Amsterdam?
> *Register:* Yes, how much would you?
> *Anabaptist:* Six pennyworth.
> *Register:* Lay your money down. Read, Thomas.
> (3.2.123–5)

And Thomas reads, from an English manuscript translation of a Dutch print coranto, a ridiculous and ridiculing cluster of 'saintly' prophecies. Just this morning Thomas was Pennyboy's barber; his present activity as clerk of the Staple places him on the print-cultural cusp between his discarded past as gossip and his desired future as factor. Manuscript constitutes in some respects a middle term between talk and print: it bears many traces of the hand and body that produced it and so retains a residuum of the physical presence necessary for conversation. Samuel Richardson would later call this phenomenon 'the Converse of the Pen,'[13] and the manuscript newsletters of the seventeenth century often cultivated the impression of epistolary 'voice' by beginning each copy with a calligraphically elaborate 'Sir,' calculated to foster the illusion (or in rarer cases the actuality) of individual address.[14] Tom, reading aloud from the manuscript, reinforces the sense of 'presence'; he becomes momentarily the kind of 'brief chronicle' Hamlet envisioned. But when he finishes, the customer will take the sheet away with her; at that moment the vocal and the present are transmuted (and literally muted) into the visual and portable. 'Seal and deliver her her news,' the Register commands (152).

The seal itself is the trademark and chief instrument of the Staple's monopolistic aspirations. In the future, the managers boast to their prospective investor Pennyboy, 'All [news] will come from the mint – Fresh and new stamped – / With the Office seal: Staple Commodity' (1.5.62–3). Here again, through an echoing of adjectives, Jonson draws the link between the new text enterprise and the old appetite for tattle. By means of their new-minted, fresh-stamped manuscripts, the Staple hopes both to approximate and to supplant the kind of talk-based authority of which Gossip Tattle boasted at the beginning of the play. 'Look your news be new and fresh, Master Prologue,' she warned, 'I shall find them else, if they be stale or flyblown' (Induction 25–7). The imperative 'Look' (i.e. 'see that') becomes resonant too: the Staple managers argue to Pennyboy that it is the *look* of manuscript that will preserve the sense of freshness that consumers like Tattle crave – an effect that, in the managers' reckoning, printing cannot match. 'It is the printing we oppose / ... for when news is printed, It leaves, sir, to be news. While 'tis but written / ... it runs news still' (1.5.46–50). Pennyboy responds with surprise and a counter-argument:

> See divers men's opinions! Unto some,
> The very printing of them makes them news,
> That ha' not the heart to believe anything
> But what they see in print.
>
> (51–4)

Of course, what is at stake in this exchange is a competition between modes of authority, one based in the physical presence, slower distribution, and consequent 'freshness' of talk and manuscript, the other in the permanence, uniformity, and pervasiveness of print. As it happens, this is the only stretch of dialogue that Jonson transposed direct and unaltered from his earlier masque to his present play. It enacts a confusion current in the culture – one that would persist a good while longer – and Jonson, representing the confusion, leaves it intact. The interlocutors do not resolve their debate either way.

In effect, though, Jonson damns the debate altogether. Those who hunger for news, whether they invest its authority in talk, script, or print, are prey to a fundamental confusion of ungoverned, unsorted appetites which Jonson dramatizes by several means in the scene set at the Staple, beginning with the Staple-Master's name: 'Cymbal,' a little tinkling instrument, here figuring the triviality of the fellow's output. When spoken on stage, though, the name would be barely distinguishable from 'symbol,' a term apt to the innovatively visual emphasis of the Master's business and its instrumental trademark: Staple Commodity. As text, the name enacts a sound; as sound, text: the operations of eyes and ears, which the playwright in the Prologue sought to sort, are indistinguishably merged in the name that heads the new enterprise. Jonson moves mouths into the same mix. Throughout the Staple scene, any talk that does not deal with the news concerns instead an elaborate celebratory dinner that Pennyboy is planning that afternoon. His cook, Lickfinger, dashes through the Staple 'bespeaking but a parcel of news / To strew out the long meal withal' (3.2.182–3); his language, here and later, leaves unclear whether the guests are intended to hear the news, read it, or eat it. (You shall have 'two bales of it,' Pennyboy is assured, as though the news were hay and its consumers horses [4.1.39].)

In the Intermean at the end of the Staple act, the Gossips pick up on this culinary confusion: 'But how like you the news?' asks Mirth, meaning the many satiric bulletins which Jonson has scattered throughout the dialogue. 'O,' replies Censure, 'they are monstrous. Scurvy and stale! And too exotic; ill cooked and ill dished.' 'They were as good,' answers Expectation, 'as Butter could make them' (Third Intermean 12–16) She means of course, Nathaniel Butter, the real-life newsbook entrepreneur for whom Jonson's Cymbal serves as stand-in. In Butter's name Jonson found a maximally expressive emblem of sensory confusion, for the condemnatory conflation of food and news: precariously 'fresh,' easily adulterated, often 'ill-cooked,' soon 'stale.' At the end of the previous Intermean, immediately before the Staple scene, Jonson provides for the Gossips a twenty-line riff on Nathaniel Butter's name. Having heard so much talk about the Staple, Gossip Expectation longs to watch it in action: 'Would Butter would come in,' she says, 'and spread itself a little to us.' Tattle: 'When it is churned and dished, we shall hear of it.' Expectation: 'If it be fresh and sweet butter; but say it be sour and wheyish?' Mirth: 'Then is it worth nothing, mere pot butter, fit to be spent in suppositories or greasing coach wheels, stale stinking butter, and such I fear it is' (Second Intermean 50–8). And so forth. Jonson frames the Staple scene in 'Butter' on either side, because Butter so conveniently encapsulates the problem that the Staple has produced: an indiscriminate consumption that dazzles, confuses, and ultimately consumes the consumer.

Just how that confusion and consumption operate, Jonson has meanwhile demonstrated in the person of Pennyboy, whose very first encounter with the news-trade catapults him into a comic crisis of self-perception and self-location. Upon first meeting Cymbal on the morning of his own birthday, Pennyboy decides to test the freshness of the Staple's product: 'What news ha' you,' he asks. 'News o' this morning? I would fain hear some / Fresh from the forge (as new as day, as they say).' Cymbal: 'And such we have, sir' (1.5.79–81). The news Pennyboy hears is indeed very fresh; it is read from a manuscript headlined 'The Heir' and it tells the story of Pennyboy himself – his father's death a week ago, his own coming of age this morning. Ecstatic to find his story thus purveyed, Pennyboy turns to his barber and, pointing to the manuscript, exults: 'I am here, Tom!' (88). The stage picture is brief but telling: the audience sees the living body of a young man, but hears his voice insisting that his presence inheres not in the body but in the ink. The age and body of *his* time (to rework *Hamlet*) has been formed and pressured, with his enthusiastic consent, onto paper. Moments later, Jonson expands on Pennyboy's misprision over a whole bewildered line of verse: 'Founder,' Pennyboy shouts to the beggar/father who accompanies him: 'We are in, here, in – i' the News Office! / In this day's roll, already' (96–7). The sticking at the preposition makes clear that he can no longer quite tell *where* his essence lies: in elegant clothing (as he thought at the play's beginning); in his body; 'i' the News Office', or in its paper product. Gossip Censure picks up on this uncertainty when she tries to summarize the action at the end of the scene: 'Here's nothing but a young prodigal come of age, who makes much of [his] barber, buys him a place in a new Office, i' the air, I know not where' (First Intermean 3–6). The latent pun on 'air' (the element) and 'heir' (the 'prodigal' legatee) rounds out the impression that in his enthusiasm for the news business, the heir has disappeared into thin air, or into a manuscript called 'The Heir.' Gossip Censure knows there is no there there.

Jonson, meanwhile, contrives countermeasures designed to rouse the audience to the difference between texts and bodies – one of the crucial distinctions between news and plays. The moment when Pennyboy points to the news-roll shouting 'I am here' is one such instance; that in which he tells the beggar '*we* are here' is a more complicated one. For though the beggar is written about in the news-manuscript, he is not, like Pennyboy, possessed by it; he is preserved from that peril by his secret identity as Pennyboy's father, which neither the newsmongers nor Pennyboy (nor at this point the audience) know anything about. By keeping his own counsel, he is able to remain 'in' his paternal body, and to resist metamorphosis into a news-representation. Jonson caps this motif in the play's last act: at the moment when Pennyboy learns to repent his self-indulgence and self-delusion, and to recognize himself regretfully as 'Prince of Prodigals' (5.1.10), the Staple News Office suddenly blows up, off-stage, as though by a kind of sympathetic magic: 'This awakes me from my lethargy,' Pennyboy remarks when he receives word of the explosion (53). The News Office, which Jonson has made so palpably inimical to self-knowledge, self-destructs at the instant self-knowledge is attained.

Such moments form part of a larger system Jonson has devised to prevent the audience from making Pennyboy's mistake, from forgetting where they are and hence who they are. In this endeavour he enlists the Gossips as allies. By sitting and talking on the stage, they remind the audience emphatically that they are in a theatre; by commenting on the play both astutely and comically – in some ways that invite assent and in others that excite laughter – they doubly reinforce in the audience precisely that critical distance which Pennyboy loses when he becomes absorbed in (and as) Staple Commodity. The news business, so this skein of the argument suggests, consumes its susceptible adherents (and blows up in their faces); the theatre leaves them comparatively free.

Perhaps too free, or too susceptible. In a note 'To the Readers' that he included in the folio edition of *The Staple*, which he prepared five years after the play's sole, short run, Jonson confesses that all his countermeasures failed dismally in the theatre.

> ...[T]he allegory and purpose of the author hath hitherto been wholly mistaken [i.e. by the audience] ... [H]e prays you thus to mend it. To consider the news here vented to be none of his news, or any reasonable man's, but news made like the time's news.
>
> (To the Reader 2–9)

Evidently, then, the audience's error consisted in mistaking Jonson's satiric news bulletins for the 'straight dope' of the corantos. The note goes on to marvel that they missed the point: the time's news, Jonson argues,

> could not be fitter reprehended than in raising this ridiculous Office of the Staple, wherein the age may see her own folly, or hunger and thirst after published pamphlets of news ... than which there cannot be a greater disease in nature.
>
> (9–14)[15]

The note implicitly confesses that the play has fallen prey to the infection.[16] Coming into contact with the audience's 'hunger and thirst,' the play, pitched against news, has in the audience's mind become news, in spite of its author's intention and design.

What is perhaps most striking about the note is not its outrage at audience incomprehension (familiar enough in Jonson, and particularly in his prefaces), but its placement. It appears not at the play's beginning but just before Act 3, the centrepiece set in the Staple office: the very scene that has given rise to the confusion Jonson now writes to correct. The odd location imparts additional urgency – Jonson intrudes to administer a very local antidote at the precise site of the interpretive infection – but it also accomplishes an extraordinary gesture: a pure print intervention in the midst of a theatrical script, consisting of instructions addressed not to the performers (as in the case of stage directions) nor to the audience (as is often the case in theatrical prologues), but to persons envisioned as ideally absent from the theatre and withdrawn from its entire *modus operandi*. The critical distance Jonson tried to foster in the theatre turned out to be neither distant nor critical enough; only in the further detachment of the printed page can Jonson hope to 'mend' the interpretation that went awry at the playhouse.

Yet even as he attempts to compound distances, Jonson enacts continuities; his printed note bears a striking resonance with the Prologue spoken at the beginning of the performance. There Jonson repeatedly declared his preference that his audience become 'wise, / Much rather by your ears than by your eyes.' Now, in the caustic note about *The Staple*'s actual audience, Jonson ominously recombines the faculties that he had earlier hoped to separate. He suggests that the playhouse crowd came up with their 'sinister [i.e. left-handed, twisted] interpretation' because

> the souls of most of the spectators lived in the eyes and ears of these ridiculous gossips that tattle between the Acts.

Which is to say that the audience's appetite for transient information was so 'gossipaceous' (to quote James Joyce on Anna Livia),[17] and so sensorily confused (in the manner that the play has mapped) that in their craving for news they have consumed Jonson's subtle preparation as though it were the worthless fare he sought to mock off the cultural menu. By the logic of his present phrasing, the Gossips' indiscriminate mingling of the faculties – eyes, ears, mouths – has produced a further, and less wholesome fusion: in the scrambled sensorium of the theatre, the audience has 'become' the Gossips, just as in the scrambled sensorium of the Staple, Pennyboy 'became' the piece of paper that narrated him.

In his note 'To the Readers,' Jonson attempts an urgent unscrambling. By its substance, its form, and its striking placement, the note implies that print may after all sort things out differently and better than the playhouse, by means of a kind of faculty exchange, in which the eye, fixed upon the page, may accomplish that which Jonson wishes the ear to do in the theatre, but which it cannot because it is there overwhelmed by sight and talk: to foster and sustain the focused attention to pure language that the poet apparently had in mind when he wished his audience 'to hear, not see, a play.' The eye now functions not merely instead of the ear, but *as* the ear. Walter Ong has written of how, in the crossing from talk to print, 'hearing-dominance yields to sight-dominance'.[18] In his note, Jonson varies that formula in this way: he moves towards sight-dominance in print as a means not of supplanting but of recovering the effects of hearing-dominance, which he values above all but now deems impossible in the theatre. He would take this logic much further after the failure of his next play, *The New Inn* (1629). His published play text opens with a 'Dedication to the Reader' in which Jonson appoints that personage as his new 'Patron' on the grounds that: 'If thou canst but spell there is more hope of thee, then of a hundred fastidious *impertinents*, who were there present the first day, yet never made piece of their prospect the right way' – that is, could not make sense of the play.[19] The edition ends with Jonson's oft-quoted 'Ode to Himself,' which begins, 'Come leave the loathed stage,' and concludes with a fantasy of the poet not as playwright but as ancient bard: 'Leave things so prostitute, / And take the Alcaic lute.'[20] In concert with the opening dedication, this closing poem achieves a layered rhetoric: Jonson is urging the reader, as well as himself, first to abandon the stage for the printed page, and finally (albeit figuratively) to abandon print, the eye, and reading, for the pleasures of verbal music, the ear, and pure audition.

But for all the anxious, injured apparatus that frames the text of *The New Inn*, the folio *Staple of News* proves the less stable, more volatile compound, precisely because it has depicted so damningly the pernicious commerce of news, eyes, and mouths, of talk, manuscript, and print. For a play so alert to and alarmed by the debasements of the new print culture, print itself can supply at best a provisional refuge. In the fifteen years since 1616, when Jonson first sought such security in his published *Works*, the field of print had been irrevocably reshaped by the advent of the periodical press. Joseph Loewenstein sums up one of Jonson's much earlier forays into print (1604) by way of a pun: 'Against the "multitudinous presse" [i.e. the crowd that attended and sometimes impeded live performance of his work] … Jonson counterposes the bulwark, the polemical stability of the Press.'[21] But now that the gossip of the multitudes – perpetual, abundant, but at least evanescent – has been commodified as text, in manuscripts and newsbooks purveyed relentlessly in a 'weekly' (and very successful) 'cheat to draw money,' the Press itself is newly 'multitudinous' and unstable. Under such conditions, mere literacy ('If thou canst but spell, there is more hope of thee …') cannot ensure immunity against the 'great disease,' the culture-wide 'hunger and thirst after published pamphlets of news.' The very readers Jonson addresses may be in receipt of the Staple's commodity. Though he 'prays,' in his note to them, that they 'mend' both the playhouse audience's misprision and the news-appetite that impelled it, his wording measures his misgiving. He knows his 'prayer' is (as the Latin root implies) precarious.

Such precariousness, though, is part of Jonson's stock in trade as playwright. In his two-part assault on the news-trade, as in so much of his writing, he persistently courts those difficulties he would defeat. The very titles that he chooses for both his masque and his play appear almost willfully to foster that failure of interpretation that he decries in his note 'To the Reader': the mistaking of the playwright for just another newsmonger. *News from the New World* sounds like a coranto headline, *The Staple of News* like that company's new trademark; both rubrics trick the ear into 'seeing' text on paper – precisely the sensory transfer Jonson sets himself against. He designs these fusions as small traps, in which to catch the audience and instruct it in the distinction between news and plays. But in the works as in the titles, these distinctions keep dissolving. Both the fictional Gossips and the real-life audience take his play for news. Jonson implies that in the nine years since his last stage play, the news business has rendered the audience unfit to hear and interpret a piece of theatre. True to the title's implication, the Staple has already set up shop in the playhouse; where (in the words of the folio note) 'the hunger and thirst' for news signal that the 'great disease' has carried over in a contagion of consumerism. Nor are the audience the only ones affected. Even the actor performing the Prologue is compelled to cut his own words short when he finds himself coming under the sweet sway of gossip, carried away with the enumeration of such items as the coaches in Hyde Park and the fare at Medley's. The playwright tries to distance himself further, switching the pronoun from 'ours' to 'his' in the second speaking of the play's first line, and thereby cutting himself off from actors as well as audience; seeking in a printed note redress for the wounding miscarriage of the play on stage. Still, Jonson's retreat to the folio sheet is a retreat in both senses of the word: an implicit surrender as well as a calculated withdrawal. To rely so explicitly on the eye in a play that has set itself so vigorously against the eye is to admit at least a partial failure of the project. In *The Staple of News*, Jonson depicts himself as troublingly implicated in the intimacy between news and plays that he seeks to sunder. He endeavours to construct an implacable opposition; he ends by discovering precarious affinities.

Sheridan, by contrast, cheerfully reckons this intimacy ineluctable from the first. He puts news-print on stage, for his audience to 'read,' at the play's outset; he knows they do so anyway, every day. His scene soon moves from the breakfast table to the theatre, where the rehearsal for a preposterous tragedy is in progress, and the overt object of mockery shifts from news to plays. But the satire on the newspapers persists, in the person of Mr Puff, the tragedy's author, director, and indefatigably admiring commentator. As his name suggests (it means blurb, or puff-piece), Puff is a creature made of newsprint. He first made his living by writing ads in which he solicited charitable contributions to be donated to himself as a person subject to numerous (and fictitious) misfortunes: 'bankruptcies, fires, gouts, dropsies, imprisonments, and other valuable calamities' (1.2.29–30). He went on to produce puff-pieces for himself and anyone willing to pay. Sheridan makes clear that Puff's new enterprise of playwriting is both a logical successor and mere subsidiary to all the previous playacting for which the newspapers have provided so congenial and lucrative a venue. Puff speaks unceasingly in the diction of publicity, a language both ventriloquized (he has absorbed it from the newspapers) and ventriloquizing (as publicist he must work so that others will speak his language too). Puff's energetic presence maps the historical distance between Jonson's *Staple* and Sheridan's *Critic*. Jonson produced a play about the news business, swathed in talk; Sheridan presents a play about the theatre business, wrapped in newspaper.

Notes

1 Quoted, with modified punctuation and typography, from *The Dramatic Works of Richard Brinsley Sheridan*, Cecil Price, ed. (Oxford: Clarendon Press, 1973), 2:478; act 1, sc. 1, lines 4–7. Subsequent citations will appear parenthetically: (1.1.4–7).

2 On the *Chronicle* and its extraordinary 'intelligence,' see Charles Harold Gray, *Theatrical Criticism in London to 1795* (New York: Columbia University Press, 1931), 222–6 and 267–78.

3 On the earliest English-language corantos, see Folke Dahl, *A Bibliography of English Corantos and Periodical Newsbooks* (London: The Bibliographical Society, 1952), 31–54.

4 *Hamlet*, William Shakespeare, ed. Harold Jenkins (London: Methuen, 1982), 2.2.519–20. Subsequent citations will appear parenthetically.

5 I am grateful to Derek Hirst for this suggestion.

6 For an overview of the modes of printed news current in London at the time of *Hamlet*'s debut, see M. A. Shaaber, *Some Forerunners of the Newspaper in England, 1476–1622* (1929; reprint, New York: Octagon Books, 1966).

7 *The Diary of Samuel Pepys*, Robert Latham and William Matthews, eds (Berkeley: University of California Press, 1970–73), 1:19.

8 For a classic parsing of the dispute, see D. J. Gordon, 'Poet and Architect: The Intellectual Setting of the Quarrel between Ben Jonson and Inigo Jones,' in *The Renaissance Imagination: Essays and Lectures by D. J. Gordon*, Stephen Orgel, ed. (Berkeley, University of California Press, 1975), 76–101. For a recent reassessment, see A.W.

Johnson, *Ben Jonson: Poetry and Architecture* (Oxford: Clarendon Press, 1994), 4–6 and 13–17.

9 *The Staple of News*, Anthony Parr, ed. (Manchester: Manchester University Press, 1988), 77: 'The Prologue for the Stage' ll. 1–2. Passages from the play will be cited parenthetically, from this edition.

10 For a compact, brilliant analysis of contemporary news-operations (both manuscript and print), of the pioneering operators, and of Jonson's alarm at their new enterprise, see D. F. McKenzie, *The London Book Trade in the Later Seventeenth Century*, Sandars Lectures, Cambridge 1976 (unpublished), 4–9. For comparable studies of the news-satire in *News from the New World*, see Sara Pearl, 'Sounding to Present Occasions: Jonson's Masques of 1620–25,' in David Lindley, ed., *The Court Masque* (Manchester: Manchester University Press, 1984), 61–77; and Paul Sellin, 'The Politics of Ben Jonson's *Newes from the New World Discover'd in the Moone*,' *Viator* 17: 321–37. For a sustained study of the scriptoria and their cultural impact, see Harold Love, *Scribal Publication in Seventeenth-Century England* (Oxford: Clarendon Press, 1993).

11 Parr cites the passages from Chaucer (*The House of Fame*, line 1960) and Ovid (*Metamorphoses*, 12.45) in his edition of *The Staple*, 165 n. 115.

12 *Ben Jonson: The Complete Masques*, Stephen Orgel, ed. (New Haven: Yale University Press, 1969), p. 292, lines 20–21. Subsequent citations will appear parenthetically.

13 *Selected Letters of Samuel Richardson*, John Carroll, ed. (Oxford: Clarendon Press, 1964), 65.

14 Stanley Morison, *The English Newspaper: Some Account of the Physical Development of Journals Printed in London between 1622 and the Present Day* (Cambridge: Cambridge University Press, 1932), 50.

15 The vituperative energy of Jonson's language here sufficiently refutes Julie Sanders's argument that the play 'potentially legitimizes' all forms of news, that it 'does not condemn the expanding print culture of the age,' and that 'in his depiction of the news-staple or office Jonson embraces the form's possibility for both elite and popular cultural practice' (*Ben Jonson's Theatrical Republics* [New York: St. Martin's Press, 1998], 124–5). Nowhere in her chapter on the play does Sanders quote Jonson's note. For a profound and persuasive reckoning of Jonson's pessimism, see McKenzie, *London Book Trade*, 1–10, and '*The Staple of News* and the Late Plays,' in William Blisset et al., eds., *A Celebration of Ben Jonson* (Toronto: University of Toronto Press, 1973), 83–128. What Sanders reads as Jonson's openness to new news-forms, I see as his dismayed awareness that news and plays have much in common – chiefly their appetitive audiences. Such awareness impels Jonson not to an endorsement of newsprint, but to an ever-heightening exasperation with the theater, and a dawning suspicion about the security of print as a place of refuge.

16 Many seventeenth-century writers represented news addiction as a contagious illness; see Ian Atherton, 'The Itch Grown a Disease: Manuscript Transmission of News in the Seventeenth Century,' in Joad Raymond, ed., *News, Newspapers, and Society in Early Modern Britain* (Portland, Oregon: Frank Cass, 1999), 39 and n. 1.

17 *Finnegans Wake* (New York: Viking Press, 1939), 195.

18 Walter Ong, *Orality and Literacy: The Technologizing of the Word* (New York: Methuen, 1982), 117.

19 *The Complete Plays of Ben Jonson*, G. A. Wilkes, ed. (Oxford: Clarendon Press, 1982), 4:367.

20 *Ibid.*, 471, 472.

21 Joseph Loewenstein, 'Printing and the "Multitudinous Presse": The Contentious Texts of Jonson's Masques,' in Jennifer Brady and W. H. Herendeen, eds, *Ben Jonson's 1616 Folio* (Newark: University of Delaware Press, 1991), 187. Loewenstein quotes the phrase 'multitudinous presse' from the volume in which Jonson published the texts of entertainments and speeches he had composed in celebration of the newly crowned James I and his family: *B. Jon: His Part of King James his Royall and Magnificent*

Entertainement ... (London, 1604). There Jonson introduces an address to England's new queen by recalling that, at the country-house festivities for which it was intended, it was 'hindred' (i.e. prevented from being delivered) 'by reason of the Multitudinous presse' (Part 2, B3r).

2 The guises of dissemination in early seventeenth-century England

News in manuscript and print

Sabrina A. Baron

Midway through the seventeenth century and beyond, print and manuscript were equally viable and relevant modes of dissemination, not just for literary texts as Arthur Marrotti, Henry Woudhuysen, and Harold Love have shown, and not just as a coterie phenomenon, but for political information relevant to most classes across the social spectrum of early seventeenth-century England.[1] There is no evidence that print carried more influence on the formation of public opinion than did manuscript as at least one modern historian has insisted.[2] Indeed, the early modern evidence quite often points to the opposite conclusion: much of the rhetoric about print and its functions in the period were negative rather than positive. Take, for example, the admittedly early sentiment: 'The pen is a virgin, the printing press is a whore.'[3] Suspicion of print endured through the age of the handpress, and manuscript retained a cachet. John Donne, for example, was notoriously hesitant about print and believed manuscript would endure when print had faded away and was forgotten.[4]

Seventeenth-century contemporaries were fully aware of the vitality of manuscript publication which modern cultural historians have ignored, especially in the genre of news, where the symbiotic yet competitive relationship between print and manuscript dissemination is particularly visible and instructive. Writing advice for Charles II in the early 1650s, William Cavendish, duke of Newcastle explained that:

> There is another error that does overheat your people extremely and does your Majesty much harm, that every man now has become a statesman, both home and abroad, merely due to the weekly gazette. Domestic or foreign gazettes, therefore, should be forbidden, as also such fellows, as Captain Rosingame, who made £500 a year by writing the news to several persons. This did as much hurt as the other, if not more, for in a letter he might be bolder than they durst in print. Such people are not only to be absolutely forbidden but punished severely if they offend in this way. This will cool the nation so much and quiet state spirits that your Majesty and your subjects will find great benefit from it. Then all our discourses will concern hunting, hawking, bowling, cocking, and such things, and we will always be ready to serve your Majesty.[5]

This is clear evidence that the interest the Crown and its advisers had in regulating news was founded on concern about its content and the social discontent it might inspire. This was more than just a commercial regulatory impulse as many publishing historians have argued.[6] It also shows an awareness that the content of manuscript publications was just as dangerous as that of print publications. Newcastle was advising the king to suppress not only those news publications issued via the printing press, but perhaps even more so, the news published in manuscript: 'for in a letter [writers] might be bolder than they durst in print.' While the contents of manuscript newsletters, both professional and private, indicate this freedom of expression in manuscript was understood throughout virtually all levels of the reading population of early seventeenth-century England, it is an attitude that paradoxically the Crown and its officials developed toward manuscript newsletters somewhat late in the day.

The paradox lies in the fact that from the 1620s, the Crown was increasingly concerned about controlling the content of printed materials and printed news publications in particular. Some of my earlier work discusses the growing politicization of the printed news reporting events in the Thirty Years' War, an issue at the centre of early Stuart domestic and foreign policy which the Crown did not want debated publicly. And news, wrote Roger L'Estrange (a government licenser for the press later in the century), was dangerous because it made 'the multitude too familiar with the actions and counsels of their superiors.' In the case of the Thirty Years' War and early Stuart domestic policies, a large portion of the multitude increasingly disagreed with the actions and counsels of their superiors.[7] C. John Sommerville points out in his work on printed news another dimension of its impact deriving from the regularized periodicity of news achieved in the same period: this 'gave a new urgency to the mundane … creating excitement [political excitement among the general populous, I would argue] – agreeable or otherwise.'[8] So making information about events available to an audience of more than a few people on a regular, sustained basis clearly had social and political consequences in early modern England, of which the Crown was well aware.

As the Crown's anxiety over the impact of printed news on public opinion increased, Crown officials became convinced that the best way to curb the news publications (and so opinion which ran contrary to policy) was to prevent news from being printed in the first place. But despite the best efforts of the Crown, the Church, and the Stationers' Company of London, regulating printing was only erratically successful. The regulatory structures were archaic and obscure, and thus easy to ignore, circumvent, or manipulate, especially by news publications which often were produced overnight and sold quickly – even before the sheets could dry, according to John Milton.[9] Still, print was more susceptible to regulation than manuscript because it was the product of an established, organized trade requiring cumbersome machinery for its manufacture. Pen and paper were easier to conceal, move, or dispose of – not to mention obtain – than was a printing press; and it could always be argued that pen and paper were used for other activities – mundane, personal, private, not necessarily political activities. Beyond monitoring the output of printing presses, the government also tried to restrict the number permitted to operate at any given time, in the 1620s and 1630s arriving at the number of twenty master printers allowed to operate presses in London.[10]

It is clear that prior to 1640 early Stuart governments were equally aware of dangerous political information disseminated in pamphlets, many of which were published in manuscript rather than, or as well as, print. One well-known example is *Leicester's Commonwealth* which the Crown successfully prevented from being printed in England until regulatory processes and bodies broke down in 1641, but which circulated widely in manuscript, copied either from other manuscripts or the 1584 edition printed in Paris.

Another well-known example is *Vox Populi* which attacked James I's subservience to Spain in blunt, seditious language.[11] *Vox Populi* circulated in manuscript before, while, and after it was printed in more than nine editions in London and the Low Countries in 1620, and it was a recognizably disruptive text.[12] Sir Simonds D'Ewes recorded in December 1620 that he had

> perused a notable book styled 'Vox Populi', penned by one Thomas Scott, a minister, marvellously displaying the subtle policies and wicked practices of the Count of Gondomar, the resident Ambassador here from the King of Spain, in prevailing with King James for connivance toward the papists, under the colourable pretence of our Prince's matching with the Infanta Maria of Spain; and that he laboured to accomplish two things, without which the state of England could not be ruined; the first, to breed distaste and jealousies in the king towards his best subjects under the false and adulterate nickname of Puritans, and so to prevent all future parliaments; and secondly, to nourish jars and differences between Great Britain and the United States of the Low Countries, that so being first divided each from the other, they might afterwards be singly and assuredly ruined by Spain and the House of Austria.
>
> There were also contained in this book many other particulars of singular notion and of moment, which made it to be generally approved of, not only by the meaner sort that were zealous for the cause of religion, but also by all men of judgement that were loyally affected to the truth of the Gospel, and the Crown and the throne. But the king himself, hoping to get the Prince Elector, his son-in-law, to be restored to the Palatinate by an amicable treaty, was much incensed at the sight of it, as being published at an unseasonable time, though otherwise it seemed to proceed from an honest English heart.[13]

This passage illustrates that contemporaries believed *Vox Populi* was revealing a conspiracy, in which their king was likely a participant, to strike at the foundations of their country, their church, and their society. It also illustrates that contemporaries, including James I, understood that the political atmosphere at the time any news was published (whether in manuscript or in print) was the most important factor in determining how it would be received and what impact it would have on political opinion, as well as how regulatory authorities would respond. D'Ewes suggested that James would not have been so incensed about *Vox Populi* had it not appeared at a crucial point in his negotiations with Spain.

Secretary of State Sir George Calvert was searching in November 1620 for the author of the politically incorrect tract. He hauled in Captain Thomas Gainsford who had been discovered in possession of a manuscript sequel to *Vox Populi* entitled 'Vox Spiritus, or Sir Walter Raleigh's Ghost.' Gainsford was a natural target for the Privy Council, 'a suspitious person' because he edited the printed news corantos published by Nathaniel Butter and Nicholas Bourne. The corantos were implicitly critical of James I's foreign policy by their very existence. It was an easy assumption that Gainsford had written *Vox Populi* and the sequel. Calvert sent the manuscript to James I himself to see how the king wanted him to proceed. As we know from D'Ewes, James was not pleased, but despite the seditious nature of 'Vox Spiritus' and the accompanying fears that the house of the Spanish Ambassador was about to be attacked, Calvert was called off the case to attend the king at Woodstock.[14] A few months later, the manuscript news writer John Chamberlain reported that 'the author of Vox Populi is discovered to be one Scot a minister, being betrayed by the printer, who thereby … saved himself.'[15] Thomas Scott was another known troublemaker, and when the Privy Council came after him this time, he fled England just ahead of the Council's pursuivant for the relative safety of the Low Countries. From there he continued to harass the Crown with a stream of anti-Spanish writings until his assassination by a fanatic minister in 1626. Gainsford remained in England and carried on with his editorial duties unmolested until he succumbed to a disease, possibly the plague, in 1624. The Council had a limited success in controlling manuscript dissemination in this instance: Scot got away, but 'Vox Spiritus' was available only in manuscript until the 1980s, and Gainsford seems to have limited his activities to the printed, licensed corantos thereafter.[16]

This sort of attention devoted by the Privy Council to *Vox Populi* and 'Vox Spiritus' and similar print- and manuscript-published pamphlets was never devoted to the manuscript dissemination of news, even though it was recognized by more contemporaries than Newcastle that the manuscript news was potentially if not actually more incendiary. Close official scrutiny was reserved for the printed news.

One possible explanation for this dichotomy was that there was no apparent conjunction of manuscript news with a specific political cause as there was in the printed news. The publishers of the printed news corantos and the supporters of the Palatine cause in the Thirty Years' War, that is to say the supporters of Protestants in the war against Catholics, intersected significantly. Nathaniel Butter, the premiere publisher and vendor of printed news, displayed the coat of arms of the Elector Palatine – the war's leading Protestant protagonist – on the title page of his coranto series, leaving little doubt where his sympathies resided or what policy he was seeking to influence. It is clear that contemporaries read this symbol in the same way. John Rous, the Norfolk clergyman, recorded in his diary an acquaintance's analysis that 'every man's religion is knowne by his newes; the Puritan talkes of Bethlehem Gabor, &c.'[17] Other arguments about general fear of information in the hands of the lower orders of society and the concomitant fear of the political activism they were developing as articulated by contemporary observers such as D'Ewes above and in the work of later historians, notably Richard Cust's study of the forced loan, also illustrate the role and effect of news dissemination and developing contemporary notions about that role and effect.[18]

But the troubling question of why the manuscript newsletters were not regulated by the Crown in the same way as print remains. The difficulty of policing the mode of production of manuscript was discussed earlier. Beyond that, there was no immediate, particular political cause associated with manuscript news. Still, the manuscript newsletters are filled with fears of interception and pleas to commit the letters to the most confidential secretary in the world, the fire, but no evidence has come to light which indicates that newsletters were ever intercepted or disrupted in any other way by government intervention.

This is even more surprising in view of the connections between the closely scrutinized printed news industry and the manuscript news business.[19] Manuscript news, both in private letters and in letters written for hire, certainly predated the 1620s boom of printed news publishing generated by the Continental religious war, but the two were intimately connected. The Stationer Nathaniel Butter and his long-time acquaintance and collaborator John Pory were central figures in the development of both genres. Pory was a prominent subscription writer who sent and received his letters from Butter's shop at the sign of the Pied Bull in a prime location between the two centres of information gathering in early Stuart London – St Paul's churchyard and the Royal Exchange in Cheapside. Pory's manuscript newsletters would have been in line with other manuscript publications such as separates which Butter sold off his shop board or as copies-on-demand. Undoubtedly anyone interested in news could have read Pory's reports in the shop as well. Pory not only exchanged foreign news he had collected from foreign correspondents, personal contacts, and in the London gossip markets with Butter's print operation, but he likely also replaced Gainsford as the editor of Butter's corantos after the Captain's death in 1624.

Pory was free with his descriptions of most aspects of his multifaceted life and career, even the unflattering ones, but he was remarkably coy about his activities while the corantos flourished. He had consistently experienced financial difficulties, primarily due to his fondness for drink, but from 1624 to 1632 he was remarkably solvent and secure, although not visibly employed other than in writing manuscript newsletters and perhaps some secretarial duties for Robert Rich, earl of Warwick.[20] When the corantos were suppressed in 1632, Pory's was one of the few voices raised in protest, in manuscript, about 'this smothering of the Currantoes.' '[W]ee … be muzled, and our mouth stopt,' he wrote. This was more than a sales pitch or sympathy for the Protestant cause; these were the words of a man who recognized the correlation between information and power and who had used the printed and written word to great advantage on behalf of a number of causes. It was also the voice of a man who had just lost a significant portion of his livelihood. If manuscript news had been his sole source of support and interest, Pory should have welcomed the suppression of the corantos as good for business.[21]

The same people who produced the printed news produced the commercial manuscript newsletters, and these newsletters generally included reports of foreign news (especially while the Thirty Years' War dominated current political events) which the Crown scrutinized so closely in print. In fact, in 1627 the Crown had set up a special government licenser, Georg Weckherlin, a member of a Secretary of State's staff, to exercise particular over-sight of printed news. At the same time, the Crown also tightened regulations to be enforced by the Stationers' Company to further control the printed news. But the underlying purpose of the manuscript newsletters was to report domestic events of political significance – something the corantos did not do, but for which there was clearly a market.

In the modern scholarship on news and publishing history a fiction somehow arose and has been perpetuated that domestic news could only be reported in manuscript letters because a law or a decree or a proclamation somewhere along the line had banned the printing of domestic news. While there are statutes dating back to Richard II which prohibit the spreading of rumours and false news, there was no prohibition on the printing of domestic news as such, something only Sheila Lambert has recognized hitherto.[22] It is possible that domestic news was confined to manuscript in deference to a clause in a statute of 23 Elizabeth, cap. 2 stating that, 'yf any p[er]son or persons … shall advisedlye and with a maliciouse intente againste our said Soverigne Ladye, devyse and wrighte printe or setforthe, any manner of Booke Ryme Ballade Letter or Writing, conteyning any false sedicious and slaunderous Matter to the Defamacon of the Queenes Ma[tie] that nowe ys, or to the encoraging stirring or moving of any Insurreccon or Rebellion,' they were liable to prosecution for felony which carried serious penalties including mutilation and execution by hanging.[23] The Crown clearly believed 'stirring' insurrection and rebellion was the intent of news, especially of news which reached a wide audience as did the printed news. But there is no law or proclamation explicitly prohibiting the printing of domestic news in England.

The Elizabethan statute cited above echoes the law of seditious libel, and potential prosecution under this law may have been chiefly responsible for the locating of domestic news dissemination in the realm of manuscript rather than that of print. Many literary scholars have concluded this is why certain literary forms such as lyric poetry and political satire were published only in manuscript.[24] The law of seditious libel was enshrined in a Tudor statute and historically had been used to great success by the Crown, particularly as a method of controlling potentially seditious printing. The work of Philip Hamburger shows this plainly.[25] Further, in the period under discussion here, several notable cases of printing which the Crown found repugnant were prosecuted under the law of seditious libel to ensure some of the Crown's greatest seventeenth-century successes in the regulation of print. A prime example is the case of Henry Burton, John Bastwick, and William Prynne, indiscriminate authors of printed works that enraged the Crown through a variety of attacks, who were finally silenced under the law of seditious libel in 1637 after more than a decade of attempts to accomplish this through other measures. Their prosecution for seditious libel worked so well that at the same time the long, drawn-out power struggle between Bishop John Williams of Lincoln, Lord Keeper under James I, and his opponents in the Caroline regime was ultimately concluded by tarring him with the same brush as Burton, Bastwick, and Prynne. Williams too was convicted under seditious libel for having authorized the printing of his own doctrinally controversial book, *The Holy Table, Name and Thing*. As Williams' case in particular illustrates, almost anything could be construed to be seditious libel and there was a clear way of proceeding against it at law with significant pains and penalties attached.[26] But however successful they were, these kinds of legal proceedings were expensive in terms of expending valuable time, money, energy, political capital, and popular appeal with the people.

The dissemination of politically volatile information in manuscript newsletters was as much subject to the pains and penalties of the law as was news in print. It is clear that the Crown believed rebellion and sedition were the results of disseminating any kind of news in any format in early modern England. But while the manuscript newsletters were known to, read by, contributed to, and relied upon by high-ranking members of the Privy Council and the upper levels of society, and were viewed in retrospect by them as a major contributing factor to Charles I's troubles, still the Crown made no move against them during the reign of Charles I.

Perhaps this was because many manuscript news subscriptions looked on the surface to be no more than ordinary correspondence of letters written by both parties in the exchange. It is plausible that the newsletters therefore could not be divorced from the fact that they were formatted and transmitted in the same way as all letters, making them personal rather than public, more closely associated with the private individual who wrote the letter and the private individual who received it, than the public actions described in the letter and the public opinion influenced and inspired by these letters.

Another plausible, if less probable, explanation is that the manuscript news writers were not interfered with because they took pains to hide their identities. Their letters were often anonymous, unsigned, or as in the case of the letters of Captain Edmund Rossingham, who took over his cousin John Pory's subscription enterprise in 1634, signed almost exclusively with initials. Gerald Aylmer has recently speculated that the subscription writer John Flower, who supplied John viscount Scudamore with newsletters as well as separates, proclamations, corantos, books, and verses over a period of five years, was a fictitious persona constructed to protect the news writer should his letters fall into hands other than those for which they were intended.[27] The more prominent writers such as Chamberlain, Pory, and Rossingham were, however, well-known figures widely recognized in London, familiar presences in St Paul's and at the Exchange, acquainted with Privy Councillors, aristocrats, and Secretaries of State. The activities of these manuscript news writers at least were well-known, yet also unregulated.

But if the manuscript news writers did employ measures to avoid detection and prosecution, it should be noted that the manuscript letters did not resort to codes, ciphers, or shorthand as letters filled with sensitive information would do during other periods of high political stress such as the civil wars.[28] Furthermore, while it was perfectly within the prerogative of the Crown to intercept letters in the earlier decades of the seventeenth century as it did in the middle and later decades, and there is ample evidence that news writers like Pory believed his letters were destined to fall into hostile hands, there is no evidence that manuscript newsletters were intercepted or the authors arrested. The Crown completely ignored the dissemination of subscription manuscript newsletters in the 1620s and 1630s.

It may be argued as well that the Crown ignored the letters because of the audience they addressed – an audience that could afford the price of a subscription, or custom copies from a Stationer's or scrivener's shop. Harold Love has argued that manuscript production in general was more expensive than print production due to the price of paper and ink (although the work of Peter Blayney and others shows that the price of paper was a major outlay for print operations as well, on average being one-third to three-fourths of a printer's total production costs). Still, there is no doubt that a subscription to a London manuscript newsletter was expensive. At the end of his career, Pory charged his clients anywhere between £5 and £20 a year for his weekly letters, depending on how long they had been subscribers. Scudamore paid the shadowy Flower £11 for one years' services in 1633.[29] In 1634 Rossingham charged one of his best and most enduring clients, Algernon Percy, tenth earl of Northumberland, £10 yearly; by 1636, Northumberland's rate was up to £20. And, in fact, £20 was the price a competitor quoted for Rossingham's subscription in 1640.[30] Northumberland's brother-in-law, Robert Sidney, second earl of Leicester, paid Rossingham £10 in 1637 and was still paying him the same in 1640; at that time, however, Rossingham demanded his payment in gold.[31]

Newcastle claimed that Rossingham had had an income of £500 a year from his news writing. At £10 per subscription, that would be fifty clients; at £20, twenty-five clients. Sixteen subscribers to Pory's letters, most of whom Rossingham inherited with the business, can be identified, and a further eight who were original clients of the Captain are also known.[32] Undoubtedly, there were more than these twenty-four identifiable subscribers. So a £500 income for Rossingham is not unrealistic; it is, in fact, a rather accurate estimate based on available evidence. Rossingham's successful career alone serves to refute Joad Raymond's assertion that there was no printed domestic news product because there was no market for it. According to Raymond, the

English consumer of news simply preferred foreign news over domestic. This was clearly not the case.[33]

Thus, it may be argued that the manuscript newsletters were in essence self-policing because these high prices limited circulation to only members of the elite who could afford an annual subscription. This seems a reasonable argument in light of the cost of a Rossingham subscription and the predominance of nobility and gentry among his clients. That said, Scudamore with his multiple subscriptions is singular evidence against the prohibitive expense argument.[34] There were also ways for those less wealthy to cut the cost of a newsletter subscription. Sir Thomas Puckering and Sir Thomas Lucy, Warwickshire neighbours and long-time clients of Pory and Rossingham, shared a subscription, and thus its cost. On occasion they split the cost even further with a third neighbour and co-subscriber, Lord Brooke. Many subscribers refused to accept letters, suspending the subscription, if they were in London themselves or otherwise away from home, presumably in order to deduct from the annual fee the cost of letters they might have received during those times. Some subscribers such as William Cecil, second earl of Salisbury, in his business relationship with Pory (just one of the writers to whom the earl subscribed) received only occasional letters. For example, Salisbury paid Pory the low sum of two shillings six pence over one six-month period in the early 1630s.[35]

There are also questions surrounding the relevance of information disseminated in the manuscript newsletters to the increased political awareness and engagement of early modern English society, and in particular, to that of the lower social orders who could not afford to buy the letters and who were largely unable to read. Yet if only a small group at the top of the social order could afford to buy the letters for themselves, or had the capability to read them for themselves, there was nothing to prevent the dissemination of the information in the manuscript letters by other means to sectors lower down the social scale.[36]

There were ways to obtain the contents of the manuscript letters other than having a personal subscription. Manuscript newsletters were sold off the shop boards of Stationers and scriveners in London. It must also be noted that multiple copies of the manuscript letters were available not only from the Stationers' and scriveners' copies, but also from other sources. Harold Love writes of the 'chain-copying' of newsletters such as the Reverend Joseph Mead at Cambridge did for his friend Sir Martin Stuteville in Surrey and others of his acquaintance. Stuteville also sent Mead information from unique letters that he received. Mead sent the original newsletters along to Stuteville just as Scudamore's archive contains newsletters to which he did not subscribe personally but that were passed on to him by friends.[37] The peripatetic George Garrard also digested his newsletters for his wide group of correspondents, as had Chamberlain for Sir Dudley Carleton earlier in the century. There was another sort of 'chain' newsletter as well. For example, Sir Simonds D'Ewes wrote a letter of news to Sir William Spring, but D'Ewes sent it first to Mead, unsealed, so he could read it. Mead then sent the letter to Stuteville who was also to read it, then seal it, and finally send it on to Spring. These examples indicate that Sheila Lambert was mistaken when she asserted that Pory's request to Scudamore to burn his letters was an effort to preserve the exclusivity of his subscription rather than to conceal any contents the government might find objectionable. L'Estrange believed in 1688 that the news writer Dyer distributed 500 copies of his manuscript newsletter weekly. Given the accuracy of contemporary estimates of Rossingham's income and thereby distribution, and the many methods that existed for copying newsletters, such speculations must be given credence.[38]

The chain of oral dissemination of information from the manuscript newsletters also played an important role in a society where oral transmission remained paramount and the cost of a personal subscription and custom copies perhaps prohibitive. Anyone looking for news could go to a Stationer's or scrivener's shop to read letters for themselves, or to discuss current news and pick up relevant gossip. Letters such as those written by Sir Edward Mountagu to his brother Viscount Mandeville are riddled with such comments as 'it is said,' 'they say,' 'I hear,' 'I have heard.' The Montagu correspondence and other examples of newsletters offer numerous occasions where individuals went to the centre aisle of St Paul's Cathedral and the book shops in its yard or the Exchange to hear the latest news in the form of conversation, gossip, or read aloud from proclamations or other documents including newsletters to the large groups that gathered in those public places.

In fact, much of what the manuscript letters disseminated was information gathered from oral transmission, from personal conversations, or from overheard conversations. John Pory frequented locations and events where he was likely to hear important information to report to his subscribers, for example dinner with George Abbot, the archbishop of Canterbury, at Lambeth Palace or attending county elections with the earl of Warwick. A coranto publisher in 1630 complained that those who gossiped in the aisles of St Paul's were less likely to buy the printed news, a comment that is more than vaguely reminiscent of the admonition to readers of the First Folio of Shakespeare's works to please buy it themselves rather than reading a borrowed or rented copy. The diarist Rous was clearly a consumer of both written and printed news, but he also heard a large amount of his news from people whom he encountered. News received from the earl of Warwick's coachman is a prominent example that features in his diary. This same mode of dissemination can also be found in Mead's correspondence with Stuteville. Mead was a voracious consumer of the printed and written news from London, having multiple subscriptions and multiple suppliers of printed news, yet he still reported to Stuteville what he had heard from the cheese man when he made a delivery. The very well-informed Thomas Crosfield at Oxford received some of his news from Mr Smythers' son who had it from his father who undoubtedly had also received it verbally from another individual. Joad Raymond notes that the printed news was filled with the nuances and characteristics of oral speaking – laughter, exclamation, etc.[39] Early modern England, despite a long existence of manuscript transmission and an explosion of print transmission, remained a society in which most transmission of information was oral.

It should also be noted that news reached marginal members of early modern English society, such as women, through print, manuscript, and oral dissemination. Lord Poulett wrote to Secretary Dorchester that Lady Poulett read all the news she could find, hoping to learn who the Secretary's next wife would be. Lady Barrington's nephew sent her corantos. Garrard read newsletters he wrote and received aloud to the countess of Northumberland when she was bedridden awaiting the birth of a child. Her sister, the countess of Leicester, swapped news with Rossingham when he visited Penshurst and she read the Captain's subscription letters before her steward sent them on to her husband in France. Dorothy Shawe, wife of the Puritan divine John Shawe, had an appetite for news as did the mistress of one of the resident Spanish Ambassadors in London, who offered the latest news rather than gold in exchange for her sexual favours.[40] News published via print, manuscript, and speech reached the four corners of the kingdom as illustrated by the diaries of Rous in Norfolk, Walter Yonge in Devon, Crosfield in Oxford, William Whiteway in Dorset, and the correspondence of the Wynn family in Wales.[41]

Thus the terms 'small' and 'elite,' when applied to the audience for manuscript newsletters, must be considered carefully within this context. Indeed, some seventeenth-century contemporaries, including news writers like Pory, believed the lower orders were better informed than the nobility – the natural governing classes. He entreated Scudamore to read newsletters so he would be at least as informed as his social inferiors. Underlying this is the implication that information is power and that the ruling classes needed to always be on their toes, to know what information reached the lower levels of society in order to anticipate the actions of their inferiors. The earl of Leicester, subscriber to Rossingham's newsletters, English Ambassador in Paris receiving regular dispatches from the Secretaries of State, member of the Privy Council, brother-in-law to the Lord High Admiral with another brother-in-law (Sir Henry Percy) and sister-in-law (Lucy Percy Hay, countess of Carlisle) in the queen's household and inner circle, and thus plugged in to some of the best informed networks in the kingdom, still implored his steward for any news 'of great or small importance it is no matter. The knowledge of anything is welcome.'[42]

It is also useful to compare the size of the potential audience for manuscript newsletters with that of the potential audience for printed news. The average print run of a printed newsbook in the 1640s – more widely disseminated, more popular, and more politically effective than the corantos twenty years earlier – was between 200 and 250 copies. This in theory was the capacity to reach an audience five to ten times the size of Rossingham's putative audience, for example. However, if we take into account that there were more news writers than Rossingham and that there were more ways than one of getting news, the disparity between the two potential levels of circulation was not so great. With adjustments, it might be considered that the newsbooks had the potential to reach two or three times the audience reached by the manuscript news. But it should also be noted that the average newsbook print run was half the size of Dyer's manuscript news production in the later seventeenth century. The cost of printed news relative to that of the manuscript letters should also be considered. Printed corantos, for example, cost 2p each.[43] At £5 a year, Pory's weekly manuscript letters cost ten times as much. But there were cheaper options as noted in detail above. Furthermore, while Harold Love refuses to speculate on the cost of copying in manuscript as a rule, he has noted some cases where copying was done for as little as 2p per page.[44] The cost of manuscript did not always make it inaccessible to those of lesser means.

That said, an audience who could afford Pory's and Rossingham's rates, for example, was by and large an audience drawn from the upper orders of society, and in the seventeenth century, this was a self-regulating audience. The common concepts of a hierarchical society and the predetermined and rigid roles of the various strata in such a society were expected to dictate the actions of individuals within those classes, upper as well as lower. But if the audience that had access to manuscript newsletters was indeed limited to a group of twenty-five or fifty among the higher ranks, the Crown completely miscalculated their ability and furthermore, their desire and need, to regulate themselves politically. If, as seems to be the case, the Caroline regime believed the upper orders of society impervious to what Richard Cust has called the politically polarizing effect of news – which the examples given here show that seventeenth-century contemporaries understood quite well – the regime exhibited a *naïveté*, insularity, and insensitivity that revisionist historians continue to insist was not possible in the decades prior to civil war.[45] But they should note that no one was more surprised that Charles I when overwhelming support for his wars was not forthcoming from the nobility and gentry in the late 1630s and early 1640s. If he was not cloistered in palaces and absorbed in fantastic collections of art, he was at the very least out of step with popular political opinion in his realm. The king's deep belief in the divine sanction of his office undoubtedly made it impossible for him to comprehend such growth and shifts in political opinion as England clearly experienced between 1620 and 1640. This is the most likely reason for Charles I's regime to have ignored the manuscript newsletters and their potential dangers, and the reason they proved so harmful to the success of his policies.

Harold Love found that manuscript dissemination defined 'communities of the like-minded,' whether royalists or Catholics or poets or music lovers.[46] It is clear that the readily identifiable readership of the manuscript newsletters constituted such a community. Attention must be drawn to the fact that this community exhibited the same attributes that Cust has identified as a common denominator among refusers of the Forced Loan in 1626–7 who were becoming more politically aware and more politically active than ever before. These attributes were zealous Protestantism, support for the defence of the Low Countries and the restoration of the Palatinate, and involvement in the exploration and colonization movements – all of which were distinctly anti-Spanish, anti-Catholic, and increasingly non-traditional sentiments.[47] To these can be added an appetite for information in the form of news, in manuscript, in print, and in speech. These were the underpinnings of political polarization not only in the 1620s but in the 1630s as well. These were, in fact, one and the same community.

Revisionist historians insist there were few if any expressions of dissatisfaction with the Personal Rule in private correspondence, diaries, or in the subscription newsletters of the time, and further, that there was no significant news reporting that would have engendered such feelings. This is based on a one-dimensional view not only of the actual political climate of the Personal Rule, but also of the nature of the manuscript newsletters. It is simply not true that the 1630s was a period where there was little or no relevant news reporting.[48] If Rossingham served up no analysis of events with a political slant to his readers, as Pory and others most definitely did to theirs, surely the fundamental information the Captain provided was raw material well-suited to the construction of politicized public opinion, a great deal of which inevitably opposed the reported actions of Charles I's regime during the Personal Rule.

It is worth noting that the identifiable readership of manuscript newsletters included a number of elites who were disillusioned in the 1620s and 1630s and who were parliamentary supporters in the 1640s and 1650s, among them the radical Lord Brooke, Viscount Saye, Sir Thomas Lucy, and the earls of Northumberland, Salisbury, Huntington, and Warwick. In some ways, as Wallace Notestein argued long ago, the manuscript newsletters and Parliament's desire for an acknowledged role in the government of the kingdom were indelibly linked. It was after all the reporting of events in and surrounding Parliament sessions that seems to have been the original reason that manuscript newsletters proliferated in the late sixteenth and early seventeenth centuries.[49] It is tempting to make the case for a correlation between the sorts of information reported in the manuscript newsletters, the rise of parliamentary concern over the survival of its ancient rights and privileges, and the growth of the same fears among the population at large.

There is evidence that towards the end of the Personal Rule at least one person in Charles I's government was becoming aware of the threat posed by manuscript news – and moving to do something about it. That person was William Laud, archbishop of Canterbury, not coincidentally the chief advocate and, by virtue of his position in the Church and consequently the civil government, the chief enforcing officer of the regulations attempting to restrict printed materials. In July 1640 Laud and his most prominent henchman in the regulation of print, Sir John Lambe, through the machinery of the High Commission for Ecclesiastical Causes, were preparing to move against John Castle, the signet clerk who wrote newsletters to the earl of Bridgwater among others.[50] But Laud and Lambe were stopped short by the Long Parliament's attack on the episcopacy and the prerogative courts in the Long Parliament, which stripped them of their power. Laud was imprisoned in the Tower in December 1640 and Lambe fled the country for fear of prosecution. There is no evidence that their fledgling campaign against manuscript news ever went forward.

Ironically, the Long Parliament also provided unprecedented material for the manuscript news writers to report in their letters. Rossingham advertised to his clients that he would provide the fullest coverage possible of events in the House of Commons, of which he was not a member. The manuscript newsletters thus laid the groundwork for the tide of printed domestic news that flowed out of the presses of London after 1641 – and they had done so well before the appearance of 'Diurnall Occurrences.' The manuscript newsletters of the 1630s must also be recognized as a vital link between the mentality behind the printed corantos in the 1620s and the purpose of the printed newsbooks in the 1640s.

While printed news in the middle of the century was perhaps beginning to come into its own as a method of dissemination, the manuscript newsletters also continued to be a vital mode of dissemination well into the eighteenth century. Little is as yet known of their history during the Civil War and Interregnum, but Rossingham, for example, continued to sell his letters full of political information to at least the earl of Northumberland well into the 1650s. The manuscript letters remained important in dissemination of information in the Restoration era as well when Newcastle's advice and experience of the past were heeded and Charles II's government undertook to police manuscript news as well as printed news for the first time.

Notes

1 Arthur F. Marotti, *Manuscript, Print, and the English Renaissance Lyric* (Ithaca, NY, 1995); H. R. Woudhuysen, *Sir Philip Sidney and the Circulation of Manuscripts 1558–1640* (Oxford, 1996); and Harold Love, *Scribal Publication in Seventeenth-Century England* (Oxford, 1993).
2 Joad Raymond, *The Invention of the Newspaper: English Newsbooks 1641–1649* (Oxford, 1996), p. 96.
3 Filippo De Strata, *Polemic Against Printing*, eds Shelagh Grier and Martin Lowry (Birmingham, 1986).
4 Love, *Scribal Publication*, p. 169.
5 Gloria Italiano Anzilotti, *An English Prince: Newcastle's Machiavellian Political Guide to Charles II* (Pisa, 1988), pp. 156–7.
6 See, for example, the various work of Sheila Lambert.
7 Roger L'Estrange was the Crown licenser for the press after 1663. Quoted in Christopher Hill, 'Censorship and English Literature,' in *The Collected Essays of Christopher Hill*, 3 vols (Amherst, MA, 1985), 1: 33.
8 C. John Sommerville, *The News Revolution in England* (Oxford, 1996), pp. 8, 10.
9 [John Milton], *Areopagitica: A Speech of Mr. John Milton for the Liberty of Vnlicenc'd Printing, To the Parlament of England* (London, 1644), [Wing M2092], p. 744.
10 [July 1637], Dell's list of master printers, Public Record Office (henceforth PRO), State Papers, Domestic 16/364/111; *A Decree of Star Chamber Concerning Printing. Made July 11, 1637* (London, 1637); *An Order of the Lords and Commons Assembled in Parliament. For the Regulating of Printing ...* (London, 1643).
11 Woudhuysen, *Sir Philip Sydney*, pp. 17, 148–9; Sheila Lambert, 'Coranto Printing in England: The First Newsbooks,' *Journal of Newspaper and Periodical History* 8 (1992): 3–19.
12 *Short Title Catlogue* (henceforth *STC*), 2: s.v. Scott, Thomas; *A Companion to Arber*, ed. W. W. Greg (Oxford, 1967), pp. 176–8.
13 *The Autobiography and Correspondence of Sir Simonds D'Ewes, Bart., During the Reigns of James I and Charles I* (London, 1845), 2 vols, ed. James O. Halliwell, 1: 158–60.
14 Simon L. Adams, 'Captain Thomas Gainsford, the "Vox Spiritus" and the *Vox Populi*,' *Bulletin of the Institute for Historical Research* (henceforth *BIHR*) 49 (May 1976): 141–4;

Calvert to Buckingham, 28 November 1620, *The Fortescue Papers* ... (London, 1871), vol. 1, ed. S. R. Gardiner, pp. 143–4.

15 Chamberlain to Carleton, 3 February 1620[21], PRO, SP14/119/64.

16 Chamberlain to Carleton, 19 February 1620[21], PRO, SP14/119/99; *The Dictionary of National Biography* (henceforth *DNB*), s.v. Gainsford; Adams, 'Captain Thomas Gainford,' pp. 141–4.

17 *Diary of John Rous, Incumbent of Santon Downham, Suffolk, From 1625 to 1642* (London, 1861), ed. Mary Anne Everett Green, p. 43.

18 Richard P. Cust, *The Forced Loan and English Politics 1626–1628* (Oxford, 1987).

19 Arthur F. Marotti, 'Manuscript, Print, and the Social History of the Lyric,' in *The Cambridge Companion to English Poetry: Donne to Marvell* (Cambridge, 1993), ed. Thomas N. Corns, p. 56; Marotti, *Manuscript*, p. 68; Woudhuysen, *Sir Philip Sydney*, p. 8.

20 William S. Powell, *John Pory 1572–1636: The Life and Letters of a Man of Many Parts* (Chapel Hill, NC, 1977), *passim*; S. A. Baron, 'John Pory,' *The History of Parliament: The House of Commons 1603–40* (London, forthcoming), eds J. P. Ferris and A. D. Thrush; and Pory's letters in Powell's typescripts and the British Library (henceforth BL), Harleian Manuscripts (henceforth Harl. Mss) 389, 390, 7000 and PRO, Chancery (henceforth C) 115.

21 Pory to Scudamore, 20 October 1632, PRO, C115/M35/8415; Pory to Brooke, [25 Oct 1632], BL, Harl. Mss 7000, fols 389–90; Pory to Scudamore, [27 October] 1632, C115/M35/8424; Pory to Lucy, 1 November 1632, Harl. Mss 7000; 9 November 1632, *The Diary of Thomas Crosfield M.A., B.D. Fellow of Queen's College, Oxford* (London, 1935), ed. Frederick S. Boas; Raymond, *Invention of the Newspaper*, p. 93.

22 Lambert, 'State Control of the Press,' p. 2. Compare, for example, Raymond, *Invention of the Newspaper*, p. 10; Woudhuysen, *Sir Philip Sydney*, p. 183.

23 *Statutes of the Realm* (London, 1819), 4: 23 Eliz. c. 2.

24 Josephine A. Roberts, 'Lady Mary Wroth's *Urania*: A Response to Jacobean Censorship,' in *New Ways of Looking at Old Texts* (Binghamton, NY, 1993), ed. W. Speed Hill, pp. 125–9; Woudhuysen, *Sir Philip Sydney*, p. 12.

25 Philip Hamburger, 'The Development of the Law of Seditious Libel and the Control of the Press,' *Stanford Law Review* 37 (1985): 661–765.

26 In the third information against Williams in Star Chamber, one of the charges against him was that he had received letters from Osbaldeston which libelled Laud and not done anything to punish Osbaldeston; another of the charges was that the letters contained false news. John Hacket, *Scrinia Reserata: A Memorial Offer'd to the Great Deservings of John Williams, D.D.* ..., 2 vols (London, 1693), [Wing H171], 2: 131.

27 Gerald Aylmer, unpublished paper delivered at 'The Putney Debates,' Folger Shakespeare Library, Washington, DC, October 1997; Ian Atherton, 'John, 1st Viscount Scudamore 1601–71: A Career at Court and in the Country, 1602–43,' Ph.D. thesis, Cambridge University, 1993, p. 264.

28 I am grateful to Michael Mendle for discussion on this point. His forthcoming work on shorthand in the seventeenth century will shed further light on this topic. See also Chapter 3 below.

29 Peter W. M. Blayney, 'The Publication of Playbooks,' in *A New History of Early English Drama* (New York, 1997), eds John D. Cox and David Scott Kastan, pp. 407–9; Raymond, *Invention of the Newspaper*, p. 234; BL, Cecil Papers (Hatfield), Boxes G-H, H-8, Private Expenses, January–September 1631; Pory to Scudamore, [15?] 25 December 1632, PRO, C115/M35/8422; Alnwick Castle Mss, General Household Accounts, 1631–40, M390; Atherton, 'John, 1st Viscount Scudamore,' pp. 264, 269. I am grateful to the Marquess of Salisbury for permission to consult material on microfilm at the British Library.

30 Alnwick Castle Mss, General Household Accounts, 1631–40, M390; Robert Crane to Sir Robert Crane, 29 May 1640, Bodleian Library (henceforth Bodl L), Tanner Mss 65, fols 78r-v and endorsement.

31 Leicester to Hawkins, 6/16 January 1636[37], Historical Manuscripts Commission (hereafter HMC), *Report on the Manuscripts of the Right Honorable Viscount De L'Isle, V. C. Preserved at Penshurst Place, Kent: Sidney Papers 1626–1698* (henceforth *D & D*) (London, 1966), ed. G. Dyfnallt, VI: 78; Hawkins to Leicester, 19 January 1636[37] and 26 January 1636[37], BL, Egerton Mss 807, fols 61v, 65v; Hawkins to Leicester, 1 August 1639, *D & D*, VI: 171; Hawkins to Leicester, 29 October 1640, *D & D*, VI: 336.

32 Pory's clients included: Sir Robert Cotton, Sir Dudley Carleton viscount Dorchester, John Chamberlain, the earl of Newport, Sir Thomas Puckering, Sir Thomas Lucy, Lord Brooke, Reverend Joseph Mead, George Garrard, the ninth and tenth earls of Northumberland, the first and second earls of Salisbury, John viscount Scudamore, Robert Lord Rich, Sir Nathaniel Rich, Robert Rich, first earl of Warwick, possibly Sir Thomas Wentworth, first earl of Strafford, and persons in Virginia. Rossingham's clients included: the tenth earl of Northumberland, the second earl of Salisbury, Viscount Saye, Lord Brooke, Sir Christopher Egerton, Scudamore, Edward second viscount Conway, Garrard, Robert Crane, Robert Sidney, second earl of Leicester, Puckering, Lucy, Henry Hastings fifth earl of Huntington, Gervaise Clifton, Sir Henry Vane, and possibly Wentworth.

33 Raymond, *Invention of the Newspaper*, p. 145.

34 Scudamore received letters from: Ralph Starkey, John Flower, John Pory, Edmund Rossingham, Georg Weckherlin, Amerigo Salvetti, Sir Henry Herbert, James Palmer, John Burghe, Robin Reade, and possibly others. Atherton, 'John, 1st Viscount Scudamore,'; PRO, C115, and BL, Additional Mss (henceforth Ass Mss) 11045, *passim*.

35 BL, Cecil Papers (Hatfield), Boxes G-H, H-8, Private Expenses, 1630.

36 Richard P. Cust, 'News and Politics in Early Seventeenth-Century England,' *Past and Present* 112 (1986): 65.

37 Atherton, 'John, 1st Viscount Scudamore,' p. 103.

38 Love, *Scribal Publication*, pp. 11, 14; 27 May 1626, Mead to Stuteville, BL, Harl. Mss 390, fol. 66; Lambert, 'Coranto Printing,' p. 5.

39 BL, Harl. Mss 390, *passim*; Raymond, *Innvention of the Newspaper*, pp. 1, 5, 156; HMC, *Buccleuch and Queensberry, Montagu House, Whitehall* (London, 1899), vol. 1., *passim*; for example, [Pory] to Mead, 17 August 1626, Harl. Mss 390, fol. 114; Pory to Mead, 21 November 1628, Powell typescripts, 132.

40 1 May 1629, John Lord Poulett to [Dorchester], PRO, SP16/14/23; Sommerville, *News Revolution*, p. 30; Raymond, *Invention of the Newspaper*, p. 245; Hacket, *Scrinia Reserata*.

41 Rous and Crosfield (see notes 17 and 21 above), *op. cit.*; *Diary of Walter Yonge, Esq. Justice of the Peace, and M.P. for Honiton, Written at Colyton and Axminster, Co. Devon, from 1604–1628* (London, 1868), ed. George Roberts; *William Whiteway of Dorchester His Diary 1618 to 1635* (Dorchester, 1991), Dorset Record Society, vol. 12; *Calendar of Wynn (of Gwydir) Papers, 1515–1690, in the National Library of Wales and Elsewhere* (Aberystwyth and London, 1926).

42 *D & D*, VI: 79.

43 Raymond, *Invention of the Newspaper*, p. 230.

44 Love, *Scribal Publication*, pp. 126–34.

45 See, for example, Kevin Sharpe, *The Personal Rule of Charles I* (New Haven, CT, 1992).

46 Love, *Scribal Publication*, p. 33.

47 Cust, *Forced Loan*.

48 Raymond, *Invention of the Newspaper*, p. 89; Sharpe, *Personal Rule*, *passim*.

49 *Commons Debates for 1629* (Minneapolis, MN, 1921), eds Wallace Notestein and Frances Helen Relf, Introduction.

50 Laud to Lambe, 17 July 1640, *The Works of the Most Reverend Father in God, William Laud, D.D. Sometime Lord Archbishop of Canterbury* (Oxford, 1860; reprinted New York, 1975), 7: 605.

3 News and the pamphlet culture of mid-seventeenth-century England

Michael Mendle

To contemporary observers, as to many historians, the flood of small printed books and broadsides reporting, commenting upon, or even sometimes themselves constituting the news, was among the most extraordinary developments of the era of civil war, regicide, and interregnum. In their first appearance, in spring 1641, these unbound little books were a sign that the old regulatory apparatus of the courts and Stationers willing to assist the government to protect their monopoly had failed, essentially because it had lost its nerve.[1] Much of the contents – texts of parliamentary speeches and satires – were familiar enough to those with access to manuscript political culture of the 1620s. By the end of 1641, printed relations of the week's news – the newsbooks – added another genre to the list of materials crossing the social and cultural divide separating manuscript from print.[2] The main novelty here was market availability: what had previously been restricted by cost and by cultural assumption to an elite was now instantly available to anybody with a few pennies to spend.

There were other aspects, however, that were new. The printed texts of monthly fast sermons of politically favoured preachers (though not unknown before) became virtually an announcement board of clerical concerns: late in 1641 and into 1642, a petitioning wave creating an important new form of printed news (sometimes, indeed, creating it). Along with the newsbooks, occasional news pamphlets (often feigned) covered the Irish Rebellion and other non-English developments, and in spring and summer 1642, as war approached, the war of words between king and Parliament generated printed text after printed text of civil collapse as well as the first great wave of political pamphleteering. The favoured genres would fluctuate over the next twenty years. For example, freestanding texts of parliamentary speeches all but dried up, while the newsbooks grew in importance. Shifts in demand and in supply – little news, fewer pamphlets – and changes in the tolerance level of the authorities affected output. But a news-driven pamphlet culture remained from 1641 to 1660, and a possibility thereafter, a chilled yeast only needing a thaw to be reactivated.

For those in the metropolis, the pamphlet culture was impossible to ignore. For as little as a penny, a weekly newsbook, a broadside, a printed petition, or some urgent war news could be had, as likely from a new network of street vendors (the 'mercury women' and other unfortunates) as from traditional booksellers.[3] For people in the provinces, the costs of carriage or postage could double or triple the price, perhaps putting these items beyond the reach of ordinary people, but for the more fortunate a steady stream of pamphlets was well within their means.[4] Amongst the gentry, letters and packages of food or sundries sent to friends and family often had one or two tracts or newsbooks included, almost as a modest gesture of affection, like a bag of sweets sent to a child today, or a clipping or a magazine to a friend.

From any perspective, by any definition, news was the hub of the pamphlet culture. There is, however, a problem in delimiting what was or was not news. This is not a sterile logomachy, but a reflection of the depth of the impact of news upon mid-seventeenth century England. Some items seem obvious: for example, a report of battle was news, the text of a speech in Parliament was news. So was a plain-vanilla summary of the week's happenings in Parliament, in the war, in the country at large, or in London's sometimes politically tense streets – that being the staple fare of many newsbooks. But even here there are fuzzy edges. Is a *reprinting* of a parliamentary speech news? And some so-called newsbooks or 'mercuries' contained little or no news: they were primarily or entirely vehicles for political persuasion, for satire, or *ad hominem* attacks upon the editor-writers, whose activities in a few cases made them public personalities.

It was also true that news was used, as it were, to make news. Publicly presented petitions to Parliament were critical to public affairs at moments in 1641–42 and 1647, and the printed texts certainly would seem to qualify as news. But the printed texts sometimes *preceded* the events they memorialized, and Leveller agents more than once used printed texts to rally a crowd.[5] The sources for some of the early newsbooks came pretty clearly from inside the Commons; while all publication of parliamentary proceedings without specific authorization was technically against the privilege of Parliament, it would seem inevitable that some 'leaks' were quite deliberate. Leaks join what amount to press releases as press-manufactured news (one will be noted later in this chapter). The capture of Charles I's papers after the battle of Naseby was an event within an event; what made it news was their very damaging publication, as *The King's Cabinet Opened*,[6] perhaps the most celebrated tract of the period before *Eikon Basilike*, Charles' apologia rushed to the streets within days of his execution. Parliamentary corruption (imagined or, often enough, real) spawned another variety of journalist-manufactured news: the exposé.[7]

Finally, a phenomenon scarcely noticed in the modern literature opened a whole new family of possibilities for news manufacture: shorthand. Amongst the most fascinating but least studied developments of the 1640s was the emergence of what today would be called the reporter – the agent of a publisher or interested party who attended a trial or an execution or other event to capture as much of it as possible and report it, as the basis for a free-standing tract. While this was possible to some extent without shorthand, the stenographic adepts who captured the very words of the key trials and scaffold speeches not only immeasurably added to the immediacy and verisimilitude of their reports but also, by their very presence, subtly transformed them.

Some of the categorical indistinctness is both explained and further muddled by a feature no less characteristic of the infancy and childhood of English journalism as it is of the modern world's electronic media. News was news, but it was also understood as the raw material of history; no sooner was there news than there were morgues to preserve it. The archival significance of one day's speech, declaration, or newsbook in the next month, year, decade, or era, was *immediately* perceived, and to the extent that it was, part of what made an item 'news' was its evaluation as future history. From the beginning they were, in the most literal and the common sense of the word, 'collectors' items.' This was part of one fascinating feature of newsbooks, their serialization and consecutive numbering. 'Separates' of speeches, petitions, and declarations were collected and published in convenient packaged editions within months or a year of their first appearance. From the beginning, collectors, most famously George Thomason, declared war on the ephemerality of little news pamphlets, collecting, preserving, organizing them, as Thomason had it, for 'posteritie.'[8]

Given the elasticity of the boundaries, it seems best to give the category of news a fairly wide compass. The transformative effects of printed news on other kinds of expression and communication cannot always be filtered out, the phenomenon of the news business creating news is too central to omit, and the dual, even simultaneous role of published news as momentary scoop and enduring record impossible to ignore. What follows is a closer examination of the major kinds of news and news-making in mid-seventeenth-century England, and how people responded to it, above all by preserving it.

The first printed news: 'separates'[9]

The first defining moment of what historians confidently used to call the English Revolution was the summoning of the Long Parliament on 3 November 1640. In the months following, members, driven by ambition, vanity, or tactical goals, arranged to have their set speeches, or what purported to be their set speeches, printed. Separate texts of this sort had floated through the country house manuscript collections since the days of Queen Elizabeth. Now, for the first time, they were printed, and sometimes reprinted.[10] The collector George Thomason, who only rarely violated his strictly chronological ordering scheme for all tracts within a size category, did so for these little speeches. He not only segregated them from other materials but gave them pride of place in his collection, designating them as the first four volumes of small quartos in his collection, a tacit homage to their special status.[11] Their effect on the public must have been striking. What had been accessible hitherto to a few was now available to the many, and although they retained textually the general attributes of elite communication, the publication of these speeches appealed to the voyeuristic impulse catered to by the plebeian and scurrilous illustrated little squibs against Laud and Strafford so common at the time.

Parliamentary documents were also issued as separates, particularly in the early months articles of impeachment against Laudian churchmen and the earl of Strafford. Later, the debates over the publication of a central text in the deteriorating relations between the politicians dominating the two houses and Charles – known as the Grand Remonstrance of November 1641 – proved to be the most acrimonious ever. The text itself was one matter, making it public through print entirely another.[12] The Grand Remonstrance is usually understood to have been the clarion calling for the pro-parliamentary petitions that followed. That, in turn, provoked petitions supportive of the prayer book, bishops, and, at least indirectly, the king. The activities of both sides were appeals to the country, and also measures of support from it. The side with the most numerous expressions of support – in printed words, in crowds of petitioners accompanying delegation leaders to the Lords or the Commons – won the war of public opinion. This was obviously a bonanza for the printers, who had a whole new genre of 'separates' to keep them busy. The spate of petitions also led to their collection, both privately and in one central instance, in a printed collection.[13]

In spring 1642, the publication of the declarations and messages exchanged between the two houses and the king (the 'war of words') created yet another round of 'separates,' as a half-sheet broadside or several sheets in quarto. Meanwhile, events outside the houses required treatment: first, events in Scotland and Ireland, then news of the armed confrontations of the king's partisans and parliamentary commanders at Hull, finally war news itself.

So it continued. The newsbooks, however great their impact, never eliminated the need for separates (in the broad sense). Partly this was a matter of periodicity: newsbooks, appearing weekly, were inevitably 'scooped' by separates that could appear overnight. Partly it was a matter of length: the ingenuity of printers and use of small type could not entirely overcome the space limitations that the editorial format imposed. And partly it was a matter of opportunism. Whatever their style or content, newsbooks were almost uniformly grey and sober, with dense text on the first page and little or no indication of interior content. Separates, though, had informative, sometimes illustrated, and occasionally gaudy title pages. They sold themselves: the urgency of war news, or a juicy crime or scandal could entice a penny or two with just a glance from the buyer.[14] Nor is it coincidental that the inundation of separates marking the great events of 1641 and 1642 was matched only by the tidal wave of the first months of 1660: separates flourished when the news was densest and when the measure of public opinion, as expressed by petitions or public declarations, was the scale. And as will be seen later in this chapter, for certain kinds of news, the separate was the only possible format.

The English revolution of the press: the newsbooks

The importance of the newsbooks cannot be overestimated. But that is unlikely to happen: a rich and expert literature has treated their emergence and flourishing in fond detail.[15] As Joad Raymond has insisted in *Making the News: An Anthology of the Newsbooks of Revolutionary England, 1641–1660*, the essence of the printed newsbook was its periodicity, not only achieved by a predictable, usually weekly, publication schedule but also by continuous signatures and pagination. The effect could be startling. While some long-running newsbooks reset the sequence every new year, and new editors or simply style shifts could disrupt earlier practice, one run of Marchamont Nedham's *Mercurius Politicus* topped 6,000 numbered pages. Anticipation of the next issue was one consequence of periodicity, archivalization the other. Readers responded. Outside of Thomason's nonce collection and his no less remarkable methods, where newsbooks survive in quantity, they survive in runs. A fill-in or two aside, it is impossible to see how these runs could have been compiled *ex post facto*; the explanation seems that the famous newsbooks were objects of preservation from the beginning.[16] Writer-editors encouraged the sense of continuity. A new issue often began only a fresh breath removed from the last: *Mercurius Aulicus* frequently began an issue with a reference to the last week's story, and carried it forward. Here is one typical case: 'You heard last weeke of the affrights and terrours which the prevailing faction in the pretended *Houses* were fallen into, by reason of the sad conditon of their affaires in most parts abroad; and shall now heare of the confusions and distractions they are in at home. …'[17]

Early on in the newsbook explosion, in January 1642, Thomason noted to his surprise, '2 diurnalls this weeke'; toward the end of March he counted seven.[18] Nehemiah Wallington, a London turner in perpetual financial difficulties, remorsefully looked upon the litter of newsbooks about his house as 'theeues that had stole away my mony.'[19] Until the mid-1650s, competition was intense. Newsbooks came and went, some surviving only for short runs of several weeks or months; like restaurateurs, the editors might reappear in a new venue. Naturally, newsbooks sought to space themselves across the week – a news addict might well plunge for a 'fix' on Mondays and Thursdays.[20] They also differentiated themselves by their favoured topics and by their political and religious commitments. *Mercurius Aulicus* was the leading Royalist journal, *Mercurius Britanicus* and *Mercurius Politicus* the most famous pro-Parliament and pro-Protectorate weeklies (both edited by Marchamont Nedham). *Mercurius Militaris* catered to one clientele, *The Scottish Dove* (with its Presbyterian slant) to another. Others were less overtly partisan, and adopted the role or the mask of reportorial objectivity.[21] Some, like the radical weekly perhaps ironically called *The Moderate* and the salacious Royalist *The Man in the Moon*, were less *news*books than vehicles for political expression, more like modern opinion magazines than first-resort news sources.

Though most newsbook writers resemble the unthanked, inky drudges of modern journalistic lore, the most celebrated newsbook writers acquired followings or, rather more strongly expressed, cult-like antipathies. The principal writer of the first great royalist newsbook, *Mercurius Aulicus*, Sir John Berkenhead, simply *was* 'Aulicus,' whose voice had an authority stemming not so much from its obvious and effective partisanship but from its status as a semi-official organ of the royalist party, not unlike the Voice of America, the BBC World Service, or the old Radio Moscow.[22] No less significant was the heroics of its distribution. Written in Oxford, it was either printed there and smuggled into the metropolis, or also surreptitiously printed in London. The 'look' of the two versions was all but identical: by hook or by crook, *Aulicus* made the rounds. John Milton, whose plea in *Areopagitica* for free publication was distinctly circumscribed, specifically taunted the authorities for their inability to stop the circulation of the still-wet sheets of London-printed editions of *Aulicus*.[23]

The most astonishing of all newsbook writers was Marchamont Nedham.[24] His first effort, *Mercurius Britanicus* (so misspelled throughout its entire run), was fiercely pro-Parliament, and a direct challenge to the acerbity of *Aulicus*. Royalists often paraded their superior literary skills as an advertisement of the worth of their cause; the parliamentarian stalwart Henry Parker acknowledged the superiority of their 'able men' in the universities to the 'sots' and 'prevaricators' of his own camp.[25] This, of course, overstated things, by judging Parliament's worst against the king's best. But with Nedham, parliamentarians found a pen as barbed as any wielded in Oxford. They also found in Nedham a stalwart for the win-the-war party and, if not precisely religious independency, then a fierce and visceral anti-Presbyterianism.

It was, therefore, with astonishment that all sides received the news in 1647 that Nedham had joined the king's camp, now as editor of the royalist *Mercurius Pragmaticus*, a weekly that like *Aulicus* before it and other royalist papers gained much of its notoriety from its underground status. That work dried up, though, with the events leading up to the king being brought to London to face trial and execution. In 1650 Nedham began his third phase as journalist-to-all-persuasions, as 'Pol,' the editor/writer of *Mercurius Politicus*, which ran very nearly to the Restoration. *Mercurius Politicus* was both a support and a critique, if sometimes guarded, of the successive regimes of the Commonwealth and Cromwellian Protectorate; at the end, inside and out of it, Nedham desperately tried to hold onto the Good Old Cause.[26] Then, after a close brush with the new authorities, Nedham did what he could to ingratiate himself with them.

These celebrated names should not obscure the truth that behind them stood many others, a few only scarcely less talented. All required an infrastructure of producers, distributors, and investors, as well as the expectation – or perhaps more truthfully, the hope – that a public existed for their work. The publisher John Thomas, who turned a manuscript newsletter into a pioneering newsbook, certainly deserves mention.[27] Eccentrics such as the sectarian scribbler Henry Walker and the railing and obscene royalist newsbook writer John Crouch tethered opposite ends of the political and religious spectrum.[28] As is often the case, their opposition was also a kind of symbiosis. The author of the brief but effective radical newsbook *The Moderate* continues to attract modern students. He may have been John Harris, an extraordinary character who was variously an actor, an army printer, a radical London printer-publisher, political organizer, and a bold though inept con man.[29]

The reporter and the emergence of shorthand reporting

The strongly flavoured personalities and the derring-do of the newsbook editor-writers have tended to obscure the most obvious function of a newsbook – that is, to report on events. How was the news gathered? Sometimes the answers are explicit or inferentially clear: a letter from a distant correspondent, a 'leak' from the Commons and Council of State, or simply some other source's recycled information. Sometimes, though, particularly for metropolitan events, the newsbooks and the separates seem to have been based on eyewitness reporting, either that of the editor-writer or someone at only one remove, the editor's agent or representative – the reporter. For example, the events surrounding the attempts in December 1642 of royalist sympathizers in London to rally support for a petition they offered for 'peace' (a code term at that moment for a quick settlement on terms favourable to the king) and the equally determined efforts of Parliament's partisans to scuttle that effort were variously reported by observers on the scene. Each, of course, had selective vision – but, equally, several accounts seem to have relied on the account of an eyewitness.[30] Similarly the newsbooks had different but, in the end, aggregatively revealing accounts of a hideous event of 9 August 1643, when an unruly crowd of royalist women in Palace Yard were charged and some killed by panicked parliamentary mounted troopers.[31]

A revolution in information technology of the mid-seventeenth century radically expanded the possibilities of reportorial journalism, irrevocably changing the expectations readers had of news accounts – and, to an extent, changing the events themselves, as participants 'performed' both for the immediate readership beyond the boundaries of the event and for posterity. This was the coming of age of shorthand.

The Renaissance brought a revival or interest in the ancient symbologies – the Ennian and Tyronian *notae* – that had served as its 'tachygraphy' or 'brachygraphy' (two of the more common synonyms for shorthand). What remained a curiosity of the learned elsewhere became in England something of a national craze, when, in the seventeenth century, the rapid development of English shorthand systems made it possible for a few people – perhaps no more than a dozen at a time out of the many dozens or hundreds of teachers, and many thousands of learners – to 'take' speech at the rate or nearly the rate at which it was spoken. The early systems show clearly the bias of their presumed likely application: though in principle phonetic, the systems had extensive tables of 'logograms' (special brief symbols) for the terms of art of sermons – for example, for the 'grace of God,' or for 'sacrament.' The Czech reformer-educator Comenius was astonished, in 1641, to see 'large numbers of men and youths' taking shorthand notes at sermons, and wrote home (with considerable exaggeration) that 'almost all' learned tachygraphy 'as soon as they have learnt at school to read the Scriptures in the vernacular.'[32] John Phillips' anti-Puritan *A Satyr Against Hypocrites* mocked '*Will* [who] writes short-hand with a pen of brass, / Oh how he's wonder'd at by many an asse / That see him shake so fast his warty fist, / As is he'd write the Sermon 'fore the Priest / Has spoke it,' and similarly the well-dressed women 'With Bibles in plush jerkins and blew garters, / The silver Inkhorn, and the writing book, / In which I wish no friend of mine to look.' Of the whole scene, he jibed: 'And I could see that many Short-hand wrote, / Where listning [*sic*] well, I could not hear a jote; / Friend, this is strange, quoth I, but he reply'd, / *Alas! your ears are yet unsanctifi'd*.'[33]

Shorthand's utility was perceived beyond the circles of zealous private note-takers and the professionals who began to publish their transcriptions of popular divines' sermons.[34] Secretaries to the powerful regarded shorthand as a valuable instrumentality; this ran across political and religious boundaries. One of the most famous of the early stenography masters, Thomas Shelton, in 1634, 'came to Oxford & profess'd to instruct Schollars in short-writing wch he did in a short space; his pay 10s & 2s 6d a booke.'[35] In 1650 the Verney boys were 'sent 1 Shelton in blew papr to teach [them] to write short hand.'[36] Shelton's shorthand system was used by John Rushworth, was probably learned by William Clarke while he was Rushworth's deputy as under clerk of the Commons, and was used by Samuel Pepys. Robert Boyle also learned it. Sir Edward Nicholas, the king's secretary, used about fifteen common logograms and an occasional contracted syllabic form from the influential system of Edmund Willis.[37] The secretary to the royalist Oxford Parliament of 1643, Noah Bridges, used his adaptation of the pioneering scheme of John Willis, which he later published.

As Bridges' case shows,[38] those who used shorthand instrumentally as a means to other ends could by degrees elide into another category: those who by profession, craft, or trade – call it what you will – used their shorthand abilities directly to earn a living, as teachers or practitioners. The most important reason why there were so many, often trivially distinct systems of shorthand published was not (as is sometimes supposed) that they did not work very well;[39] rather, the published systems were linked to the teaching practices of the shorthand masters. An extremely high percentage of these books were published 'for the author' and were to be sold by him.[40] Two leading systems had not only their own textbooks but what amounted to workbooks as well; practice was also to be had by comparing shorthand versions of the New Testament or metrical psalms with the ordinary printed texts. Such professional stenographers – and perhaps their most expert students – had skills on a different order of magnitude than the stenographers (or, one suspects, the would-be stenographers) in the church pews. The difference was supplied by time: some of the leading masters could claim, by the time of their deaths, thirty, forty or even more years of shorthand teaching and practice – which is also to say, that in their prime, they already had decades of experience.

In the 1640s, the shorthand and the news revolutions fused. While John Rushworth's large, child-like italic can be found in private members' diaries, he kept many of his own notes in shorthand. He was 'purposely placed near the Earl [of Strafford, at his trial in 1641], to take in Characters whatsoever should be said, either against or for him.' The results were the foundation of his account later published as *The Tryal of Thomas Earl of Strafford*.[41] He was not alone. Another 'ready writer' published his notes, in 108 quarto pages, in 1647.[42]

Rushworth also took in shorthand the king's brief speech in the Commons on 4 January 1642, during his failed attempt to arrest the Five Members. Charles later required Rushworth to give him a transcription, while Rushworth was in the king's presence, which Charles slightly amended.[43]

These were, though, behind-the-scenes or after-the-fact transactions. That would shortly change. William Laud's scaffold speech, taken by the shorthand master John Hinde, was subtly but unmistakably altered by the stenographer's very presence:

> Then turning to Master *Hinde*, [Laud] said, Friend, I beseech you hear me, I cannot say I have spoken every word as it is in my Paper, but I have gone very neer it, to help my memory as well as I could; but I beseech you, let me have no wrong done me.
>
> *Hinde.* Sir youshall [*sic*] not, if I doe any wrong let it fall on my own head. I pray God have mercy on your soul.
>
> *Cant.* I thank you: I did not speak with any jealousie, as if you would so do, but I spake it onely as a poor man, goeing out of the world, it is not possible for me to keep to the words in my paper, and a phrase may do me wrong.[44]

Since those mainly liable to the scaffold for political crimes were royalists, a cottage industry developed around shorthand reportage of the events. Hinde was prominent enough, or perhaps simply vain enough, to write himself into the billing of the royalist Henry Hyde's and the Presbyterian-royalist Christopher Love's dying words.[45] In the first case, Hinde backhandedly boasted of his prowess by claiming that although Hyde had 'some abrupt brakings off, and other expressions not so smooth as might have been, yet I could not with honesty alter a word.' The scaffold speech of the century, of course, was Charles I's, on 30 January 1649. The only record of the king's remarks was, 'what was taken in shorthand, on the Scaffold, by three several Gentlemen, who were very exquisite in that Art,' who later compared and collated their copies to produce the standard version.[46] Collaboration was also involved in the production of the dying words of the royalist peers who, on 9 March 1649, followed Charles to the scaffold. Hamilton confessed to his chaplain that had he known that 'writers' would take his speech, he would have produced a better one: characteristically, that too was recorded.[47]

Other condemned royalists surely would know better. Shorthand writers were integral to the emergent royalist martyrology. With the Restoration, the 'separates' reporting their last moments were published in an important collection, *England's Black Tribunall*. The publisher was John Playford, remembered today largely as a music publisher, but from 1649 to 1660 he was frequently involved with Peter Cole (the publisher of Jeremiah Rich's earliest shorthand treatise, *Charactery*) and, on occasion, the law publisher Francis Tyton in shorthand-derived publications, usually speeches or trials.[48]

Takers of scaffold speeches were reporters: in addition to the words of the speech itself, the takers described the setting and delighted in the reproduction of extempore dialogue. In many cases they and their publishers resorted to dramatic typography – speakers identified usually in italic, followed by their marks in roman type, with dashes occasionally used to indicate the interruptions of one speaker's words by another's. Such facility was to be severely tested in the taking of trials, which were characteristically much longer than the scaffold scenes, often had more potential speakers, and took place indoors, where the ambient noise of onlookers and crowds could be much more distracting. Nevertheless, trials were taken successfully from Strafford's onwards. Though unpublished, William Clarke possessed (and perhaps took) a distinctive and self-evidently stenographic report of Laud's trial; he also possessed a still-unused report of the trial of royalist peers.[49] One trial that demonstrated the possibilities of stenography was not political at all: *The Arraignment and Acquittall of Sr. Edward Moseley Baronet, Indicted at the Kings Bench for a Rape, upon the body of Mistris Anne Swinnerton. January 28, 1647. Taken by a Reporter there present, who heard all the Circumstances thereof, whereof this is a true Copy.*[50] The 'reporter' summarized some of the proceedings but at other moments he attempted to reproduce through the flow of talk word by word. Not using play typography, he or his printer had a few problems, but the result was clear enough. In one exchange, Mrs Swinnerton's loyal maid began by telling the court that she told Moseley that if he would not be

> more civill, I would call my Master, and if hee came hee would crack his crowne for using my Mistris so uncivilly, Sir *Edward Mosely* answered hee cared not a fart for my Master, and that for mee I was a base Jade, and hee would make mee kisse his, &c. what said the Court, but the Maid having some modesty could not bring it out, then said her Mistris, he said she should kisse something that was about him, what was that the court said againe, Master *Swinnerton* answered, he said he would make her kisse his Arse, then the Court said to the Maide, you must not be so nice in speaking of the truth, being upon your Oath. ...[51]

Such exchanges made the possibilities of the medium only too obvious. However, a titillating and mildly salacious trial would not long linger in the public memory, and with the passing of interest in the subject, there would be a parallel fading of interest in the reporting technique. The three great show trials of 1649 were each taken in shorthand; two were published, to the enduring memory of the events and what amounted to a perpetual advertisement for the technique.[52] The first in time was the trial of Charles I. The demand for information, obviously, was enormous; no less large was the state's need to control that information. While several accounts were put out at the time of the events, the finest was the state-authorized stenographic *Perfect Narrative*, which appeared in three parts, with 24- to 48-hour turnaround.[53] It was licensed by Gilbert Mabbott, who also seems to have had a financial interest in the project. The stenographer, one 'C. W.', was perhaps William

Clarke, Mabbott's brother-in-law and Rushworth's one-time deputy, who used shorthand in his capture of the famed Putney Debates of 1647.[54] John Bradshaw's remark at the trial that Charles had written the meaning of his actions in 'bloody Characters' – 'characters' being one of the many terms for shorthand – may comment as much upon the information technology as upon the king.[55]

The year's greatest stenographic triumph, though, was the edition/transcript of the trial of John Lilburne, 'as exactly pen'd and taken in short hand, as it was possible to be done in such a crowd and noyes.'[56] Unlike the king's trial, which was relatively short and needed to get out quickly, the record of Lilburne's trial was massive. Nevertheless, its 150 pages (mostly of transcript, with a few appended documents) appeared within six weeks of the event, serving to share and to celebrate his victory.[57]

Typographically, it went one step beyond the play format that would become the standard: Lilburne's words were presented in Roman type, all others' in italic. In the verbal byplay, the reproduction of the testiness of the judges, and the scenic apparatus, the printed text was the finest example yet extant of shorthand reportage. One example may serve for many. Late in the final day's lengthy proceedings, Lilburne pled for a little time to rest and prepare his concluding remarks to the jury. He was denied it. After a momentary fright when some seating scaffolding fell, Lilburne resumed his plea:

> Sir, if you will be so cruell as not to give me leave to withdraw to ease and refresh my body: I pray you, let me do it in the Court. Officer, I entreat you to help me to a chamberpot; which whilst it was fetching, Mr *Lilburne* followeth his Papers and books close, and when the pott came, he made water, and gave it to the *Foreman*.[58]

Lilburne's 1649 trial's influence as a text and as model was considerable. One trial spectator was the Royalist conspirator Christopher Love. When Love's trial came up in 1652, he consulted Lilburne, used the 1649 trial record extensively in developing his own case, and secured the services of the shorthand adept John Farthing to take his own trial.[59] Lilburne's second trial, in 1653, was attended by several shorthand writers, including the celebrated shorthand master Jeremiah Rich. One writer boasted that when he finished collating his preliminary account with those of the other writers, he would produce a composite larger than the magnificent edition of the 1649 trial.[60] With the Restoration, the regicides' friends arranged for the astonishingly vivid *An Exact and Most Impartiall Accompt of the Indictment, Arraignment, Trial, and Judgment (According to Law) of the Twenty Nine Regicides*.[61] In scarcely over a decade, close stenographic reporting of key public events had become almost the expectation. The next great spate of political trials would see a revival of this kind of reportage, and with it a new level of respectability through imprimaturs granted by trial judges.[62] The stenographic reporter, working for a publisher or one of the parties, had become 'normal.'

The news and the old: collection and archiving of news[63]

Like Janus, the news-driven pamphlet culture faced both ways, looking forward and backwards at the same time. As to the first, timeliness was everything. News spoiled, but freshness sold. Thomason's famous handwritten dates began in imitation of a practice that became the rage in summer 1642 – day-dated imprints, designed to hook the buyer by their up-to-the-minute immediacy.

The correlative of immediacy, however, is ephemerality. As separate replaced separate, newsbook succeeded newsbook, contemporaries reflected on and responded to their dizzying procession. One highly cultivated writer thought the little books needed to be preserved precisely *because of* their ephemerality. He compared them to the most obvious use-and-lose objects of the era: there was need of 'praeserving the memory, both of greater, and more especially lesser tracts and treatises (which are commonly lost like pinns and needles, and never recovered again).'[64] A compiler of a published collection of country royalist declarations in 1660 said he collected them to prevent their being put to new duty in the privy.[65] And Thomason's day-dates, begun in apparent sympathy with the presentistic mode of mid-1642, became in their own era the close markers of the past, just as they have become for historians an invaluable resource.

The historicity of news was appreciated from the beginning. William Cooke gathered and published the little separates as *Speeches and Passages of this Great and Happy Parliament.*[66] That volume would have a future beyond its compiler's wildest expectations, serving as a vertebra of John Rushworth's account as well of the relevant portions of that large and still useful eighteenth-century compilation, the 'Old Parliamentary History.'[67] Another publisher, Edward Husbands, provided the continuation, *An Exact Collection*, the 'book of declarations' of the war of words that perhaps more than any other such volume reflected and encouraged the primacy of text over event.[68] Such collections became an occasional feature of the pamphlet culture. Sir Thomas Aston republished conformist church petitions in an important collection.[69] Husbands continued his compilation. Army declarations later received similar treatment.[70] At the Restoration, a flurry of royalist petitions generated a collection of them within weeks of their appearance.[71] Soon John Playford issued a collection of the scaffold speeches of royalist martyrs, from Charles on down, *England's Black Tribunall*, the importance of which for the story of shorthand reportage has already been noticed.[72]

Meanwhile, private collectors gathered their own harvests. There is simply no way to calculate the number of contemporary collectors of pamphlets – people who bought pamphlets for their news, but preserved and ordered them for their memory. But the great piles of pamphlets in research libraries are themselves one sort of witness, for, as Peter Blayney has sagely remarked, the chances of a book's survival increase enormously if it was an object of collection.[73] And among the commonest of all contemporary reader's marks on a pamphlet is the part number in the upper right-hand corner of a title page, indicating that its owner had gathered, ordered, and bound together a number of separate (and as we shall see, often chronologically or topically related) items in a single volume.[74]

Two great collections have survived almost intact. Sir William Clarke, the shorthand writer and army secretary, accumulated vast stocks of pamphlets (perhaps 6,000 in all), mostly from the 1640s and 1650s, which he bound together, for economy's sake, in very large volumes, and which his son donated to Worcester College, Oxford.[75] Newsbooks he kept together as serials; his sets are among the most complete that have survived. Otherwise he kept his news separates together, in a fairly tight chronology, usually segregating them from volumes of public acts, sermons, tracts of theology or ecclesiology, or pertaining to political and constitutional matters. Inevitably, there were more miscellaneous compilations. The grandest collection, though, was George Thomason's, now to be found in the British Library. A London bookseller (essentially a wholesaler of expensive, foreign, and scholarly volumes, who had extensive business connections with Oxford University), Thomason collected some 22,000 titles, overwhelmingly the little books and smaller tracts that were at the opposite end of the publishing business from his own relatively rarefied traffic. From mid-1642, he dated almost all of them that did not bear an imprint date; even the earlier items were kept in chronological series that generally allow them to be pinned to a time period ranging from a week to a fortnight. Moreover, he bound them carefully, in convenient and manageable size- and format-determined volumes that have beautifully preserved them across the centuries. Thomason also accounted for the disposition of every item in two identical eight-volume manuscript catalogues.[76]

There were others. John Rushworth's collection was sold by auction after his death, although it was partially reassembled later by the heirs of Sir Thomas Fairfax.[77] In 1645–6 the Bodleian Library, though focused upon the high scholarship of the day, nevertheless bought from Richard Branthwayt's estate, for £1.12.0, '8 bundles of pamphlets … conteyninge the occurances of the times.'[78] The London bookseller William Miller's personal tract collection was sold by his widow and business continuator Susannah Miller in 1695; although it ranged from the late sixteenth century to the 1680s, many volumes and bundles were from the 1640s and 1650s and could only have been based on someone's (not necessarily Miller's) own vast, contemporaneously assembled holdings for these items, as, for example, the seven bundles of folio acts of state from 1648 to 1659 and the twenty-three quarto volumes (some double-sized) of newsbooks from 1641 to 1660.[79] Further evidence is provided by the earliest English book auction catalogues, of which the first was that of the library of the bibliophile-divine Lazarus Seaman in 1676. While his books included substantial numbers of Civil War-era political tracts (but apparently no large compilations of news), other collectors assembled substantial runs of newsbooks and tightly chronologized runs of separates, usually by year – and these are simply inconceivable unless accumulated and preserved at or near the time of publication. There were also compilations by author, as well as the predictable miscellanies. By the later 1670s and 1680s (times themselves of news and high political drama), the interested and relatively well-heeled could seek out and purchase as 'history' what had earlier been fondly compiled and saved as 'news.'

Examining the auspices: the press releases of General Monck

In the seventeenth century, as among some historians today, it was commonly (and generally correctly) assumed that high politics was conducted in privacy if not secrecy, and if in writing, then in manuscript, not print. Titles such as *The King's Cabinet Opened*, *Cabala ... Mysteries of State and Government*, and *Scrinia Reserata* (unlocked boxes) encapsulate the prevailing attitudes.[80] John Rushworth, who in point of fact relied extensively upon his 'Printed Pamphlets' of news in composing his own documentary histories, nevertheless juxtaposed their unreliability with the prima-facie trustworthiness of Rushworth's private records of 'the Debates in Parliament, and to the most secret Results of Councils of War.'[81]

But this is not a rule without its exception. Early in 1660, the highest of all possible politics was conducted by means of that sub-species of news, the press release, and the 'most secret' councils of government became all but obsessed with the correct interpretation of public words. The episode bears close examination as a high water mark of the 'politics of information,' as practised in England's mature pamphlet culture on the eve of the Restoration.

The story focuses on a sheet in quarto, *A Letter of General George Monck's, Dated at Leicester 23 Ian.*[82] This letter, directed to Mr Robert Rolle, was to be communicated to Devonshire notables who had written to the Parliament from Exeter on 14 January 1660. The great General's letter was never private, Monck himself arranging to have it read in Parliament, and then printed. On 23 January, Monck personally forwarded a copy of the *printed* text with a covering letter to Rolle, and sent a copy as well to Sir William Morrice, a man who was simultaneously in Monck's entourage and a royalist agent. The arrow found the mark: Monck's letter to Morrice ended up in Clarendon's papers.[83] The amplitude of the Clarendon manuscripts allows us to trace the effects of that printed document upon royalist hopes, fears, and calculations.

The Devonshire gentlemen had written to Monck pleading for a free Parliament – in particular that the secluded members (those removed at Pride's Purge in 1648) be permitted to resume their seats.[84] This was only one of a large number of published items of similar sentiments.[85] In the universal reckoning, the return of the secluded members would lead to dissolution of the Long Parliament, issuance of writs for new elections with few or no political disqualifications for royalism, and return of a parliament sympathetic to a Stuart restoration.

Monck replied to 'my friends and relations' with a lecture on the past twenty years. Before 1642, 'the Government of these Nations was Monarchical in Church and State,' he began, but the wars generated new 'interests.' In religion these were the 'Presbyterian, Independent, Anabaptist, and Sectaries.' In the new state they were the purchasers of royal and ecclesiastical lands and all those 'engaged in these Wars against the King.' The different groups were really one, 'interwove by purchases and intermarriages.' Loosely echoing James Harrington, Monck argued that no 'Government' could be 'good, peacefull, or lasting' that did not 'include and comprehend' these interests' 'security and preservation.' But since the new interests were 'incompatible' with kings and bishops, the only possible government was a 'Republique'. Therefore Monck could not support readmission of the secluded members. It would only restart the wars, for 'the Army ... [would] never endure it.' He urged his friends to accept a reformed 'Commonwealth.'[86]

Nothing could be clearer, and yet nothing was less so. Royalists were astonished. They, Hyde included, had assumed that Monck himself had asked his neighbours to write to him.[87] To summon the *vox populi* from his own countrymen and then exhibitionistically dash their hopes was inexplicable.[88] The royalist press rushed to limit the damage. Five answers appeared within a week of the date of Thomason's purchase of the original, one from William Morrice himself.[89] All took Monck's response as a denial, though two grasped at straws. One suggested lamely that the letter might have been a fake; another found comfort from the tone if not the content.[90] Private reflections varied. One of Hyde's correspondents thought Monck's intentions could 'be disputed bothe wayes.' Another remarked that while Monck's words left 'noe roome' for doubt, some republicans continued to distrust him. A third was wholly despondent: Monk 'pul'd off his maske' and showed himself 'republiqueall.'[91] Another said that Monck could not reveal his true intentions because Sir Arthur Haselrigg's republican agents Scot and Robinson shadowed his every move.[92] Hyde was angry and discouraged: Monck's 'lewd carriage' was 'very melancholique.' If Monck did not give way, restoration would require a 'forrainge army.'[93]

So Monck's answer – the manufactured news of a press release – was studied in the royalists' innermost councils with the intensity that Sovietologists once reserved for the entrails of *Pravda.* What was Monck up to? My view is that Monck was neither a reactive temporizer nor a Cavalier mole working to demolish the Commonwealth. Rather, he was an independent political presence seeking in January 1660 not to engineer *the* Restoration (as if only one were possible), but one that accommodated the 'interests' (to use his word) he would protect. There was a restoration scenario he sought proactively to promote, and others he would as determinedly avoid. His words bear another look. Monck declared himself opposed to restoration for contingent, changeable reasons – because it was incompatible with Presbyterians and other dissenters, with the interests of those who had purchased tainted lands, with indemnity for those who had fought against Charles I. But what if restoration provided protection to dissenters, if an arrangement could be worked out for land purchasers, if a general indemnity could be relied upon – would the army object to that, especially if arrears were paid and there was some prospect of continued employment? In explaining why he opposed the return of the secluded members, Monck was outlining the terms later known as the Declaration of Breda, Charles II's promises on the eve of the Restoration.

Monck continued to communicate to inner-circle royalists through the press and his later printed addresses continued to receive the same sort of oracular scrutiny. Until he got what he wanted, Monck negotiated, as he had in his response to the Devonshire declaration, through the news. Nothing could be more wrong than to think that Monck was merely posturing for the public, having already come to secret understandings. If so, Hyde knew nothing of them. Even in early March (two months before the final deal was settled), Hyde did not know if 'any reasonable hope' could be entertained of Monck. He advised Lady Willoughby to be 'prepared for the worst.' When she urged that Monck's press releases were but 'vizards,' Hyde retorted they were 'made with the most terrible of aspects ... that ever vizards were.'[94] The irony cannot be ignored: the most public of media, either valued or scorned for its popularity in 1641, had become the conduit of information from Monck to Hyde. Of all outcomes, that cheap little books of news should have so shaped the restoration of a dynasty was perhaps the least imaginable.

Notes

1 Michael Mendle, 'De Facto Freedom, De Facto Authority: Press and Parliament, 1640–1643,' *Historical Journal* 38 (1995): 307–32.

2 For political communication and news in the 1620s, see Sabrina Baron's chapter in this book, and Richard Cust, 'News and Politics in Seventeenth-Century England,' *Past and Present* (1986): 60–90. While the newsbooks of domestic affairs that emerged in the 1641–42 have some relation to the brief allowance in the 1620s of printed 'corontoes' of foreign news, Joad Raymond has convincingly shown that the newsbooks owe far more – even in the beginning – to the very words of private subscription manuscript summaries: see his *The Invention of the Newspaper: English Newsbooks 1641–1649* (Oxford, 1996), pp. 100–7, 314–20.

3 For ordinary pieces, the price seems to have been a penny a sheet (most commonly a quarto, a sheet folded into four leaves or eight pages). The best resource for pamphlet prices has scarcely been touched: the collection of pamphlets collected by the parliamentary and army clerk William Clarke, now at Worcester College, Oxford. For many pamphlets (presumably the ones Clarke had to buy), Clarke listed the price asked, and, frequently at variance, the lower price Clarke actually paid. How Clarke so frequently obtained his pamphlets below the asking price – through quantity purchase, use or misuse of his official position, or otherwise – is not clear. Why many routine political and news tracts carried no price is another question impossible to answer.

4 The cost of carriage is an important issue discussed by Raymond, *Invention of the Newspaper*, p. 239.

5 For example, *Certaine Petitions Presented to the Lord Maior, and Commonalty of the Citie of London ... Shewing, the Great Inconveniences of Protections* (London, 1641); see the tipped-in slip announcing an organizational meeting adjacent to Thomason's copy, British Library (henceforth BL) E. 197 (4). The petition of 'many thousand poore people' of 30 January 1642 printed by William Larnar, a Lilburne associate, and the radical-friendly printer Thomas Banks (BL 669. f.4 [54]), contained directions for assembly and instructions that the petitioners should carry the printed text in their hands, a political gesture later associated with the Leveller draft constitution, *The Agreement of the People*. In 1647, Thomason acquired a Leveller petition (BL 669. f. 11 [21]) on behalf of some imprisoned royalists currently allied with the Levellers that came with a little slip indicating how canvassers were to obtain subscriptions.

6 London, 1645. Annotations were made by Henry Parker, Thomas May, and John Sadler. For the context and other details, see Michael Mendle, *Henry Parker and the English Civil War* (Cambridge, 1995), pp. 25–6; for the tract's contemporary significance, see Lois Potter, *Secret Rites and Secret Writing: Royalist Literature, 1641–1660* (Cambridge, 1989), pp. 59–64.

7 Some examples: Amon Willbee, *Prima Pars, De Comparatis Comparandis* (1647); [John Wildman], *Putney Projects* (1647); M[ercurius]. E[lencticus]. [viz., George Wharton], *A List of the Names of Members of the House of Commons* (1648), and its sequel *The Second Centurie* (1648); *Westminster Projects, or the Mysterie of Darby House Discovered* (1648). The Wharton list was perpetuated by reprinting in Clement Walker's influential *History of Independency*.

8 Borrowing from the continuation (by Thomas Nabbes) to the fifth edition of Richard Knolles' *General Historie of the Turkes* (London, 1638), p. 1628. Thomason drew his collection's motto to the effect that actions that might be 'presidents' for 'posteritie' deserved careful preservation (BL C. 38. h.21, vol. 1 A1 recto [small quartos]); compare Thomson's unpaged prefatory note in the same volume, that his collection would 'prove a great Advantage to Posteritie.'

9 The term was devised by Wallace Notestein and Frances Relf, *Commons Debates for 1629* (Minneapolis, MN, 1929), where its use was restricted to parliamentary speeches. For purposes of comparison with the news digests of the diurnals and mercuries (newsbooks), the meaning of 'separate' can be extended to include almost any discretely issued news item.

10 A. D. T. Cromartie, 'The Printing of Parliamentary Speeches November 1640–July 1642,' *Historical Journal* 33 (1990): 23–44, is useful on many points. However, it is defective and misleading largely for its failure to use the substantial body of licences to print issued by important individual members (notably John Pym and Oliver St. John) and by Sir Edward Dering (in his capacity as chairman of one of the committees of the Commons to oversee printing), which the Stationers' Company kept in its book recording orders from various public authorities, Liber A. See Stationers' Hall, London. Record of the Stationers' Company. Liber A.

11 The modern shelfmarks of these volumes, BL E. 196-E.199, like most of the modern shelfmarks, have only an accidental relation to the volume numbers assigned by Thomason. The original numbers remain embossed on the spines of the Thomason volumes, having been preserved in all rebindings. The disposition of every tract in the collection according to original position and modern shelf-marking, and in some cases, tract-shuffling and rebinding, is indicated in the notations made in one copy of Thomason's twelve-volume manuscript catalogue, BL C. 37. h. 13; for the speeches, see vol. A (small quartos nos. 1–100), nos. 1–4. Small quartos constitute the bulk of the collection, filling eight of the twelve catalogue volumes.

12 In one instance before 1641, publication of a parliamentary text assumed similarly large implications. See Elizabeth Read Foster, 'The Printing of the Petition of Right,' *Huntington Library Quarterly* 28 (1972). For the tensions connected with the debates on printing the Grand Remonstrance, see Willson Coates, ed., *The Journal of Sir Simonds D'Ewes* (New Haven, 1942), pp. 184–7, 295.

13 Nehemiah Wallington, *Historical Notices of Events Occurring Chiefly in the Reign of Charles I* (London, 1869), 2 vols, ed. R. Webb, 2: 1–22, lists over 100 petitions collected by puritan stalwart Wallington. Sir Thomas Aston, *A Collection of Sundry Petitions* (1642), 'The Collector to the Reader' (sig. A2 recto) indicates that this pro-episcopal and pro-prayer book collection was a response to the impression of mass support left by the spate of petitions on the other side. The precision of reference of Aston's scorn for the anti-episcopal petitions implies that he had texts of the offending petitions at hand. Edward Hyde, earl of Clarendon, *The History of the Rebellion and Civil Wars in England*, 6 vols, ed. W. Dunn Macray, 2: 537–44, 548–53, includes substantial excerpts

from the radical petitions of this period. Wallington, it might be noted, also collected newsbooks to the point of financial distress.

14 One genre is indicated in Jerome Friedman, *The Battle of the Frogs and Fairford's Flies: Miracles and the Pulp Press During the English Revolution* (New York Press, 1993), a book, however, that must be used with caution.

15 In addition to what is now the primary account, Raymond, *Invention of the Newspaper*, the more recent published literature includes Joad Raymond, ed., *Making the News: An Anthology of the Newsbooks of Revolutionary England, 1641–1660* (New York, 1993); Joseph Frank, *The Beginnings of the English Newspaper 1620–1660* (Cambridge, Mass., 1961); Carolyn Nelson and Matthew Seccombe, *Periodical Publications 1641–1700. A Survey with Illustrations* (London, 1986), Occasional Papers of the Bibliographical Society, no. 2. Bibliography is fully and expertly handled in Nelson and Seccombe, compilers, *British Newspapers and Periodicals, 1641–1700: A Short-Title Catalogue* (New York, 1987). See also the studies of individual journalists cited below, nn. 22, 24, and 25.

16 See below, p. 68–70.

17 BL E. 65 (26) (Nelson and Seccombe 275.132).

18 BL E. 201 (6), E. 201 (32). In the intervening weeks Thomason reported generally increasing numbers of newsbooks. In May–September 1642, Thomason did a similar count, peaking with five diurnals in the third week of July (E. 202 [20]). For a detailed monthly census, see *British Newspapers and Periodicals, 1641–1700*, pp. 622–3.

19 BL Add. Mss. 40883, fol. 15b. On Wallington, see Paul Seaver, *Wallington's World* (London, 1985).

20 Indeed, from 1655 the officially sanctioned newsbook appeared on Monday and on Thursday under different titles. For this development, see Nelson and Seccombe, *Periodical Publications*, p. 98.

21 The possibilities and ambiguities of 'factual' reporting are usefully discussed by Raymond in *Invention of the Newspaper*, pp. 130–6, 141–4, 158–63.

22 P. W. Thomas, *Sir John Berkenhead 1617–1679* (Oxford, 1969). Raymond, in *Invention of the Newspaper*, p. 149, is sceptical about the influence of *Mercurius Aulicus*.

23 *Areopagitica*, in John Milton, *Complete Prose Works* (New Haven, 1953–82), 8 vols, 2: 528. Sheets of paper were dampened before they were put into the press, and then hung up like laundry to dry. Milton's comment about the wet sheets of *Mercurius Aulicus* thus refers specifically to the London editions. See also Nelson and Seccombe, *Periodical Publications*, pp. 62–5.

24 The literature on Nedham is increasingly valuable. Joseph Frank, *Cromwell's Press Agent: A Critical Biography of Marchamont Nedham, 1620–1678* (Lanham, MD, 1980) has been largely superseded. For a brief introduction of many excerpts, see Raymond, *Making the News*, pp. 332–79. But above all see the recent essays of Blair Worden: 'Marchamont Nedham and the Beginnings of English Republicanism,' in David Wootton, ed., *Republicanism, Liberty, and Commercial Society, 1649–1776* (Stanford, CA, 1994); 'Milton and Marchamont Nedham,' in David Armitage, Armand Himy, and Quentin Skinner, eds, *Milton and Republicanism* (Cambridge, 1995); ' "Wit in a Roundhead": the Dilemma of Marchamont Nedham,' in Susan Dwyer Amussen and Mark A. Kishlansky, eds, *Political Culture and Cultural Politics in Early Modern England: Essays Presented to David Underdown* (Manchester, 1995).

25 Parker, *The Contra-Replicant* (London, 1642), pp. 1–3.

26 Also his *Interest Will Not Lie* (London, 1659) and *Newes from Brussels* (London, 1660).

27 Raymond, *Invention of the Newspaper*, pp. 108–11, 314–20.

28 Walker: Raymond, *Invention of the Newspaper*, *passim*; Ernest Sirluck, 'To Your Tents, O Israel: A Lost Pamphlet,' *Huntington Library Quarterly* 19 (1955–56): 301–5. Crouch: David Underdown, *A Freeborn People: Politics and the Nation in Seventeenth-Century England* (Oxford, 1966), pp. 90–111.

29 I hope to report on John Harris and his royalist wife Susannah in another place. For Harris see the article on him by Barbara Taft in Robert Zaller and Richard L.

Greaves, eds, *Biographical Dictionary of British Radicals in the Seventeenth Century* (Brighton, 1982), 2: 59–60. See also Margo Heinemann, 'Popular Drama and Leveller Style, Richard Overton and John Harris,' in Maurice Cornforth, ed., *Rebels and Their Causes* (Atlantic Highlands, NJ, 1979); J. B. Williams (pseudonym for J. G. Muddiman), *A History of English Journalism* (London, 1908), pp. 106–7; H. N. Brailsford, *The Levellers and the English Revolution* (Stanford, CA, 1961), especially p. 416 n.4, where Harris is proposed as the author of key issues of *The Moderate*; Joseph Frank, *The Beginnings*, pp. 165–5, 192–3, 204, 356 n. 23.

30 I discuss this episode in *Henry Parker*, pp. 112–33; see the sources there cited in n. 3, 4.

31 See Sir Simonds D'Ewes' moving account of the event in his diary, BL Harl. 165, fol. 150 recto (1255b), which S. R. Gardiner, *The History of the Great Civil War, 1642–1649* (repr. New York, 1965), 4 vols, 1: 186–7 quoted *in extenso*. Gardiner relied partly upon the newsbook *Certaine Informations from Severall Parts of the Kingdome*, 7–14 August 1643, p. 231. The event was covered by at least three other newsbooks, the fullest effort being the *c.* 1,500-word account carried as an extended lead story in *The Kingdomes Weekly Intelligencer*, 8–15 August 1643, pp. 227–30. Tending to exculpate the Parliament guards, the report was rich both in context and significant on-the-scene detail. Rushworth, *Historical Collections*, 5 (part 3, vol. 2): 357–8, upon which Gradiner also relied, drew heavily and sometimes verbatim (though not entirely from) *The Kingdomes Weekly Intelligencer*.

32 Robert Fitzgibbon Young, *Comenius in England* (Oxford, 1932), p. 65; cited in Vivian Salmon, *The Works of Francis Lodowick* (London, 1972), pp. 61–2.

33 *A Satyr Against Hypocrites* (London, 1655), pp. 5, 8, 9. In Phillips' *Speculum Crapegownorum, the Second Part* (London, 1682) sig., c2 recto, Priestlove (a scorner of dissenters) says that in 'a Meeting House' in sermon time, 'you shall see a company of People, Young and Old, rich and Poor, sitting upon their Bums, their Hats pull'd over their Eyebrows, with their Pens, and their Books, and their blotting-Papers, all so busily employed, as if they were so many men Copying of news-Letters, and this in such a strange Ethiopic Character, that no-body cann tell what they Write: They may be setting down their last Weeks gains and Expences for ought I know. Nay, I saw one so wedded to his Hat, that after the Minister was in his last Prayer, he would not stir from his Head, till he had concluded what he had to Write, wiped his Pen, screw'd his Inkhorn, fix'd his Blotting-paper, clasp'd his Book, and put it in his Pocket: and by that time the Minister had almost done.'

34 Thomas Shelton, *Zeiglographia* (London, 1650), sig. a1 verso, indicates that the sermons of John Preston, Richard Sibbes, and Day (presumably Martin Day) were preserved through shorthand. Launcelot Andrewes' were similarly published, though with some disapproval about the results of the 'legerdemain of brachygraphy': Sir Gyles Isham, ed., *The Correspondence of Bishop Brian Duppa and Sir Justinian Isham, 1650–1660* (Lamport, 1955), p. 157. The reference is Andrewes' *Apospasmatia Sacra.*

35 *The Diary of Thomas Crosfield M.A., B.D. Fellow of Queen's College Oxford*, ed. F. S. Boas (London, 1935), p. 74. I owe this reference to Sabrina Baron.

36 *Memoirs of the Verney Family* (London, 1894), 4 vols, ed. Margaret M. Verney, 3: 69. Shelton's second system, published in 1650 as *Zeiglographia*, never attained the popularity of his first, *Tachygraphy*, which was the one presumably meant here, and was in fact resented by those who committed to his earlier system.

37 Nicholas' parliamentary diary for 1624 (PRO SP 14/166) uses these characters, though perhaps less often and less consistently than later. SP 16/97 is the 1628 diary, with a reading key to some of the symbols on the front. An example of the use of the characters in 1642 is SP 16/488/53. Traditional shorthand historians probably would not consider Nicholas to be a true shorthand writer, because his use was restricted to common forms. The shorthand is noted in John Westby-Gibson, *The Bibliography of Shorthand* (London and Bath, 1887), p. 53, and in *Proceedings in Parliament 1628* (New Haven, CT, 1977–83), 5 vols, eds Robert Johnson, Maija Jansson *et al.*, 1: 29–30.

38 In a related though distinct way, Rushworth's shorthand skills were essential to one of his printed volumes, the one covering the trial of the earl of Strafford.

39 This is not to deny that the systems had severe limitations, and that an ethic of progressive, incremental improvement was a prominent feature of shorthand culture.

40 In addition, systems circulated in manuscript, partly because the books were very expensive to produce, since they required the services of an engraver. See William Mason, *La Plume Volante* (London, 1707), 'To the Reader,' unpaged, unsigned, that this revision of his older system circulated in manuscript for fifteen years prior to printed publication. William Facy's *The Complement of Stenography. Or, the Power of the Pen Displayed, in a New Art of Charactery* (London, 1672), though printed, had its shorthand characters hand-entered by the author.

41 London, 1680, sig. c2 verso; see also sig. b2 recto, and Rushworth, *Historical Collections* (London, 1682), Part 1. Preface sig. b1 verso – b2 recto. On Rushworth's use of shorthand, see Frances Henderson, "Posterity to judge': John Rushworth and his 'Historical collections,' *Bodleian Library Record* 15 (1996): 246–59; and the examples in *The Fairfax Library and Archive. The Property of the Lord and Lady Fairfax* (Sotheby's sale catalogue, 14 December 1993), illustrations to Lot 70, and Raymond, *Invention of the Newspaper*, p. 139.

42 *A Briefe and Perfect Relation of the Answers and Replies of Thomas Earle of Strafford* (London, 1647), p. 1, identifies the reporter as a ready writer, another term for stenographer. It was derived from Psalm 45:1, 'my tongue is the pen of a ready writer.' Wencelaus Hollar's contemporary engraving of the trial scene BL 669. f. 4 (12) shows a number of note-takers (whether shorthand or not) amongst the front-row spectators.

43 Rushworth, *Historical Collections* (1721), 4: 477–8. Rushworth's copy, with the king's emendations, is SP 16/488/15. In his *Historical Collections* text, Rushworth largely complied with those emendations and excisions.

44 *England's Black Tribunall. Set Forth in the Triall of K. Charles,* [sic] *I. ... Also the Several Dying Speeches of the Nobility and Gentry, as were Inhumanely Put to Death for their Loyalty* (London, 1660), p. 113.

45 *A True Copy of Sir Henry Hide's Speech on the Scaffold ... the 4th of March 1650* [viz. 1651]. *Taken in Short-hand from His mouth, By John Hinde* (London, 1650), p. 3; *Mr. Love's Case: ... Printed from an Exact Copy, Taken in Short-hand by John Hinde* (London, 1651).

46 *England's Black Tribunall*, p. 65 (sig. F1 recto).

47 James Hamilton *et al.*, *The Several Speeches of Duke Hamilton Earl of Cambridg,* [sic] *Henry Earl of Holland, and Arthur Lord Capel upon the Scaffold ... 9 of March* (London, 1649), p. 9.

48 *England's Black Tribunall.* While the texts of the various editions by Cole, Playford and Tyton of the king's trial and scaffold speech and the speeches of the royalist peers were essentially stable, there were some changes in reported details and in the scenic apparatus, probably reflecting the predominantly royalist market for these items after their initial general-interest appearance as news, and after they had passed the commonwealth's censors.

49 Clarke possessed (a) a distinctive manuscript (reel 17, item 4/9 appendix = Worcester Coll. ms. 71) of Laud's trial, which G. E. Aylmer believed was undertaken by Clarke as Rushworth's assistant [Introduction/reel guide to microfilm edition of *Sir William Clarke Manuscripts 1640–1664* (Harvester Press, 1979), p. 45]; (b) a unique and very full account of the Hamilton, Holland, Capel, etc. trials (reel 9, item 2/10 = ms. 70), which though known to Hilary Rubinstein, *Captain Luckless*, was not used; Rubinstein relied solely on Bishop Burnett's account, which was the one reproduced in *State Trials*.

50 London, 1647. Though not set up play-style, and relying at points upon summary, central speeches are presented, or at represented as, verbatim reports.

51 *The Arraignment and Acquittall*, p. 6.

52 The trial of the royalist peers was not published; see n. 49 above.

53 This is a perfect instance of the necessity of separates, given the inherent limitations of newsbooks. For the various trial versions, see C. V. Wedgwood, *The Trial of Charles I* (London, 1964), pp. 125–6, 227–8. The first part (*A Perfect Narrative*), covering 20 and 22 January, bore an imprint date of 23 January 1648[49]. The *Continuation of the Narrative*, part 2, covered 23–24 January, with an imprint date of 25 January; part 3 covered 27 January (a Saturday), with an imprint date of 29 January (Monday).

54 The suggestion that C. W. is Clarke was made to me by Frances Henderson, the student of Clarke's shorthand papers in the Worcester College manuscripts, and by Lesley Le Claire, the former librarian of the college. Their suggestion is strongly buttressed by Clarke's role as witness at the trial of the regicides, and in particular by Clarke's own words that his testimony was based in part upon what he took notice of 'in a Book': *An Exact and Most Impartiall Accompt of the Indictment, Arraignment, Trial, and Judgment (According to Law) of the Twenty Nine Regicides* (London, 1660), p. 43.

55 *England's Black Tribunall*, pp. 29–30.

56 *The Triall, of Lieut. Collonell John Lilburne* (1649). The role of the self-styled 'publisher' Theodorus Verax (viz., Clement Walker) is not perfectly clear. Walker is not known to have been a shorthand writer. A remark on p. 65 implies that Walker used others' notes ('the best imperfect notes the Publisher could pick up'); but compare p. 154, where the publisher claims to have been 'indifferent in writing and transcribing'. The latter passage also notes the possibility of 'exacter Copies'; there are fragments of the trial in the Clarke Mss. (Worcester College Ms. 71, 12 loose unnumbered pages), showing many gaps but only a few differences with the printed text. A 'John Hinde' (otherwise 'Captain' Hinde) was among the grand jurors summoned to return a true bill antecedent to the trial proper. This Hinde was reported in a later addendum to the trial to have 'writ down the words' that one of the judges had used, and to have read them back: *The Second Part of the Triall of Lieut. Col. John Lilburn ... Being Exactly the First Dayes Work ... (which was not inserted in the last)* (London, 1649 1650 [*sic*]), pp. 3, 11. It is possible that this Hinde was the shorthand writer, and could well have taken the trial as a spectator once the grand jury's work was completed.

57 The trial was concluded on 26 October 1649; Thomason, exceptionally, did not hand-date this item, but its place in the sequence of small quartos yields a date of 1–4 December.

58 *The Triall, of Lieut. Collonell John Lilburne*, p. 120. The point about the books is that Lilburne had been angling for time to gather his citations. With equal stupidity, the court denied a request of the jurors for some sack shortly before they were to render their verdict; *ibid.*, p. 150.

59 Farthing was prevented from publishing his text at the time of the trial, although other accounts emerged, as did Love's scaffold speeches. *The Triall of Mr Christopher Love Before a Pretended High Court of Justice in Westminster Hall* (London, 1660). The title page indicates the trial was 'Published by *John Farthing* Citizen of *London*, who took the Triall in the said Court in Short-Writing for Mr. *Love*, and at his own request.' For the circumstances of publication, sig. A2; for Love's use of Lilburne's argument and the judges' reluctance to allow Love to turn what they regarded as the exceptional characteristics of Lilburne's trial into precedents, pp. 3–13. For Farthing, see the very good material in W. J. Carlton, 'Part 4, Shorthand Books, with Biographical and Bibliographical Notes,' in *Bibliotheca Pepysiana: A Descriptive Catalogue of the Library of Samuel Pepys* (London, 1914– [no end date supplied]). For another case of the influence of Lilburne's trial record, *The Triall of the Honourable Iohn Penruddock of Compton in Wiltshire*. ('Printed by order of the Gent. intrusted. 1655.'). This report, however, shows little sign of stenography.

60 Rich's claim was made in his *Semigraphy: or, Arts Rarity* (London, 1654), sig. A6 recto. But this cannot be connected with any of the several accounts of various parts of the trial. For the boast, see *The Triall of Mr. John Lilburn ... upon Wednesday, Thursday, Friday, and Saturday, the 13, 14, 15, & 16 of July 1653* (London, 1653), p. 26.

61 London, for Andrew Crook and Edward Powel, 1660. There was a similar compilation made in 1662 for those then executed: *The Speeches and Prayers of John Barkstead, John Okey, and Miles Corbet Together with Several Passages at the Time of their Execution at Tyburn, the Nineteenth of April, 1662* (London: for Nathaniel Brook and Edward Thomas, 1662). For a positive indication that the trial of the regicides was taken in shorthand, see *A Brief Narrative of that Stupendious Tragedy Late Intended to be Acted by the Satanical Saints of these Reforming Times* (London, 1663). The title page notes, '*exactly taken in Short-Hand Characters, by the same Person that wrote the late Kings Iudges Tryals.*' Most, though not all, of the related cases were reported wholly or in part through shorthand.

62 For example, *The Proceedings and Tryal in the Case of the Most Reverend Father in God William Lord Archbishop of Canterbury* (London, by Thomas Bassett and Thomas Fox, 1689). This is explicit that the record was procured by the six bishops for their own use, and then presented to Judge Powel for his approval.

63 I expect to provide a fuller treatment of the collection of pamphlets in *A Cultural History of Reading*, edited by Jennifer Andersen and Elizabeth Sauer (Philadelphia, PA: forthcoming).

64 *The Correspondence of Bishop Brian Duppa and Sir Justinian Isham*, p. 117.

65 *A Happy Handful* (London, 1660), sig. A2 verso: '*The best of papers ... are oft consigned to the worst of uses.*'

66 *Speeches and Passages of this Great and Happy Parliament: from the Third of November, 1640, to this Instant June, 1641. Collected into One Volume, and According to the Most Perfect Originalls, Exactly Published* (London: for William Cooke, 1641). Cooke then published a continuation, with a new emphasis on deed over word: *The Diurnall Occurrences ... of Both Houses ... from the Third of November, 1640 to the Third of November 1641. With a Continuation of all the Speeches from June Last, to the Third of November, 1641* (London: for William Cooke, 1641).

67 Raymond, *Invention of the Newspaper*, pp. 302–10 (where Raymond stresses Rushworth's ideological skewing of his sources). *The Parliamentary or Constitutional History of England* (London, 1751–61), 24 vols, vols 9 and 10. I owe this point to Maija Jansson, of the Yale Center for Parliamentary History. The methodological introduction to vol. 9 (pp. iii–ix) does not, however, mention the volume.

68 Edward Husbands, ed., *An Exact Collection* (1643). For its importance, see Andrew Sharp, 'John Lilburne and the Long Parliament's Book of Declarations: A Radical's Exploitation of the Words of Authorities,' *History of Political Thought* 9 (1988): 19–44. See also Michael Mendle, *Dangerous Positions* (1985), p. 179, n. 30.

69 *A Collection of Sundry Petitions Presented to the Kings Most Excellent Majestie* (London, 1642).

70 *A Declaration of the Engagements, Remonstrances, Representations* (1647).

71 *A Happy Handful*, sig. A2 verso; see also Thomason's title page note to his copy (BL E. 1021 [17]).

72 See above, pp. 63–8.

73 Peter M. W. Blayney, *The Texts of 'King Lear' and their Origins* (Cambridge, 1982), vol. 1, p. 38.

74 Steven Zwicker, who has done a study of readers' marginalia in seventeenth-century books, has confirmed to me the accuracy of this observation.

75 On Clarke, see the essays by Frances Henderson and Lesley Le Claire in *The Putney Debates of 1647: The Army, the Levellers, and the English State*, ed. Michael Mendle (Cambridge, forthcoming).

76 For a brief indication of Thomason's methods (though with several points needing modification), see Michael Mendle, 'The Thomason Collection: A Reply to Stephen J. Greenberg,' *Albion* 22, no. 1 (Spring 1990): 85–93.

77 Henderson, 'Posterity to judge'; *The Fairfax Library and Archive*. There are also a few instances of Rushworth's characteristic annotations of tracts now in Clarke's collec-

tion, and most importantly a volume compiled, listed, and numbered by Rushworth: Worcester College AA.2.6.

78 *The Bodleian Library Account Book 1613–1649* (Oxford, 1983), ed. Gwen Hampshire, Oxford Bibliographical Society Publications, New Series 21, p. 150. These were not the only contemporary works received through purchase or donation, but they are the ones that by their description are self-evidently news or news-related. At 1p. a sheet, the going rate for such items, the sum would purchase as many as 384 standard-size quarto newsbooks or separates, and as many as 3,072 pages.

79 *The Famous Collection of Papers & Pamphlets of All Sorts, from the Year 1600. Down to this Day, Commonly Known by the Name of William Miller's Collection* ... (London, n.d.). Anthony Wood purchased his copy for 1 s. on 10 May 1695.

80 *The King's Cabinet Opened* (London, 1645), cited above, n. 5; *Cabala, sive, Scrinia Sacra: Mysteries of State and Government* (1654); John Hacket, *Scrinia Reserata: a Memorial Offer'd to the Great Deservinge of John Williams, D. D. ... Ld Archbishop of York* (1693).

81 John Rushworth, *Historical Collections*, Part 1 (London, 1682), Preface, sig. b1 verso – b2 recto: he wrote of the 'impossibility for any man in After-ages to ground a true History, by relying on the Printed Pamphlets in our days.'

82 London, 16[59]60. Despite the date of 23 January on the title, the letter was dated 21 January on p. 7. Thomason's copy is dated 27 January, and the title page of this edition notes that the letter was read in Parliament on 26 January.

83 The letter to Morrice (Morris) is in Bodl. Libr. Clar. Ms. 69, fol. 3; see also *The Dictionary of National Biography* article on him. The letter to Rolle is in *The Clarke Papers* (London, 1891–1901), ed. C. H. Firth, 4 vols, Camden Society Publications, New Series 49, 54, 61, 62, 4: 258–9, where Monck indicates that he had also written to 'Cozen Morris' to provide Rolle with assistance. Monck did venture to Rolle that while the printed text made room for the 'giddy interests,' Monck intended only 'their just rights as men and Christians,' not 'martiall and civill trust.'

84 According to Thomas Rugg, this letter was publicly known on 17 January: *The Diurnal of Thomas Rugg 1659–1661* (London, 1961), ed. William L. Sachse, Camden Society Publications, third series, vol. 91, p. 29.

85 In addition to the predictably rich gathering of these in the Thomason Collection, there is a thick deposit of printed petitions and declarations in the State Papers: PRO SP 18/219; cf. the editorial comments in *Calendar of State Papers Domestic, 1659–1660*, pp. x–xi.

86 *A Letter*, pp. 3–7.

87 See Clar. Ms. 68, fols 138, 205–5; Clar. Ms. 69 fols 9–10. F. J. Routledge, the editor of volume 4 of the *Calendar of the Clarendon State Papers* (Oxford, 1932), described Monck's 'connexion' to the Devonshire declaration as 'at the least that of connivance' (p. xv).

88 For comparison's sake, it might be noted that a conference with Lords on 25 January 1642, John Pym hectored the Lords on their responsibilities to the nation by using petitions exemplifying the *vox populi* from his own tiny borough, Tavistock, and elsewhere in Devon.

89 *To his Excellency, Generall Monck* (669. f. 23 [23]); Trev., J., *The Fair Dealer: Or, a Modest Answer* (E. 1015 [11]); R. M., *A Letter to General Monck* (E. 1015 [1]); *A Letter of Advice to his Excellency the Lord General Monck* (E. 1013 [23]); M. W. (viz., William Morrice, according to Thomason's own attribution, using the form 'Moris'), *Animadversions upon Generall Monck's Letter*. A copy of this item, attributed by the modern editors to 'Moris William' is in the State Papers: SP 18/219/27.

90 BL 669 f. 23 (33); E. 1015 (11), p. 3.

91 Clar. Ms. 68, fol. 204; Clar. Ms. 69, fols 58, 78.

92 Clar. Ms. 69, fols 37–8.

93 Clar. Ms. 69, fol., 67.

94 Clar. Ms. 70, fols 27 recto, 61 recto, 83 recto. Of course, Hyde too was negotiating. In finding no hope in Monck he was declaring that he had yet to accept Monck's terms.

4 News, history and the construction of the present in early modern England

Daniel Woolf

In *Before Novels*, his important cultural history of the late seventeenth- and early eighteenth-century literary milieu, J. Paul Hunter suggests that when the novel began to emerge in the early eighteenth century, it did so amid 'a developing concern for contemporaneity, a wish to recognize the momentous in the momentary and to feel the power of all time in its most fleeting moment.' England had developed, he continues, 'an urgent sense of now' and a preoccupation with novelty; but, he concedes, 'it is hard to say exactly when the present time became such an urgent issue in the English cultural consciousness.'[1] Hunter is undoubtedly correct both as to the existence of this phenomenon of present-mindedness, and its clearest expression in the journalism of the Augustan era. His account raises a number of problems, not least (as he admits in the latter quotation) the beginnings of a strong sense of the present, and that present's connections to the past. In noting, for instance, the obvious etymological link between the French word *jour* and 'journalism' (a word that did not itself appear until the early nineteenth century), he suggests that by the 1690s, English culture had become so intoxicated by 'the potential significance to human consciousness of any single moment that an immediate written record was required.'[2] This correctly and astutely identifies the relationship, but puts the cart before the horse. The newspaper was not merely the creation of a cultural obsession; it in large measure created that obsession, which cannot have sprung *ex nihilo*. To make this point, it is necessary to go well back beyond the 1690s and link the Augustans' concern with contemporaneity to the creation of that contemporaneity over the preceding century.

The perception of the present

The modern sense of the present as a segment of time experientially distinguishable from past or future differs sharply from that which existed in the mid-sixteenth century. This is owed in large measure to the progressive shrinkage that has occurred over four centuries in the length of time deemed minimally necessary for a series of events to unfold, to be fashioned into formal or informal narrative (or even into competing and mutually contradictory narratives), and dispersed over a wide geographic field.[3] The indulgence of a recent example may serve to illustrate how presentness is manufactured in our own time, by way of contrast with the pre-electronic era. In January 1986, as I left my home for the university to teach an afternoon class, I saw on the television the first report of the *Challenger* space shuttle disaster. This had been flashed only moments earlier from Cape Canaveral, Florida nearly two thousand miles to the south. Within thirty minutes, the time it took me to walk to campus and get into the classroom, the entire university, including my students (not normally the group of people most conscious of events outside their scholastic and recreational universe), was abuzz with talk of the catastrophe. When I flew to England for the mid-term break three weeks later, the shuttle was still the main subject of conversation, dwarfing Mrs Thatcher's latest attacks on the unions and the impending fall of Philippine dictator Ferdinand Marcos. What was already a 'past' event, existentially, was still talked of, understood, and treated as part of an extended present. Having lost none of its shocking immediacy over the preceding weeks, it was still 'news,' and not yet 'history.'

News of some kind – oral or written communication of some new event, some fluctuation in the 'normal' process of things – is of course as old as civilization. There has always been an interest in new events, something to enliven the boredom of daily life, and bad news often has the added appeal to *schadenfreude*. News stands on the cusp between past and future; it arouses recollection, anticipation, expectation, or apprehension. But the *means* by which it has been communicated, and consequently the ways in which it has been perceived, have evolved over the millennia, in response to developments in transportation and technology. Our perception of news is very different from that of early modern people, because both our technology and our relationship to that technology is radically different; theirs, in turn, differed from that of the pre-print era. Stephen Kern's panoramic study of European culture in the pre-First World War era, as it made use of new instruments of communication such as the telephone and Marconi wireless, points to the *simultaneity* of experience as a critical mark of a culture's tacit recognition of a public present in which a wide range of experience can be shared by many people over wide distances. Commentators on the wireless news reports of the *Titanic*'s last hours in April 1912 noted 'with a sense near to awe that we have been almost witness of a great ship in her death agonies.' The process that Kern notes has been magnified by technology in the course of the century, but its antecedents can be pushed back to the seventeenth century.[4]

Because major events now reach a wide audience through the print and, especially quickly, the electronic media, they can almost instantaneously form a common currency in local, national and international discourse – a 'public sphere,' to borrow Jürgen Habermas' terminology – that they could not have done as easily two centuries ago, and scarcely at all three centuries before that.[5] And because they do reach listeners or readers so quickly, they are now deemed 'current events,' rather than history, at the point at which they are perceived, cognitively processed, and discussed. As one student of the psychology of memory and time has put it, 'the psychological present is a duration, not an instant.'[6] Since this would appear directly to contradict the formal, philosophical understanding of the present as a brief moment among most commentators since St. Augustine, some explanation is needed of the shift toward an experientially-defined sense of the present as meaningful duration. In the West, at least, we now have a very strong sense of the present (and hence of an immediate past flowing into but distinct from that present) because our lives, and the society that shapes them, have themselves been pre-narrated by the public institutions that organize and convey information. As Pierre Janet, a pioneer in the study of the psychology of memory, noted in 1928 by way of studying the phenomenon of *déjà vu*, the sense of duration is largely intellectual, its preciseness impeded by our construction of the present.[7] In other words, our present is as much a social fabrication as our past, but it is seen as independent of that past, even if it draws on that past through memory, and even if we acknowledge that it will, *in the future*, become past, and hence a matter of history.

People of all classes in the Middle Ages and in the sixteenth century inhabited a remembered past (enhanced for the then-relatively small number of literate by reading) and an expected future. In contrast to us, they conceived of the present as an instant rather than a duration, through most of the period recognizing no 'present' beyond that instant. This lack of a sense of the present as duration was owed less to intellectual theories about the nature of time than to the reality of its experience, and in particular to the limitations constraining the perception of news. These limitations will figure prominently in the argument I wish to make about precisely how the printing press affected news. They can be enumerated as follows:

1 speed: the slow rate at which people learned of remote events, a velocity that increased in inverse proportion to their geographical distance from the event itself;
2 flow: the discreet, blip-like and erratic way in which news reached them and had then to be sorted out from rumour;
3 commonality: the degree to which knowledge of a particular event is shared simultaneously among persons or communities separated by geography; and
4 density: the number of aural and visual cues to sudden change, most obviously represented in the printed media and in the public world of conversation, but most often in combination of these.

Our own experience of these limits is not monolithic, but conditioned by race, class , gender, family, occupation and other factors. On the whole, however, it is very different from that of our ancestors of four centuries or so ago. We do not learn of news in the way they did, which was normally slowly, sporadically and sparsely, unless they were directly caught up in the events by proximity. Rather, we are enveloped by it, and the plots of our own lives are absorbed into an ongoing social narrative (the medium-term 'march of events,' or 'today's big story') – whether we choose to take an interest in them or not.[8] It is in the seventeenth century, however, that the social and psychological experience of news first acquired something like its modern form, with the only major changes still to come falling under category 1 (speed), as communication became virtually instantaneous beginning with the telegraph.

Modern technology has increased our awareness of news but perhaps also deadened our sensitivity to it, as theorists of boredom such as Klapp suggest, so that we now need a major event like Kennedy's assassination or the Princess of Wales' death to jolt us into engagement with a present beyond our domestic and professional lives.[9] Nevertheless, it is possible to trace the origins of the communications trajectory that has ended in the present back to the last great revolution in communications, the printing press. How printing affected the perception of news is less obvious than it might seem: any advances in the velocity of news transmission prior to that time were very modest, and approaches that emphasize the 'speed' of the print era are emphasizing an attribute that the press did not in fact possess. In terms of the four constraints on news mentioned above, the press did not materially increase the speed at which news travelled (it was still sometimes slower than a fast horseman). However, it did expand the number of people simultaneously reading or discussing variant versions of the same news (commonality); it presented multiple – even if conflicting – reports of those events (density); and it eventually regularized the rate at which events were transmitted and the intervals between transmissions (flow).[10]

Time and the speed of news

From the point of view of a person receiving news of a great event, and recording it or passing it on to an acquaintance, there was an unbridgeable temporal gap between the event itself and his or her perception of it. This is a gap which contemporaries did not often remark on, since they were accustomed to it, but it made their understanding of what was present and what was past fundamentally different from our own. At the end of the seventeenth century something like a modern understanding of temporal relations had been achieved, so much so that Richard Steele made it the subject of a satire on the verb tenses, cast in the form of a mock letter from a Civil War prisoner who is about to be executed by Roundhead captors. In a final letter to his wife, the captive Royalist reports his death as *past* rather than impending, since he knows she will not receive this news until his head has fallen; this produces farcical complications since she weds again soon after receiving the letter, unaware that her husband had in the meantime been rescued.[11]

It was literally impossible before the advent of the telegraph for an event to be noted at great distance almost immediately, in what is now colloquially termed 'real time,' after its occurrence. In addition, the period before 1641 (the year Crown restrictions on publication effectively ceased, or were at least considerably loosened) also lacked the enhanced density and flow of news conducive to the experience of 'current events,' except once again for those situated in close proximity to those events. To individuals who believed that the present was only an existential instant, an ephemeral joint between a dead past and an unborn future, a delay of several days or more meant simply that the event they had heard about *already belonged to the past*: a recent past, perhaps, but past none the less. The principal difference, then, between the period before 1640 and that after was not the greater *speed* of printed news, nor a noticeable change in overall reception times (the time elapsed between an event and a person's learning about it, by whatever means, at a distance). Rather, the sense of an enveloping present owed its development to changes in the other limits on news reception that I sketched out above: flow, density, and commonality. All of these substantially altered during the seventeenth century, and particularly in periods of continuous activity, publicized through multiple media (printed, oral and written) such as the 1640s. It is this, not print's superiority over oral or manuscript transmission, that accounts for the changing relationship between past and present, and the establishment of the latter as a free-standing locus of social experience. These changes had profound implications for the modernization of the sense of time, and for the development of new media such as the novel (Hunter's point, above) and, slightly earlier, the diary; the latter genre was the literary consequence of individual attempts to record and order life-experiences according to a faster-moving diurnal and hourly experience in a new world dominated by clocks and watches. They also occasioned the decline and disappearance of older media such as the chronicle, whose capacity to record rapid change on an annual basis seemed by the mid-seventeenth century as inadequately slow as daily news now seems to users of Internet news servers and CNN.[12]

By way of illustrating the dispersal of a major news event and the importance of geography, let us look at one well-known example, the announcement to the world of the death of Elizabeth I. The old queen died at about three in the morning on the last day (as it was reckoned then) of 1602, 24 March, which was a Thursday. According to the young barrister John Manningham (whose friendship with the late queen's chaplain, Dr Parry, gave him inside knowledge), the Council had met at Whitehall and by ten o'clock, had proclaimed James VI of Scotland as the new king of England. Sir Robert Cecil read this proclamation aloud outside Whitehall; he then journeyed to Cheapside to read it there. Two districts of the city thus heard of this major event separately but immediately, and without any interposing media commentary, from the same high official. Over the course of the day, most of London discovered the death of the queen, though reports were fragmentary and coloured by rumour. Would there be a civil war over the succession? Had the queen, already the subject of numerous plots, finally been assassinated by Jesuits? Would the new king of Spain attempt another invasion – or had Spanish troops indeed already landed in the south? Those who could read would, some days and even weeks later, have the opportunity to discover answers to some of these questions as proclamations were issued by the Council, and as city hacks wrote poems and processionals about the queen in anticipation of her funeral, or of her successor's arrival.

So much for the city. Because London, and especially the royal court, served as a kind of clearing-house for news from all points of the kingdom and beyond, the closer one was to the metropolis the sooner one was likely to hear of most events.[13] The rest of the nation had to wait much longer to discover this news, as did the expectant heir, several hundred miles to the north, despite the hurried departure of Sir Robert Carey and his famous breakneck ride (at about seven miles an hour) across country to Edinburgh. Carey reached Doncaster, 162 miles away, that night, and Berwick (184 miles) on Saturday; he then 'poasted on to Edenburgh' (fifty miles), after stopping to refresh himself, change horses, and acquaint his brother, Sir John, with the news. He got to Edinburgh later that night, having covered about 400 miles in three days. Consequently, lowland Scotland, or at least Edinburgh, may have learned of the change of dynasty before some parts of England. It took considerably longer for the news to travel to rebellion-torn Ireland; the earl of Tyrone, his armies worn out and his supplies exhausted, surrendered to the late queen on 3 April, still in ignorance of her death.[14]

News travelled as quickly or slowly as the men or women who carried it in the early modern era, which is to say that it did not normally travel quickly at all. Fernand Braudel estimated that until the major road improvements of the mid-eighteenth century, the average speed of all types of transport was a maximum of 100 kilometres (sixty miles) per twenty-four hour day.[15] This may be overly pessimistic (depending on the terrain), since an estimate derived from Kentish postal speeds in the later part of the seventeenth century indicates that an average journey could take place at no greater than four and a half miles per hour, somewhat less during the winter – considerably slower than Carey's mad gallop of 1603 – but the general point stands.[16] Between England and the Continent, delays were longer, though perhaps one ought to be surprised that they were not even greater. The news of Francis I's defeat at Pavia on 24 February 1525 first reached England in late March, in a letter of 15 March to Cardinal Wolsey from the English ambassador to Madrid, who himself had heard the news five days earlier from 'a currier, that passyd throw France be [*sic*] the Frence kings salve conduict.'[17] Sir Thomas Barrington complained to his aged mother in 1632 that 'newes comes so uncertaynely and slowly to hand.' Sir Thomas was able to relay to her the spectacular victory of Gustavus Adolphus over the forces of Maximilian of Bavaria at Lech, which occurred on 5/15 April, only on 15 May, having just heard it in London; others had to wait for newsbooks to report it over the course of the next week. Bad news may have been fleeter of foot: a year earlier, the burning of Magdeburg by Tilly's troops on 10/20 May 1631 reached Oxford a mere three weeks later, on 30 May.[18] From more remote areas, news took even longer. Samuel Pepys first learned from his patron Edward Montagu of the death of Charles X of Sweden on 3 March, 1660, exactly a month after the king had died. Running in the other direction, word of the battle of Worcester (3/13 September, 1651), which destroyed Charles II's Scottish army and sent him into exile, reached Paris nine days later, on the night of 12/22 September.[19]

Nor did the regular newspapers of the Restoration much improve the speed of foreign news, since they could only print material as they received it by packet boats from across the channel. Although more contact as well as back and forth travel between England and the colonies took place in the seventeenth century than has often been acknowledged, the ocean remained an even greater divide.[20] Word of the dreadful earthquake in Lima, Peru (20 October 1687) took the whole winter to cross the Atlantic, appearing in the *London Gazette* only on 24 May 1688.[21] On 20 September 1705 Nicholas Blundell in Lancashire heard, for the first time, of the death of his brother in Maryland nearly ten months earlier.[22]

Provincial papers remained heavily dependent on the London press or on handwritten newsletters from the capital well into the eighteenth century.[23] The same was true of news going in the opposite direction as information from the country was sent to city newsletter writers, and eventually newspapers, by post or rider; the principal difference between foreign and provincial news throughout the period was the considerably greater dependence of London news-writers on the foreign printed press for international news, supplemented by diplomatic dispatches and material supplied by newly-returned merchants, sailors and travellers.[24] In contrast, news from other English and Welsh towns or even further afield in Scotland and Ireland could be sent by a system of regular correspondents.[25]

Information and the flow of news

Like the sense of time itself, the ways in which news intruded on an individual's mental horizon could undoubtedly be shaped by such factors as social degree, gender, religion, or occupation. But the most influential determinant was without a doubt geography. Because towns, especially London, served as national or regional clearing-houses, those living in them were apt to think that there was an over-abundance of news, a chaos of passing events which had to be understood and mentally categorized, and which threatened to disturb the orderly passage of time. In a celebrated passage of his *Anatomy of Melancholy*, Robert Burton commented, from the perspective of an Oxford college room, on the variety of new information reaching his ears and eyes from different sources every day:

> I hear new news every day, and those ordinary rumours of war, plagues, fires, inundations, thefts, murders, massacres, meteors, comets, spectrums, prodigies, apparitions, of towns taken, cities besieged in France, Germany, Turkey, Persia, Poland, &c. … A vast confusion of vows, wishes, actions, edicts, petitions, lawsuits, pleas, laws, proclamations, complaints, grievances, are daily brought to our ears. New books every day, pamphlets, currantoes, stories, whole catalogues of volumes of all sorts, new paradoxes, opinions, schisms, heresies, controversies in philosophy, religion &c. … To-day we hear of new Lords and officers created, to-morrow of some great men deposed, and then again of fresh honours conferred. … Thus I daily hear, and such like, both private and publick newes.[26]

So great was the flow of information that the news-conscious town-dweller was obliged to come to terms with the relative importance of an event, its national, international or local significance, or be overwhelmed by it. Burton's comments on this 'vast confusion' are a pungent reminder that the anxiety induced by too great a stream of information is merely the flip side of the feelings of boredom, melancholy or ennui which were first being articulated at the same time.[27]

In the country, the case could be much different, though rural gentry and clergy, at least, were able to keep themselves informed of events elsewhere, especially during times of crisis. In the comparative isolation of her husband's Yorkshire estate, Lady Margaret Hoby appears to have heard from a visiting friend of the execution of her former brother-in-law, the earl of Essex, on 25 February 1601, within a day of the event. More trivial news, though coming a shorter distance, could take much longer. Through one Mr Pollard, the high constable of Pickering Lythe, Lady Hoby heard, a month after it happened, of the death from drunkenness of a York parson and 'some other thinges of lesse moment.'[28] National events were received and noted together with those of familial or parochial interest. If they came in slowly and sporadically, as they generally did, they did not much disrupt the gentle trickle of time through daily, weekly and yearly routines. The diary of an Essex minister, Ralph Josselin, may serve as an example of the way in which extraordinary news could be quietly noted, its occurrence meshing with facts of everyday life such as planting or the weather. On 24 February 1678, Josselin made the following entry:

> Lovely growing weather, a million granted the King to begin the war with France (,) wee are a people peeled and polled, help lord, see the issue of things.[29]

Josselin, an articulate and intelligent observer, was clearly aware of the significance of events taking place outside the tiny world of his Earls Colne home to a greater degree than would have been his humbler parishioners. This awareness would still have been somewhat limited and conditioned by geographical isolation, though in Essex Josselin was relatively close to the capital. Even in the mid-seventeenth century, when newsbooks had proliferated, news travelled slowly into the provinces, thereby making 'current events' that much less current. It is best not to overstate this distinction between centre and periphery: a shocking event was a shocking event, wherever one heard it, and recent studies of the circulation of political news and of the attitude of the 'county communities' suggest that they were considerably less narrow and localist in interest than was once believed. In his brief autobiography, John Evelyn recalled, as one of his Sussex childhood memories, being awakened abruptly one morning in 1628 with the news of the duke of Buckingham's assassination. One of the earliest memories of Abraham de la Pryme was of the death of Charles II in 1685; as a small boy in Yorkshire he had 'heard a gentleman say that came from London, that the citty was in tears, and most of the towns through which he came.'[30] For both men, these morsels of 'news,' unconnected blips on their youthful horizons, occurred too early in their lives to shape their immediate futures, yet still occupied a privileged status in their retrospective understandings of their own pasts.

Density and commonality: Multiple modes of transmission of news

Thus far, I have argued that print affected the reproduction of news, and its effect on consciousness of present events, less by the speed at which it could record or disseminate events – which was still much slower, in the era of the hand-press, than writing or speech – than because of its mass-reproduction capacity, and the consequent rapidity with which it could replicate itself. This capacity was itself realized slowly, and until the late seventeenth century both the creators and receivers of news continued to rely heavily on more conventional media such as manuscript newsletters.[31] Within England, visual and aural signals such as bells and bonfires (the latter set up in relay form) offered the easiest means to 'flash' news from one part of the country to another. Although they were unable to indicate exactly what that news was, some events (or rather, the outcomes of ongoing events) were already anticipated, so that the significance of a bonfire or bell-ringing would be understood in most places.[32] This system remained in place half a century later: the proclamation of James II and the defeat of the duke of Monmouth were signalled at Leicester by a bonfire paid for by public money, as was the birth of the king's son in 1688.[33] A slower but more informative route was to rely on a network of correspondents for 'retransmission' of news across the country and on the Continent. In such a manner did the Protestant reformer Richard Hilles, living in Strasbourg in 1547, pass on to Heinrich Bullinger, in Zürich, the news of the death of Henry VIII and the coronation of his son, 'which they write me word from England is all true.' In the 1620s, the Cambridge scholar Joseph Mead subscribed to private newsletters as well as to the newer corantos which that decade produced; he in turn was a tireless recirculator of their contents to his own contacts.[34]

News continued to be conveyed by oral transmission throughout and long past the end of the period under discussion here.[35] During Elizabeth I's reign and through the early Stuart period, however, this was increasingly complemented by a variety of graphic forms including official and unofficial manuscript newsletters, libels,[36] and 'separates,' written or printed sheets sent from London to the provinces and giving details of foreign affairs, parliamentary speeches, and court scandals, as well as the regular diet of broadsheet ballad accounts of marvels and prodigies.[37] Written and printed news reports were often sent together, a coranto adjoined to a personal newsletter, a practice that would continue after 1641.[38] An important recent study by Alastair Bellany of the spread of news about the early Stuart court has exploited family muniments and especially diaries and commonplace books to demonstrate the breadth of circulation of oral, written and printed news concerning such *scandala magnata* as the Thomas Overbury murder and the career and assassination of the duke of

Buckingham.[39] As Bellany perceptively remarks of the early seventeenth century: 'A vibrant news culture created the space in which increasing numbers of people were able to engage with and become agents in the political process.'[40]

Oral news lost no ground to its graphic counterparts after the collapse of Caroline censorship in 1641. If anything, its relationship with both print and manuscript became more symbiotic as each medium provided checks and confirmations on the others. The ballads published shortly after events such as the defeat of the Armada, the destruction of Charing Cross in 1647, the execution of the king, the Great Fire, and the Battle of Sedgemoor, which found their way into the collections of readers like Samuel Pepys, were successful in part because they could mediate between the oral and written. Other forms of printed news tended to complement rather than replace oral communication.[41] In Elizabethan and Jacobean London, one simply had to go to a central meeting place such as Lincoln's Inn Fields, or 'Paul's Walk' in the Cathedral environs, to hear the latest news. The Royal Exchange was ideal for this purpose since there, as one Jacobean writer noted, 'from all countreys there was dayly newes to be heard by one meanes or other.'[42] In rural areas, markets and fairs served the same function. When the diarist John Rous tried to obtain news of the king's siege of Coventry in August 1642, he consulted both newsbooks and Coventry men whom he encountered at Stourbridge Fair in Worcestershire. The Yorkshire cleric Abraham de la Pryme went to nearby Brigg to 'heare the newse' in 1696; since he also writes of going there to '*see* the newse,' it is probable that, like Rous, he was picking it up from both newspapers and casual conversation.[43]

Couriers, ambassadors and private messengers, travelling by foot, ship and mainly on horse brought news at widely varying rates,[44] and the development of a more sophisticated postal system in the seventeenth century did not, in the short term, greatly alleviate the irregularities in news circulation that were worsened in times of disaster or upheaval like the plagues that struck London in 1603, 1625 and 1665, or the Great Fire (which in addition to burning down the Letter Office, halted publication of the *London Gazette* for a week, while utterly destroying its rivals). The Civil War on the whole propelled the spread of news (of which it was the dominant though not exclusive subject), the energies and resources devoted to communications more than compensating for the countervailing disruption occasioned by the existence of hostile camps and the blockage of major roads and bridges. These retardants should not, of course, be underestimated, as contemporary complaints suggest. Writing to the earl of Essex on 26 May 1645, Sir Samuel Luke provided the Parliamentary commander with news from the garrison at Newport Pagnell, though he warned that it might be 'stale by the slowness of the messenger.' At other times news could travel very fast. Luke wrote to his brother, Sir Oliver, three weeks later, that his bearer had come in 'good time,' and had been dispatched back again almost immediately.[45] Yet the very slowness and unreliability of ordinary channels – the local officials who were supposed to keep the government informed – contributed to improvements, forcing central officials like the Cromwellian Secretary,

John Thurloe, to employ networks of agents and spies, much as his Elizabethan predecessor Sir Francis Walsingham had done in peacetime.

The gathering of information and the careful control of its release in the press indeed became one of the Secretary of State's major functions after the Restoration, as illustrated in the newsletters regularly dispatched in the 1660s and 1670s, at a subscription cost of about £5 a year, by individuals such as Henry Oldenburg or Henry Muddiman, and especially by writers working for the Secretaries of State, Henry Bennet earl of Arlington, his colleague, Sir William Morrice, and Arlington's subordinate and then successor, Sir Joseph Williamson.[46] Caroline and Commonwealth improvements to the postal system were maintained at the Restoration with the 1660 Post Office Act (12 Car. II cap. 35), which made permanent the removal of the office from private hands and set standard rates. The Act was accompanied by a purge of the office's suspect ex-Cromwellian leadership; the use of the post to send and receive news was further aided by the exemption of news-factors like Muddiman from the inland postage cost of 2d for the first eighty miles and 3d for anywhere else in England and Wales, a relatively high cost by contemporary standards.[47]

Beginning with certain royal proclamations and with the short chronicles published by men like William Rastell and Richard Grafton in the early to mid-1500s, news had begun to make its way into print, albeit initially at a turgid rate. The next step, taken in the early seventeenth century, was the publication of monthly and then weekly 'newsbooks,' such as the foreign corantos that crept into England slowly prior to 1620 and thereafter much faster.[48] These initially had to be imported from Antwerp or from the Dutch Republic. In 1621, the government permitted their printing in London (so long as they stuck to foreign news and left domestic matters alone) thereby further reducing the time between the occurrence of events and their printing, since the news could travel faster across the channel in pre-print form, and increasing the volume of copies that could be quickly distributed. Beginning in October 1623, the first of several numbered series appeared, initiating a tentative regularity – of titles rather than intervals of publication – to the production of news.[49] Pamphlets such as *Mercurius Britannicus* (not to be confused with its parliamentarian namesake of the 1640s, *Mercurius Britanicus* with one 'n') began to proliferate.[50] By the early 1640s, according to one estimate, about 1,000 separate issues of a number of these corantos had been published, though only about one-third of these have survived.[51] For various reasons, including complaints from the Spanish ambassador, Charles I suppressed the corantos in 1632, thereafter allowing only slower 'annuals' like the *Swedish Intelligencer* to be printed in the kingdom. Once again the letter-writers had to fill the void for their gentry customers, though the corantos were revived in 1638, under their earlier printers, Nathaniel Butter and Nicholas Bourne.[52]

In his play *The Staple of News* (1631), Ben Jonson asked the question whether news remained news once it was committed to print, thereby identifying a distinction between history and current events that, I have posited, was emerging at exactly this time. Indeed, even a decade earlier, in his Twelfth Night masque,

News from the new world, discovered in the moon, Jonson had already raised the same issue. In this masque, two characters, a printer who prints newsbooks and corantos, and a factor who writes letters to correspondents in the countryside, debate the proper medium for the conveyance of news. The factor claims to be offended at the printing, rather than the writing down of news, 'for when they are printed they leave to be news; while they are written, though they be false, they remain news still.' The answer of the printer is that: 'It is the printing of them makes them news to a great many who will indeed believe nothing but what's in print.' It is these customers who keep his presses running, and his writers writing; and every ten years or so he recycles his stories as the age 'grows forgetful' of their contents.[53]

One has only to examine the heading 'Newsbooks' in the revised *Short-Title Catalogue* to notice how, by 1640, print had already largely formalized the recording and transmission of news and begun to accustom readers to regular reports. Whether print caused an increased appetite for quicker, more regular news or simply responded to an interest that was already there is a chicken-and-egg question of little significance. The issuing of proclamations and the publication of statutes and letters patent, or the circulation of other pieces of information in sermons and at meetings of the Assizes from the late Middle Ages through the seventeenth century must certainly count as a form of the transmission of news, as did the return of MPs from parliaments, albeit news so spread was both sparse and irregular.[54] There can similarly be little doubt, from the reception end, that the gentry, clergy and aristocracy had already been growing acclimatized to semi-regular news, in non-printed form, through diplomatic letters and private correspondence (for which the letters of the Pastons in the fifteenth century, as much as those of John Chamberlain to Dudley Carleton or of Henry More to Anne Conway, offer well-known examples), and through the services of professional letter-writers such as Rowland White, who during the turbulent 1590s, with an aged queen, Irish rebellion, and the Spanish lurking across the channel, had kept paying correspondents in the country in touch with developments in London and elsewhere.[55] But it is also apparent that without print and its rapid-replication capacity, any wider public appetite for information would have remained severely constrained by the transmissional limits of oral and handwritten reports. In 1600, the provincial citizen or rural subject was more or less entirely at the mercy of oral reports, visitors, and correspondents. In 1728, by contrast, the mayor of remote Durham could supply himself with a year's worth of printed news for a mere shilling.[56]

At first sight it might be argued that one effect of the newsbook and the newspaper was to silence the news, making it something to be perceived quietly by the reader, in isolation from others, rather than a part of ordinary conversation. This would be a mistake, since news could run freely between speech and writing or print. It is true that in reading a newspaper or letter in privacy, one is confined simply to comprehending and acknowledging the message contained therein: a solitary reader may surely read between the lines to discern hidden intent, but texts cannot fill in nuances, clarify details, or answer questions. In contrast, to converse about the news – even about a newspaper one has just read and has in hand – is not only to possess knowledge of its contents but also to be able to respond to it directly and dialogically. In conversation with the provider of oral news, one can evaluate the messenger as well as the message, and judge from gesture, facial expression, and intonation whether the news is true, or at least whether its spokesperson believes it to be true. It is no wonder, then, that early modern people long preferred to have their news by mouth when possible. Henry VIII often read diplomatic letters to himself, but at other times he would read them aloud, or have them read to him, and converse with the messenger. Sir Thomas More reported in 1529 that the king had received and read a foreign letter which 'mencioned credence to be geven to the bringer in the declaring of the same.' On another occasion, five years earlier, More noted that the king had read a dispatch from Richard Pace aloud to the queen and court, 'and furthwithe he declared the newes and every materiall point, which uppon the reding his Grace well noted un to the Quenys Grace and all other abowt hym who were mervelouse glad to here it.'[57]

Writing in 1580, John Lyly commented that 'the eare is the caryer of newes.'[58] A century later print, an upstart competitor, had challenged the ear's monopoly but not overthrown it, aural news being among other things less demanding on its recipients (something that remains true today when newspapers have lost ground to less time-consuming media like radio and television). In fact, though print allowed for private digestion of the news, it just as often promoted discussion. This is best demonstrated by the interplay between oral, written and printed news at that most characteristic of Restoration and Augustan institutions, the coffee-house, which one scholar has, in the wake of Habermas, called 'the architecture for the emergence of the public sphere.'[59] These were not limited to London. In larger towns, one simply had to go to the nearest coffee-house to consult the papers, read letters, *and* hear and discuss news. Rowland Davies, dean of Ross, who visited England in 1689, records going to a coffee-house and 'reading the news' throughout his journal as part of his ordinary daily activities. But he also, while at dinner with a friend, 'heard an account of the Turks being defeated.'[60] The West country physician Claver Morris heard of the peace terms with France in 1709 at a coffee-house (news which seems, however, to have been of less interest than that which he heard while at music later in the day, 'of poor Molley Mills's being scalded to death in Cornwall, in a kettle of water').[61] These remarks all come from the gentry and professional classes, but the expanded literacy of the later seventeenth century makes it nearly as applicable to their social inferiors. If one listens to such contemporary comments as those of the Swiss-French visitor César de Saussure in 1729, the coffee-houses attracted 'workmen' who began their day 'by going to coffee-rooms to read the latest news' and 'discussing politics and topics of interest concerning royalty.'[62] Lewis Theobald thought it 'provokingly ridiculous' to hear a haberdasher in a coffee-house 'descant on a general's misconduct, and talk of an army's passing a river with the same facility as he himself could go over Fleet-bridge.'[63]

The degree to which the recipient of news did not distinguish between information conveyed orally and that conveyed in writing, even in the early eighteenth century, appears in the detailed record afforded by one diarist in the reign of Queen Anne, Henry Prescott. The deputy registrar of the diocese of Chester, Prescott was a lazy functionary with a higher devotion to drink and conversation than to ecclesiastical law. He was, however, an inveterate news-hound who daily recorded the bits of information that came his way through personal contact, conversation at alehouses and coffeehouses, correspondence, and what he called 'the public news.' Figure 1 breaks down the news that he recorded by subject.

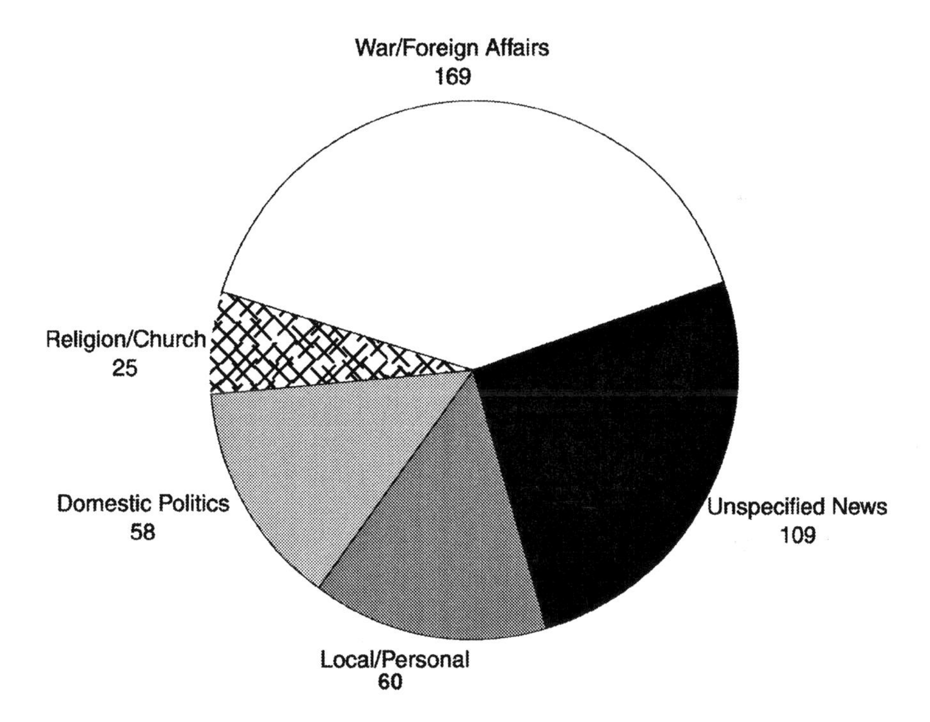

Figure 1 The circulation of the news at Chester: subjects of events heard of or read of by Henry Prescott, 1704–11

Note: Sources include personal information, letters, alehouse/coffeehouse discourse and the 'public news'

Source: The Diary of Henry Prescott LL.B, vol. 1, J.M. Addy, ed., Record Society of Lancashire and Cheshire, 127

Aside from a large unspecified category of general 'news' that he records without further detail as to its subject (about one quarter of all references), he paid about the same attention to local matters, or those involving his immediate family, as he did to domestic British politics. Either despite or because of his employment as a lay official of the Church, he had little interest in recording news involving religion and the Church. But the chart makes it crystal clear that in the relative isolation of Chester, the news that regularly had the greatest impact on him was that of foreign affairs and especially war. In all, 169 references in the diary are concerned with international affairs. War had an ability to puncture the flow of time so effectively and shockingly that it could overwhelm the intake of other forms of news. Let us now see if some earlier cases of war had an equivalent effect on the sense of the present.

News and current events

By the late 1620s, the production of corantos had become serialized and more systematic. Just as letter-writers such as Chamberlain gave their correspondents weekly updates on the events at court, so the publishers of newsbooks at home and abroad realized that they could sell more copies if they retained an audience from one week, or month, to the next. The repeated use of names like the *Swedish Intelligencer* or *Mercurius Britannicus*, suggests a nascent 'brand loyalty' among the readership, as readers bestowed their trust, and their pennies, on a publication that appeared at intervals. After 1641, ideological conflict would further the division and redivision of the readership of news along political lines: John Cleveland, the royalist poet, denounced parliamentary diurnals as 'urinalls,' as different from royalist newsbooks 'as the Devill and his Exorcist; or as a black Witch doth [differ] from a white one, whose office is to unravell her inchantments.'[64] The proximity of events and the need to keep informed about them in turn affected the speed at which newsbooks were produced, since publishers wished their products to keep pace with events, rather than simply responding to them on an *ad hoc* basis. *Regularity* was thus added to newness and truth as a quality for the successful newsbook, something demonstrated once again by the increasing number of dated and numbered corantos in the *Short-title Catalogue* and later in the Thomason Tracts.[65]

The Thirty Years' War did much to increase the importation of foreign news on a regular basis. Gustavus' victories or the atrocities of Tilly's troops remained remote events; though Protestants might fear the possible outcome of an imperial victory for the Reformation throughout Europe, though they might shudder at accounts of babies hurled into the flames by marauding Spanish soldiers, they had little sense of these events having an immediate effect on English life. Yet troubles for Protestantism in Germany were potentially deadly to Englishmen apprehensive for the future, their memories still fresh with Bloody Mary, the Armada, and the Gunpowder Plot. Even if they did not resonate in the same way as a crisis on home soil, they involved English mercenaries and money, an English princess in distress (the Electress Palatine), and rising fears about the future of reformed religion in England.[66]

The vigour of public discussion of foreign affairs and court scandals in the 1620s and 1630s, whether in corantos, newsletters, or private correspondence, is difficult to deny. Yet it is possible to argue that the activities of the Long

Parliament, the Irish Rebellion, and the Civil War that ensued in 1642 marked events different in kind as well as degree from anything that had preceded them, and that they produced in the 1640s newsbook a printed mirror that is just as distinguishable from its early Stuart predecessors.[67] For the first time in 200 years, and the first time ever since the advent of printing, large armies were fighting battles not across the Channel but right at home, on British soil, and in all three kingdoms at the same time. This would happen only on a much smaller scale after 1660 and would cease altogether with Culloden in 1746. To read of military, religious and political developments became not just a matter of interest (though that it surely was), but also potentially one of survival; to publish such accounts offered not simply the prospect of a small monetary gain but an opportunity to fight a propaganda campaign that was unprecedented, at least in scale and duration, in English history. And once the hand of the censor was lifted in 1641, even the shaky control of news exercised by the Elizabethan and early Stuart regimes ceased to exist. The result was a veritable flood of pamphlets, parliamentary speeches,[68] and especially newsbooks, beginning with *The Heads of Severall Proceedings in this Present Parliament* (22–29 November 1641), produced with weekly regularity, each presenting an account of recent events that was both up to date and, from the point of view of the side generating it, 'true.' In 1642 came greater regularity as a few newsbooks established themselves under titles like *A Perfect Diurnall*, and as each day of the week became the publishing territory of rival series.[69] The printed word was occasionally supplemented by woodcuts, the effectiveness of graphic representations having been demonstrated much earlier in such Elizabethan works as Foxe's *Acts and Monuments*.[70]

The distribution of news was not, even then, confined to the newsbooks, as testified by the continuation of pre-war practices, such as the dispatching of manuscript newsletters by professional writers who specialized in providing weekly information to rural subscribers; booksellers now took on extra copyists or employed scriveners in order to service their swelling subscription lists.[71] Alastair Bellany has rightly remarked that the news culture of the half century before 1640 had set the stage for the 'phenomenal growth of political expression and debate' after the end of censorship.[72] With such favourable conditions in place, the volume of printed and written material was in itself sufficient to carry news through different parts of the realm in an unparalleled volume and with unprecedented regularity; and, as Joad Raymond points out, even in small runs of 250 to 1,000 copies, the same newsbooks would be re-read by several readers over a period of days elsewhere in the provinces.[73] This represented a major increase in the flow, density and commonality of news even though it brought with it, as we will see further below, added problems for recipients unable to distil truth from propaganda, reality from rumour.

The flip side of a current event is 'public opinion,' the collective if discordant responses of the readers or hearers of news to what that news means, whether it is good or bad, and, most important, what should be done about it. The petitions produced on the eve of and throughout the Civil War represent among other things a more concerted and direct provincial response to events in Westminster than had ever occurred previously; and the conflicts between rival newsbooks further fuelled the political flames.[74] The same environment for ideological response to events would be achieved again during the Exclusion Crisis, where it has recently been studied by Mark Knights, with the volume of pamphlets published in 1680, about 1,800, representing double the number published three years before.[75] News thus does much more than recount events that are part of a longer story, still in play; it solicits possible resolutions to that story. Where history relates acts which are complete with a narrative beginning, middle and end, news is Janus-faced, simultaneously peering into the past and the future. The literate public of the 1640s were aware that the events through which they were living were incomplete and that, subject to providence, they would be called upon to shape their final disposition.

This had lasting consequences for the future development of news in England: Figure 2 illustrates the stages in the expansion of the present from the early sixteenth to the early eighteenth century, with relation to the national events occurring at that time and the printed media wherein they were related.

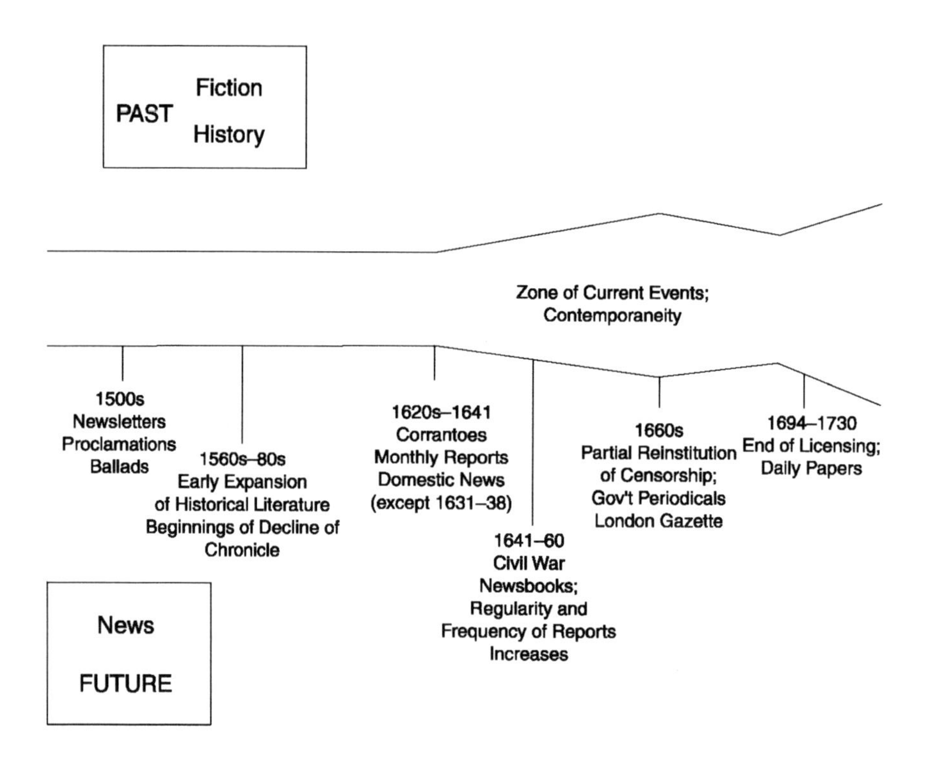

Figure 2 News and the expansion of the present, 1500–1730

The desperate urgency with which the newsbooks were greeted may have abated with the temporary cessation of armed hostility in 1646, but not the appetite for their information. Despite the ban on newspapers other than the official *Gazette* from 1666 to 1679 and again from 1682, the attempts of successive regimes throughout the Interregnum and Restoration to restrict the publication of all domestic news proved largely futile, notwithstanding the scrutiny of watchdogs like Sir Roger L'Estrange, Charles II's Surveyor of the Press. The proclamation issued by Charles II's government in 1680, at the height of the Exclusion Crisis, which attempted to suppress the unlicensed printing and distribution of news, was a desperate barn-door locking after the horse had escaped. Nailed awkwardly back into place in 1682, the door squeaked open again in 1688–89. It would come off its hinges for good in 1695, though the use of 'general warrants' issued by the Secretaries of State remained a frequent but controverted practice until the time of John Wilkes and the North-Briton in the 1760s.[76]

On the theory that the best defence lay less in a sieve-like censorship than in the good offence of an official and Crown-friendly publication, the later Stuart period saw the advent of L'Estrange's own *Intelligencer* (1663) and then the *London Gazette* (1665), which for its first few months, while the Court was in Oxford fleeing the Plague, was published both there and in the City. That the government felt compelled to supply an official outlet for news at all – not something done under any preceding regime (if we exclude proclamations) – is a mark of how news-oriented English society had become in the ensuing two decades These papers to some degree competed for the most interesting stories with the manuscript newsletter services largely controlled by L'Estrange's rival, Williamson, and by Henry Muddiman, whose own *Current Intelligence* was put out of business by the Great Fire within weeks of its initiation.[77] The *Gazette* was the monarchical successor to two Marchamont Nedham-run official publications of the 1650s, *Mercurius Politicus* and the *Publick Intelligencer* (which enjoyed an official monopoly after the Cromwellian crack-down on newsbooks in 1655), and to Nedham's 1659–60 successors *Mercurius Publicus* and the *Parliamentary Intelligencer*, run by General Monck's client Muddiman. Boasting the barred rubric 'published by authority,' the *Gazette* first appeared in a double-column broadsheet, before evolving into a four-page format. It enjoyed special status as an official publication, despite the relative sparseness of domestic news and outlasted most of its contemporary rivals, holding a virtual monopoly between 1666 and 1679. In May of that year, the expiration of the 1662 Licensing Act owing to Charles II's prorogation of Parliament permitted a brief window of three years during which nearly forty different papers were published, many of them short-lived.[78]

Both the *London Gazette* and the other papers that sprang up briefly during the Exclusion Crisis signify that the old weekly or bi-weekly newsbook was on its way to becoming, in form and frequency, the new newspaper. By the turn of the seventeenth into the eighteenth century, the transition to a daily issue of the same series had been achieved in such titles as the *Daily Courant* (a morning paper) and the *Evening Post*.[79] With the dailies came the thrice-weekly *Posts* of William III's reign, and then the literary periodicals such as the *Guardian*, *Tatler*, and *Spectator.* These functioned as the printed link between members of different clubs and coffee-houses, which were themselves active agents in the dissemination of news, blending oral rumour with writing and print into a pastiche of contemporaneity.[80] The dailies even introduced an early sort of stop-press instrument to allow up-to-the-hour additions, in the form of 'postscripts' which began as handwritten notes in the margins of printed papers, and soon became printed sheets separately issued, albeit without an explicitly advertised connection to their parent paper.[81] Only further improvements in communications, in the nineteenth century, would seriously reduce the lag between an event and its recounting in the press.

News and history

There was one further consequence of the creation of a meaningful present, which was the amicable but permanent separation of news from history. The corantos and early newsbooks of the 1620s speak of news as history and often were published under the rubric of history, a further reinforcement of the argument that at its earliest stage the published news was perceived as a record of the recent past, not of an ongoing present. During the 1640s and later, writers such as John Cleveland drew a sharp contrast between the dignity and truthfulness of history – at a time when it was losing both – and the vulgarity, lack of elegance, and sensationalism of the newsbooks, 'the embrio of history slinckt before maturity.' Cleveland would not have been pleased at the manner in which the contents of yesterday's newsbooks reappeared, from the late 1640s onward, as today's histories in writers from Joshua Sprigge through William Dugdale and John Rushworth.[82] References to the word 'history' in newspapers of every sort decline sharply in the second half of the century, though the term 'chronicle,' no longer in vogue among historians, would enjoy a second life as a purveyor of news, and though, too, the former close relation of the two is conveyed in Steele's reference to newsbooks as 'weekly historians.'[83] It is perhaps significant that when two formerly independent papers, the *Post-man* and *The Historical Account* were merged in 1695 and for a time published under both titles, the 'historical account' subtitle was soon dropped.[84] There were, naturally, exceptions. But even in a paper of the 1730s entitled *The Historical Journal*, the serialized *History of England from the Earliest Accounts of Time Down to the Reign of his Present Majesty King George II* that it provided readers (an adaptation of Paul de Rapin-Thoyras' popular history) was deliberately kept separate from the news, and printed as a detachable half-sheet supplement.[85]

News had not, of course, displaced history as a subject of discussion. But it had definitively established the present as a zone of activity, as narratable as the past, but distinguishable from it, and thereby constructed a public space within which events could enjoy their ephemeral life before slipping into the maw of history. A very clear expression of the proper spheres of history and news comes from 1733, when Eustace Budgell tried to evade the latest (1725) Stamp Tax on newspapers. Successive governments since 1712 had been obliging the publishers of newspapers carrying recent intelligence to use stamped paper.[86] Budgell was the author of *The Bee; or, Universal Weekly Pamphlet*, and he had neglected to apply to the Commissioners of the Stamp Revenue for exemption by virtue of his publication being a three-sheet pamphlet rather than a newspaper proper (pamphlets over a certain number of sheets were counted as books and exempted). Accordingly, *The Bee* was taken as a 'Weekly Collection of news' and entered at the Stamp Office as a newspaper, which should be printed on a half-sheet with the half-penny stamp. Budgell protested that his publication, insofar as it contained news at all, as opposed to other matter, was not a newspaper but a magazine, like the *London Magazine* or *Gentleman's Magazine*. The publisher of the *London Magazine*, however, was keen to defend the commercial advantage of his own exemption. He therefore made the case that his publication was qualitatively different from Budgell's because as a monthly its news was *by definition* no longer current, hence not news at all but history:

> The true *Import* and *Meaning* of the Word *NEWS* is the Return of Intelligence of any Kind, by the Posts *Foreign* or *Domestick*. But all Transactions of a Month's standing, are, long within that Time, recorded in the *Secretary* of *State's Office*, then, by the Law of Nations, become *Memorials*, and all future Recitals of them, fall under the proper, and only, Denomination of HISTORY.

At the end of a month, Budgell's enemy pointed out, all intelligence collections were bound up and indexed – essentially turned into history books. Any attempt to include such materials under the coverage of the tax was in his view ludicrous and 'might as well include *Josephus*, Rapin's *History*, and Baker's *Chronicle*,' all three of which works had recently been serialized.[87]

The removal of news from the realm of the historical was not absolute – since the present inescapably emerges from the past it never can be. The diarist Lady Sarah Cowper indiscriminately classified her snippets of news together with stories under the marginal rubric 'histories,' and she makes a telling comment in 1713 that speaks to news and history being close relations, but not identical because of the temporal spheres in which they operate:

> History and news are so nearly alli'd that the only difference seems to be; the one informs us of what was done in times remote from us, and the other of what is so late as may be properly call'd present and in being; if anything which depends on time may deserve that name. It serves to shew how like the several ages of the world have been to one another, what warrs, and revolution monarchy's erected, empires pull'd down; cittys built and destroy'd. Ravages, alliances, treatys, and all the other variety's wee see in our daye, have gone on in a course of succession since the earth has been inhabited.[88]

The past helped Cowper, like most readers, to make sense of the present, and the present to understand the nature of events in the past.

By the end of the seventeenth century, events were seen to be part of an ongoing historical process continuing into the future, a process that could be broken down into weekly, daily or even smaller units. Various links between the media that conveyed the present and those that commemorated and interpreted more remote events continued to exert an attraction to readers, not least of all the family of genres that includes the salacious 'narratives' or 'true narratives' or 'true accounts,' as they often titled themselves, of crime and punishment, scaffold speeches, and reports of marvels and miraculous cures, as well as the occasional *chronique scandaleuse* of misconduct among the famous. An examination of the 'news' contained in one major collection, the Pepys ballads, indicates a concern with events ranging from the apparently trivial, such as the cow that ran into Clerkenwell church during a sermon in 1689, or the 'Somersetshire wonder,' a calf born with the face of a woman, to major political and military events.[89] As Paul Hunter writes, there is a strong sense in the titles of most such works that they are 'helping to write the full history of the times and ultimately of reality itself.'[90]

News, rumour, distrust, and anxiety

The presence of the present in news was not universally welcomed. In addition to the anxiety occasioned by the onrush of information, there remained throughout the period a deep distrust of news because it was both new and difficult to verify. News lacked the air of authority that surrounded old texts. Vocalized, it could scarcely be distinguished from rumour, *a fortiori* when it emanated at second hand, or from a less than credible source.[91] Print did not help since for many readers and writers in the first two centuries after Caxton, printed publication constituted a 'stigma' that made a communication or utterance inherently less trustworthy than a manuscript text.[92] 'When a piece of false intelligence gets into one paper,' reported the *Craftsman* in 1734, 'it commonly runs thro' them all, unless timely contradicted by those who are acquainted with the particular circumstances.'[93] Steven Shapin has argued that in the realm of science, truth was increasingly thought to issue exclusively from the mouths of the social elite, and particularly from those of good 'credit.' Shapin's point can be supported from fields other than science, news among them. In the credibility of news, however, other elements more than social degree were important, such as political and religious affiliation: put simply, one inclined to believe one's friends and disbelieve one's enemies. Dudley Ryder, a constant reader of newspapers and haunter of coffee houses, was keen to get a good seat at the execution of the Jacobite earl of Derwentwater in 1716. Ryder discounted the news presented by his lodging-house maid, to the effect that the earl and his condemned comrades had been reprieved, because its original source had been a fellow lodger of Tory persuasion, and 'the Tories love to deceive themselves with agreeable news.' He was uncertain enough, however, to go straight into town and make sure of his facts, arriving just in time to get a perfect view of the falling heads.[94]

Such distrust existed throughout the early modern period, but it did little to kill the appetite for news. As Thomas Cromwell remarked to John Creke in 1523, 'news refresheth the spirit of life.'[95] Throughout the period, thirst for news, like innovation in general, provided a target for wits. In about 1516, the court poet John Skelton commented that news had made men worse gossips than women:

> For men be now tatlers and tellers of tales;
> What tidings at Totham, what newis in Wales,
> What shippis are sailing to Scalis Malis,
> And all is not worth a couple of nut shalis.

Bishop John Jewel, writing to Bishop John Parkhurst in 1553, refused to report any news, punningly remarking that, 'the old is more than enough.'[96] In Chapman's play *The Revenge of Bussy d'Ambois*, Renel tells Clermont that if he wishes to be considered a 'gentleman well-qualified,' he must ask 'what the news is.' Clermont, in reply, refers to the Locrian princes who punished any newcomers who enquired as to the news,

> Since commonly such brains are most delighted
> With innovations, gossips' tales, and mischiefs.[97]

A sermon preached at Whitehall in 1619 denounced the quest for news, which had become so widespread that 'Every man's religion is known by his news; the puritan talkes of Bethlehem Gabor, &c.'[98]

Such satires became more common in the 1620s, the decade of the corantos. In Jonson's *News from the New World*, to which I have already referred, the anti-masque opens with a discussion between two heralds (the purveyors of oral news), a factor of news who writes letters to clients in the country, a printer and a chronicler.

1st herald: News, news, news!
2nd herald: Bold and brave news!
1st herald: New as the night they are born in.
2nd herald: Or the phant'sie that begot them.
1st herald: Excellent news!
2nd herald: Will you hear any news?

The printer then enquires as to the price of the news and is asked if anyone ever buys the news: has it, in short, become a commodity, like fish or corn? He responds that he is all in favour of selling it; in fact, being a printer, he makes his living hunting out news wherever it may be and selling printed versions of it. 'I'le give any thing for a good Copie now, be't true or false, so't be newes.'[99] In 1626

Jonson returned to these themes at greater length in *The Staple of News*, performed in that year and first printed in 1631. In this work we meet a woman called Tatle, one of a quartet of 'gossips' including Mirth, Censure and, significantly, Expectation. She enjoins Prologue to 'Looke your Newes be new, and fresh, Mr. Prologue, and untainted, I shall find them else, if they be stale, or flye-blowne, quickly!' It is not clear that 'untainted' necessarily means 'truthful.' Another exchange between several characters emphasizes the theme of information overload or 'vast confusion' we have seen in Burton's *Anatomy*, before raising a related concern: the lack of any rubric by which to distinguish true and false, amid the Babel-like noise of the newest events.[100] News addicts presented as inviting a target as those who fed their habit; with allowances for the greater prominence of printed news, there is a close family resemblance between Skelton's early Tudor remarks on news-hunger and an essay of two centuries later by Joseph Addison. This features an impoverished Political Upholsterer who is 'the greatest newsmonger in our quarter.' Up before dawn to read the *Postman*, he walks up and down town to check for Dutch mails. More anxious about the welfare of King Augustus than that of his own family, 'He looked extremely thin in a dearth of news, and never enjoyed himself in a westerly wind.'[101]

But there was more to object to in news than simply its promotion of a perceived popular addiction to novelty. Another, and major, reason why commentators from one end of the period to the other were so suspicious of news – in whatever medium – was that it was so often either false or out of date.[102] To counteract such well-established distrust, the newsbooks (rather like another, less regular, medium of news, the ballad, which was also subject to distrust), very early commonly emphasized two qualities in their titles. First, they stressed their newness, the excitement to be gained from reading them. In 1614, Philip Gawdy remarked to his nephew, Framlingham, 'That newes is best in season, when it is newest, whether it be true, or false.' Exactly a century later a letter printed in *The Spectator* made a comparable comment, but used the shorter time span of an hour as the measure of freshness. 'A piece of news loses its flavour when it hath been an hour in the air.'[103] Title-page set-ups quickly developed the marketing technique of stressing the newness of their contents in a graphic anticipation of the modern headline, thereby predetermining the reader's sense of what had become an important event. Second, they assured readers of their truth, each book claiming that it was the most up-to-date and reliable account of the events being related. Thus the most accomplished newsmonger of the 1640s, Marchamont Nedham, felt obliged in 1645 to declare that he was reporting events independently and without interference from his parliamentary masters; other pamphlets carried encouraging names like *The Moderate* or *Perfect Passages*.[104] Both truth and newness were necessary claims, as the volume of such material increased. Publishers and booksellers began to compete for a still relatively limited literate market, and in order to persuade readers to buy one account rather than another it was essential to persuade them that the account was genuinely 'new,' in the sense of most recent and that it was truthful, both in the sense of having not committed deliberate falsification, and in the different but no less important sense of having not been overtaken by further events. It might seem strange that writers had to make a special plea for the veracity of their accounts. That is because in democratic countries with a free press we now take it for granted that this should be so (though we are often disappointed) and demand immediate editorial retractions when it is not. The early modern mind, with its deep distrust of anything new and unsanctioned by authority, needed reassurance that what was contained in the newsbook was not idle rumour, or fancy. Not only was early modern news explicitly biased, it was also widely expected to be so. The modern goal of 'objective' and unopinionated reporting (whether or not it is ever, in practice, really achieved), would have seemed strange to news readers and writers of 300 years ago.

Rumour and report, said the Jacobean MP Sir Walter Cope, are 'two bastards begotten by the people; the author seldom knowne.'[105] It was easy to invent tales, or simply to let one's imagination creatively edit a piece of information and pass it on in greatly changed form. Robert Crowley pointed out some of the ill consequences of false news in the mid-sixteenth century, in words reminiscent of Skelton's earlier comparison between news and women's gossip:

> Some men do delite
>   straunge newes to invente,
> Of this mannes doynge,
>   and that mannes intente;
> What is done in Fraunce,
>   and in the Emperours lande;
> And what thyng the Scottes
>   do nowe take in hande;
> What the kynge and his counsell
>   do intende to do;
> Though for the most parte
>   it be nothing so.

Such men cause murmuring, discontent, even sedition – a gloss on this epigram points out, 'We sawe the experience of thys of late,' referring to the rebellions of 1549.[106]

It is not difficult to see why the incompleteness or uncertainty of news aroused anxiety. The godly steward of Northampton, Robert Woodford, expressed a grave sense of public fear of rumoured French and popish conspiracies in 1639, a good two years before the advent of a real cabal, the Army Plot, during the earl of Strafford's trial. 'The times in the apprehencon of all seeme to be very doubtfull, and many feares we have of dangerous plotts by French and papists.'[107] Tudor and Stuart governments, always acutely conscious of the danger of rumour and report, were consequently strict in the punishment of rumour-mongers. English law had long admitted the possibility of treason by words as opposed to acts; while the dissemination of false news was less obnoxious than treason, it was also much more commonplace. Statutes against false news date from the late fifteenth century and were revived and enhanced under Elizabeth I. Lord Keeper Egerton noted in 1596 the dangers that false reports posed to due process. 'Thought is free, but the tongue should be governed by knowledge'; a false accusation could lead easily to the miscarriage of justice since 'on common voice and rumour a man may be imprisoned.'[108] In 1628, Sir John Coke complained to the House of Commons that discussions of the Petition of Right had caused various rumours abroad, thereby damaging the king's reputation; he claimed that news of it had 'flown so far that I have a copy of it in Spanish in my pocket, that the people of England will not rely upon the King's word.'[109]

A single example from the late seventeenth century suggests that governments were not mistaken in being concerned about the overly free travelling of news, even if they were relatively powerless to do much about it. On the eve of the Revolution of 1688, rumours flew about the country of murdering armies of Irish, of popish conspiracies, and of 'ferocious Laplanders clad in bearskins' serving in William of Orange's army. The Irish rumour – not the first of its kind – caused a minor panic in Yorkshire. As Abraham de la Pryme put it, 'all was up in arms, yet nobody knew where they were to fight.' What is most striking about this case is the degree to which, even in the age of printed news, such rumour moved much more quickly and furtively by voice.

> This newse or report ran, as I sayd, quite through the country, and for all it was some weeks a running northward, yet no one letter appear'd out of the south concerning any such thing there till it was always gone past those places where these letters were to go.

What clearly began as orally-communicated rumour had thus made its way into written form, which inevitably appeared, as Jonson had long before noted, to stamp it with a specious authority in the eyes of the foolish. Pryme soon learned, however, to be equally sceptical of the letters that followed the verbal reports north, which told of buried copper pots full of oil for boiling heretics, and of wild horses kept underground for years and fed on human flesh so that when the papists rose they would tear Protestants to pieces.[110]

Deliberate distortion was not necessary for the truth of news to be lost amid competing rumours, fears and speculations. The degree of falsity often grew in direct proportion to the distance from the event, as the number of relayers of news expanded and the means of checking for accuracy diminished. Small wonder, then, that country gentry and Englishmen abroad were suspicious of any sort of news, but especially of that which came *exclusively* in oral form – not because print and writing were inherently more trustworthy but because letters and newspapers could provide a check on or confirmation of oral reports. The English Catholic Richard Verstegan, who lived much of his life in Antwerp, was confronted with conflicting information concerning recent anti-Catholic persecutions in England when visited by two co-religionists in 1602. As he in turn wrote to Father Robert Parsons, the information from these men did not concur with earlier reports, 'yet had I rather write uppon the relation of thease two gentlemen, beeing knowen and of credit, then uppon other reportes of lesse certainty.' During the anticipatory period of the Spanish Match in November 1623, the Norfolk gentleman Thomas Knyvett could only write that there was 'a great deal of uncertaine newes.' The court, however, was not much better informed: Sir John Coke received a message from London on 14 June that there was 'as yet no news, no marriage,' noting that 'the scenes and the actors are so far off.'[111] Sometimes the problem was too many reports, and no basis for choosing one over another. Following developments in the Low Countries, the Norfolk gentleman and future judge, Francis Wyndham, was perplexed and anxious at contradictory accounts reaching him both direct from Flanders and via informants in his own county.[112] Brilliana Harley had difficulty ascertaining, from her home in Herefordshire, the truth about negotiations at Westminster between the English and the Scots in March 1641. 'Many rumors are in the cuntry' she noted; two months later, she wrote to her son reporting that 'in the cuntry they have in report hanged the archbischope.' In fact, Laud was still under safe-keeping in the Tower: the rumour of his death was probably a confusion of reports concerning the execution of Strafford on 12 May.[113]

Extraordinary circumstances might intervene to make news even harder to obtain and verify. The home counties, close to London, were normally in a good position to receive accurate reports. But in 1625, as the planned match of Charles I and Henrietta Maria drew near, the Suffolk incumbent John Rous, an assiduous reader and collector of corantos, was frustrated by a lack of news concerning this. 'Newes of her arrivall, and the occurrences thereof, was very litle and very uncertaine in Norfolk,' he observed, blaming this on the fact that the plague had forced Parliament to abandon London for Oxford, and was making travel dangerous. In October of the same year, Rous recorded from his corantos that Mansfeld had defeated the emperor and slain the duke of Friedland (Wallenstein); he was inclined to believe this last rumor because 'many corantoes confirmed' it.[114] Once again the greater density of news reports, and the ability to compare them, rather than their speed, was the decisive factor that invested the story with credibility.

The births and deaths of notables lent themselves most easily to rumour-mongering. Often reports of death were either 'distorted' or at least premature, if a person were known to be ill. The death of Jane Seymour was turned by rumour into a report of the death of the king himself. The London merchant tailor, Henry Machyn, recorded reports of the death of Edward VI in 1553, including the tale that 'he was poyssoned, as evere body says, wher now, thanke be unto God, ther be mony of the false trayturs browt to ther end. ...' Two years later, the city was alive for a day or two with news that Queen Mary had given birth to a son:

> The xxx day of Aprell and the last day of Aprell thydynges cam to London that the Quen['s] grace was delevered of a prynce, and so ther was grett

> ryngyng thrugh London, and dyvers plases *Te Deum laudamus* songe; and the morow after yt was tornyd odurways to the plesur of God.[115]

Philip Gawdy noted anticipatory rumours concerning the fate of Mary Stuart in 1587, climaxing in the unconfirmed reports of her beheading, which unlike other Tudor executions had not been public. 'Much uncerteyne newes touching the Queene of Skottes, in that she should have hidd herself in the topp of a chymney, and so by that meanes not being founde that they should have made presently great search for her and then she might have escaped,' he wrote. 'It is muche bothe thought and reported that she is executed, but the truthe not directly knowen.' In June 1633 a rumour reached Oxford that the earl of Arundel (who died in 1646) had fallen from his horse while riding with the king's progress into Scotland, 'and being trod upon so dyed.' The diarist who recorded this rumour, Thomas Crosfield, never remarked on the falsity of the information, and three years later noted that Arundel was about to visit the emperor in Vienna to negotiate restoration of the Palatinate.[116] Late seventeenth-century letter-writers regularly report and then un-report such deaths as rumours were either verified or disproved. Richard Lapthorne warned his Devonshire client Richard Coffin that although the bishop of Oxford had been twice declared dead, he was merely ill. 'Sir William Norrie's brother is not dead, as was reported,' wrote one of Lord Wharton's correspondents, adding, a touch hopefully, 'but 'tis true he is very sick.'[117]

The tendency to report news before it had actually happened or before the facts were fully known was thus by no means an invention of the newspaper error. But the 'determination to be first' that characterized the papers of the late seventeenth century, and which always had to be balanced precariously against the urge to be 'freshest,' made rumour and error a public institution.[118] The regularization of printed news reports and their greater availability in the second half of the seventeenth century did little to prevent such errors; if anything the pressure of producing to pre-established deadlines increased the likelihood that a published news report would be based on incomplete facts and require revision in subsequent issues. In September 1696, the news was abroad that the queen of Spain was dying, or was dead, or had died but had a living foetus cut out of her stomach (an heir to the idiot Charles II), and that Louis XIV had died of boils and gout. Men laid wagers on the truth, only to discover days later that both Louis (who, unfortunately for the nations of Europe, had two more decades in him) and the Spanish queen (who lived until 1740) were still alive. On 17 June 1699, the *Flying-Post*, bearing news from the Continent, prematurely described the death of the duchess of Mazarin; in this case, the informants were only slightly ahead of the game since the duchess did in fact expire a week later.[119] And in 1711, the *British Mercury* reported a tremendous defeat for the French that had never occurred.[120] This could happen, on a shorter time-scale, with domestic news as well. Thomas Benskin tried to take advantage of his paper's (the *Domestick Intelligence*) appearance on Thursdays to report on the Oxford trial and expected conviction of Stephen College, the 'Protestant Joiner' on

Wednesday 17 August 1681, but was defeated by College's own eloquence in his defence, which stretched the trial into the small hours of Thursday morning, too late for Benskin's paper.[121]

It is difficult to resist the hypothesis that by the end of the seventeenth century news and its readers existed in a love-hate relationship: the news was indispensable because it was now a critical channel by which individuals situated themselves within the social present. But neither could it be altogether trusted, whatever the medium. It is surely no coincidence that the trope of news's uncertainty became such a commonplace at about the same time that both writers and readers of history were beginning to have serious doubts about the status of the historical record, and even of such hitherto unimpeachable sources as the Bible. Sir Walter Ralegh, at the beginning of the seventeenth century, was said to have torn up the continuation of his gargantuan *History of the World* in a Pyrrhonist pique after he observed two eyewitnesses to a recent event unable to agree in their accounts of it. Defoe, one hundred years later, defended *Robinson Crusoe*'s claim to historicity – taken by at least one critic as a meretricious attempt to cover up a lie – by turning Ralegh's frustration on its head. In a passage anticipatory of Hayden White, Dominick LaCapra, Hans Kellner, and the current 'linguistic turn,' Defoe pointed out that *no* story could be absolutely congruent with the events it purports to represent. 'Nothing is more common, than to have two Men tell the same Story quite differing from one another, yet both of them Eye-witnesses to the Fact related.'[122]

Both of these occasions point to a fundamental problem that eighteenth-century historical thought would inherit: if no agreement is possible on the present through witnesses, if the news can be shown to be mere rumour, then how much stock can be placed in the accounts of more remote pasts by historians? This is nowhere better expressed than by Sarah Cowper, whose remarks on the close relation of news and history have already been noted. Cowper was a prodigious reader of history who also had her ear to the ground for the public events that she recorded in her diary (though she claimed, disingenuously, never to read printed news). She would comment in 1702 (with reference to disagreement among William III's physicians as to the condition of his body at his death a few days earlier): 'This age is enough to destroy the credit of history of remote past times, and places; when wee can scarce attain any certainty of things present near hand, and matters liable to demonstration.'[123]

Conclusion

The availability of news reports, through oral, written and especially printed media, in the second half of the seventeenth century, had consequences for historical thought that we have not yet addressed. By focusing public attention on the present, and on the hinge whereby present became past, the news also occasioned interest in the converse: how the past evolved into or 'caused' the present. It is no coincidence that historians during and after the Civil War turned their attentions away from depicting long-dead medieval monarchs and toward the study of very recent events, with news reports in many cases turning into verbatim fodder for their historical accounts. One further by-product of this attention to the contemporary was the restructuring of temporal connections between past and present. In medieval and humanist historical thought, these had been founded on similarity, comparison and metaphor rather than, as in the modern historical tradition, proximity, continuity, and metonymy. Historiography after 1640 also reveals the high degree of ideological fractiousness, the competing perspectives, that are the hallmark of the newsbooks, and which occasioned similar concerns about objectivity and truth.[124] These developments might well have occurred without the mid-century proliferation of news. It is probable that the Civil War would have found its aspiring Thucydides sooner or later: Clarendon, who came closest to that ideal, relied more on personal knowledge of the actors than on published reports. But it cannot be doubted that the obsession with the present that marks public discourse from the 1640s on helped to create a market for 'contemporary history,' a sub-genre that early Stuart historians had expressly avoided.

Over the course of the seventeenth century, the news had also generated an extended present of duration, not instant. Or, to put it another way, it had carved out a 'detemporalized zone' between past and future, a zone that offered a space for the discussion of current events analogous to Habermas' emergent public sphere. Within this zone, novelties cease to be mere 'marvels,' passively absorbed into the fabric of tradition like a stucco wall. They become matters of ongoing concern, actively discussed and engaged with, disruptive, anxiety-provoking, and potentially significant steps in the movement toward newness and modernity.[125] The monsters and marvels that feature in the news and in pamphlet literature of the 1640s and 1650s become signs of the times, not mere random instances of natural caprice or divine intervention.[126] As one modern psychologist has observed, 'a present orientation involves reflecting on the past and expecting the future.'[127] The discussions of foreign affairs in the 1620s and 1630s, and especially of the civil wars of the 1640s and early 1650s, dominated public discourse for an extended period. They thereby encouraged the spread of news on a regular basis and became the subject of that news. The evolving relationship between news and history, and the redefinition of the connection between past and present, is intimately connected to seventeenth-century people's considerably enhanced awareness of the moving currents within which they swam.

Notes

The place of publication of all works is London except where otherwise noted. I am indebted to the Social Sciences and Humanities Research Council for support between 1993 and 1996, when this article was first researched, and to the Institute for Advanced Study, Princeton, for the membership (1996–97) during which it was largely written. I wish also to thank members of the History Department seminar at Dalhousie University, and the editors of this volume for their comments on earlier drafts of this chapter. Oriel MacLennan of the Killam Library at Dalhousie, and my student Elena Culshaw helpfully tracked down a few stray references for me in the winter of 1999 during my recovery from an immobilizing accident.

1 J. Paul Hunter, *Before Novels: The Cultural Contexts of Eighteenth-Century English Fiction* (New York and London, 1990), p. 168. My interpretation of the relationship between contemporaneity and pastness, hence between history and other genres (including but not limited to prose fiction) has profited a great deal from Hunter's work though, as will be seen, I differ from him sharply in a number of respects. I have also found helpful the very different though not incompatible (with Hunter) account in Michael McKeon, *The Origins of the English Novel, 1600–1740* (Baltimore and London, 1987).

2 Hunter, *Before Novels*, p. 172.

3 The wideness of dispersal is crucial here: it was certainly possible for many people to experience the same event simultaneously in earlier times, in close proximity, the diaries of Renaissance merchants recording urban affairs being one example. But such common experience did not extend very far geographically.

4 Stephen Kern, *The Culture of Time and Space 1880–1918* (Cambridge, MA, 1983), pp. 65–7.

5 Jürgen Habermas, *The Structural Transformation of the Public Sphere: An Inquiry into a Category of Bourgeois Society*, trans. T. Burger with F. Lawrence (Cambridge, MA, 1989; first published 1962), pp. 16, 21–2, 254n. In Habermas' study, Britain represents an 'ideal case' of the public sphere, and the regularity of news a crucial distinguishing mark separating news reports of the sixteenth century with those of the seventeenth and eighteenth centuries. While Habermas' historical analysis is often simplistic and occasionally misleading, I have none the less found his treatment of the public sphere very useful. An application of his ideas to French politics after the Estates General of 1614 can be found in J. Sawyer, *Printed Poison: Pamphlet Propaganda, Faction Politics, and the Public Sphere in Early Seventeenth-Century France* (Berkeley, 1990). For a critique of Habermas which brings out the importance of print, see David Zaret, 'Religion, Science, and Printing in the Public Spheres of England,' in Craig Calhoun, ed., *Habermas and the Public Sphere* (Cambridge, MA, 1992), pp. 212–35.

6 Donald A. Norman, *Learning and Memory* (San Francisco, 1982), p. 10; compare M. Edlund, *Psychological Time and Mental Illness* (New York and London, 1987), pp. 11–12.

7 Pierre Janet, *L'Evolution de la mémoire et de la notion du temps* (Paris, 1928), pp. 321–4; cited and discussed in G. J. Whitrow, *The Natural Philosophy of Time* (Oxford, 1980; 2nd edn.), pp. 74–83.

8 It will be obvious from this that I do not agree with the more pessimistic analysis of C. John Sommerville, *The News Revolution in England: Cultural Dynamics of Daily Information* (New York, 1996), which work nevertheless I have found a highly stimulating encouragement to my own thinking about news and time. Sommerville, operating in a tradition deriving from Walter J. Ong, and, beyond that, Marshall McLuhan (and ultimately Ben Jonson, for whom see further on) is of the view that the realities of daily information, and the need to produce news to fill daily newspapers, had an atomizing and disintegrative effect on the perception of reality. I would agree that this possibility existed but would argue that the results of daily flow were, to the contrary, socially and temporally integrative. My position on this is thus much closer to that of Habermas in *The Structural Transformation of the Public Sphere*.

9 Orrin E. Klapp, 'Creeping Banality,' in his *Overload and Boredom: Essays on the Quality of Life in the Information Society* (New York and London, 1986), pp. 53–70. Geographical proximity is still, of course, a factor: the tragic crash of Swissair flight 111 in early September 1998, about fifteen miles from my house, was the present-defining event there weeks after it had faded from the front pages and first thoughts of places and people outside Nova Scotia.

10 My term 'flow' is thus comparable to the 'periodicity' that Joad Raymond argues rapidly became an expectation of 1640s' readers: Raymond, *The Invention of the Newspaper: English Newsbooks 1641–1649* (Oxford, 1996), p. 120.

11 *The Tatler*, 164 (27 April 1710), ed. George Aitken (1898–9) 4 vols, iii, p. 268.

12 On the diary and its relationship to changing perceptions of time, especially daily, clock-influenced time, see, for the post-1660 period, Stuart Sherman's wide-ranging book, *Telling Time: Clocks, Diaries and English Diurnal Form, 1660–1785* (Chicago, 1997). On time, the press, and the decline of the chronicle, see my article, 'Genre into Artifact: the Decline of the English Chronicle in the Sixteenth Century,' *Sixteenth Century Journal* 19 (1988): 321–54.

13 Richard Cust, 'News and Politics in Early Seventeenth-Century England,' *Past and Present* 112 (August 1986): 60–90; Kevin Sharpe, 'Crown, Parliament and Locality: Government and Communication in Early Stuart England,' *English Historical Review*, 101 (1986): 321–50; F. J. Levy, 'How Information Spread Among the Gentry, 1550–1640,' *Journal of British Studies* 21 (1982): 11–34; Andrew Mousley, 'Self, State, and Seventeenth Century News,' *The Seventeenth Century* 6 (1991): 189–204.

14 *The Memoirs of Robert Carey* (Oxford, 1972), ed. F. H. Mares, pp. 62–3; *The Diary of John Manningham of the Middle Temple, 1602–1603* (Hanover, N.H., 1976), ed. R. P. Sorlien, pp. 208, 247; John Nichols, *The Progresses, Processions, and Magnificent Festivities, of King James the First, his Royal Consort, Family, and Court; Collected from Original Manuscripts, Scarce Pamphlets, Corporation Records, Parochial Registers, &c.* (1828), 4 vols, I: 55–6. Nine decades of improvement in the transportation system improved the situation somewhat: the Reverend Thomas Brockbank, in the north-west, heard of Mary II's death in 1694 within twenty-four hours of its occurrence: *The Diary and Letter Book of the Rev. Thomas Brockbank 1671–1709* (1930), ed. R. Trappes-Lomax, Chetham Society, new series 89, p. 76.

15 Fernand Braudel, *Civilization and Capitalism, 15th–18th Century: Volume I, The Structures of Everyday Life* (New York, 1979), trans. S. Reynolds, pp. 424–8; Gerhard Dohrn Rossum, *History of the Hour: Clocks and Modern Temporal Orders* (Chicago and London, 1996), trans. T. Dunlap, pp. 324–50, especially p. 325, follows Braudel in minimizing the degree to which this situation changed prior to the eighteenth century.

16 Brian Austen, *English Provincial Posts* (Chichester, 1978), pp. 32–3; for more on the postal system and news see further below. On the varieties of news available in the earlier period, and their shading into printed news, M. A. Shaaber's *Some Forerunners of the Newspaper in England, 1476–1622* (Philadelphia, PA, 1929) remains highly useful.

17 *Original Letters Illustrative of English History* (1834), ed. H. Ellis, I: 260; Norman J. G. Pounds, *Hearth and Home: A History of Material Culture* (Bloomington and Indianapolis, IN, 1990), p. 356.

18 *Barrington Family Letters 1628–1632* (1983), ed. A. Searle, Camden Society, 4th series, 28, pp. 235, 241 and n. 1; *The Diary of Thomas Crosfield* (1935), ed. F. S. Boas, p. 54. All dates in this section are old style, except where noted.

19 *The Diary of John Evelyn* (Oxford, 1955), 6 vols, ed. E. S. De Beer, III: 44; *Calendar of the Clarendon State Papers preserved in the Bodleian Library* (Oxford, 1869–1970), 5 vols, II: 107.

20 The case for continuing contact is well made by David Cressy in *Coming Over: Migration and Communication Between England and New England in the Seventeenth Century* (Cambridge, 1987).

21 *Diary of Samuel Pepys* (Oxford, 1970–81), 11 vols, eds R. Latham and W. Matthews, i, pp. 76, 83: more definite information came through the diplomatic grapevine on 8 March; Evelyn, *Diary*, IV, pp. 585–6; *London Gazette*, 24 May 1688.

22 *The Great Diurnal of Nicholas Blundell of Little Crosby, Lancashire* (Record Society of Lancs and Cheshire, 1968–72), 3 vols, eds Frank Tyrer and J. J. Bagley, I: 93.

23 Jeremy Black, 'The British Press and Europe in the Early Eighteenth Century,' in Michael Harris and Alan Lee, eds, *The Press in English Society from the Seventeenth to the Nineteenth Centuries* (London, Toronto, and Cranbury, NJ, 1986), pp. 64–79.

24 Diplomatic dispatches had been a staple for newsletter writers such as John Pory from early in the seventeenth century; I am grateful to Sabrina Baron for reminding me of this point.

25 For country news during the Restoration, see James Sutherland, *The Restoration Newspaper and its Development* (Cambridge and New York, 1986), pp. 91–122; for foreign news, *ibid.*, especially pp. 130–3.

26 Burton, *Anatomy of Melancholy*, p. 14. On the other hand, lack of news could also excite comment from the bored. William Adams of Christ Church, Oxford apologized to Thomas Tanner for his lack of significant news in 1699. 'If I could send thee a ream of paper full of news I would; but there is none here, but that Randal of Oriel has powdered his hair in order to be Bishop Talbot's chaplain': Adams to Tanner, 4 May 1699, Bodl. MS Tanner 21, fol. 39r-v.

27 Klapp, *Overload and Boredom*, pp. 53–70; M. Csikszentmihalyi, *Beyond Boredom and Anxiety* (San Francisco, CA, 1975), pp. 35–6; compare Georg Simmel's classic study of the overload of sensation in urban life, in *The Sociology of Georg Simmel*, ed. K. H. Wolff (Glencoe, IL, 1950), p. 415. Michael Hobart and Zachary Schiffman, *Information Ages* (Baltimore, MD, 1998) is an incisive overview of the relationship between knowledge, its vessels, and human capacity, over several millennia; I am indebted to Professor Schiffman for sharing sections of the work with me prior to publication, and also for many conversations on this subject.

28 *Diary of Lady Margaret Hoby 1599–1605*, ed. Dorothy M. Meads (Boston, MA, 1930), pp. 165, 193, 282–3 n. 524. As Meads observes, a high constable such as Pollard would be a 'mine of information' since he had to get regular information from the constables of each parish in his area to pass on to the Quarter Sessions.

29 *The Diary of Ralph Josselin*, ed. Alan Macfarlane (1976), p. 608.

30 Evelyn, *Diary*, I, p. 8; *The Diary of Abraham de la Pryme, the Yorkshire Antiquary* (1869–70), ed. Charles Jackson, Surtees Society, 54, p. 7.

31 As will be argued below, the newsletter, already commonplace during the Hundred Years' War, interacted with the chronicle in the Middle Ages. But by the mid-seventeenth century, it was the diary's turn. For an example, see John Evelyn's summaries or paraphrases of events culled from newspapers: *Diary*, iii, p. 361, account of translation ceremony of Gilbert Sheldon from London to Canterbury.

32 David Cressy, *Bonfires and Bells: National Memory and the Protestant Calendar in Elizabethan and Stuart England* (Berkeley, CA and London, 1989); Ronald Hutton, *The Rise and Fall of Merry England: The Ritual Year, 1400–1700* (Oxford, 1994).

33 *Records of the Borough of Leicester* (Cambridge, 1923), ed. Helen Stocks, p. 584.

34 *Original Letters Relative to the English Reformation* (Cambridge, 1846), Parker Society, 27, p. 257; Thomas Cogswell, *The Blessed Revolution* (Cambridge, 1989), p. 22. Sir John Newdigate received the proclamation of the Parliament of 1628, of which he would be a member, as well as manuscript newsletters and other pamphlets from London, such as Thomas Scott's inflammatory anti-Catholic *Vox populi* (1622) during the 1620s: Vivienne Larminie, *Wealth, Kinship and Culture: The Seventeenth-Century Newdigates of Arbury and their World* (1995), pp. 161–3.

35 See especially the work of Dr Adam Fox, in particular, 'Aspects of Oral Culture and its Development in Early Modern England', Ph.D. thesis, Cambridge University, 1993.

36 Harold Love, *Scribal Publication in Seventeenth-Century England* (Oxford, 1993), pp. 9–22. On libels and popular perceptions of political figures see a recent case study by P. Croft, 'The Reputation of Robert Cecil: Libels, Political Opinion and Popular Awareness in the Early Seventeenth Century,' *Transactions of the Royal Historical Society*, 6th series, 1 (1991): 43–69; the subject is dealt with more generally by Adam Fox, 'Ballads, Libels and Popular Ridicule in Jacobean England,' *Past and Present* 145 (1994): 47–83.

37 C. H. Firth, 'The Ballad History of the Reigns of the Later Tudors,' TRHS, 3rd series, 3 (1909): 51–124; *idem*, 'The Ballad History of the Reign of James I,' TRHS, 3rd series, 5 (1911): 21–61. Firth notes that ballads about contemporary events first begin to outnumber traditional ballads about the remote past under the later

Tudors; both then and in the early Stuart era, however, ballads (in contrast to Jacobean and Caroline libels and newsletters), generally steered clear of discussing the monarch and his policies.

38 Raymond, *Invention of the Newspaper*, pp. 9, 90.

39 A. J. Bellany, 'The Poisoning of Legitimacy? Court Scandal, News Culture and Politics in England' (Ph.D. dissertation, Princeton University, 1995), pp. 32–166.

40 Bellany, 'The Poisoning of Legitimacy,' p. 163. Elsewhere (p. 150), Bellany points out that the copying habits of the gentry 'helped prolong scandals, transforming items that originally circulated as news into artefacts [*sic*] of recent history.'

41 For example, *Cheapsides Triumphs, and Cyrones Crosses Lamentation* in *The Pepys Ballads* (Cambridge, 1987), 5 vols, ed. W. G. Dray, facsimile vol. I: 66; *The Manner of the Kings Tryal at Westminster-Hall, by the High Court of Justice*, which versified the proceedings of the High Court of Justice: *ibid.*, facsimile vol. II: 204–5; *Englands Miseries Crown'd with Mercies* (one of several ballads on the Popish Plot), *ibid.*, II: 225. For other examples of such news ballads, see the brief selection in R. Palmer, *A Ballad History of England from 1588 to the Present Day* (1979). This remains the case today, since most people hear about an event at second hand and subsequently buy a newspaper or tune in to the evening news to find out about it in more detail. Raymond, *Invention of the Newspaper*, pp. 156–8, points out that many mid-century newsbooks presented their materials in ways that imitated speech.

42 H. Roberts, *Englands Farewell to Christian the Fourth* (1606), in Nichols, *Progresses of King James*, II: 78.

43 *Diary of John Rous*, Camden Society, original series, 66, p. 122; *Diary of Abraham de la Pryme*, pp. 97, 122, emphasis mine.

44 See, for example, the complaints by Philip Gawdy to his father concerning carriers in the late sixteenth century. 'I knowe not whether the carryar hath performed his dutye or no, in that I heard not from any of yowr howse' (14 December 1587); and 'If any newes els there be either I have not heard of it, or els it hathe escaped my memory. Some uncertayne speaches touching the poysoning of thre or fower great Kingges and princes of late' (9 May 1588). *Letters of Philip Gawdy of West Harling, Norfolk, and of London to Various Members of his Family 1579–1616* (1906), ed. I. H. Jeayes, pp. 30, 36.

45 *The Letter Books 1644–45 of Sir Samuel Luke* (1963), ed. H. G. Tibbutt, Historical Manuscripts Commission joint publications, IV: 287, 578.

46 P. Fraser, *The Intelligence of the Secretaries of State and their Monopoly of Licensed News, 1660–68* (Cambridge, 1956), pp. 28–34 and appendices; Alan Marshall, *Intelligence and Espionage in the Reign of Charles II* (Cambridge, 1994), pp. 30, 60; Steven C. A. Pincus, *Protestantism and Patriotism: Ideologies and the Making of English Foreign Policy, 1650–1668* (Cambridge, 1996), pp. 276–88.

47 The first postal 'system' dates back to Henry VIII's reign, and under several Tudor and early Stuart Masters of the Posts, six basic 'roads' or routes having been established by James I's reign, at which time a foreign postmaster was appointed for international posts. This system operated in parallel with informal measures such as private messengers and the 'common carrier.' The government system was not for private use initially but was opened to the public in the reign of Charles I, under whose regime standard rates for postage were first instituted and 'byposts' (subroutes off the main roads) first established under the direction of Thomas Witherings, a London merchant placed in charge of what was then called the Letter Office in 1637. See Kevin Sharpe, 'Thomas Witherings and the Reform of the Foreign Posts, 1632–40,' *Bulletin of the Institute of Historical Research* 57 (1989): 149–64; see especially pp. 160–1 for average postal times to or from major centres like Vienna, Brussels, and Naples. The first Post Office Act was passed by the second Protectorate Parliament in 1657, creating the first General Post Office; the measures in this Act were confirmed by the Convention Parliament in 1660. From 1678 through the eight-

eenth century the Post Office was housed on Lombard Street in London. For the development of the post, see the following: M. Ashley, *John Wildman: Plotter and Postmaster* (1947); *idem*, 'John Wildman and the Post Office,' in R. Ollard and P. Tudor-Craig, *For Veronica Wedgwood These* (1986), pp. 204–16. More general accounts can be found in J. C. Hemmeon, *The History of the British Post Office* (Cambridge, MA, 1912), pp. 3–33; H. Robinson, *The British Post Office: A History* (Princeton, NJ, 1948), pp. 3–112; and K. Ellis, *The Post Office in the Eighteenth Century* (Oxford, 1958), pp. 1–8. A new study of the post in the seventeenth century would be welcome. The difficulties of and procedures used in the inland posts emerge from the document summaries (principally references to the State Papers and Acts of the Privy Council) in J. W. M. Stone, ed., *The Inland Posts (1392–1672): A Calendar of Historical Documents* (1987) and in R. M. Willcocks, *England's Postal History, to 1840* (1975); local posts are discussed, principally for Kent, in Austen, *English Provincial Posts*. For the use of the posts in the circulation of news into and out of London, and Muddiman's exemption, see Sutherland, *The Restoration Newspaper*, p. 92.

48 Shaaber, *Some Forerunners of the Newspaper in England*, pp. 35–64, on 'official' news under Elizabeth and its circulation into the provinces; L. Hanson, 'English Newsbooks, 1620–1641,' *The Library*, 4th series, 18 (1938): 355–84; Jerzy Limon, *Dangerous Matter: English Dramatists and Politics in 1623/24* (Cambridge, 1986), pp. 6–7; Theodore K. Rabb, 'English Readers and the Revolt in Bohemia, 1619–1622,' in *Sefer ha-yovel le-Aharon Mosheh Rabinovits* (*A.M.K. Rabinowicz Jubilee Volume*) (Jerusalem, 1996), pp. 152–75. I am grateful to Ted Rabb for providing me with a copy of his article.

49 Joseph Frank, *The Beginnings of the English Newspaper, 1620–1660* (Cambridge, MA, 1961), pp. 8, 13, estimates an initial circulation of between 250 and 500 copies of each number; a comparison of this with the figure of 6,000 copies per number of the *Gazette* alone (only one of many papers and not the most popular) in 1704, or of E. Dobrée's weekly *London Journal* (15,000 per week in its proprietor's 1722 estimate) is about as effective an illustration as can be found of the increase in news circulation during the seventeenth century: J. R. Sutherland, 'The Circulation of Newspapers and Literary Periodicals, 1700–30,' *The Library*, 4th series, 15 (1935): 110–24.

50 From the mid-seventeenth century, towns often kept newsbooks and papers available for the public: the chamberlain's accounts for Leicester contain numerous references to funds disbursed 'for newes bookes and other things,' generally at a cost of £3 17s or £4 a year: *Records of the Borough of Leicester* (Cambridge, 1923), ed. Helen Stocks, pp. 518, 534; when one John Ley provided the mayor with twenty-one newsbooks in 1661–62, he was paid 5s. 9d.

51 Folke Dahl, *A Bibliography of English Corantos and Periodical Newsbooks, 1620–1642* (1952); compare the bibliography of 1640s' newsbooks included in Raymond, *Invention of the Newspaper*, pp. 324–35.

52 Frank, *Beginnings of the English Newspaper*, pp. 1–18; Stanley Morison, *The English Newpaper, 1622–1932* (Cambridge, 1932), p. 14.

53 *News from the New World Discover'd in the Moon*, in *Ben Jonson* (Oxford, 1925–52), 11 vols, eds C. H. Herford, P. Simpson, and E. Simpson, VII: 514–15; *The Staple of News*, I. v., 45–50 (*ibid.*, vi, p. 295); Mark Z. Muggli, 'Ben Jonson and the Business of News,' *Studies in English Literature* 32 (1992): 323–39.

54 P. R. Coss, 'Aspects of Cultural Diffusion in Medieval England: The Early Romances, Local Society and Robin Hood,' *Past and Present* 108 (1985): 35–79.

55 Levy, 'How Information Spread Among the Gentry,' p. 20 ff.; Bellany, 'Poisoning of Legitimacy,' p. 64. On the other hand, the transmission of such materials could be frustratingly slow, since it was dependent not only on the vagaries of transportation (worsened if cross-channel travel was involved), but on the speed at which the correspondent wrote. John Chamberlain wrote to Dudley Carleton on 6 March 1619, to convey the news of Queen Anne's death 'about four o'clock that morning, being the second of this month.' Carleton did not even commit his news to letter for four days

after the event; it would be a week to ten days before Carleton, at the Hague, would receive it, at which time the event would no longer be, in any meaningful sense, 'current': *Letters of John Chamberlain* (Philadelphia, PA, 1939), 2 vols, ed. N. E. McClure, II: 219 (Chamberlain to Carleton, 6 March 1619). For More's letters to Anne, viscountess Conway, see *The Conway Letters: The Correspondence of Anne, viscountess Conway, Henry More, and their Friends, 1642–1684* (Oxford, 1992; revised edn.), ed. S. Hutton (orig. ed. M. H. Nicolson).

56 Durham Record Office, Du 1421 (mayor of Durham's account book), sub. 1728.

57 *Original Letters Illustrative of English History*, ed. Ellis, I: 298; *The Correspondence of Sir Thomas More* (Princeton, NJ, 1927), ed. E. F. Rogers, p. 312.

58 John Lyly, *Euphues and his England (1580), Complete Works of John Lyly* (Oxford, 1902), II: 159.

59 Pincus, *Protestantism and Patriotism*, pp. 279–80; *idem*, ' "Coffee Politicians Does Create": Coffee Houses and Restoration Political Culture,' *Journal of Modern History* 67 (1995): 807–34, at p. 822. For an older account, see A. Ellis, *The Penny Universities: A History of the Coffee-Houses* (1956).

60 *Journal of the Rev. Rowland Davies* (1857), ed. R. Caulfield, Camden o.s. 68, pp. 39, 48. In 1698, when the London owner of a parrot discovered that it was repeating oaths and curses heard in Billingsgate Street, he placed it in a coffee house on another street, where it learned to say 'Where's the news'; unfortunately, on returning home its old language returned. *Diary of Abraham de la Pryme*, p. 176.

61 *The Diary of a West Country Physician, A.D. 1684–1726* (1934), ed. Edmund Hobhouse, pp. 52–3 (23 May 1709); for other examples at the same time, see *The Diary of Dudley Ryder 1715–1716* (1939), ed. W. Matthews, *passim*.

62 César de Saussure, *A Foreign View of England in the Reigns of George I. & George II. The Letters of Monsieur Cesar De Saussure To His Family* (1902), trans. and ed. Mme van Muyden, p. 162. Saussure's ascription of news-hunger to the lower orders was already remarked on nearly a century earlier by Peter Mundy, who commented of London in 1639 that it was full of 'lords, knightts, gentry posting and riding to and fro, some aboutt businesse, butt most to see and hear newes. For this latter purpose went multitudes off the common sort.' *The Travels of Peter Mundy in Europe and Asia 1608–1667* (1925), vol. IV, ed. R. C. Temple, Hakluyt Society, 2nd series, 55, p. 41.

63 Lewis Theobald, *The Censor* (1717), 3 vols, ii, p. 214. Further examples of the attendance of the lower orders at coffee houses and their engagement in discussion of politics are provided by Pincus, 'Coffeehouses and Restoration Political Culture,' p. 825 and note.

64 John Cleveland, *The Character of a London-diurnall* (1647; first published 1644: Wing C4664), p. 1.

65 For example, *The Ordinary Weekly Curranto from Franckford* (1639, STC, newsbooks, 18507. 285, 283, 287 *et seq.*); F. S. Siebert, *Freedom of the Press in England, 1476–1776: The Rise and Decline of Government Controls* (Urbana, IL, 1952), pp. 147–61; Joad Raymond, *Making the News: An Anthology of the Newsbooks of Revolutionary England, 1641–1660* (London and New York, 1993), p. 18; G. A. Cranfield, *The Press and Society from Caxton to Northcliffe* (1978), pp. 6–11, an account vitiated to some degree by a weak grasp of the sixteenth- and seventeenth-century political and cultural context.

66 Thomas Cogswell, *The Blessed Revolution* and 'The Politics of Propaganda: Charles I and the People in the 1620s,' *JBS* 29 (1990): 187–215; Jerzy Limon, *Dangerous Matter*, Marvin Breslow, *A Mirror of England: English Puritan Views of Foreign Nations, 1618–1640* (Cambridge, MA, 1970); Godfrey Davies, 'English Political Sermons, 1603–1640,' *Huntington Library Quarterly* 1 (1939): 1–22.

67 Raymond, *Invention of the Newspaper*, p. 81 argues persuasively that the 1640s newsbooks were not the result of decades of censorship-restricted news hunger, nor the direct descendant of the corantos, but rather 'a response to something new' in the charged atmosphere of late 1641. I would agree, but would add that that some-

thing new included the sense of currency and immediacy to the events being captured therein.

68 A. D. T. Cromartie, 'The Printing of Parliamentary Speeches November 1640–July 1642,' *Historical Journal* 33 (1990): 23–44.

69 Raymond, *Invention of the Newspaper*, pp. 108–11. Frank, *Beginnings of the English Newspaper*, pp. 21, 29, 67, 219. Like any new industry, the process of news publication had both winners and losers as many series fell by the wayside while others achieved greater stability: by 1653, under the stewardship of John Rushworth and Samuel Pecke, *A Perfect Diurnall* was able to rename itself *The Perfect Diurnall*. On Rushworth's later career as a transformer of the newsbooks into his *Historical Collections*, see Raymond, *Invention of the Newspaper*, pp. 296–312.

70 Tessa Watt, *Cheap Print and Popular Piety, 1550–1640* (Cambridge, 1991), pp. 90–1 and *passim*.

71 For example, Bodl. MS Carte 228 (Wharton-Huntingdon collections), a set of newsletters to Philip, Lord Wharton, from various informants between 1656 and 1701; a set of these specifically devoted to news and in the same hand, from 1698 to 1701, is at fos. 253r–408v; BL MS Sloane 3925, fos. 1–356, collection of newsletters apparently intended for insertion in printed newspapers, 1690–92; BL MS Sloane 3929, newsletters collected by Henry Coley, 1670s–1680s.

72 Bellany, 'Poisoning of Legitimacy,' p. 679; compare Michael Mendle, 'De Facto Freedom, De Facto Authority: Press and Parliament, 1640–1643,' *HJ* 38 (1995): 307–32.

73 Raymond, *Invention of the Newspaper*, pp. 233–38.

74 Anthony Fletcher, *The Outbreak of the English Civil War* (1981), pp. 91–227; Raymond, 'Introduction' to his *Making the News*, p. 7.

75 Mark Knights, *Politics and Opinion in Crisis, 1678–81* (Cambridge, 1994), pp. 156–92.

76 *A Proclamation for Suppressing the Printing and Publishing of Unlicensed News-books* (1680: Wing C.3428).

77 Fraser, *Intelligence of the Secretaries of State*, pp. 35–56; Marshall, *Intelligence and Espionage in the Reign of Charles II*, p. 60. These works supersede the older study by J. G. Muddiman, *The King's Journalist 1659–1689* (1923).

78 Sutherland, *The Restoration Newspaper* is definitive on the papers of the period 1679–82; P. M. Handover, *A History of the London Gazette 1665–1965* (1965), pp. 9–51; Thomas O'Malley, 'Religion and the Newspaper Press, 1660–1685: A Study of the *London Gazette*,' in *The Press in English Society from the Seventeenth to the Nineteenth Centuries* (London, Toronto, and Cranbury, NJ, 1986), pp. 25–46 suggests that the *Gazette* included more domestic news than is usually thought and defends its value as a source, especially for official Anglicanism.

79 Morison, *The English Newspaper*, pp. 5, 43; Sutherland, *The Restoration Newspaper*, pp. 30–1.

80 Robert J. Allen, *The Clubs of Augustan London* (Cambridge, MA, 1933). For the coffee house as meeting ground for the exchange of news, and in particular for its blurring of the distinction between oral and written news, see Hunter, *Before Novels*, p. 173. Robert Darnton has advanced a similar argument with regard to the interplay between oral news, rumour, *libelles* and books in the two or three decades prior to the French Revolution, and I am grateful to him for a discussion on this point.

81 Morison, *The English Newspaper*, pp. 62–70.

82 Raymond, *Invention of the Newspaper*, pp. 193, 269–312, quotation at p. 276 from Cleveland, *A Character of a Diurnal-Maker* (1654), p. 3.

83 *The Tatler*, 3 and 12 [16 April and 7 May 1709] (1898–9), 4 vols, ed. George Aitken, I: 31, 106. In this usage, 'history' is given a new meaning as the record of *current* events, like the 'chronicle' or 'herald,' while, conversely, the period of time worth historicizing in public is reduced to a week.

84 Morison, *The English Newspaper*, pp. 60–1.

85 R. M. Wiles, *Serial Publication in England Before 1750* (Cambridge, 1957), p. 61.

86 The first stamp duty, intended to reduce the number of newspapers as the Tory government of 1712 was bringing the War of the Spanish Succession to a close, imposed .5d on a half sheet or less and 1d on a whole sheet, with a duty of 1s on printed advertisements. The 1725 Act increased the duty to .5d on every half sheet, forcing a change in format from the standard six-page paper to one made of a single half-sheet of large paper in order to minimize the effect of the duty: Sutherland, *The Restoration Newspaper*, p. 32.

87 Italics in original, quoted from Wiles, *Serial Publication*, pp. 55–8, citing J. Wilford's *London Magazine*, the principal source for Budgell's own claims and the attacks on them.

88 Hertfordshire RO, DEP F. 34 (Panshanger MSS), diary of Sarah Cowper, vol. 6, p. 269 (1 August 1713). Addison, ever a trick-mirror of contemporary cultural practices, was only half in earnest when he satirized the mayfly quality of news by making it into history, referring to descriptions of the War of the Spanish Succession as 'weekly historians.' *The Spectator*, no. 445 (31 July 1712), ed. Bond, IV: 63.

89 *The Frightened People of Clerkenwell* and *The Somersetshire Wonder*, in *The Pepys Ballads*, facsimile vol. IV, 343, 363; for ballads containing news of political events, which Pepys arranged chronologically under the rubric 'State', see *ibid.*, vol. II, pp. 201–374. The effect of this is to create a virtual ballad history of events from the execution of Charles I through the major crises of the next three reigns – Popish Plot and Exclusion Crisis, Rye House Plot, Monmouth's rebellion and Jeffries' Assizes, and the Revolution – culminating, at the end of Pepys's life, in William III's victories against Louis XIV.

90 Morison, *The English Newspaper*, pp. 59–60 for the merger of these two papers, without comment on this point; Hunter, *Before Novels*, pp. 185–6, 188.

91 On news and rumour, see Adam Fox, 'Rumour, News and Popular Political Opinion in Elizabethan and Early Stuart England,' *HJ* 40 (1997): 597–620, and *idem*, 'Aspects of Oral Culture,' ch. 5.

92 Love, *Scribal Publication*, brings this point out well; more recently, see the thorough debunking of the 'authority' and 'integrity' of printed texts in Adrian Johns, *The Nature of the Book* (Chicago, 1998).

93 *Craftsman* (17 July 1734), quoted in Black, 'British Press and Europe,' p. 65.

94 *The Diary of Dudley Ryder 1715–1716* (1939), ed. W. Matthews, p. 187; Steven Shapin, *A Social History of Truth* (Chicago, 1994); Shaaber, *Some Forerunners of the Newspaper in England*, pp. 236–42. The partisan politics of Augustan news, which contributed to distrust, are discussed by W. A. Speck, 'Politics and the Press,' in *The Press in English Society from the Seventeenth to the Nineteenth Centuries* (London, Toronto, and Cranbury, NJ, 1986), pp. 47–63. As Speck points out, the distrust was not unfounded, particularly on the reporting of parliamentary activities and elections. On the other hand, readers did not ignore newsbooks and newspapers written by those of differing opinions: Raymond, *Invention of the Newspaper*, p. 255 and *passim* offers several examples of readers deliberately seeking out the newsbooks produced by the opposing side.

95 *Life and Letters of Thomas Cromwell* (Oxford, 1902), 2 vols, ed. R. B. Merriman, I: 313, cited in G. R. Elton, *The Tudor Constitution* (Cambridge, 1982; 2nd edn.), p. 242.

96 John Skelton, 'Against Venemous Tongues,' ll. 63–6, *Complete English Poems of John Skelton*, ed. Scattergood; *The Letter Book of John Parkhurst, Bishop of Norwich* (1974–5), ed. R. A. Houlbrooke, Norfolk Record Society, 43, p. 77.

97 *Revenge of Bussy D'Ambois*, III, ii. 6–16, *The Plays of George Chapman: The Tragedies* (New York, 1961), 2 vols, ed. T. M. Parrott, I: 105.

98 *Diary of John Rous*, p. 44. Even if this were an overstatement, it is true that enquiries for news, to say nothing of relations of it, could illustrate religious attitudes. Father Robert Southwell complained in 1591 that any news or rumor directed against

Catholics was 'currant, and goeth presently abrode *cum privilegio*,' adding that 'many poore printers and needy libellers make the best part of their living by our slaunders': *Letters and Despatches of Richard Verstegan* (1959), ed. A. G. Petti, Catholic Record Society, 52, p. 4.

99 *News from the New World Discover'd in the Moon*, in *Ben Jonson*, VII: 514.

100 *The Staple of News*, Induction and III, ii, 14–50, in *Ben Jonson*, VI: 328.

101 *The Tatler*, 155 (6 April 1710), iii, pp. 218–20.

102 McKeon, *Origins of the English Novel*, p. 50

103 Gawdy to Framlingham Gawdy (February 1614). *Letters of Philip Gawdy*, p. 175; *The Spectator*, no. 625 [26 November 1714], (Oxford, 1965), 5 vols, ed. Donald F. Bond, V: 137.

104 Frank, *Beginnings of the English Newspaper*, p. 77. The protest of truthfulness and newness goes back beyond the 1620s newsbooks to their more sporadic Tudor precursors. Compare an Elizabethan title such as *Certayn and tru good nues, from the syege of the isle Malta* (STC 17213.5, 1565) with specimens from after 1620, e.g.: *The Last Newes* (STC, *sub* 'newsbooks', 18507.111, 113); *The Certaine Newes of this Present Weeke* (STC 18507. 68, 72); *The 2 of September. Two great battailes very lately fought* (STC 18507.74).

105 Sir Walter Cope, 16 April 1614, *Proceedings in Parliament 1614 (House of Commons)* (Philadelphia, 1988), ed. Maija Jansson, p. 90.

106 Robert Crowley, 'Of Inventers of Straunge Newes,' *Epigrams* (1550), in *Select Works of Robert Crowley* (1872), ed. J.M. Cowper, Early English Text Society, extra series, 15, p. 38. False news could occasion major embarrassment. John Evelyn noted with some amusement in 1690 that Louis XIV, having heard the news that William III had been slain in battle in Ireland, held a magnificent triumph in Paris, only to have the disappointing truth of the matter brought to him in person by the defeated James II: *Diary of John Evelyn*, V: 32. Louis only heard of his army's defeat at Blenheim after a week's delay: John B. Wolf, *Louis XIV*, pp. 537–8.

107 Historical Manuscripts Commission [hereafter HMC] *Ninth Report*, II, p. 498: diary of Robert Woodford, steward of Northampton, 22 March 1639; J. Fielding, 'Opposition to the Personal Rule of Charles I: The Diary of Robert Woodford, 1637–1641,' *HJ* 31 (1988): 769–88.

108 I. Thornley, 'Treason by Words in the Fifteenth Century,' *EHR* 32 (1917): 556–61; J. Hawarde, *Les Reportes dels cases in Camera stellata, 1593–1609* (1894), ed. W. P. Baildon, p. 66.

109 *Commons Debates 1628* (New Haven, CT, 1977–83), 6 vols, ed. Robert C. Johnson *et al.*, iii, p. 276.

110 *Diary of Abraham de la Pryme*, pp. 15–16; Pryme believed such rumours had helped the cause of the Revolution, but he expressed amazement at their invention and the velocity at which they travelled.

111 *The Letters and Despatches of Richard Verstegan*, p. 39; *The Knyvett Letters (1620–1644)* (1949), ed. Bertram Schofield, p. 63; HMC, *Cowper*, i, 142.

112 Francis Wyndham to Nathaniel Bacon, 13 October 1572, *The Papers of Nathaniel Bacon of Stiffkey, I, 1556–1577* (1978–9), ed. A. H. Smith *et al.*, Norfolk Record Society, 46, pp. 37–8.

113 *The Letters of the Lady Brilliana Harley, wife of Sir Robert Harley, of Brampton Bryan, knight of the Bath* (1854), ed. T. T. Lewis, Camden Society, original series, 58, pp. 118, 130.

114 Wallenstein was in fact killed, by imperial assassins, only in 1634. For these and other 'news' recorded by Rous, who complained of the quantity of 'foolish reportes' in 1628, see *Diary of John Rous*, pp. 1, 18, 25, 59.

115 *Diary of Henry Machyn*, pp. 35, 86; Helen Miller, *Henry VIII and the English Nobility* (1986), pp. 67–8.

116 *Letters of Philip Gawdy*, p. 10 (Gawdy to his mother, 8 February 1587); *The Diary of Thomas Crosfield*, pp. 64, 88. Crosfield also reports (*ibid.*, p. 83) the rumour, in January

1636, that the lord deputy of Ireland had been 'kild in ye feild by a muskatier yt bare him a grudge, but it was another.'

117 Devon Record Office Z19403, Lapthorne to Coffin, 19 February 1687/88; Bodl. MS Carte 228 (Wharton-Huntingdon collections), fol. 259v, anon. to Wharton, 5 January 1678/9.

118 The phrase is Sutherland's, *The Restoration Newspaper*, p. 135.

119 *London Gazette*, 31 August, 10 September; *Flying Post*, 1, 8, 12 September 1696; *Diary of John Evelyn*, V: 330; Evelyn records similar reports in the *Post-Man* for the same day.

120 Sutherland, *The Restoration Newspaper*, pp. 135–6.

121 *Ibid.*, p. 231.

122 Daniel Defoe, *Serious Reflections During the Life and Surprising Adventures of Robinson Crusoe* (1720), quoted in McKeon, *Origins of the English Novel*, pp. 120–1.

123 Herts RO, DEP F.29 (Panshanger MSS), diary of Sarah Cowper, vol. 1, p. 199 (12 March 1701/2); compare p. 129 for her comment about not reading printed news, a clear exaggeration given her references elsewhere to what the newspapers report.

124 For the shift in focus in historiography from the past to recent events, and the parallel advent of competing ideological perspectives in place of the consensual approach adopted by early Stuart historians, see the final chapter of my book, *The Idea of History in Early Stuart England* (Toronto, 1990).

125 Habermas, *Structural Transformation of the Public Sphere*, dates the true emergence of the public sphere in England to the aftermath of the Glorious Revolution; Pincus, 'Coffeehouses and Restoration Political Culture,' pp. 819, 833–4 endorses Habermas in general but pushes the emergence of the public sphere back into the Restoration, while nevertheless holding the pre-1640 news circulation insufficiently public and regular to meet Habermas' test for a public sphere. This is a view supported by Raymond, *Making the News*, p. 9, and one which I am inclined to endorse, without discounting the enormous weight of public dialogue over foreign affairs and court scandal in earlier decades.

126 On monsters and miracles during the same period see Jerome Friedman, *The Battle of the Frogs and Fairford's Flies: Miracles and the Pulp Press During the English Revolution* (New York, 1993).

127 Thomas J. Cottle, 'The Time of Youth,' in Gorman and Wessman, *The Personal Experience of Time*, pp. 163–89, at pp. 178–9.

Part II
The Continent

From Copenhagen to Messina, from Wittenberg to Madrid, from Vienna to Paris, the political information business spanned the Continent. The following chapters portray a world in constant motion, a context of roiling political and social turmoil, where information was fed by convulsive changes of rule – in Naples, in Catalonia, in Holland; and where communication persisted in spite of repressive censorship mechanisms in some of these places.

Was there a Continental model of political communication, in contrast with the English model, in the age of absolutism? Jürgen Habermas thought so. And the French and Spanish journalism discussed in the following section, respectively, by Jean-Pierre Vittu and Henry Ettinghausen, seems to correspond closely to the type of celebratory rhetoric characterized by Habermas as a feature of the public sphere of absolutism. However, the chapters here offer a widely varied panorama of the media landscape of the age.

Thomas Schröder focuses on the birth of printed journalism in Europe, which occurred in the German-speaking cities of Wolfenbüttel and Strasbourg in 1609. Sparked by the demand for news about the events preceding the Thirty Years' War, these first attempts did not sweep away the pre-print genres at a stroke, but contributed to a many-sided menu including newsletters, handbills and newsbooks, prose and poetry. At this early stage, government interest in the invention was negligible. A systematic survey of the contents of the first papers gives ample evidence of bias and error, but nothing systematic enough to indicate deliberate manipulation or intention to mislead. What purpose, then, did it serve? Since the news was rarely fresh enough or local enough to be of much practical use, Schröder suggests that it must have served chiefly to satisfy a growing curiosity about the world, as the press critics constantly complained.

In the Dutch Republic, beginning with the Amsterdam-based *Courante uyt Italian*, published from 1618, printed political information quickly became a main product of one of the most vital printing industries in Europe. Otto Lankhorst shows how municipal governments favoured the development of an information industry by making heavy use of newsletters and newspapers for their own needs. The States-General and the States of the Provinces refrained from pre-publication censorship, giving writers and entrepreneurs considerable freedom. However, strict laws governed what could and could not be said about political affairs that directly interested the Republic and its neighbours. The Republic's reputation as an oasis of toleration was mainly earned in comparison with elsewhere; and specific cases of government intervention illustrate official opinions about the press in relation to particularly vital points of public policy.

Similarly in the Spanish Netherlands, Paul Arblaster shows, a vigorous printing industry made news a major product. The Spanish administration imposed more invasive censorship here than its counterparts did in the Dutch Republic. But the very issue of censorship itself became part of the struggle between the Spanish and the local authorities. And already by the 1630s, local authorities managed to usurp control over the press, initiating a period of considerable independence. In the 1650s, in spite of Spanish negotiations with the French, the Low Countries press began a campaign of preventive attacks on the French-based statesman Mazarin, motivated by fears of invasion and of extended involvement in French-Spanish hostilities.

Jean-Pierre Vittu places the career of the first French newspaper writer and publisher, Théophraste Renaudot, in the context of existing seventeenth-century media for the diffusion of political news. He outlines the various forms of publication then available, printed and manuscript, tracing the contexts where political information of each type was habitually discussed in public. He then examines Renaudot's strategies for creating a monopoly on news publication in Paris and the provinces with help from Richelieu. His evidence shows that the increased circulation of news in the midst of the late seventeenth-century wars led the monarchy to pay far more attention than before to the image of itself as projected in the press, suggesting a new role for public opinion.

Although Spain was in the rearguard of Europe as far as the formation of newspapers was concerned, it participated fully in the development of other genres, as Henry Ettinghausen shows in his chapter. Manuscript newsletters purveyed information and commentary critical of the regime of Philip IV. Printed publications were more cautious, and purported to deliver the usual store of ceremonial facts, battle reports and sensationalism to more credulous audiences. Criticism was not absent from the forum of print; but in Philip IV's reign, such was most likely to be found in reference to the previous monarch, as a foil to exalt the virtues of his successor, in an interesting and self-conscious game of representations and re-representations. The *Gaceta nueva* newspaper, published from 1661 by a secretary to the king's natural son, promised to place the task of political advocacy on a wholly new footing.

Mario Infelise analyses the circulation of political information in Venice during a particular conjuncture: the wars against the Ottoman Turks from the liberation of Vienna to the conquest of Vallona. Each new event, he shows, created a powerful new demand. To show how information became news, he identifies the sources of many stories among rumours and obscure reports penned by soldiers in the field. He then traces the way these were picked up in diplomatic correspondence and secret government reports. Newsletter and newspaper writers alike depended on a pan-European information network for compiling their publications; and from Venice, such publications quickly diffused to the rest of Europe, where they were pirated, copied and emulated. At the local level, the effects of information were unmistakably evident in raucous and occasionally violent collective actions celebrating victories and bemoaning losses.

Paul Ries shows how cultural and political differences between the two neighbouring absolutist states of Sweden and Denmark determined significant variations in newspaper production. In the information network connecting both places with the rest of Europe, postmasters played a key role, and this chapter traces the distribution of foreign news, particularly from the German-speaking press in Hamburg. A Swedish-language derivative of the German newspapers emerged early, in 1645, urged by authorities in Stockholm who hoped for advantages to state and economy from a controlled press. Danish-language news publication emerged no earlier than the 1660s, after locally printed German-language papers had already primed the market; and in a much freer environment. A product of the competition for readership between various firms, *Den Danske Mercurius* was published in verse. To achieve a more direct rapport with readers, it offered a higher proportion of local news than its earlier counterparts, initiating the inward turn that was characteristic of mature journalism all over Europe.

While tracing the pan-European spread of news in each of its various settings in the seventeenth century, these chapters also point to the future. They furnish information about major sources that may help lay the groundwork for future comparative studies. And they offer new insights concerning some of the conceptual problems of media research in general.

5 The origins of the German press

Thomas Schröder

The story of the German press in the seventeenth century is one of success. The oldest remaining weekly newspapers mark the beginning: the Strassburg *Relation* (documented since 1605) and the Wolfenbüttel *Aviso* from 1609. Other newspapers appeared just a few years later, for example in Frankfurt am Main (1615), Berlin (1617), and in Hamburg (1618). It has been shown that by the middle of the century, there were at least thirty cities in which German-language newspapers were published. It is also estimated that a total of 200 German-language newspapers in more than seventy cities were founded in the course of the century. Toward the end of the century, however, almost every larger German city had its own newspaper, many of which already appeared more than once a week. At the same time, the number of readers is estimated to have reached up to 250,000.

The reasons for this success are many, and range from the special qualities of the newspaper itself, to the often deplored *Neuigkeitssucht*, that is, addiction to news in the seventeenth century. One important reason was also that the development of the newspapers was supported, among people, by the political powers of the time, which were interested in this new medium for many reasons. First, they profited from the newspapers as a supplement to the existing system of information. For example, the press quickly became one of the most important sources of information for the smaller courts of the Holy Roman Empire. Second, they were interested in newspapers as an instrument of power. There is evidence from quite early on of the first attempts at using newspapers as an instrument for politics. For example, they might be used to spread rumours or launch one-sided information campaigns. Finally, and most important, the political powers of the time supported newspapers in order to control them. Apart from censorship, the granting of privileges was the most important means for making the press accessible to the state.

Nevertheless, the press was always more than just an instrument of power. This became more obvious in the later stages of development, in which newspapers, together with other changes, proved to be an important factor for social and political change. The potential for this development was embedded in the very concept of a newspaper. True, specific references to this concept cannot be discovered by studying the biographies of the people involved or the programmes they announced. Nevertheless, it can be deduced from the practice of news coverage, in the efforts not to patronize or educate the readers, but rather to offer them multifarious and far-reaching information. This concept is recognizable in the first newspapers, and its future impact is inevitable. Of course, the path from these first beginnings to a press that would function as an organ for democratic opinion-formation, or as a tool in the service of a critical public, was as long as the path to this democratic society itself. And newspapers themselves changed significantly as time went on. However, newspapers also did their part in establishing this itinerary from the very beginning.

Characteristics of news coverage

One reason for the rapid, sweeping success of newspapers in the seventeenth century was that this new medium proved to be highly effective from the outset, and at the same time was structured flexibly enough to meet whatever changes proved to be necessary. The most important characteristics become apparent in the analysis of news coverage. The following account is based on the results of a comparative study, in which two newspapers from 1609 (*Aviso* and *Relation*), as well as three other newspapers from 1667, are analysed (the last remaining year of the Strassburg *Relation*, plus the Frankfurt *Ordentliche Wochentliche Post-Zeitungen*, and Greflinger's *Nordischer Mercurius* from Hamburg).[1]

News structure

News coverage in the early press was based on the reporting of correspondents strewn throughout Europe. In their letters, they compiled whatever news was available to them in their cities. In addition to news from the city itself, they often covered very large geographical areas. The Venetian correspondent, for instance, covered an area that reached into the heart of the Ottoman Empire. Although such correspondents are supposed to have provided newspapers with most of their information, the individuals remain largely unknown. For example, Philipp Hainhofer from Augsburg is said to have been active as an important correspondent for both newspapers from the year 1609.[2] However, no further information confirming this can be derived from the reports. Information appeared anonymously. It is not even possible to prove with any certainty that the correspondence from one city all originate from the same author.

Newspapers received information from their correspondents regularly by mail, usually once or twice per week.[3] The largest amount of correspondence came from a few cities. In 1609, these were Antwerp, Cologne, Prague, Rome, Venice, and Vienna. The most important cities of correspondence in the year 1667 were Hamburg, Vienna, Cologne, Paris, and Venice. Every issue of the newspaper was made up of an average of six to eight letters of correspondence, which meant an average issue contained approximately 1,500 to 1,900 words.

The letters from the correspondents were given a heading in the newspapers, which included the city of origin and a postmark date. They were printed in the order in which they were received, and, in fact, without much editing aside from the furnishing of headings and the cutting of texts to fit the space provided.[4] Therefore, the newspaper of the seventeenth century consisted of a sequence of letters, patched together, each of which was in turn compiled from various reports usually covering many different topics. This simple organization had an advantage over more elaborate schemes. It allowed rapid production, responding to the pressure to stay up to date, and at the same time it created a fixed layout for contents that varied week by week. This gave the newspaper a characteristic look, easy for readers to recognize, and provided the reader with at least a rough orientation within the structure of the text. The letter-based format remained the determining factor for the arrangement of news material until well into the nineteenth century.

Content structure

The content structure of news coverage was marked above all by its geographical variety. The first newspapers included news from all of Europe, as well as occasional reports from America or the Far East. Certain cities of correspondence, however, produced larger quantities of reports than others. In newspapers from the year 1609, approximately two-thirds of all news originated from the Empire (particularly from Prague and Vienna). Throughout the course of the century, however, news from other European countries was given an increasing amount of space.

More than half of all news covered ongoing events. In 1609, repeatedly covered topics included the armistice talks in the Netherlands, conflicts between rulers and estates in Vienna and Prague, as well as the succession crisis concerning Jülich, Kleve, and Berg. Again in 1667, there were four topics of great importance: the second English-Dutch Naval War, the start of the French War of Devolution of the Spanish Netherlands against Spain, attacks by Eastern European nations upon Poland, and the Venetian-Ottoman War over Candia (Crete).

Political and military topics prevailed – not only in the number of stories of this nature concerning continuous events.[5] Altogether, two-thirds of all reports consisted of such topics. Political topics were most important. However, differences did appear in the distribution. Whereas domestic policy conflicts dominated in the year 1609, 1667 proved to be a year of international and military conflicts. Accordingly, the number of reports covering actual armed military encounters rose distinctly. There was also a noticeable increase in press coverage of events at the sovereign courts throughout the course of the century. Whereas state and constitution were still strongly influenced by the older corporative structures, especially in the Empire at the beginning of the century, absolutism had already gained considerably in the second half of the century. Absolutist rulers were the centre of their countries' attention – reason enough for newspapers to print detailed reports about 'horse ballets,' court hunting expeditions, and similar events.

However, aside from these main areas of interest, there were numerous reports on other topics. For example, trade reports covered the arrival and departure of merchant ships, gold and silver shipments, and the issuing of loans. News concerning the Church and religion focused on processions, pilgrimages, or the occupation of a bishopric, to name a few examples. The crimes and punishment of criminals were reported, alongside reports of natural catastrophes, a flying dragon, ghost-riders, or the collapse of a house. Indeed, the news coverage was characterized by a considerable variety of themes.

Information structure

Most of the reports were brief. Approximately two-thirds of them in the 1609 newspapers contain less than fifty words. Related to this no doubt is the purely factual nature of approximately one half of all reports. The reader was only told that a certain event took place; the information was limited to the basics: who, what, when, where. But also other texts, which contained additional components, had a predominantly factual function. Complex facts or background information (for example, why something occurred, and what the consequences were) are mentioned in half of the reports, but they are given prominence in only one-fourth of the texts. Accounts of events with detailed information about people, proceedings, or additional details were given even less importance. The news coverage of the early press was predominantly fact-oriented event coverage.

Differentiation according to types of journalistic texts (announcements, reports, commentaries, or reportage) was not yet known. Different types of text, which share an underlying pattern, are only partly recognizable. These can be seen as the point of departure for later standardization and differentiation. One striking feature from today's vantage point, is the printing of official documents verbatim, and therefore with different vocabulary, syntax, and style from the language of news texts.

Sections of text devoted to assessment and commentary are especially interesting. On the one hand, they show that in the news coverage of the early press there was no clear separation between information and judgement. More than one-third of all reports contained value judgements. On the other hand, even in these cases the informative function is almost always in the foreground. It is quite rare to find a report, for example, which can be viewed primarily as a commentary. Therefore, an 'emancipation of information' was definitely under way, in comparison with older types of media, like pamphlets. In the sixteenth century, according to Schwitalla's analysis, events were reported not for the sake of the events themselves, but rather to establish opinions, to engage the reader for or against something, or to show the reader how good or bad this or that action was.[6] In contrast, it is quite obvious that the informative function dominated in the newspapers of the seventeenth century.[7] In addition, it is interesting to note that, on further study, a considerable number of commentary elements prove to be second-hand accounts. The comments of the reporter himself had an explanatory rather than a judgmental function, and critical comments with regard to people or their actions, if these occurred at all, were almost always made from a non-partisan standpoint. Therefore, events and behaviour were criticized, for example, which endangered peace, the peaceful resolution of a conflict, or internal security and order. On the other hand, partisanship praise or criticism was limited almost entirely to the reproduction of comments from those affected or involved.

Predecessors and competitors

Written news: newsletters and Geschriebene Zeitungen

One important foundation for all information media of the seventeenth century was news transmitted through letters. Its beginnings can be traced to the fifteenth century.[8] Three different stages mark the development from private to 'public' news. *Brief-Nova* was the earliest form; here, news about daily events would be added at the end of a personal letter. In the next stage, more extensive 'news supplements,' in the form of loose pages, would be sent along with the letter, no longer written solely for the addressee. And finally, in 'newsletters,' the communication of news was the main reason for the entire letter; transmission and trade of this information was expected and intended.

The most important groups interested in this growing exchange of news were government officials and merchants. Both required reliable, current information, particularly about political, military, and economic events. The famous *Fugger-Zeitungen*, or newsletters, are a notable example. However, noblemen also corresponded with one another, and passed news on to friendly or allied courts. They also used scholars and other people, who worked as paid correspondents in the various news centres, to guarantee a less haphazard flow of news.[9]

For the most part, this news belonged to a largely self-contained and closed-circuit system of communication. However, as collected and copied communications were offered for sale more and more, this situation began to change. Handwritten news commerce flourished as early as the first half of the sixteenth century. People who did not belong to the closed-circuit system received access to information in growing numbers. Commercial trade with news stepped into the foreground at the turn of the century, as the first periodical handwritten newsletters appeared. In accordance with the rhythm of postal delivery, news correspondence was put together in weekly intervals and *Geschriebene Zeitungen* (written newspapers) were delivered regularly to subscribers.

The history of *Geschriebene Zeitungen* can thus be read as the history of a common root shared by written and printed newspapers. The development of a handwritten correspondence service was the deciding factor in the emergence of periodical news coverage, whether of the written or printed sort. While *Geschriebene Zeitungen* offered their readers current, thematically varied, and even periodical news coverage, they also anticipated some central characteristics of the early weekly press and contributed to the development of a form of news coverage that could provide a reference point for the weekly press. In many cases the connection between written and printed newspapers was even closer. Handwritten newspapers were the most important sources of news for the weekly press. Even Johann Carolus, publisher of the *Relation*, did business with handwritten copies of news before his 'invention' of the weekly press.

Geschriebene Zeitungen were not only precursors to the weekly press, they were also an independent medium and the printed paper's greatest competitor. At the beginning of the seventeenth century, they obviously had many advantages over the printed paper. For example, *Geschriebene Zeitungen* were not subject to censorship to the same degree as printed material, and could more easily evade the censorship regulations. Moreover, the editors of *Geschriebene Zeitungen* were able to choose the news to suit each individual subscriber.[10]

The most important difference between the handwritten and printed sheets, however, lay in the essentially different claim to a public role. In the beginning, neither form of media was a mass production meant for everyone. The cost of both was prohibitive, as were the educational prerequisites for comprehension by readers. But whereas *Geschriebene Zeitungen* were, and always remained, an exclusive medium (the price stood at about five times higher than that of the average printed newspaper),[11] the aim of the printed sheets was always to gain the largest possible circulation. Limiting readership opposed their economic principle. Differentiating information for varying interests opposed their underlying concept. It was the principle of equality that mattered in the weekly press. This claim to a public role was continually reinforced, and the press eventually became the 'press for everyone.' Contrary to this, the absolutist state, with its ministers and diplomatic services, developed a news system for internal communication independent from the weekly press. Therefore, functions which were still connected in the *Geschriebene Zeitungen* as a result of their historical development – functions such as providing information and facilitating government – would be clearly separated during the course of the seventeenth century.

Single prints: flyers, pamphlets, Neue Zeitungen

The spread of news in printed form is of course not as old as the exchange of news via handwritten personal letters and newsletters. Nevertheless, quite a considerable tradition existed at the beginning of the seventeenth century. The first single prints came into existence around the same time as Gutenberg's invention. Printed pamphlets experienced their first heyday in connection with the Reformation, and they reached a rate of increase that was even higher than that of the wildly expanding book production industry. The age of the illustrated flyer stretched from the middle of the sixteenth century to the middle of the seventeenth century. Early on, individual copies of written newspapers were also published in printed form.[12]

During the course of the sixteenth century, a greatly varied field of non-periodical, printed journalism developed, in many characteristic forms. Formal criteria permit the identification of two basic types. The first, *Flugblätter* (flyers), were one-sided printed pages, which were usually in large format (folio or large folio) and included a large share of illustrations. *Flugschriften* (pamphlets), on the other hand, are best described as brochures made up of at least two pages. These were usually printed in a smaller format (quarto or octavo), and there were a minimal number of illustrations. The contents of the single prints ranged from purely factual information to propaganda and agitation. Other important functions of the single prints included entertainment, education, or edification. The repertoire of text genres and styles of writing was correspondingly diverse. Official documents and announcements were printed alongside satires, polemics, and lampoons. Some of the more important topics covered included religion and confessional disputes, and politics, as well as news about miracles, catastrophes, and crimes. However, topics to do with natural history and moral or social problems were also taken up.

Imprints with an informational function were very important in both of the above basic types. Early on, such single imprints with informational claims received the generic name of *Neue Zeitung*, roughly translated as 'Current News.' Numerous sheets used this as their title or used similar terms such as *Erschreckliche Zeitung*, *Erbärmliche Zeitung*, or *Glückliche Zeitung*. In 1480, the *Neue Zeitungen* first appeared in the German-speaking areas and subsequently spread throughout Europe. The latest known copies date from the end of the seventeenth century.[13]

The main difference between the weekly press and the *Neue Zeitungen* lay simply in the latter's lack of periodicity. Before the advent of the newspaper *per se*, serial newspapers existed that were purely occasional, covering an event sequentially in individual numbered issues. What was missing, in this case as well as in the case of the *Neue Zeitungen*, however, was the planned regularity of a periodical publication with fixed publication dates. The *Neue Zeitungen*, furthermore, were always occasional publications. Correspondingly, they were not sold by subscription, as was the case with the weekly press, but were sold individually on the street. This was a decisive factor in determining the type of layout. Illustrations, together with stylistic and textual characteristics, were used to stimulate sales and appeal to a large audience, whose reading ability was assumed to be rather limited. Thus the *Neue Zeitungen* were able to reach a social class for which the weekly papers were most certainly too expensive.[14]

Lack of periodicity could sometimes be an advantage, to the extent that it made government and censorship control more difficult. *Neue Zeitungen* often appeared anonymously, contrary to legal regulations. Weekly papers, however, depended on government approval, and it is probably for this reason that they were characterized by a cautious reserve, an unbiased impartiality. The *Neue Zeitungen*, by contrast, welcomed a polemical or satirical style of presentation. Another difference lay in the selection of topics. Since they were single imprints, *Neue Zeitungen* concentrated upon a single event; their lack of periodicity meant that they could not follow the unfolding of long-term events. This also meant an emphasis on more sensational news, since, as a rule, this style of reporting justified their production.

Despite these central differences, however, a close relationship existed between both types of media. *Neue Zeitungen* covered many different kinds of events, as did the weekly papers. *Neue Zeitungen* were often used as a source for the weekly newspapers; and indeed, cases are known of publishers who switched from one side to the other.[15] Most importantly, the *Neue Zeitungen*, for many years, had tested many related forms of news coverage and news presentation, which could serve as examples for the newly developing weekly press. In this sense, then, *Neue Zeitungen* can be described as the root of the modern press. At the same time, however, they were also more than merely a forerunner to the modern press, lacking the key characteristic of periodicity. Logically, they were neither thrust aside nor replaced by the newly emerging weekly press: *Neue Zeitungen* appeared throughout the seventeenth century. Indeed, many features of the *Neue Zeitungen*, for example front-page stories, headlines, illustrations, masthead, and street sales, remained unique to the form; the periodical press had to reinvent them in the nineteenth century.

Periodicals: Messrelationen *and monthly magazines*

A third news medium, one that earned a secure position next to *Geschriebene* and *Neue Zeitungen* in the media landscape of the seventeenth century, were the *Messrelationen*.[16] *Messrelationen* ('Fair Reports') normally appeared biannually, in time for the spring and autumn trade fairs (hence the name), where they were offered to the public for sale. The contents included the most important events that had occurred in the previous months. In 1583, Michael von Aitzing established the genre in Cologne, with his *Relatio historica*, and the *Messrelationen* soon began flourishing elsewhere. For the *Messrelationen*, too, the weekly press was not a fatal blow. They continued to be published and sold well into the eighteenth century; and in Frankfurt, they even managed to survive until 1806.

Like the weekly papers, *Messrelationen* appeared periodically. Along with calendars, which already enjoyed large popularity in the sixteenth century, and in many cases also included a chronicle-like summary of annual events, *Messrelationen* are the first evident periodical print medium. The second important similarity to the weekly press lies in the thematic variety of news coverage. Emphasis was placed on important political and military incidents of the period, and less attention was paid to crimes, sensational facts, or miracles, the staple topics of the *Neue Zeitungen*.

The main difference between the *Messrelationen* and the weekly press was the longer intervals between publications of the former. The retrospective viewpoint allowed the *Messrelationen* not only to offer a stronger selection of news, but also to present a clearer outline of events, though on the whole this was chronological. At the same time, the limited amount of space necessitated a concise form of news coverage and an avoidance of excessive detail. The lower level of topicality opened up a larger scope for editorial elaboration, evident in design characteristics not found in the weekly press of the seventeenth century. Content-specific headlines drew attention to the material. Moreover, introductory texts, in which the previous history of an event was summarized, or additional information, including important background knowledge, might be found – elements which in the weekly press obviously became victims of the need for topicality. It must be pointed out, however, that all of these structural possibilities were realized to different degrees and in different forms by the various *Messrelationen*.

At the turn of the sixteenth century, the growing mass of available information, faster transmission, and a growing need to be informed allowed for the appearance of a periodical with shorter intervals of production than the biannual *Messrelationen*. However, before the first printed weekly papers emerged, publishers experimented with a monthly form. Although there are indications regarding the existence of more than one monthly magazine, only one has survived. It was printed in 1597, in Rorschach on Lake Constance, and is known as the *Rorschacher Monatsblatt* or *Annus Christi*.[17] The author was the journalist and poet Samuel Dilbaum of Augsburg, and the *Annus Christi* was printed by Leonhard Straub the Elder. In comparison with the *Messrelationen*, the monthly publication schedule of the *Annus Christi* represented an enormous acceleration. Still, if we take into consideration that a weekly schedule of news transmission was possible at this time, the most current level of information transmission relative to the given possibilities had not yet been reached. This may also be one reason why the *Annus Christi* was only produced for one year. Production was apparently discontinued with the December issue from 1597. Apparently, a monthly schedule could no longer satisfy the demands of the time. On the other hand, the *Annus Christi* was obviously quite successful. A comparison of all six surviving copies shows that there must have been reprints, from which it can be assumed that there was a comparatively large demand.

Weekly papers

It is thus clear that weekly papers did not develop in a vacuum. At the time newspapers were developing, all elements that made up the character of the weekly press were already well known and in use by other forms of media. The characteristics of periodical publication had already been developed by *Messrelationen* and *Geschriebene Zeitungen*, much earlier than the weekly press. Current affairs were the defining element for at least some of the *Neue Zeitungen*. Even versatility and variety in the content of news coverage was not a new development: *Messrelationen*, *Annus Christi*, and written weekly papers all indicated the variety of news in their titles. A public role, the fourth and final criterion defining the modern press, characterized all types of media. In view of the social structure of readerships this was most pronounced in the *Neue Zeitungen* or *Flugblätter*.

That newspapers could fall back on the work of their predecessors and were very closely related to other media of the time explains how they could present themselves as a well-functioning news medium from the very first (preserved) issue. At the same time, *Geschriebene Zeitungen*, *Neue Zeitungen*, and *Messrelationen* were not only the roots or predecessors of the weekly press. They were also independent and functioning elements of the media landscape of this time. They distinguished themselves through different possible functions and effects, and were not only competitors, but also partners in the practice of journalism.

Despite the relationship with its competitors, once the weekly press joined this media system, it could only hold its own and prevail on a long-term basis because of its own individual profile. After all, the newspaper was indeed a new kind of medium – not because of its individual characteristics, but rather on account of the previously unknown combination of them. First, the early press combined periodical publication with the demand for the most current news coverage possible. At the same time, in its printed form it targeted an ever-increasing public and, in response to the demand, covered the entire spectrum of available news. There was no model and no predecessor for these characteristics in their entirety. Today's press can be described using the same characteristics. In this sense, it is correct to say that the modern press was born with the emergence of the weekly press.

Existing circumstances

Prerequisites for the development of newspapers

The technical and organizational requirements for a periodical press already existed long before the beginning of the seventeenth century. Let us not forget the printing press itself, with moveable metal letters, since this made fast and rational printing possible in the first place. In addition, paper production increased dramatically toward the end of the sixteenth century. Moreover, improvements were made in printing techniques and type founding.[18]

Just as important for the development of up-to-date periodical newspapers was the existence of functioning systems of news production and transmission. Indeed, before the development of the weekly press a vast network of commercial news exchange already involved all important European trade centres. That a continuous supply of news could be furnished to a news service was already proven by the *Geschriebene Zeitungen*. Newspaper publishers at the beginning of the seventeenth century knew they could supply themselves with information from correspondents or news writers. According to the analysis provided by Kieslich, correspondents were normally found in higher social positions.[19] Their positions or corresponding contacts gave them access to valuable information. As a rule, correspondents composed and sent this information in their spare time in return for payment. Full-time news writers provided a more reasonably priced, though less exclusive, supply of news. The first news agencies were founded as early as the sixteenth century. As a result, the business of written news experienced a dramatic upward trend. News writers supplied and collected news – often through mutual exchanges with colleagues in other cities – and conveyed this information by letter to newspaper publishers on the basis of fixed contracts.

Courier networks and the postal service ensured the regular, rapid transmission of news.[20] As early as the fourteenth and fifteenth centuries, some courier services, for example the so-called *Ordinari-Boten*, had fixed routes and stations. At the beginning of the seventeenth century, private messenger services were still very important for the transportation of news. But the postal service played an ever larger role, since it was not only less expensive but also faster and more reliable. At the end of the sixteenth century, a strong phase of expansion began with the institution of the *Reichspost*. The appointment of Leopold I von Taxis as Imperial *Reichsgeneralpostmeister* in 1595, as well as the imperial postal regulations of 1597, marked this development and, at the same time, made it clear that the government was interested in expanding and controlling communications during this period.

As a means of transmitting and acquiring news, the postal service was of central importance for the emergence of a periodical press. In spite of their key role in this system, the postmasters appear to have left the job of actual newspaper publication largely to merchants and publishers. Of the forty newspaper publishers from 1609 to 1650 whose careers have been reconstructed by Kieslich, twenty-seven were full-time printers or owners of printing presses. As printing production capacities continued to grow, newspapers became economically interesting to people in these categories. A newspaper that appeared periodically seemed to offer more advantages than the usual sporadic orders in book production, in terms of the chance for constant and predictable employment of their businesses. Johann Carolus, publisher of the *Relation*, justified his application for the privilege of producing printed newspapers using arguments of business administration: the printed duplication of news was clearly less expensive than handwritten duplication.[21]

The newspaper business

Newspapers were only good business ventures if their sales were secure. In view of their rapid success, there can be no doubt that there was considerable interest in weekly papers and that their publication paid off economically, as early as the beginning of the century. The printing of newspapers even appears to have been the most lucrative form of business for book printers. Profit margins of more than 500 per cent were not uncommon. The average newspaper circulation, according to Welke, was 350 to 400 copies per issue, whereas certain newspapers reached an average of as many as 1,500 copies per issue. By using a constant format and printing procedure, up to 600 copies could be printed on a printing press in one day.[22]

Who might subscribe? The courts of the high nobility must be mentioned first.[23] It is known that an average of approximately thirty complimentary copies of each newspaper had to be delivered to court. And records from the first half of the seventeenth century indicate that periodical newspapers were sent to princes, their officials, or to their governmental councils. Courts of the high nobility, however, were not the only target group. Letters from 1611 show us, for example, that the Wolfenbüttel *Aviso* was not only known at the local court, but that jurists and aristocrats were also subscribers.[24] The *Aviso* was circulated into the countryside by private messengers, and even outside of the territory. In the country, aristocrats, pastors, estate managers, mayors, and governors are said to have been subscribers to the weekly press. In cities, the number of potential customers was even higher. Scholars, booksellers, students, and merchants are also shown to have been customers. According to Welke's calculations, not only patricians and wealthy citizens, but also journeymen, and even labourers and servants could afford at least the less expensive papers.

Communal subscription was also known, lowering costs for individuals. Private reading circles have been traced from the beginning of the seventeenth century. Even aristocrats and wealthy patricians might make subscriptions in common. If we take into consideration that newspapers were not only subscribed to by nobility, but also by monasteries and convents, charitable institutions, and municipal councils, this suggests a considerably wider range than the number of copies in circulation might imply. On this basis, Blühm estimates readership at between 24,000 and 60,000 people in the time before the Thirty Years' War, and Welke estimates between 200,000 and 250,000 readers in the period following the war. In addition, it can be supposed that in reality a much larger public was reached through practices of reading out loud and other oral forms of circulation.

The success of newspapers in the seventeenth century can be measured not only by the number of readers, but even more clearly by the expansion of the newspaper business itself.[25] The first wave of newspaper establishments began with the first newspapers and lasted well into the second half of the 1620s. The Thirty Years' War seems to have been rather favourable for the expansion of the press. It has been shown that, especially in the 1630s, numerous new newspaper businesses were established. Following the war, however, a slowdown in the development of newspapers can be observed as a result of pauperization. Only in the 1670s did such large numbers of new establishments appear again.

These developments occurred more quickly and powerfully in the Empire than in other European States. The Empire's special structure, with its internal confessional strife and its great variety of reigning sovereigns, not only favoured the development of newspapers, but possibly even represented an essential prerequisite.[26] Throughout the course of the century, approximately 200 German-language newspapers came into existence in more than seventy cities. Although only a fraction of this newspaper production has survived, today there are at least 60,000 known issues.[27] At the end of the century, there were weekly papers in all of the important commercial and capital towns. Newspapers that were published more than once a week became popular. The first daily paper, the *Einkommenden Zeitungen*, appeared in Leipzig in 1650.

The press and the government

By 1609, the crucial importance of reliable and current information for every government was well known. Thus, Gregor Wintermonat cited a Turkish saying in the preface of his *Zehnjährige Historische Relation*, in which newspapers were described as 'der Herren und Potentaten Steuerruder' (a helm for lords and potentates).[28] According to Wintermonat, the Ottoman Empire, as well as the Republic of Venice, owed their success to their precocious recognition of the important role that current information played in the administrative duties of lords and potentates. Officials of the Holy Roman Empire had long been aware of the important role of communications, and did their best to improve the supply of information. The expansion of the *Reichspost* at the beginning of the seventeenth century was a symptom of this.

The ruling groups were naturally interested in what the development of the press could contribute to the emergence of a more complete and effective form of communication. The press quickly took on an important role in the supply of information to the smaller courts of the Empire, which could only afford their own envoys to a limited extent. The following anecdote is narrated by Johann Peter von Ludewig in his treatise *Vom Gebrauch und Missbrauch der Zeitungen*: 'On this occasion I recall that a well-known secretary at the Court of Württemberg once joked that the Emperor could be dead for several months before they received the news from Vienna, if they didn't have the Frankfurt Paper.'[29]

Newspapers, however, were not only a central source of information for the ruling classes, but increasingly a political tool in themselves. They fit perfectly with the various strategies being used by the developing absolutism to win control over subjects' bodies and minds. This possibility was also recognized early on. For example in 1610, Cardinal Khlesl of Vienna encouraged the government to influence political decisions with help from the press. The idea was to put the Emperor under pressure through controlled publication of rumours about King Matthias' readiness for battle.[30] Such obvious political manipulation of information can only be proved very rarely, at least during the early period of the press. Other propaganda tools were more important for public relations.[31] Nevertheless, the development of the press represented a significant improvement in government communications, and offered new possibilities for influencing subjects.

Before this new medium could be successfully utilized, it had to be effectively controlled. The means to do this were available in the form of censorship and the granting of privileges. In the seventeenth century, all publications were subject to the Imperial Supervision of Books and Press Within the Empire.[32] Pre-publication censorship had already been introduced with the imperial edict of 1521, by which every document going to press had to be inspected and approved before permission to print was granted. Implementation of the rules was passed on to the regional sovereigns and respective local authorities. As a rule, universities or religious institutions were then commissioned to perform the inspections. This system was consolidated and intensified with the Imperial Diet of Speyer 1529, and in the Imperial Police Regulations of 1548. On the whole, it existed until the end of the Empire in 1806. The main emphasis of the inspections was on religious works, with the aim of controlling the flood of inflammatory and slanderous pamphlets that emerged in the course of the confessional disputes of the sixteenth century. However, newspapers were specifically mentioned as early as the Erfurt Diet in 1567.

Aside from censorship regulations themselves, the right to grant printing privileges on behalf of the Emperor and regional sovereigns was an especially effective means of exercising control over newspapers.[33] These privileges were supposed to protect the publisher's economic interests by granting a monopoly over the sale of a particular printed product and protecting the grantee against reprints. In the face of growing competition in the newspaper business, the granting of privileges grew into an effective means for the government to influence the press. Especially sought after were monopoly privileges for newspaper publication in a given city. The importance of such privileges was demonstrated by the numerous conflicts between potential grantees.

Last but not least, the granting of privileges in the seventeenth century shows that newspapers were regarded as more and more important, and that a new form of public role was part of this process. At the same time, the government's not always successful control policies betray an ambivalence in its relationship with the press. On the one hand, the government supported the press for its improvements on the existing communication system. On the other hand, the new medium's public role began the break-up of the old, self-contained system of information. That newspapers could break away from the governmental interests that contributed to their emergence, and go on to become an important instrument in the emancipation of the emerging bourgeoisie, is a dialectical development that is worthy of note. The image of newspapers as a tiller in the hand of the rulers proved to be an attractive slogan[34] and a desirable goal, unrealizable in the end.

Assessments

The development of the newspaper was one of the central and most important events of this epoch for modern-day press historians.[35] Its importance, however, was apparently not known to contemporaries. A public debate on the uses and dangers of the new medium began a half century after the appearance of the first newspapers.[36] One of the most important points of discussion reproached the uselessness of the papers: newspapers only satisfy the public's 'news addiction.' They contain meaningless news that the public wastes its time by reading. The second line of argumentation questioned the newspapers' claim to truth and non-partisanship. These topics can only be touched upon here. In any case, newspapers clearly made new demands upon readers, while offering special advantages and creating special opportunities. Together, these components make up the character of the modern press, and point to an emancipatory potential which is founded upon the very concept of the press.

The benefits of reading newspapers

If we are to believe the press critics who grappled with the benefits and dangers of newspapers toward the end of the seventeenth century, then the population of this time must have fallen victim to a real newspaper craze. A widespread 'news addiction' was mentioned; a 'horrible curiosity of certain people to read and hear new things.' The more avid did not refrain from reading newspapers in church, while listening to recitations from the Holy Scripture; even the clergymen suffered from the 'craving to hear new things.' This ghastly scenario, in Ahasver Fritsch's polemical *Discursus de Novellarum quas vocant Neue Zeitungen hodierno usu et abusu* of 1676,[37] was considerably exaggerated. Here, Fritsch distinguished himself as one of the most severe press critics, and gave reasons why the publication of newspapers should be, if not completely prohibited, then at least subjected to strict censorship and regulation with penalties imposed. Other authors took up milder or explicitly pro-newspaper positions. For them, the supposed addiction to news was really a thirst for knowledge, and in their eyes newspapers did not bring about the downfall of society, but rather its edification. One of the most famous defenders of the newspaper was Christian Weise, who claimed that the chief benefit of the press was its effectiveness as a source of knowledge. In his work *Schediasma curiosum de lectione Novellarum*, also published in 1676,[38] he gave a detailed presentation of the diverse advantages of reading newspapers.

Were newspapers only a means of entertainment, a senseless and dangerous pastime? Or could one learn and profit from them? As in all such discussions, the arguments were exaggerated and simplistic. Then as now, not everything that was labelled a newspaper was the same. Some of the *Neue Zeitungen* were more like today's tabloid press. Sensational occurrences, crimes, and catastrophes were their main topics, and the entertainment value was certainly much higher than the informational value. Such sensational reports appeared only rarely in newspapers, such as the *Aviso* or *Relation*. Comparisons between articles concerning the same event in *Neue Zeitungen* and the weekly papers show how concise and (relatively) fact-oriented were the reports in the latter.

The accusation of news addiction and uselessness, however, was not only inspired by sensationalist reporting. It had a much more fundamental meaning and also referred to the basic material of the regular newspapers. Critics like Fritsch were of the opinion that the public was not seriously interested in news, but merely succumbed to a feverish addiction. What they objected to, in this connection, was the concept of a 'newspaper for everyone.' Some also criticized the concept of 'current information' in general. According to this view, newspapers that gathered new information in weekly (or even shorter) intervals were not able to differentiate between what was useful and what was useless. The competence of the 'journalists' was occasionally questioned. Especially, the journalists' preoccupation with current events was regarded as fundamentally improper.

Historical writing was the standard of comparison for such judgements. Tobias Peucer, who composed a dissertation on the topic in 1690, for the first time at a German university ('De Relationibus Novellis'), compared newspaper publishers with historians. He wrote:

> The individuals who collect the insignificant things which make up the largest part of certain newspapers can be forgiven. Unlike historians, these people do not write for posterity so much as for the curiosity of the people, who yearn for novel information. These people write hastily and indiscriminately. If important events are missing, in order to feed these masses, then it is enough to add insignificant and occasionally unreliable news.[39]

Peucer argued his moderate position regarding the press against Weise's much more positive assessment. Weise especially emphasized the scholarly advantage of reading newspapers and the value of the press as an indispensable source of historical information. Peucer insisted on the weaknesses of newspapers compared to the work of an historian. However, he opposed the notion that these weaknesses made newspapers so worthless or dangerous that they should be completely rejected. In his view, the supposed weaknesses of newspapers certainly existed and were to be deplored, but they were also avoidable or could at least be limited. The predominantly insignificant news content in most newspapers was not an inevitable characteristic of the medium, but rather a typical problem that occurred in 'certain newspapers' to an exaggerated extent. In the end, Peucer went beyond the misleading issue of whether newspapers could attain the quality of historical writing. Historical writing for him was an impossible standard. He focused attention instead on the varying quality of newspapers and how this could be improved.

The proper object of criticism, according to Peucer, was not newspapers in general, but rather 'certain newspapers,' which mainly consisted of insignificant and unreliable news, put together randomly. Indeed, the fact that all newspapers contain insignificant news, at least in comparison to historical writing, merely points to the differences between an historical representation and a current periodical chronicle. We now realize that this turn to the 'insignificant' formed an important part of the new concept of newspaper. What appeared to be a weakness in comparison to historical writing was in fact a strength from the reader's perspective, a potential for a completely different type of use.

Indeed, if the newspapers were to be judged by the standard of the historical importance of their contents, they would be seen to be full of much that was 'insignificant' or barely memorable. Peucer suggested that they did not contain enough 'res graves' (significant events). Yet such was one of the necessary characteristics of a medium at once current and periodical, that had to be compiled each week whether or not enough important things happened. Hartnack had also observed this in his 1688 book, *Erachten Von Einrichtung Der Alten Teutschen und neuen Europäischen HISTORIEN*. One could scarcely demand great battles every week, he pointed out, just so that all pages in the newspaper could be filled.[40] Today newspapers typically have a variable repertory of news that is allowed into print according to importance, and issues tend to contain news of varying importance. Both are facts that originate directly from the concept of periodical newspapers. The same held true in the early press. The fewer events there were of a sensational nature in a given period, the more room there was for news that, for example, dealt with the travel plans of a little-known Venetian aristocrat. In every issue we find, next to the doubtlessly important reports on peace negotiations or military confrontations, less spectacular announcements about some envoy who had finally arrived, was still expected, or who was not going to come at all.

Though newspapers clearly reported other things besides matters of importance, this is no proof that news was put together at random. On the contrary, careful attention was paid to the content structure of news coverage. As we have seen, coverage of politics was more prevalent than coverage of other topics. Particularly, important political events were reported in detail on a regular basis. The early press is, therefore, characterized not by a lack of selectivity, but rather by an 'excessive' supply of news, which contained much insignificant information along with the significant information. The readers were thus largely left to choose for themselves what was interesting to them. The fact that newspapers did not target one specific audience meant that readers' expectations were likely to vary greatly. The enormous variety of news on offer, which was a fundamental characteristic of the early press, certainly made up a large part of its attraction, if not its advantage.

Another effect of newspapers' main characteristics of currency and periodicity was the reporting of particularly important current events episodically. Because the events took place over longer periods of time, they were broken up into many smaller individual events in the weekly news coverage. Over time, although the individual reports often remained disappointingly uninformative, the weekly papers established a far more complete and differentiated picture of events than the *Messrelationen*. The reasons for this were the total amount of information and the treatment of the topic from different perspectives. Making connections between the often completely isolated single news reports, and recognizing their meaning, was largely left up to the reader. The total news coverage was not so much an artistically arranged painting, as it was a mosaic, which the reader had put together himself.[41]

Many of the individual news stories in the mosaic of news had no special importance. Messengers were sent out continually, others were expected, were travelling through, or had just arrived. Everything connected in some way with an important event seemed *ipso facto* newsworthy. Ongoing stories raised constant questions: Has anything new happened on the topic? How will things continue to develop? The individual importance of each piece of new information was not an issue. Even the fact that there was nothing new to report was often reason enough to write about it. What was to be counted as significant, therefore, was newly defined within the framework of continuous news coverage. The reader was thus placed in the position of an observer of the event. Bit by bit, he was able to discover who was where at which point in time, when and where negotiations occurred, who had an audience with whom, and who had given an official statement. Current and periodical news coverage laid special stress on the 'everyday.' Not in the sense that the daily life of readers was reported, but rather in the sense that abstract and complex political processes were broken down into small, and therefore understandable everyday occurrences.

Furthermore, current news coverage about an ongoing event that had not yet reached closure inevitably had limited validity. It contained much information of no importance in historical hindsight: plans never carried out, events which had no results, developments which took a different course. All of these 'detours' were unavoidable parts of current news coverage, and had to be reported before an event came to a conclusion. For the reader, this not only meant that he learned about a great number of things which, in comparison to historical writing, he could later simply forget. It also meant that he could observe historical events from up close, seeing how they evolved, how they developed. Not only the results, but also the processes themselves were subjects of news coverage.

Truth and non-partisanship

The accusation that newspapers lie is as old as the medium itself. Just as old, however, is the protest of newspaper publishers that the accusation does not apply, at least not to *their* product. Two issues were continually mentioned: the credibility of the sources and the reliability of transmission. Together, both should have guaranteed that the reader found out, 'what is going on and what happened,'[42] and not 'groundless and untrue narrations,' according to the formulation that Michael von Aitzing used in the preface of the second edition of his *Messrelation*, in 1584.[43]

That Aitzing should have introduced the opposite term 'narrations,' emphasizes his own view that the non-fiction character of his texts was decisive. In differentiating his *Messrelation* from 'narrations,' he also opposed a view sustained in the fields of theology and literature, according to which 'truth' was understood in a 'higher' sense as belonging solely to insight into the godly world order. From this point of view, truth could not be attained through the simple representation of reality. Press texts were 'untrue' from the very beginning, and their content dangerous instead of useful. Against this 'higher' view of truth, newspaper publishers of the seventeenth century set a different, empirically-based definition. Publishers' arguments that their information originated from reliable sources or even from eyewitnesses meant, above all, that truth could be empirically verified. The particular value of newspaper reports, according to this view, lay not in a 'higher truth,' but rather in the reliable, fact-oriented rendering of reality, for which there was an intersubjectively valid criterion of verification.

One such definition of truth was not a new creation by the newspaper publishers. Long before the seventeenth century, it was advocated by non-fiction authors, chroniclers, and translators.[44] Its success was nevertheless an intricate process, which was not completed until the seventeenth century. An important stage in this process was the conceptual differentiation between truth and probability in seventeenth-century literary theory, whereby a new categorization of texts was established according to the criterion of fictitiousness. Poetry's 'higher' claim to truth was now defined in terms of probability, setting poetry apart from works belonging to the category of 'historia.' On the other hand, the claim to truth in the sense of an empirically verifiable understanding of reality remained open to historians and therefore also became a determining factor for the press. In contrast to the art of creative writing, which was beginning to accept fiction as a defining characteristic, the reference to truth became a fundamentally defining criterion for the press. If poetry can have no truth beyond probability, then newspapers can have no probability beyond the truth.[45]

Truth in the sense of an empirically verifiable representation of reality was fundamental for the press. At the same time and for the same reason, however, it became a central problem. The more or less successful fulfilment of truthful reporting became a criterion for journalistic quality. However, a press that did not, or could not, report truthfully lost its vindication. This correlation not only explains the importance of the problematic nature of truth in the press debate of the seventeenth century, but also constitutes the starting point for various assessments of the benefits of newspapers by different participants in this debate. Two different types of critics can be identified. Sceptics who painted a particularly dark picture included Besold, in his 1629 *Thesaurus Practicus*,[46] and Fritsch, mentioned above. They disputed honest efforts at truthful reporting by 'The Press,' or held the influence of structural factors, like censorship or dependence upon informants, to be so serious that successful efforts at truthful reporting were doomed from the outset. However, even defenders of the press, like Weise or Peucer, who considered truthful reporting to be an attainable goal, pointed out that violations of this maxim were a part of daily life.

The newspapers of 1609 seem to stand up well against these criticisms. It must be noted that no universally valid statements can be made, since the analyst is principally in the same position as the contemporary reader. He is dependent upon competitive information, which is available only piecemeal. Especially problematic is the fact that reports from *Aviso* and *Relation*, and even in *Neue Zeitungen*, *Messrelationen*, or *Geschriebene Zeitungen* often originated from the same source. In turn, sources from outside of the field of communications did not report events in such detail and the portrayals themselves were often quite one-sided, as they mostly originated from someone involved. To the extent that verification is possible at all, accusations of deceitfulness, especially by the harshest critics, appear baseless with regard to the early press. Of course, details in accounts often differ. Contradictions and mistakes in numerical data quite often appear, and a certain looseness in the reporting of numbers seems endemic. As a rule, however, the essential facts from the various sources are in agreement, and no events were made-up. In principle, the first newspapers prove to be thoroughly trustworthy sources of information.

Often, the question of the truth or untruth in the news is also a question of perspective. The demand for correct news coverage is connected to the demand for objectivity, balance, and impartiality.[47] A comparative analysis of the first two weekly papers shows that there are actually numerous occasions on which the *Aviso* and *Relation* convey quite different pictures of the events.[48] In the news covering a military confrontation, one newspaper reported upon the casualties suffered by one side of the conflict, while the other newspaper reported those of the opposing side. If we suppose that no falsification of the apparently shared source of information took place, then at least one of the two newspapers must have left out important information. The most likely possibility is that both papers were reporting with a bias. In another case, one newspaper limited itself to a short factual report, while the other newspaper offered numerous additional details and turned a simple death into a political scandal. Again, at least one of the two papers was clearly biased. Either the correspondent for the *Relation* left out relevant information, rendering the facts harmless. Or the correspondent for the *Aviso*, with his very definite allocation of guilt, claimed to know more than he could at that point in time. In either case it seems likely to suppose a purposefully one-sided portrayal of events. In this case, the news coverage has to be classified as biased.

In most cases, violations against impartiality were not as severe or even as clear. The most important circumstantial evidence is terminology and phrasing, from which a biased underlying foundation can be deducted without it actually being stated. These refer primarily to differing perspectives, which often originated in the city from which the correspondent wrote. Different correspondents each reported from the point of view of his own city. Their reports included characterizations and opinions reflecting the views of their governments, while not indicating either a definite detachment from or association with the latter. These are especially interesting if they included assessments or commentaries, for example, designating the results of negotiations as a success for one's own side and a failure for the other.

To be sure, even press critics like Fritsch or Stieler, who clearly supported the impartiality of newspaper publishers, did not view it as an absolute. This becomes especially clear in Stieler, who examined the problem in great detail.[49] He basically argued that newspaper publishers should be impartial, while at the same time he set limits. To some degree, his view seemed to be based on a recognition of the practical obstacles to obtaining impartial news. The effects of biased reporting in the news sources and the inability to verify it were worsened by actual official intervention. On the other hand, Stieler also recognized the limits to the application of this maxim. Impartial news coverage, in his view, was a prerequisite for reliable information; and reliable information was in the interest of one's own local government. He thus justified the demand for impartiality not by the importance of this maxim, but rather by its political usefulness; and impartial news coverage, in his view, might be sacrificed when that utility was in jeopardy. For him, political consensus was more important than press independence and impartiality. Censorship, as well as the launching of false reports, were not only unpleasant realities, but also worthy of endorsement, so long as they were in the interests of one's local government.

The 'emancipated' reader

Examples of attempts at politically one-sided government manipulation, of the sort that Stieler was disposed to permit of his local government but not of another's, are known from as early as the first phase in newspaper development. They only became an important factor as newspapers developed into an influential part of public life. To be sure, neither censorship nor politically controlled false reports can be found in the first newspapers. On the other hand, there are several examples showing that some government influence and even controlled news coverage cannot be excluded, at least at the correspondence level. Can a basic attitude of partiality in the newspapers be deduced from this? Did the newspapers from 1609, as many scholars have suggested, hold biased Protestant or royalist views, however inconsistent?[50] A systematic analysis of newspaper coverage of the Viennese Estates conflict of 1609 was unsuccessful in detecting any sustained partiality. I will now summarize some of the most important results.[51]

The Viennese Estates conflict was one of the four main events continually reported in the newspapers of 1609. Tradition demanded that the new ruler should sit down with the Estates before his accession to the throne to discuss their complaints and requests. Both sides would then sign a treaty, in which the agreements were put down in writing. How successful the Estates were at getting their own ideas accepted always depended upon their actual political power. And in the beginning of the seventeenth century the Estates enjoyed considerably enhanced power within the Habsburg empire for two reasons. First, danger from Turkey was a tremendous financial burden, which the rulers were not able to assume without the co-operation of the Estates. Furthermore, Rudolf and Matthias had to call upon the help of the Estates during critical developments in the fraternal dispute in 1608. These reasons contributed to building enough political strength for the Austrian Estates to demand the fulfilment of considerable conditions in return for their allegiance with Matthias. The central point of these conditions was freedom of religion. For purely political conflicts between Estates and rulers were now accompanied by confessional disputes. Although the Counter-Reformation had begun in the Austrian states under Ferdinand, most of the Estates were Protestant.

The course of the negotiations was reported continually and in great detail in both newspapers. Finally, on 19 March 1609, an agreement was signed between King Matthias and the Protestant Austrian Estates in Vienna. As a result, in May the homage was carried out in Linz, Protestant sermons were permitted once again, and there was a comprehensive reorganization of the government in the Autumn. Some of the king's other concessions were so vaguely formulated that they could never be fulfilled due to the ever-shifting balance of power. The historical assessment of the agreement of 1609 and how it came about has remained extremely controversial up to the present day. For example, Parker, in his portrayal of the era, placed an emphasis on the concessions Matthias was forced into making, and characterized the conduct of the Estates as extortive.[52] In the Göttingen *Deutsche Geschichte*, however, the agreement was depicted as a disappointing resolution to the Estates' legitimate demands.[53] Not surprisingly, the conflicting parties themselves also assessed the proceedings and the outcome quite differently. The question is, how balanced were the reports in the early press?

There is no proof that either of the two newspapers reported untruthfully in order to present a one-sided point of view. Errors in details are recognizable in both, but a tendentious motive can by no means be concluded from this. It was not the commentaries that put the impartiality of the news coverage in jeopardy. Of course, criticism of the lack of distinction between factual information and judgments is justified in many cases from the point of view of today's standards. However, the judgments never prevent mainly impartial points of view from coming through. The few one-sided judgments, presented in the form of commentaries in the two newspapers under examination, were not enough to establish partiality in either case. The question of news selection is more problematic. The reproduction of statements and opinions of the parties involved was a central building block for the information. Both newspapers limited themselves, as far as can be perceived, to the reproduction of official disclosures. There appear to have been no inquiries, much less investigative reporting. One of the first consequences of this particular type of source dependency can be seen in the fact that both sides were not always taken into consideration in the news coverage to the same extent.

A second problem is closely related to this. If the correspondents relied upon information sent to them from the conflicting parties, then they themselves ran the danger of becoming victims of biased accounts. A minimal claim to transparency would have been fulfilled if at least all information taken over directly from the source was clearly marked, so that the readers would be aware of its origins. However, this was not always done. The tremendous variety of information, often quite detailed, led in many cases, almost automatically, not only to an unbalanced account of one side, but even to the unintended assumption of the bias of the source. Furthermore, in their reports on official and public matters, correspondents often referred to 'public opinions' and sentiments, as well as unverified and often unverifiable rumours and statements. How much or which of such sources to incorporate was up to them. For readers, this material presented insuperable problems of reliability and verifiability. All things considered, the news coverage in many individual reports cannot be described as objective or neutral. Let us consider the practical results of this for the two papers.

In the first stage of events, both newspapers basically presented the same picture. They established the bargaining positions of the king and the Estates, showing how efforts to come to an agreement had largely come to a standstill. Both newspapers gave the conflicting parties an equal hearing. Information with a taint of one-sidedness about both sides' willingness to make concessions, or about their receiving assistance from a third party, cancelled itself out in the overall news coverage. An approximately balanced picture resulted, although individual reports were biased in many cases by the selection of information, as well as the perspectives of the writers. This is especially true of the *Aviso*. Its news coverage was not as carefully formulated and efforts at objective detachment were rare. In the *Relation*, on the other hand, balanced reporting was often sought, at least within the framework of a single correspondence.

This difference became even more noticeable in the news coverage of the second stage of events. The main points of interest were the attempts at settlement and the delays. Both sides were apparently trying to arrange the most favourable possible starting positions for the ensuing direct negotiations. In the *Relation*, events were commented upon with much more reserve. There, one-sided news was less common and was usually invalidated by a comparison of both sides. The disadvantages of such an approach are also clearly visible. By emphasizing verifiable and balanced information, the newspaper ended up providing more superficial and less revealing news coverage. The *Aviso* appears to have had better, more detailed information at its disposal. Its news coverage was more enlightening and of immediate interest.

On the other hand, in the second stage of events the *Aviso* apparently had no inhibitions about printing biased reports or even opinions in its news coverage. That first the position of the Estates and then a rather pro-Catholic assessment of events coloured the reports appears to have been primarily due to the course of events. The actors and their positions were the centre of focus. No clear partiality can be proven within the overall tendency of news coverage, although individual reports may be biased in one way or another. And here lies the difference between the *Relation* and the *Aviso*. Whereas the first appears to have sought neutrality through cautious reporting, the second appears to be a compilation of different points of view and assessments.

The differences between the *Aviso* and the *Relation* are particularly evident in the two papers' coverage following the settlement agreement. In accordance with its cautious approach, the *Relation*'s main emphasis was on comparing the concessions on both sides. The *Aviso*, on the other hand, presented the settlement agreement as an achievement by the Estates, which, for the most part, was able to enforce its demands. Which point of view corresponded more to the facts is extremely difficult to say. Both assessments could be valid, even from an historical standpoint. The difference may be less a matter of truth versus intentional misinformation than one of interpretation. Both versions are expressions of a certain point of view – on the one hand, a view emphasizing the success of the Estates, and on the other, one emphasizing the comparative aspects.

To equate these differing points of view with partiality seems misleading. The only attitude that was continually and repeatedly advocated in both newspapers was the support for peace and public security. This attitude might also be manifest in the prominent display, or even criticism, of behaviour threatening these goals, especially in the rather conflictual reporting of the *Aviso*. At the beginning of the negotiations this attitude put both papers on the side of the Estates. Toward the end, as Matthias changed his position and began to favour a settlement, both papers turned against the king's 'evil advisers.' When the king and the Estates reached a peaceful settlement, this was endorsed by both newspapers, despite slightly differing perspectives.

News coverage in the early press was by no means free of opinion, assessment, or interpretation. It was neither always balanced, nor did it always separate clearly between information and evaluation, between dispassionate reporting and one-sided opinions. However, newspapers did not submit to continuous manipulation from one or another party. They neither systematically falsified reality nor subordinated information to a higher truth. Just as newspapers contained many topics, they also contained many points of view, perspectives, and opinions. To be an 'emancipated' reader was not an easy task. Newspapers required mental processing, and the readers themselves were responsible for putting together their own pictures of events.

Conclusion

The emergence of the first newspapers at the beginning of the seventeenth century was not a sensational event in itself. What was so special about the fact that *Geschriebene Zeitungen* were now being printed? Where was the surprise, when newspapers began to appear regularly in addition to the individual issues of the *Neue Zeitungen*? Why should the world change if news was not only available biannually or monthly, but weekly? The step from the *Geschriebene Zeitung*, *Neue Zeitung*, and the *Messrelation* to the weekly press was not so great. Nor was it spectacular. What was spectacular was the initial success of the newspaper, its tremendously rapid diffusion, its continually increasing audience and its resonance throughout many different social classes. Not surprisingly, public discussion of the new medium first began only a half century later.

If the weekly press did not represent such a great technological advance, it was none the less of great consequence. That the early newspapers of the seventeenth century continued to publish and, as a result, become important factors in political and social change, was largely due to their ability to develop further and adjust to different conditions. At the same time, this outcome was also due to the new concept that the newspapers brought into the world, one that, as it turned out, reached beyond their time. As I have argued in this chapter, this was the concept of a type of news coverage that was at once true to reality, empirical, fact-oriented, and non-patronizing. This was the concept of an up-to-date and periodical chronicle, concerned with showing the everyday functions of politics. And this was the concept of a varied supply of information – the same variety for everyone, and for as many people as possible. This was, in short, the concept of a modern communications medium.

Much of what I have outlined here was only barely suggested in the press of the seventeenth century, and not actually realized. Other things were missing altogether. For example, journalistic research, objective detachment, and consideration for readers' demands. The press of the seventeenth century was a product of its time, a result of the predominant social and political relations. How could it be otherwise? In addition, because it was a product of its time, newspaper publishers did not intend to change the world. They wanted to report on the world, they wanted to be chroniclers of current events. What they ended up changing, nevertheless, was the picture of the world which their readers were able to make for themselves. At the very least they made this picture just a little more transparent and understandable. What Berns has said, in another context, is apt here: the newspaper is essentially an anti-absolutist medium, though it emerged in the midst of absolutism.[54]

Notes

1 For a more complete account of this study and its results, and for more complete bibliographical information, see Thomas Schröder, *Die ersten Zeitungen. Textgestaltung und Nachrichtenauswahl* (Tübingen, 1995); and G. Fritz and E. Strassner, eds, *Die Sprache der ersten deutschen Wochenzeitungen im 17. Jahrhundert* (Tübingen, 1996). The newspapers from 1609 are printed in complete form in W. Schöne, ed., *Der Aviso des Jahres 1609* (Leipzig, 1939), and W. Schöne, ed., *Die Relation des Jahres 1609* (Leipzig, 1940), respectively.

2 G. Kieslich, 'Berufsbilder im frühen Zeitungswesen. Vorstudien zu einer Soziologie des Journalismus zwischen 1609 und 1650,' *Publizistik* 11 (1966): 256.

3 See also H. Bibo, *Die beiden ersten Wochenzeitungen* (Oestrich a. Rh., 1933).

4 One exception to this, and on many other points, is the 'Mercurius'; see G. Fritz and E. Strassner, eds, *Die Sprache der ersten deutschen Wochenzeitungen im 17. Jahrhundert.*

5 See also J. Wilke, *Nachrichtenauswahl und Medienrealität in vier Jahrhunderten. Eine Modellstudie zur Verbindung von historischer und empirischer Publizistikwissenschaft* (Berlin and New York, 1984).

6 J. Schwitalla, *Deutsche Flugschriften 1460–1525. Textsortengeschichtliche Studien* (Tübingen, 1983), p. 46.

7 Compare P. Ukena, 'Tagesschrifttum und Öffentlichkeit im 16. und 17. Jahrhundert in Deutschland,' in E. Blühm, ed., *Presse und Geschichte. Beiträge zur historischen Kommunikationsforschung* (Munich, 1977), pp. 35–53.

8 R. Grasshoff, *Die briefliche Zeitung des XVI. Jahrhunderts*, Ph.D. dissertation, University of Leipzig, 1877, pp. 50 ff.

9 J. Kleinpaul, *Die Fuggerzeitungen 1568–1605* (Leipzig, 1921); J. Kleinpaul, 'Der Nachrichtendienst der Herzöge von Braunschweig im 16. und 17. Jahrhundert,' *Zeitungswissenschaft* 5 (1930): 82–94; M. A. H. Fitzler, *Die Entstehung der sogenannten Fuggerzeitungen in der Wiener Nationalbibliothek* (Baden b. Wien, 1937).

10 C. Prange, *Die Zeitungen und Zeitschriften des 17. Jahrhunderts in Hamburg und Altona. Ein Beitrag zur Publizistik der Frühaufklärung* (Hamburg, 1978), pp. 49 ff.; Z. Simecek, 'Geschriebene Zeitungen in den böhmischen Ländern um 1600 und ihr Entstehungs – und Rezeptionszusammenhang mit den gedruckten Zeitungen,' E. Blühm and H. Gebhardt, eds, *Presse und Geschichte II. Neue Beiträge zur historischen Kommunikationsforschung* (Munich, 1987), pp. 71–82.

11 L. Sporhan-Krempel, *Nürnberg als Nachrichtenzentrum zwischen 1400 und 1700* (Nuremberg, 1968), p. 126; M. Welke, 'Russland in der deutschen Publizistik des 17. Jahrhunderts (1613–1689),' *Forschungen zur osteurop. Geschichte* 23 (1976): 163.

12 J. Schwitalla, *Deutsche Flugschriften 1460–1525* (Tübingen, 1983), pp. 6 ff.; W. Harms, 'Das illustrierte Flugblatt im Rahmen der Publizistik der frühen Neuzeit,' in M. Bobrowsky and W. R. Langenbucher, eds, *Wege zur Kommunikationsgeschichte* (Munich, 1987), pp. 259–65; M. Schilling, *Bildpublizistik der frühen Neuzeit. Aufgaben und Leistungen des illustrierten Flugblatts in Deutschland bis um 1700* (Tübingen, 1990).

13 H. W. Lang, 'Die Neue Zeitung des 15. und 17. Jahrhunderts. Entwicklungsgeschichte und Typologie,' in E. Blühm and H. Gebhardt, eds, *Presse und Geschichte II* (Munich:

1987), pp. 57–60; P. Roth, *Die Neuen Zeitungen in Deutschland im 15. und 16. Jahrhundert* (Leipzig, 1914; repr. 1963).

14 E. Blühm, 'Die ältesten Zeitungen und das Volk,' in W. Brückner, P. Blickle, and D. Breuer, eds, *Literatur und Volk im 17. Jahrhundert. Probleme populärer Kultur in Deutschland* (Wiesbaden, 1985), p. 744.

15 H. Fischer, *Die ältesten Zeitungen und ihre Verleger* (Augsburg, 1936), p. 25.

16 K. Bender, 'Die deutschen Messrelationen von ihren Anfängen bis zum Ende des Dreissigjährigen Krieges. Ein Forschungsvorhaben,' in E. Blühm and H. Gebhardt, eds, *Presse und Geschichte II*, pp. 61–70.

17 G. Barth, *Die Rorschacher Monatsschrift. Das erste periodische Druckwerk in der Geschichte der deutschsprachigen Presse*, Ph.D. dissertation, University of Vienna, 1970.

18 K. Beyrer and M. Dallmeier, eds, *Als die Post noch Zeitung machte. Eine Pressegeschichte* (Giessen, 1994).

19 G. Kieslich, 'Berufsbilder im frühen Zeitungswesen,' *Publizistik* 11 (1966): 253–63.

20 See C. Prange, *Die Zeitungen und Zeitschriften des 17. Jahrhunderts in Hamburg und Altona*, pp. 35 ff.; M. Dallmeier, 'Die Funktion der Reichspost für den Hof und die Öffentlichkeit,' in E. Blühm, J. Garber, and K. Garber, eds, *Hof, Staat und Gesellschaft in der Literatur des 17. Jahrhunderts* (Amsterdam, 1982), pp. 399–431; K. Beyrer and M. Dallmeier, eds, *Als die Post noch Zeitung machte.*

21 J. Weber, ' "Die Novellen sind eine Eröffnung des Buchs der gantzen Welt." Die Entstehung der Zeitung im 17. Jahrhundert,' in K. Beyrer and M. Dallmeier, eds, *Als die Post noch Zeitung machte*, pp. 15–25.

22 M. Welke, 'Russland in der deutschen Publizistik des 17. Jahrhunderts (1613–1689),' *Forschungen zur osteurop. Geschichte* 23 (1976): 144 ff. and 156 ff.

23 See M. Welke, 'Russland in der deutschen Publizistik des 17. Jahrhunderts (1613–1689),' *Forschungen zur osteurop. Geschichte* 23 (1976): 160 ff.; E. Blühm, 'Deutscher Fürstenstaat und Presse im 17. Jahrhundert,' in E. Blühm, J. Garber, and K. Garber, eds, *Hof, Staat und Gesellschaft in der Literatur des 17. Jahrhunderts* (Amsterdam, 1982), pp. 293 ff.; E. Blühm, 'Die ältesten Zeitungen und das Volk,' in W. Brückner, P. Blickle and D. Breuer, eds, *Literatur und Volk im 17. Jahrhundert* (Wiesbaden, 1985), p. 743.

24 E. Blühm, 'Adlige Bezieher des Wolfenbütteler *Aviso*. Bericht über einen Archivfund von Wilhelm Hartmann,' *Publizistik* 1 (1971): 66.

25 See M. Lindemann, *Deutsche Presse bis 1815. Geschichte der deutschen Presse* (Berlin, 1969), vol. 1, pp. 93 ff. and 100 ff.; K. Koszyk, *Vorläufer der Massenpresse. Ökonomie und Publizistik zwischen Reformation und Französischer Revolution. Öffentliche Kommunikation im Zeitalter des Feudalismus* (Munich, 1972), pp. 48 ff.; M. Welke, 'Russland in der deutschen Publizistik des 17. Jahrhunderts (1613–1689),' *Forschungen zur osteurop. Geschichte* 23 (1976): 154 ff.

26 E. Blühm, 'Deutscher Fürstenstaat und Presse im 17. Jahrhundert,' in E. Blühm, J. Garber, and K. Garber, eds, *Hof, Staat und Gesellschaft in der Literatur des 17. Jahrhunderts*, pp. 299 ff.; J. J. Berns, 'Zeitung und Historia: Die historiographischen Konzepte der Zeitungstheoretiker des 17. Jahrhunderts,' *Daphnis* 12 (1983): 95; and see P. Ries, 'Staat und Presse im 17. Jahrhundert in England,' in E. Blühm, J. Garber, and K. Garber, eds, *Hof, Staat und Gesellschaft in der Literatur des 17. Jahrhunderts*, pp. 351–75.

27 E. Blühm, 'Die ersten Zeitungen Deutschlands und der Schweiz und der Beginn der europäischen Pressegeschichte,' in M. Bircher, W. Sparn, and E. Weyrauch, eds, *Schweizerisch-deutsche Beziehungen im konfessionellen Zeitalter. Beiträge zur Kulturgeschichte 1580–1650* (Wiesbaden, 1984), pp. 103 ff.

28 Quoted in E. Blühm and R. Engelsing, eds, *Die Zeitung. Deutsche Urteile und Dokumente von den Anfängen bis zur Gegenwart* (Bremen, 1967), p. 22.

29 J. P. Ludewig, 'Von Gebrauch und Missbrauch Der Zeitungen and Bey Eröffnung eines Collegii geführet. Anno 1700,' in his *Gesamte Teutsche Schrifften* (Halle, 1705), p. 94.

30 E. Blühm and R. Engelsing, eds, *Die Zeitung*, pp. 23 f.
31 See, for example, K. Vocelka, *Die politische Propaganda Kaiser Rudolfs II (1576–1612)* (Vienna, 1981).
32 U. Eisenhardt, *Die kaiserliche Aufsicht über Buchdruck, Buchhandel und Presse im Heiligen Römischen Reich Deutscher Nation (1496–1806). Ein Beitrag zur Geschichte der Bücher- und Pressezensur* (Karlsruhe, 1970).
33 See also M. Lindemann, *Deutsche Presse bis 1815* (Berlin, 1969), pp. 62 ff.
34 J. J. Berns, 'Der nackte Monarch und die nackte Wahrheit. Auskünfte der deutschen Zeitungs- und Zeremoniellschriften des späten 17. und frühen 18. Jahrhunderts zum Verhältnis von Hof und Öffentlichkeit,' in E. Blühm, J. Garber, and K. Garber, eds, *Hof, Staat und Gesellschaft in der Literatur des 17. Jahrhunderts*, pp. 327.
35 E. Blühm, 'Die ersten Zeitungen Deutschlands und der Schweiz und der Beginn der europäischen Pressegeschichte,' in M. Bircher, W. Sparn, and E. Weyrauch, eds, *Schweizerisch-deutsche Beziehungen im konfessionellen Zeitalter. Beiträge zur Kulturgeschichte 1580–1650*, p. 103.
36 Several texts are printed in K. Kurth, ed., *Die ältesten Schriften für und wider die Zeitung. Die Urteile des Christophorus Besoldus (1629), Ahasver Fritsch (1676), Christian Weise (1676) und Tobias Peucer (1690) über den Gebrauch und Missbrauch der Nachrichten* (Brünn, Munich and Vienna, 1944); see J. J. Berns, '"Partheylichkeit" und Zeitungswesen. Zur Rekonstruktion einer medienpolitischen Diskussion an der Wende vom 17. zum 18. Jahrhundert,' in F. Haug, ed., *Massen, Medien, Politik* (Karlsruhe, 1976), pp. 202–33; J. Gieseler, 'Vom Nutzen und richtigen Gebrauch der frühen Zeitungen. Zur sogenannten Pressedebatte des 17. Jahrhunderts,' in G. Fritz and E. Strassner, eds, *Die Sprache der ersten deutschen Wochenzeitungen im 17. Jahrhundert*, pp. 259–85.
37 See K. Kurth, ed., *Die ältesten Schriften für und wider die Zeitung*, pp. 117 ff.
38 See K. Kurth, ed., *Die ältesten Schriften für und wider die Zeitung*, pp. 129 ff.
39 Quoted in K. Kurth, ed., *Die ältesten Schriften für und wider die Zeitung*, p. 174.
40 D. Hartnack, *Danielis Hartnacci Erachten von Einrichtung Der Alten Teutschen und neuen Europäischen HISTORIEN* (Hamburg, 1688), pp. 82 ff.; see J. J. Berns, 'Zeitung und Historia,' *Daphnis* 12 (1983): 102 ff.
41 See the case study of news coverage of the battle of succession over Jülich, Kleve, and Berg in T. Schröder, *Die ersten Zeitungen*, especially pp. 257 ff.
42 Cover page of the *Aviso* from 1609.
43 Quoted in K. Bender, 'Die deutschen Messrelationen von ihren Anfängen bis zum Ende des Dreissigjährigen Krieges,' in E. Blühm and H. Gebhardt, eds, *Presse und Geschichte II*, p. 61.
44 See, for example, H. Kästner and E. Schütz, 'Beglaubigte Information. Ein konstitutiver Faktor in Prosaberichten des späten Mittelalters und der frühen Neuzeit,' in K. O. Conrady, ed., *Textsorten und literarische Gattungen. Dokumentation des Germanistentages in Hamburg vom 1.–4. April 1979* (Berlin, 1983), pp. 454 f.
45 J. J. Berns, 'Zeitung und Historia,' p. 110.
46 Printed in K. Kurth, ed., *Die ältesten Schriften für und wider die Zeitung*, pp. 113 ff.
47 See J. J. Berns, 'Partheylichkeit und Zeitungswesen,' in F. Haug, ed., *Massen, Medien, Politik* (Karlsruhe, 1976), pp. 202–233.
48 T. Schröder, *Die ersten Zeitungen*, pp. 305 ff.
49 K. Stieler, *Zeitungs Lust und Nutz. Vollständiger Neudruck der Originalausgabe von 1695*, ed. G. Hagelweide (Bremen, 1969).
50 For example, J. O. Opel, *Die Anfänge der deutschen Zeitungspresse 1609–1650* (Leipzig, 1879), pp. 49 ff.; G. Bialowons, *Geschichte der deutschen Presse von den Anfängen bis 1789* (Leipzig, 1969), p. 88; H. Schöne-Rieck, *Die Zeitungen des Jahres 1609* (Leipzig, 1943), p. 89.
51 For more details, see T. Schröder, *Die ersten Zeitungen*, pp. 310 ff.
52 G. Parker, *The Thirty Years' War* (New York: 1984), 38ff.

53 B. Moeller, M. Heckel, R. Vierhaus and K. O. F. von Aretin, eds, *Deutsche Geschichte. Vol. 2: Frühe Neuzeit* (Göttingen, 1985), p. 242.
54 J. J. Berns, 'Medienkonkurrenz im siebzehnten Jahrhundert. Literarhistorische Beobachtungen zur Irritationskraft der periodischen Zeitung in deren Frühphase,' in E. Blühm and H. Gebhardt, eds, *Presse und Geschichte II*, p. 200.

6 Newspapers in the Netherlands in the seventeenth century

Otto Lankhorst

When did newspaper publishing begin in the Dutch Republic? Eugène Hatin, the mid-nineteenth-century French press historian, considered the collections of the *Tydinghen uyt verscheyde quartieren* and *Courante uyt Italien ende Duytschlandt* at the Bibliothèque Mazarine in Paris to be the oldest printed Dutch papers. These collections consist of a series of issues of both newspapers from 20 June 1637 to the end of 1643. Because the oldest issue in the archive bears the number 25, Hatin concluded that earlier issues must have been published.[1]

Subsequent discoveries in libraries and archives have shifted the starting date of the Dutch newspaper industry further back. In 1880, an issue of 25 November 1619, of the *Courante uyt Italien, Duytslandt &c*, printed by Joris Veseler was recovered by W. P. Sautijn Kluit in the British Library in London.[2] Emmanuel de Bom moved the beginning a few months further back when he discovered an issue dated 31 August 1619, of the *Tydinghen uyt verscheyde quartieren*, in the Stadsbibliotheek of Antwerp in 1903.[3] Subsequently, the Swedish librarian, Folke Dahl, made another important find in the Kunglika Biblioteket in Stockholm. There, among a large collection of Dutch newspapers, presumably from the diplomatic archives in the Swedish Riksarchivet, he discovered no less than 139 issues dating from before 1626, including an issue of the *Courante uyt Italien, Duytslandt &c* of 14 June 1618.[4] To date, this is the oldest preserved Dutch newspaper. Following his find, Dahl compiled a bibliography of the infancy of the Dutch press: *Dutch corantos 1618–1650*.[5] This also contains facsimiles of all the extant newspapers between 1618 and 1625. In 1946, the complete print run of 375 copies of this bibliography was handed over by the University library of Göteborg to the Koninklijke Bibliotheek in The Hague, 'so that it could use them to exchange them for other publications or in any other way, as it saw fit.' Pleas for resuming work on this bibliography for the years after 1650 have been made regularly. G. C. Gibbs, for instance, wrote in 1971: 'The task of compiling such a catalogue [a published catalogue of the holdings of early Dutch newspapers], though immense, however, would be rewarding, and is certainly long overdue.' For the time being, however, the composition of a *Bibliografie van Nederlandse couranten vóór 1800* remains an urgent desideratum.[6]

Herman de la Fontaine Verwey, the first Dutch professor of book and publishing history and bibliography, said in his inaugural address, 'no history of the book is possible without an extensive bibliography as point of departure and substratum.'[7] This is a dictum that holds true today, and it applies even more to newspapers than to books.[8] After all, newspapers are often not only preserved incomplete, but also divided over several archives and libraries. Further research into the history of the press industry, the expansion of the Dutch newspapers in the seventeenth century for example, is seriously impeded by the absence of a good bibliography of Dutch newspapers from the period of the *ancien régime.*

We do not have much data for drawing conclusions about the rate and pattern of the industry's expansion. We do know, however, that the Dutch press started in Amsterdam, where the *Courante uyt Italien, Duytslandt* by Caspar van Hilten (carried on by his son John) and the *Tydinghen uyt verscheyde quartieren,* by Broer Jansz, were printed.[9] Apart from a Dutch edition, both soon published a French edition as well, the *Courant d'Italie et d'Almaigne* of Caspar van Hilten and the *Nouvelles de divers quartiers* of Broer Jansz. Other publishers in Amsterdam soon followed their example, and in 1645 the city had nine different newspapers, of which eight appeared weekly and one, the *Extra Europische Tydingen uyt verscheyde quartieren,* even twice a week, on Mondays and Thursdays.

Outside Amsterdam, newspapers appeared successively in Arnhem (1621), Delft (1623), The Hague (1635), Haarlem (1656), Utrecht (1658), Rotterdam (1666), and Leyden (1686). Just how haphazardly the series have been preserved becomes clear when we look at the case of the *Arnhemsche courant,* which presumably appeared weekly from 1621 to at least 1636. Of the 750 issues which must have been published with an unknown circulation, only fourteen have been preserved, divided over several archives and libraries. Putting together a bibliography based on evidence of these newspapers is, therefore, in the words of G. C. Gibbs: 'a mammoth task, which would of necessity take the whole of Europe for its oyster.'[10]

Through booksellers and peddlers, newspapers found their way to the general public in Amsterdam, and also in Holland and the other Provinces. The rare correspondence between booksellers in the seventeenth century which has survived shows that 'courantier' Jan van Hilten sent twelve copies of his *Courante uyt Italien, Duytslandt* to his Leeuwarden colleague Tjerk Claessen every week, and twenty-six copies on average per week to his Nijmegen colleague Abraham Leyniers.[11] Apart from booksellers, peddlers sold newspapers as well, even though booksellers' guilds would regularly raise objections to this practice, which continued despite counter-measures. Dutch newspapers – in particular the French- and English-language gazettes which appeared in the Republic – were also read in other countries. The first two Dutch newspapers soon appeared in French editions, as we have seen. Their successor, the *Gazette d'Amsterdam,* was to play an important role for news coverage across Europe.

The first Dutch newspapers consisted of two parts, separated by a line across the width of a column. The news which was put above the line, relating mainly to central and southern Europe, came from other, German, sources. The news below the line came from local correspondents. Seventeenth-century 'courantiers' were first and foremost concerned with collecting and printing news. They were responsible for the news service. Discussion of political issues and criticism of government policies only appeared in a continual flood of pamphlets.[12] To defend its policies, the government itself printed pamphlets as well, which it sent into the world either anonymously or officially. Only in exceptional circumstances would they use newspapers for this purpose.[13]

The government played an encouraging role in the advent of the press. First, the 'courantiers' were able to operate within a prosperous environment of booksellers and publishers. In the seventeenth century, booksellers from the Republic played a key role in Europe. The economic and cultural upsurge of the province of Holland in particular spurred an enormous production of books, learned journals, maps, musical works, and pictures which were circulated all over Europe. Apart from this, a large local market for pamphlets, songbooks, and almanacs flourished due to a high level of literacy. In addition, the technical circumstances for book production were favourable. In the Republic, an independent paper and type industry had emerged, and printing techniques had reached a high standard. This boom was also possible because booksellers did not meet with much resistance from the government. This applied to the organization as well as the control of the press. The authorities were only concerned from a distance with the internal organization of printers and booksellers in guilds. Traditionally, printers and booksellers, together with painters and other artists, had been united in the local Guild of St. Luke. In the course of the seventeenth century, however, autonomous printers and booksellers' guilds were founded in the larger cities. The government of the United Provinces took a reserved stance towards censorship of the press compared with other countries. There was no preventive censorship. After a book or a pamphlet had been published, the government would sometimes take action when complaints had been filed. The reason for this relative freedom of the press lay mainly in the lack of a powerful central authority and in the fact that the Reformed Church did not have a dominant position.

Apart from this generally profitable climate in which the press could develop, the government also encouraged the advent of printed newspapers in another way. I shall first discuss handwritten news bulletins, which preceded printed newspapers here as everywhere else.[14] The local, regional and national authorities were very much interested in receiving these handwritten news bulletins. In the archives, there are regular instances of orders for these ancestors of newspapers by government agencies. A few examples may suffice here. In 1590 the States-General decided to pay 100 guilders to the 'nouvellier' of Cologne, Engbert Pellicorne, who offered news reports from Rome and other regions of Italy and Germany. From 1592 onward, his successor, Hendrik van Bilderbeeck, was granted 200 guilders a year as a stipend for the delivery of news bulletins from Italy and Germany.[15] Bilderbeeck continued his work for the States-General until his death in 1607. At some point, his son joined him in these activities. Father and son Bilderbeeck did not only work for the States-General, their sheets were also read by other national and municipal government councils.

Often, payments would be made to the person who copied them by hand. The city of Leyden received the news bulletins from Bilderbeeck through Dirk Gool, the 'kastelein' of the Court of the Province of Holland ('Hof van Holland'), who received a payment of 36 guilders a year for them.[16] In addition, Leyden paid other news suppliers as well. In 1600, during the campaign of Prince Maurice, a correspondent in Vlissingen received a reward of 50 guilders for writing and sending 'couranten en nieumaren' (newspapers and news tidings) from the local area.[17] The Court of the Province of Holland paid an annual salary of 36 guilders to Abraham Robaert, clerk for the States of Holland, for handwritten newsletters and newspapers. Robaert supplied his news from France to the municipal authorities of Leyden and Haarlem as well.[18]

The authorities were interested in receiving news, and they were prepared to pay for it. When printed newspapers began to replace written newsletters, they sold well among the authorities. The orders can be traced in the archives. Due to space limitations, I shall give only a few examples here. Aert Meuris, a bookseller in The Hague, supplied written and printed 'nouvelles' to the amount of 1,100 guilders to the Court of the Province of Holland between 1610 and 1624.[19] On 22 April 1619, the Court of Arnhem decided from then on to order printed newspapers instead of the written newspapers from Bilderbeeck.[20] Later in the century, the States of Holland paid for thirty-nine copies of the *Haarlemsche courant*, twenty-eight copies of the *Amsterdamsche courant*, and thirty-one copies of the *Leydsche courant*. Bookseller Jan Velly from The Hague billed the 'thesauriër' of The Hague more than 1,800 guilders for his 'wekelijkse kranten en nieuwigheden' (weekly papers and novelties) between 1641 and 1650, and he received almost 1,150 guilders from the Court of Holland.[21] In 1645 the 'thesauriër' of Amsterdam was startled when he saw the amount of 6,000 guilders a year which he had to pay out for 'papieren, couranten, nieuwe tijdingen en adersints' (papers, newspapers, news tidings and other printed material). It was decided to make better arrangements for newspaper deliveries.[22]

The government's interest in written and printed newsletters undoubtedly had a favourable effect on the expansion of the new medium and, as already mentioned, the Republic had a fruitful climate for publishing and distributing books, newspapers, and magazines. It was not lenient towards the distribution of political news concerning the national government, however. It had not been liberal under the Habsburg regime, nor had it been liberal since the Seven Provinces had declared their independence and joined together in the Republic of the United Provinces in the Act of Abjuration in 1581. The government tried many times to impose restraints on the press in the young Republic by means of Acts. On 27 November 1587, for instance, the States of Holland issued a decree prohibiting the printing and distribution of newsletters, pamphlets, songbooks and other writings which could lead to disturbance and conflicts in the country, and which were seen as being detrimental to the authority of the government. It was also explicitly prohibited to publish printed material regarding the state, in order to maintain peace and quiet and 'to restrain unruly tongues.'[23] This prohibition of the distribution of printed material concerning the government was similar to the situation in neighbouring countries. In the past, it had been the sovereign's prerogative to distribute news, and private persons had to refrain from publicly expressing opinions about the authority of the state. As late as 1680 in England, Charles II forbade 'the printing and publishing of all newsbooks and pamphlets of news whatsoever not licensed by his Majesty's authority as manifestly tending to the breach of the peace and disturbance of the kingdom.'[24]

In the Republic, too, the authorities decided that the burghers should not interfere with state affairs. This meant they tried to prevent public speaking or writing about the authorities, regents, and foreign monarchs. The tenor of the Act of 1587 cited above was reiterated repeatedly by the States-General, as well as by regional and municipal authorities in the course of the seventeenth century. Obviously, more decrees were issued in times of war and unrest.[25] The proclamation of Acts arose out of concern about the security of the state as well as about the protection of foreign rulers and the prevention of difficulties arising from negative news coverage regarding these rulers or their countries. The Act of 4 January 1651 announced the prohibition of publications leading 'tot grooten ondienst van desen Staet' (to large disservice of this state), and of indecent and scandalous publications which would discredit the reputation and name of kings, republics, princes and potentates of neighbouring countries, as well as their ministers.[26] In a few cases an Act was proclaimed prohibiting a particular news category. This happened in 1652 for all news concerning the political situation in England. This was the first time newspapers were included explicitly in such a ban.[27]

The government did not just issue decrees, it also enforced them in a few cases. In 1658, Gerard Lodewijk de Maght, 'courantier' in The Hague, was banned from the Provinces of Holland and Zeeland for ten years by the Court of the Province of Holland because he had made paid enquiries about state affairs of government officials in The Hague and published them in his weekly, the *Haegsche wekelycke Mercurius*.[28] In Rotterdam, a temporary publication ban was imposed on Johannes Naeranus' twice-weekly *Rotterdamse zee- en posttijdingen* in 1666 and 1667 because he had published news about the Dutch fleet and had written too openly about English affairs, over which the English ambassador had lodged a complaint.[29] Also in 1667, Chrispijn Hoeckwater was not allowed to publish his *Haegse Post-Tijdingen* for six weeks because he had written about state affairs. In addition, he was forced to pay a fine of 200 guilders.[30]

The States-General and the States of the Provinces issued Acts; in effect, however, it was the municipal authorities who had to take action in the case of violations. However, the cities often persisted in remaining autonomous and refused to follow the course set out by the government. In 1670, for example, the Court of the Province of Holland unsuccessfully called upon the city council of Haarlem to punish Abraham Casteleyn, publisher of the *Oprechte Haerlemsche courant*, for repeatedly printing the resolutions of the States-General and the States of the Province of Holland.[31] In the last decades of the seventeenth century, the charges against 'courantiers' mainly concerned news coverage and criticism of foreign monarchs and governments, and were less frequently to do with their publications on domestic political news.[32]

In comparison with pamphlets, newspapers were more vulnerable because of their regular appearance. A pamphlet could be banned after it had appeared, but by then all the copies would have sold out. Newspapers could be punished much more effectively with a publication ban. In the Republic, 'courantiers' had become more or less dependent on the municipal authorities as a result of the system of privileges or patents. Privileges for printing books were granted on the request of the publisher by the government to offer protection against pirate editions. Partly because of the ensuing costs, publishers only requested privileges for valuable works. Privileges offered protection for newspapers as well, but they also provided authorities with a means of supervision. In Amsterdam, courantiers (at that moment probably exclusively Van Hilten and Broer Jansz) were apparently already appointed by the city council in 1624, for which they had to pay 6 guilders to the *Aalmoezeniershuis* (almshouse). In 1656 there were four authorized 'courantiers,' but this number was reduced in the following years. In 1686, Casparis Commelin was the only 'courantier' for newspapers in the Dutch language.[33] In other cities, there had been only one from the very beginning. In 1666, Abraham Casteleyn became 'courantier' of Haarlem; it was decided, however, that he was not allowed to publish on matters concerning the municipal authorities. In Rotterdam, Johannes Naeranus was granted a privilege for the publication of his *Rotterdamse zee- en posttijdingen*, yet he had to be careful not to publish any offensive material in his newspaper.[34] The guidelines for 'courantiers' were defined more strictly in the course of the century. In 1693, the regulations for 'courantier' of the city of Rotterdam listed nine entries. A courantier was not allowed to cover any news which could discredit the Pope, the cardinal, or the clergy, nor could he publish material which could offend foreign rulers. In addition, he was not allowed to include decisions made by the government, even if they were not officially secret.[35]

On 9 December 1702, the States of Holland once again decreed that every 'courantier' had to request permission for publication of his newspaper from the municipal authorities.[36] By then, they were forced to pay an annual fee, the so-called 'recognitiegeld' (recognition fee), which was to rise steeply in the eighteenth century. In 1755, for instance, this 'recognitiegeld' amounted to no less than 4,500 guilders in The Hague. In addition, publishers were forced to pay a tax of 4 stuiver (20 cents) for every printed sheet.

The wealth of publications coming off the Dutch presses in the seventeenth century, which is sometimes referred to as 'the Dutch miracle,' certainly also included newspapers. However, one needs to be cautious of painting a picture of a 'tolerant Republic'. To an extent, freedom of the press did exist in the Dutch Republic, and it was certainly the envy of neighbouring countries. But it should not be forgotten that printers and publishers, 'courantiers' and booksellers in the Dutch Republic also had to deal with authorities who supervised, took censorial measures every now and then, and were always present.

Notes

1 Bibliothèque Mazarine, Paris: Rés. 5028. See E. Hatin, *Les gazettes de Hollande et la presse clandestine aux XVIIe et XVIIIe siècles* (Paris, 1865), pp. 54–5.
2 W. P. Sautijn Kluit, 'De eerste courantier in Europa,' *De Nederlandsche spectator* 25 (1880): 59–60.
3 Emm. de Bom, 'Abraham Verhoeven de eerste courantier van Europa?,' *Tijdschrift voor boek- en bibliotheekwezen* 1 (1903): 27–51.
4 Dahl published the results of his research in a number of articles: 'Amsterdam – Earliest Newspaper Centre of Western Europe. New Contributions to the History of the First Dutch and French Corantos,' *Het Boek* 25 (1938–39): 160–97. (This is an expanded translation of his 'Nya bidrag till Hollands och Frankrikes äldsta tidningshistoria,' *Lychnos* [1938]); 'Amsterdam, Cradle of English Newspapers,' *The Library* 5(4) (1950): 166–79; 'Les premiers journaux en français,' in F. Dahl, F. Petibon, and M. Boulet, *Les débuts de la presse française. Nouveau aperçus* (Göteborg and Paris, 1951), pp. 1–15. A comprehensive study of early newspapers was announced by Dahl, but to date has not appeared.
5 F. Dahl, *Dutch Corantos 1618–1650. A Bibliography Illustrated with 334 Facsimile Reproductions of Corantos Printed 1618–1625 and an Introductory Essay on Seventeenth Century Stop Press News* (Göteborg, 1946).
6 See G. C. Gibbs, 'The Role of the Dutch Republic as the Intellectual Entrepôt of Europe in the Seventeenth and Eighteenth Centuries,' *Bijdragen en mededelingen betreffende de geschiedenis der Nederlanden* 86 (1971): 323–49, here p. 329. See also Otto S. Lankhorst, 'Bibliografie van Nederlandse couranten vóór 1800. Is het geen tijd om 'zulk een kolossaal gebouw' op te trekken?,' *Open. Vaktijdschrift voor bibliothecarissen, literatuuronderzoekers en documentalisten* 27 (1995): 232–4.
7 H. de la Fontaine Verwey, *De wereld van het boek. Rede uitgesproken ter aanvaarding van het ambt van bizonder hoogleraar in de wetenschap van het boek en de bibliographie aan de Universiteit van Amsterdam op 10 mei 1954* (Haarlem, 1954), p. 21.
8 In the Netherlands, nothing has yet been produced resembling the bibliographies published in other countries, for instance, in Germany, E. Bögel and E. Blühm, eds, *Die Deutsche Zeitungen des 17. Jahrhunderts. Ein Bestandsverzeichnis mit historischen und bibliographischen Angaben* (Bremen, 1971); in the UK, C. Nelson and M. Seccombe, eds, *British Newspapers and Periodicals 1641–1700. A Short-title Catalogue of Serials Printed in England, Scotland, Ireland, and British America* (New York, 1987); and in France, J. Sgard, ed., *Dictionnaire des journaux: 1600–1789* (Paris, 1991).
9 See F. Dahl, *Dutch Corantos 1618–1650. A Bibliography* (Göteborg, 1946), pp. 33–69.
10 Gibbs, *op. cit.*, p. 329.
11 For the correspondance with Claessen, see H. Borst, 'Van Hilten, Broersz en Claessen: handel in boeken en actueel drukwerk tussen Amsterdam en Leeuwarden rond 1639,' *De zeventiende eeuw* 8 (1992): 131–8; for the correspondence with Leyniers, see P. Begheyn SJ, *Abraham Leyniers. Een Nijmeegs boekverkoper uit de zeventiende eeuw. Met een uitgave van zijn correspondentie* (Nijmegen, 1992).
12 Catalogues have appeared of several collections of Dutch pamphlets. The best-known collection is kept in the Koninklijke Bibliotheek in The Hague, see W. P. C. Knuttel, *Catalogus van de pamflettenverzameling berustende in de Koninklijke Bibliotheek* ('s-Gravenhage, 1889–1920; reprinted with additions: Utrecht, 1978, 10 vols), 9 vols. This collection is on microfilm, published by IDC in Leiden: *Dutch Pamphlets: ca.1486–1648, 1649–1750, 1751–1853.* Section I: *The Collection in the Royal Library, The Hague* (Zug-Leyden, 1980–1998). On the role of pamphlets in politics in the Republic, see C. E. Harline, *Pamphlets, Printing, and Political Culture in the Early Dutch Republic* (Dordrecht, 1987).
13 G. de Bruin, *Geheimhouding en verraad. De geheimhouding van staatszaken ten tijde van de Republiek (1600–1750)* ('s-Gravenhage: 1950), p. 433.

14 For handwritten newspapers the most important study remains A. Stolp, *De eerste couranten in Holland. Bijdrage tot de geschiedenis der geschreven nieuwstijdingen* (Haarlem: 1938). Unfortunately, there is no inventory of these preserved newspapers.
15 N. Japikse, ed., *Resolutiën der Staten-Generaal van 1576 tot 1609: vol. 7, 1590–1592* ('s-Gravenhage, 1923), p. 294.
16 About father and son Bilderbeeck, see Stolp, *op. cit.*, pp. 36–48. Both were appointed by the States-General as 'agents' in Cologne. Hendrik senior from 1591 to 1608; Hendrik junior from 1608 to 1653. Later in that century, this office was occupied by the grandson, Hendrick. See O. Schutte, *Repertorium der Nederlandse vertegenwoordigers, residerende in het buitenland 1584–1810* ('s-Gravenhage, 1976), pp. 181–3.
17 H. A. Enno van Gelder, *Getemperde vrijheid. Een verhandeling over de verhouding van Kerk en Staat in de Republiek der Verenigde Nederlanden en de vrijheid van meninsguiting in zake godsdienst, drukpers en onderwijs, gedurende de 17e eeeuw* (Groningen, 1972), p. 186.
18 Stolp, *op. cit.*, p. 31; and M. Keblusek, *Boeken in de hofstad. Haagse boekcultuur in de Gouden Eeuw* (Hilversum, 1997), p. 120.
19 Keblusek, *op. cit.*, p. 32.
20 Stolp, *op. cit.*, p. 45.
21 Keblusek, *op. cit.*, p. 60.
22 Gelder, *op. cit.*, p. 187.
23 'Placaet, jegens seditieuse propoosten, conspiratien, heymelijcke aenslagen ende stroyen van Pasquillen. Den 27 November 1587,' *Groot Placaet-boeck, vervattende de placaten, ordonnantien ende edicten van de Hoogh Mogende Heeren Staten Generael der Vereenighde Nederlanden* ('s-Gravenhage, 1658), , vol. 1, col. 435–6. Prohibition on publication of written material leading to: 'onrust, oneenicheyt van de Lande, naedeel ofte vermindering der authoriteyt ende der Overigheyt, Magistraten, Vroetschappen, Regenten van de voorschreve Steden ofte Leden van dien, ofte oock concernerende den staet van den voorschreven Lande.'
24 Cited in G. de Bruin, *Geheimhouding en verraad. De geheimhouding van staatszaken ten tijde van de Republiek (1600–1750)* ('s-Gravenhage, 1991), pp. 85–6.
25 The most important Acts are mentioned in Bruin, *op. cit.*, pp. 414–15. For more information on censorship in the Republic in general, see S. Groenveld, 'The Mecca of Authors? States Assemblies and Censorship in the Seventeenth-Century Dutch Republic,' in A. C. Duke and C. A. Tamse, eds, *Too Mighty to Be Free. Censorship and the Press in Britain and the Netherlands* (Zutphen, 1987), pp. 63–86.
26 'Placaet, op 't selve subject als de voorgaende. Verbiedende mede eenige Acten van Staet, ende de gemeene Regieringe betreffende, te drucken, verkoopen, &c. In date den 4 Ianuarij 1651,' *Groot Placaet-boeck*, ('s-Gravenhage, 1658), vol. 1, col. 445–52.
27 Act of the States of Holland, 28.2.1652. See Keblusek, *op. cit.*, p. 284.
28 Keblusek, *op. cit.*, pp. 134–5.
29 W. P. Sautijn Kluit, 'De Rotterdamsche courant,' *Handelingen en mededeelingen van de Maatschappij der Nederlandsche Letterkunde te Leiden* (1878), pp. 3–92, here, pp. 4–17.
30 Bruin, *op. cit.*, p. 424.
31 W. P. Sautijn Kluit, 'De Haarlemsche courant,' *Handelingen en mededeelingen van de Maatschappij der Nederlandsche Letterkunde te Leiden* (1873), pp. 3–132, here, p. 19.
32 Two recent publications mainly about the French protests against the Dutch newspapers in the eighteenth century: Jeroom Vercruysse, 'La réception politique des journaux de Hollande, une lecture diplomatique,' *La diffusion et la lecture des journaux de langue française sous l'Ancien Régime. Actes du colloque international Nimègue 3–5 juin 1987* (Amsterdam and Maarssen, 1988), pp. 39–47; Pierre Rétat, 'Les gazetiers de Hollande et les puissances politiques. Une difficile collaboration,' *Dix-huitième siècle* 25 (1993): 319–35.
33 W. P. Sautijn Kluit, 'De Amsterdamsche courant,' *Bijdragen voor vaderlandsche geschiedenis en oudheidkunde* (1868), n.s., vol. 5, pp. 209–92.
34 W. P. Sautijn Kluit, 'De Rotterdamsche courant,' *op. cit.*, pp. 5–7.

35 W. P. Sautijn Kluit, 'De Amsterdamsche courant,' *op. cit.*, pp. 243–4: 'Instructie voor de stads courantier, waer naer hy zig in 't toecomende preciselyk zal hebben te reguleren.'

36 See *Groot Placaet-boeck* ('s-Gravenhage, 1725), vol. 5, pp. 691–2.

7 Instruments of political information in France

Jean-Pierre Vittu

Until about the 1970s, seventeenth-century France was usually viewed in the most contradictory terms by scholars. In the very period when new instruments of political information began to flourish in France, it was claimed, particularly strict controls regulated their use. The seventeenth century was the century of the periodical press; and while notices of every kind proliferated, improvements in the postal system aided in their diffusion. However, theories concerning absolutist order and control consigned government affairs to the realm of the 'secret of the prince.' And, scholars insisted, the theories were carried out in practice. Censored and manipulated from above, the new proponents of information functioned mainly for encouraging consensus, while critical reflection, excluded from political matters, sought expression in literary and artistic fields. There a 'public sphere' would be formed, the bearer of modernity.[1]

More recently, studies on monarchical administration, political polemic, and the periodical press have offered a more nuanced picture. We may now observe the operation of a demand for information – restricted, certainly, but by no means negligible. And we now see that the 'secret of the prince' could be sacrificed in order to gain public confidence. Political information was thus part of a complex pattern of negotiation between the king and the people of France, which created a specific field for the expression of opinion.[2]

News and information at the beginning of the seventeenth century

Monarchical news

From the beginning of the seventeenth century, political information depended largely upon the monarchy. Painful memories had been left by the powerful influence of uncontrolled news and rumours during the religious and civil disturbances of the second half of the previous century.[3] For this reason, the construction of absolutism in the first three decades of the seventeenth century had been accompanied by controls on the various types of ceremonial information and on the new forms of printed information – not only in order to publicize decisions, actions, and victories, but also to moderate the influence of parties and factions.

The celebration of the sovereign by means of public information originated in Henry IV's efforts to ensure his succession to the throne of France after the assassination of Henry III. After the king's abjuration and coronation at Chartres in February 1594, each subjugation or conquest of cities by the League forces was celebrated by a Te Deum exalting the victories and proclaiming the legitimacy of the king. Following the local processions that continued to proliferate during the reign of Henry III and during the first years of that of Henry IV, the Te Deum marked a social and spatial expansion of the celebration of the sovereign's actions, since royal letters prescribing the actions of grace (processions, bonfires, and the Te Deum) were diffused throughout the realm. These letters specified the circumstances as well as the events that had occasioned the public solemnities, and the audience for this news was expanded to the extent that civil or religious authorities caused it to be printed.[4]

While the diffusion of information by way of the Te Deum was an offshoot of state ceremonial announcements, the announcement of royal decisions followed a well-established ritual that developed according to its own internal logic. In both cases, two forms of information joined together: namely, the written and spoken public proclamation. In fact, a minor Parisian official of the Prevost of Paris was responsible for guaranteeing public notice of proclamations of laws that had first been read in the Grand Chamber of Parliament.[5] This royal position, known to have existed at least since the end of the fourteenth century, was long threatened by tribunals and administrators demanding more control over the diffusion of their decrees. In the first decades of the seventeenth century, the Chamber of Justice and the Exchequer attempted once again to establish their own system of proclamations. But the official town crier managed to obtain confirmation of his monopoly in 1630, thus reinforcing the power of the sovereign over this sort of diffusion, in spite of the pretensions to autonomy asserted by the various sovereign courts sitting in the capital.

In the exercise of his function, the official town crier rode through Paris on horseback accompanied by three trumpeters who also owned their positions; and in the appointed places, after the trumpets sounded, the officer made his proclamation. Before reading the proclamation in question, he indicated the authority from which it emanated. Finally, before continuing on the circuit that would take him down another major thoroughfare of the capital or the suburbs, the town crier posted a copy of the proclamation on a wall or fountain. The few known itineraries of royal officers do not seem to correspond exactly either to the demography or the functions of the major areas of the city. Not all the busiest areas were visited; the most densely populated areas were left out. The itinerary was modified from time to time – less in connection with the nature of the proclamations than with a series of customary practices, revealing the difference between the political space as conceived by the authorities and the real space of the capital.

Toward the middle of the sixteenth century, the use of printing contributed to the proliferation of public postings. Notices that had hitherto been hand copied in limited numbers, one for each of the sixteen quarters of the city, were now printed up in quantity: fifty to a hundred for publications regarding local affairs, 300 to 400 for urgent proclamations (for example, the calling of troops to serve under the flag), and as many as 600 for new laws. As public posting became more frequent, official sheets were printed in such a way as to attract the attention of passers-by through their *in-plano* (unfolded) format (depending on the paper manufacturer, perhaps 35 by 43–59 centimetres). The arms of France and the diction 'de par le Roy' or 'Ordonnance du Roy' in large print at the top indicated their origin.

The choice of places, the solemnity of the cry and trumpets, the public posting, and the obvious presence of royal symbols, all gave these publications significance even for those unable to read them. Readers, listeners, or passers-by received all or part of the elements of information whereby the authorities accompanied their decisions, and this varied reception created different circles of reception of events and political realities.

Besides these forms of public proclamation, the authorities also diffused their decisions and had them printed in the form of broadsheets or brochures which, according to content and circumstances, might be distributed or sold. The practice of diffusing these official publications dated from the first age of the printing press; and the pieces that have survived seem to indicate a particularly robust development during the civil wars at the beginning of the sixteenth century, setting the standard for the subsequent period. Furthermore, to guarantee the copies' fidelity to the original manuscripts, the authorities made exclusive use of a small number of printers. These printers remained attached to the monarchy and to the men who made the decisions.

This kind of official work was certainly a profitable business for the Parisian and provincial printers who engaged in it, as we know about more than 500,000 printed acts from 1598 to 1643 alone. A number of court cases indicate that the printers to the king vigorously defended their monopoly against fellow-printers who reproduced the texts; for apart from the official distribution network, there was a market for them. In March 1636, the Prevost of Paris fixed the maximum price that street vendors might demand for edicts. And in the same year a printer to the king in Paris filed counterfeiting charges against a bookseller in Troyes, before finally engaging the same bookseller as his exclusive agent. Publications subject to this wider market concerned the reformation of coinage, creation of offices, judgments concerning tax farms, or laws applicable to a particular part of the realm. Such topics might suggest a much more restricted audience than the one addressed by proclamation via cry and posting, one made up of holders of royal offices and members of the legal profession; yet there were other categories that might be equally interested: namely, merchants and property owners, or administrators.

Besides ordinances or edicts, there were also official notices concerning royal ceremonies – especially descriptions of coronations, but also royal or princely visits to major cities. These placards, distributed and sold at the location of the ceremonies, eventually entered the commercial network, as we know from the reproductions by printers in other cities.

Private networks

Thus the monarchy diffused the elements of political information by the expedient of celebrations and proclamations aiming to encourage agreement with the sovereign's decisions. But various private circuits permitted a fairly broad diffusion of news.

Private correspondence often furnishes evidence of networks of information established by a well-known personage or a literary figure. For instance, the correspondence of the Provençal scholar Claude-Nicolas Fabri de Peiresc (1580–1637) not only covered all of France but extended to England, the United Provinces, the Low Countries, the Empire, and Italy. Following the classic form of the literary exchange, his letters carried political news along with erudite reflections.[6]

Other sorts of exchanges made use of the institutional resources of bodies or communities. Great correspondence networks linked the various houses of the same religious order. Merchants and foreign students made use of similar circuits. The 'German Nation' of the University of Orleans paid its own messenger to carry letters to and from Germany; it also paid newsletter writers in Paris to send them whatever German news they might have.[7] This example demonstrates the importance of information professionals working alongside the members of a particular community who furnished news to their correspondents. Consider also the foreign agents who provided reports to merchants, or veritable postal agents, such as the Thurm and Taxis within the Empire.[8]

Information purveyors also operated within the networks of the great nobles.[9] Many persons in the service of resident foreigners – commissioners, interpreters, guides, preceptors – were also in the business of compiling manuscript gazettes. For instance, a German named Jean Epstein, living in Paris, worked for the German Nation of Orleans as well as for various nobles.[10] Literary figures belonging to the clientele of important personages exercised the same functions. From the 1630s onward, the poet Jean Chapelain played this role for the duke of Longueville and various officers.[11]

These 'agents of information' maintained two-way relations with the first printed genres of news: from them they drew some of their stories, and to them they furnished still other stories. In fact, from the beginning of printing in France, two sorts of news sheets were marketed. Special editions a few pages long, known as *occasionnels* and containing information about contemporary events, were known already in 1488; they developed particularly during the Italian wars of the subsequent decades. From 1529 another sort of publication emerged, the so-called *canards*, which offered sensationalist or shocking stories illustrated by images and distinguished by a suggestive headline that a street hawker could use as an advertisement.[12]

Both of these types of publications carried political information. The *occasionnels* reported on wars, victories, and royal ceremonies (coronations, entrances, weddings, etc.), whereas the *canards* presented prodigies and miracles in a fashion favourable to the sovereign or one of the parties (the Church, the League members, the Huguenots).[13] They were mostly printed in Paris or in Lyons, and they could be widely distributed by the street vendors who wandered the streets of the cities and the travelling salesmen who went to the fairs or rural markets.[14] And if the style of the texts sometimes appeared to indicate a supposed audience among the educated, the frightful images that accompanied them and the sensationalist cries of the vendors widened their appeal even to the illiterate passer-by.

Information and partisanship

Henry IV never succeeded in preventing the publication of handbills put out by parties in their own defence or aristocrats trying to gain support or opposing him – notably, in the conspiracy of Biron in 1602. None the less, the *occasionnels* published in this period mainly concerned foreign affairs. Thanks to the journal kept by Pierre de l'Estoile, an officer of justice who collected placards and manuscript or printed information sheets sold in Paris, we can observe, in particular, the proliferation of anti-Spanish libels. They were attributed to various Parisian personages including Guillaume, also called Mathurine, the court buffoon and king's 'fool.' The practice of using a disguise based on a real or fictitious personage, as also the procedure of mixing coarseness with literary allusions, mark these as productions aimed at cultivated circles, including notables or minor officials – just those whom the authorities hoped to shield from any League influences. And indeed, the statements of Estoile, as well as his habit of copying and reselling whatever he could get his hands on, indicate that the greatest curiosity about this kind of information was within these circles.[15]

The assassination of the king began a new period of political struggles that once again mobilized the purveyors of information. And the regency of Marie de Médicis, the campaigns of Louis XIII and the Fronde all signal noteworthy increases in the production of handbills, pamphlets and propaganda prints.[16]

The minority of Louis XIII

The meeting of the Estates General in 1614 was accompanied by a multitude of booklets and pamphlets written in the form of *occasionnels* . In fact, the number of publications in the two-year period of the Estates surpassed that of the sheets published during the ten years of the League war. Perhaps 1,500,000 copies came on the market. As the regency period offered an open field for political debate, every argument, including foreign policy, reform, taxation and the choice of ministers, was seized by the clans and parties in an effort to influence the weakened system. Royal propaganda focused on the aristocracy, the royal officers, and the privileged bodies. These pamphlets came mostly from Parisian presses, and their publication occurred especially in the key moments of the crisis. At this time, the royal party succeeded better than its adversaries in making itself heard, since it kept the Parisian presses under control and possessed the financial means for paying writers and booksellers, thanks to Sully's financial acumen. While the texts still reflected the old cleavages of the time of the League, their publication under fictitious shibboleths joined a new kind of battle; they appeared in large quantities and their argumentation included daring references to the Holy Scripture.[17]

From the time of the palace revolution of April 1617 that eliminated Concini and displaced the Queen Mother, the royal party multiplied the number of placards, handbills and prints in which the assassination and the subsequent popular disturbances were interpreted in a sense favourable to the sovereign. Euphemistic language served to erase every subversive aspect of the events and absolve the young king of any responsibility for the crime on which his power was based. In 1619 and 1620, the conflict between Louis XIII and his mother was accompanied by publications emanating from authors engaged by the various parties involved. Thus, around 1620, the king's favourite, the duc de Luynes, was attacked by a series of pamphlets, some of them produced by booksellers connected to the Protestant party.[18] In the same period, Richelieu also made use of the news sheets in his bid for power; but as soon as he entered the Council, culminating in 1625–26, he became the object of violent campaigns inspired by the Queen Mother and the Catholic party, making use of foreign printers and the black market.[19]

These battles of the books demonstrate the special role of printed information in troubled times: namely, that of justifying the positions of the parties or factions involved, in order to maintain the fidelity of the clans or to animate their patronage networks, while sapping the legitimacy of the adversary in the eyes of his partisans, and even more, in those of the king.

Richelieu and information

Richelieu must have paid close attention to the new importance of printed information in this period; and this impression must have been reinforced in the 1630s, when the *Parlement* of Paris began to produce more posters informing Parisians about their decisions as well as those of the ordinary courts or Châtelet. In publishing their decisions concerning public security, and especially, the rules protecting individuals, these posters participated in the *Parlement's* struggle to defend local autonomies against the centralizing programmes of the cardinal.[20] Not content merely to condemn the pamphlets and persecute the booksellers that diffused them, Richelieu formed his own group of paid publicists to defend his policies against the rumours circulated by his adversaries and by foreign powers.[21] Apart from clerks and magistrates, he recruited young writers seeking patronage and social improvement; and some of these, such as Hay du Chastelet and Sirmonde, were rewarded for their efforts by access to the French Academy – itself yet another propaganda instrument created by the cardinal.[22]

The notion of influencing and directing public judgments was clearly evinced also in the hundreds of publications celebrating the surrender of La Rochelle on 28 October 1628.[23] On the other hand, a veritable hunger for news is apparent in contemporary correspondence, where writers constantly copied the printed pieces or mentioned the dispatch of *occasionnels* or *canards* to a friend far from the centres of diffusion. The same hunger is apparent in the success of the *Mercure françois*, a collection published irregularly from 1610 or 1611 and containing all or part of the news sheets. By the time it became a regular annual from 1621, it too passed under the control of Richelieu.[24] And the same effort to reach the public was behind the creation of the first veritable periodical of political infor-mation in France, the *Gazette*.

In the first years of the seventeenth century, printers and booksellers elsewhere in Europe had begun to publish journals with various periodicity and based on compilations of correspondence. The first appeared soon after 1600 in Strasbourg and Wolfenbüttel; soon examples of these gazettes appeared in Basel and in the United Provinces (the famous corantos), and elsewhere.[25]

These sheets arrived in France, and the agents of information we have been discussing utilized the news in them, adding whatever they might get from the ordinary postal carriers. We can scarcely be surprised that Jean Epstein, an associate of the printer Jean Martin and the bookseller Louis Vendosme, followed this model in publishing a periodical entitled *Nouvelles ordinaires de divers entroits* from 1631 in Paris. Théophraste Renaudot, who had founded a 'bureau d'addresses' furnishing job announcements and placement services as well as small loans, seems to have begun his *Gazette* very soon after Epstein's publication, but thanks to support from Richelieu, he was quickly able to establish a monopoly for his own journal against any less-favoured competitors.[26]

Situated within the corridors of power from the very outset, the *Gazette* appeared each week, and until the end of 1631 it consisted of a single fascicle made up of a quarto half-sheet with the title at the top. Subsequently, Renaudot added a second fascicle of the same size with a title borrowed from his unfortunate competitors: *Nouvelles ordinaires*. From February 1632 to December 1633, the journalist also offered his readers a monthly supplement entitled, *Relation des nouvelles du monde receuës tout le mois de...*, containing reflections on the past month's events. But this *Relation* was short-lived, as the monarchy wished the political periodical to offer only 'reports' and no 'reflections.' The model of the gazette was thus established. It was to be a political journal with one or two pages of print, issued several times a month and presenting general information in the form of reports, often dispatches dated from the particular locations where the information originated. Renaudot gathered his information in the customary manner, by using the ordinary couriers as well as gazettes from elsewhere and occasional pieces produced in foreign countries. In addition, he relied upon professional informers, such as Jean Epstein, or government agents such as Pierre d'Hozier. To be sure, he also received statements dictated by Richelieu or by the king himself, confirming the official character of the periodical.

As the *Gazette*'s success encouraged imitations in the provinces (Aix and Rouen), Renaudot sold the right to reprint his periodical in exchange for an annual payment of £200 to £300. Thanks to these contracts, the *Gazette* was reproduced, beginning in the 1630s, in Rouen, Lyon, Bordeaux, and later in Dijon and Tours, in perhaps as many copies as the 1,200-issue printings in Paris.[27] The *Gazette*'s success did nothing to depress the market for *occasionnels*. But these latter publications eventually began to assume the *Gazette*'s in-quarto format. Likewise, in competition with the *Gazette*, the *occasionnels* began to focus even more narrowly on providing extended coverage of exceptional events.[28] Renaudot responded to the demand for more detailed reports by providing a fascicle of *Extraordinaires* each month giving 'single simple narrations of particularly noteworthy things.'[29]

Thus, in the first third of the century, the different available outlets, public and private, offered political information to an audience interested in news, particularly in urban areas, an audience mainly composed of royal officers and notables, as the registers of a bookseller in Grenoble clearly demonstrate. From 1646 to 1663, this bookseller, Jean Nicolas, sold or rented out his reprints of the *Gazette* to clients in Die, Valence, Gap, Nîmes and even in Besançon; and they included mainly members of the robe nobility and the clergy.[30] The importance of the news sheets, placards, or brochures, from the point of view of those in power, was noticed and understood by a political thinker like Gabriel Naudé. In his *Considérations politiques sur les coups d'état*, 1639, he explained the sovereign's need to distribute among the people 'clandestine booklets, manifestoes, apologies and declarations, artfully designed to lead them by the nose.'[31]

The Fronde

The Fronde overturned the entire system that had been put in place by Richelieu. The Parisian troubles were accompanied by an unprecedented mobilization of the presses, made all the more singular by the implementation of every possible form of print: pamphlets, booklets, handbills, brochures, cards, as well as broadsheets.

Between 1648 and 1653 over 5,000 pamphlets appeared, as against only 858 during the troubles occasioned by Louis XIII's coming of age in 1614–1615. Some 10 per cent of these publications emanated from outside Paris, principally Bordeaux. Called *mazarinades*, they were particularly numerous during the worst moments of the crisis when Paris was under siege: thus, 2,000 titles appeared in 1649 and 1,600 or so appeared in 1652.[32] Although the entire production was designated by the name *mazarinades*, indicating that portion of them which was hostile to the cardinal, topics varied widely. Size, too, varied widely: from handbills, occasionally including illustrations, to booklets of 8, 16, or 32 pages. And every sort of genre was pressed into the service of the political debate, including letters, discourses, narratives, poems, songs, and whatever might be provided by professional writers like Scarron (on behalf of Retz) and Sarasin (on behalf of Condé). Naudé wrote for Mazarin when the latter finally, and belatedly, began to organize his editorial counter-offensive.[33]

If the *mazarinades* adopted mainly the classic forms of the *ocasionnel* or the manifesto, they also imitated periodicals; and there are thirty or so publications entitled *Courrier*..., *Mercure*..., *Journal*... between 1648 and 1652.[34] During the first months of 1649, a periodical entitled the *Courrier françois* appeared in Paris, where the *Gazette* was circulating with difficulty; and counterfeit versions of the *Extraordinaires* of Renaudot were published in 1650 and 1651, to the greater profit of the street vendors with whom he had constantly been in conflict.

The different parties engaged in the Fronde also utilized various printed materials with a more immediate impact: bills and placards. Thus, on 11 February 1649, La Valette distributed throughout the faubourg a printed tract favourable to Mazarin and entitled, *Lis et fais*, only because he was unable to post the text in public places; and on 4 July 1652, the municipal assembly, blocked within the Hôtel de Ville by a strike, vainly tried to avoid a massacre by throwing handwritten 'scraps of paper out of the windows explaining how it had resolved and concluded the union of the princes.'[35] Printed placarding, a costly operation, was utilized by both the queen and the cardinal. When they were taking refuge in Reuil, in January 1649, they had a broadsheet posted, which they later issued as a pamphlet. But in November 1650, Mazarin's enemies posted his portrait with a noose around his neck, while hostile pamphlets were being sold.[36] Evidence of such postings comes from memorialists like Dubuisson Aubenay or Vallier, as well as from Abraham de Wicquefort, who recorded them, along with publications of pamphlets and distributions of handbills, in the handwritten newsletters he sent to the duc August de Brunswick-Lunebourg. For the latter, Wicquefort also copied 400 political manuscripts belonging to the collections of Mazarin, Séguier and the treasury of Chartes, all made suddenly accessible by the exile of the court.[37]

An examination of this impressive mass of printed material reveals two sets of connections: on the one hand, we can observe the clusters of texts that appeared in direct opposition to one another; on the other hand, we find various genres of writing or editorial forms grouped together in a single volley, including placards, pamphlets and handbills. Indeed, politics during the Fronde invaded every form of publication. Print became the chief field of battle and the pens of the various camps utilized one or another vector according to the strategy of the moment. At first these genres and these forms may appear to have functioned very well according to the criteria of Naudé: to persuade and manipulate, leading readers 'by the nose' and turning them into simple spectators of 'political theatre.' Yet they also seem to have functioned as the weapons of the actors within this theatre: as images of the force of the clans and pressure groups in the conflict, constantly calling for reiteration by new reprints.[38]

Absolutism and information

The return to order at the end of the Fronde was marked by increased control over the various instruments of information whose importance within the 'political theatre' the conflict had demonstrated so clearly.[39]

The reinforcement of control

In 1654, evoking his rebellious youth, Henri de Campion wrote, 'It is certain that when I consider the liberties that the French have always taken in their complaints and expressions of discontent ... I can hardly recognize them in the French state as presently reformed.'[40] And indeed, with the development of the administrative monarchy, surveillance of the Parisian and provincial press became more and more strict. The new legislation of 1618, 1629, and 1650 completed the structure begun with the Moulins ordinance of 1566 for the regulation of printing permissions and privileges. The newly reinforced government used this legislative arsenal effectively against the *Mazarinades* from 1656 through 1661.[41] And during the quarrel between Jansenists and Jesuits following the publication of Pascal's *Provinciales*, the government intervened directly in 1656; after that the Jansenists, deprived of their exalted protection, had to change the form and place of the edition.[42] The beginning of Louis XIV's personal rule marked a new stage in this surveillance; and the booksellers who resorted to pamphlet production as a way out of the economic downturn ended up in the Bastille.[43] Indeed, the network of clandestine presses that Madame Foucquet had engaged to multiply the pamphlets defending her disgraced husband was quickly discovered. In October 1663, royal officers arrested her Parisian typographer; and in Spring of the following year they got her provincial printers – four brothers working in Rouen, Évreux, La Flèche, and Saumur.[44]

Pamphlets might also be distributed in manuscript form; and against the news writers and hawkers who distributed such items, the monarchy exercised the same severity as against the printers. State documents and Bastille prison registers with regard to the period following the Fronde testify to a continuous persecution – of writers furnishing handwritten news to the nobility in 1660–61, of compilers of newsletters who gathered information from Germany in 1662, of writers hired by Madame Foucquet to defend her husband in 1663–64.[45] These cases give precious insights into the world of the handwritten news sheets, revealing their compilers among minor officialdom and the lower clergy, their transportation, their copying by lackeys or, in one case, by a tavern keeper, their diffusion by servants or by frequenters of the Palace of Justice, whose galleries were reputed to be thronged with newsletter writers.[46] In 1666 the *Parlement* reinforced its repressive arsenal by determining to apply to the newsletter writers the same penalties inflicted upon pamphlet printers: the whip, and then banishment, and finally galley service for repeat offenders. La Reynie, from the time of his nomination as the chief of police in Paris in 1667, built an effective system of control allowing him to respond to the concerns Colbert expressed in the following missive: 'I referred to the king what you wrote to me concerning the handwritten newsletters. His Majesty desires that you should continue your inquiries concerning the people involved....'[47]

In spite of the repeated arrests and prohibitions of 1670,[48] the newsletters continued to flourish so openly that in February 1672, in his comedy *La Comtesse d'Escarbagnas*, Molière made fun of the court's impotence in the face of news writers who had overrun even a small city like Angoulême. In this play, one character speaks thus of another: 'He showed me at first two pages of paper filled to the margins with a huge heap of twaddle from what he called the most reliable source in the world.'[49] The various wars in fact fed the hunger for news to an extraordinary degree throughout the reign of Louis XIV, as Donneau de Visé noted specifically with respect to the Dutch conflict: 'I saw news writers during the campaign of 1673 who received letters two times a week from bankers in Holland who had much to say that would have come from the field much later.'[50] Audience demands, as revealed by these episodes, in part inspired official attempts to organize the printing industry as well as official attention to royal celebrations.

Organizing the press

Under Colbert's influence, the monarchy perfected a system of press organization in which the industry was involved in its own regulation. Under the pretext of ensuring the survival of booksellers during a period of crisis, the government imposed strict surveillance, carefully distinguishing the various allied professions – printers, binders, and booksellers – and fixing the number who could exercise them, first in Paris in 1667 and then in the provincial cities in 1704. An extension of the laws on printing privileges that had been introduced in 1566 by the Moulins ordinance allowed the establishment of a system of pre-publication censorship in exchange for guarantees of monopolies on certain editions, i.e., privileges, enforced by the officials of the booksellers' corporation themselves. Finally, the statutes of 1686 completed the dispositions regarding travelling salesmen and the importation of foreign books. All of these measures strongly favoured the Parisian printers and booksellers, who were after all easier to control, as they began to turn their attention to the periodical press.[51]

Besides the *Gazette*, which had a monopoly on 'official' news, there were the *Journal des savants* and the *Mercure galant*. The *Journal*, a weekly publication founded in 1665 and specializing in the presentation of new books, diffused political information among the learned by way of extracts of books about current wars or civil disturbances, or of the latest examples of two genres that had developed during the last third of the century: namely, memoirs and histories of cities.[52] The *Mercure*,[53] founded in 1672 by Donneau de Visé, an associate of Corneille, was issued quarterly at first, and then monthly. It had two faces, so to speak. On the one hand, as a magazine of entertainment, it provided 'galant notices,' poems, doggerels, puzzles, and so forth. As a 'worldly' production, it also indicated nominations to government and church positions, exploits of officers on campaign, as well as weddings, baptisms, and deaths of 'persons of high birth' or of great merit. Not to mention contributions to heraldry and genealogy of interest from a political point of view.[54]

Monarchical information evolves

While these developments were going on in the sphere of the periodical press within the system of privileges, other developments occurred in the sphere of ceremonial and ritual information.

During the last third of the century, the posting of official proclamations in Paris experienced a transformation: whereas royal acts were less frequently displayed,[55] decisions from the lieutenant general of police were more frequent than ever before. In fact, Marc-René d'Argenson, the holder of this position from 1697 to 1718, multiplied his postings in order to make Parisians aware of his decisions as well as to inform them about the extent of his mandate. But apart from informing the populace by a sort of educational programme, what really inspired this publicity was the opposition generated among the *Parlement* and the civil and criminal officials of the Châtelet by the lieutenant general's increased powers and brutal procedures. In any case, these Parisian postings also depended upon the world of political information of which they formed a part.[56]

Throughout the reign of Louis XIV, the Te Deum became the centrepiece of royal celebrations, despite the Church's inclination to view itself as the sole body responsible for organizing religious ceremonies and its disapproval of the use of the pulpit for profane purposes. Although the king accepted an accommodation on the first point from the 1670s onward, it remained deaf to the second objection, which would have altered a ritual that had become the sovereign's fundamental instrument for reminding his people about the permanence of war after 1689. In fact, the repetition of these ceremonies and their particular frequency at important moments such as the wars of the league of Augsburg and then of the Spanish Succession (1693, 1703–1704, and 1712–1713–1714[57]) exercised the absolutist will to control while symbolically demonstrating the presence of the king to his subjects. The Te Deum belonged to the same phase of monarchical propaganda as the monumental inscriptions, the statues of the king, and especially the illustrated almanacs. The latter also enjoyed a wide distribution, especially in the large cities. Many of them offered a symbolic representation of the principal events of the preceding year (victories, peace settlements), seeking to gain the approval of the reader by the inclusion of long texts or by some pictorial image representing, for instance, 'the people or benevolent assistance.'[58]

The system of ceremonial information evident in the monarchy's efforts to situate political news within its own criteria, however, produced a contradiction: whereas the Te Deum inspired the allegiance of subjects by presenting them with information about the war, the exercise of absolute power as such reinforced the secret of the prince.[59] The monarchy's management of ceremonial information therefore could not extinguish the exercise of consensus, on which the relation between the sovereign and his people was based. The establishment of a system of periodical information based on the same exigencies demonstrates the precise limits of this system of opinion. I shall call this 'contained opinion.'

Contained opinion

Printed news

The possibility of defending book privileges in the tribunals of the whole kingdom encouraged provincial booksellers to collaborate with periodical promoters in order to share in the press market. Contracts were drawn up authorizing various reprints of the *Mercure galant*; and if the editions of Bordeaux and Nantes were short-lived, others in Lyons and Toulouse lasted some twenty years. Reprints of the *Gazette* multiplied during the War of the League of Augsburg: from 1687 to 1699 there were thirteen contracts to permit reprinting. Applications came principally from cities north of the Loire that were heavily involved in the administrative structure of the kingdom, usually bishoprics, often the home of a college, of a district's offices, or of a sovereign court.[60] These contracts created the first distribution system of a periodical on a country-wide scale, in which there was a difference of no more than twenty-four hours between the Parisian edition and that of the areas to the North and East of Paris, although up to a week passed before Parisian notices reached the Rhône valley. Thus, toward 1700, the total press run of the *Gazette* in some twenty cities might be around 7,000 or 10,000 copies, with 5,700 to 7,400 copies being added to the 1,500 or 2,000 copies printed in Paris edition.[61]

By the last third of the seventeenth century, a political press in the French language began to develop in the Dutch Republic, alongside the literary press aimed at French-speaking readers. The Huguenot diaspora furnished information for these publications, as well as a cohort of penniless writers capable of editing them. By 1685, new weekly and biweekly gazettes began publishing in Rotterdam, The Hague, and Utrecht, to accompany old standbys like the *Gazette de Layde* started in 1677. Later, the three other new Amsterdam gazettes experienced problems due to French complaints to the Dutch magistrates; and the same happened with the gazettes published in Brussels, Bern, and Geneva.

Apart from a few noisy and expensive diplomatic protests and persecutions aimed at stemming the flow of clandestine sheets into the kingdom, the French monarchy, inspired by Louvois, adopted a tolerant stance based on France's role in this market. Official authorization for the import of packages of these periodicals from Lille, Strasbourg, and some of the Atlantic ports, served to incite the foreign journalists to observe some moderation. These accommodations formed a double market for information, where the French *Gazette* presented news from abroad, concerning diplomacy or war, inspired or endorsed by the king and his ministers, while the foreign gazettes furnished, alongside their version of the same stories, information concerning what was going on in France, within the limits prescribed by the king and his government.[62] The foreign gazettes were certainly costly. In Paris in 1714 the *Gazette d'Amsterdam* cost nearly eight times that of Paris. But they circulated within the same environment of office holders, merchants, and literary figures, as attested by the catalogues of booksellers in Bordeaux, Grenoble, Toulouse, and Troyes, as well as the lists of certain private collections.[63]

Manuscript news

Because of their cost, the handwritten newsletters addressed a more restricted public. Yet the police records and the information we have concerning collections suggest that these continued to be produced, and indeed, increased in production, during the course of the wars.[64]

A recent inventory of the extant series of these newsletters testifies to a varied production, coming either from the solitary study of a single gazetteer or from a workshop filled with a whole army of copyists. These differences suggest the existence of diverse types of producers of manuscript periodicals: the pen-pusher who collects his news in a ministerial office and goes home to copy up what he has learned, the 'collector' who gathers the manuscript newsletters and re-transmits them to his correspondents, the authorized professional in the trade, such as Joachim de Lionne or the abbé Eusèbe Renaudot. The family ties of the former with the minister Hugues de Lionne allowed him to exercise the role of official informer – both in his manuscripts and in person. The latter established an official manuscript news service parallel to his printed *Gazette*, capable of responding to the particular demands of his clients, or obtainable as a supplement to the *Gazette* at extra cost.

Alongside these official workshops, a clandestine trade in newsletters flourished especially during the wars of this late period. In 1700, the Parisian authorities listed no fewer than twenty-five handwritten news writers; and in 1706 they arrested thirty employees of the Foreign service who peddled information collected in their bureaux.[65] However, the police never succeeded in discovering the source of the *Nouvelles ecclésiastiques*, a manuscript newsletter from the Jansenist camp offering information and anecdotes according to its party's interest, and circulated from 1675 by means of a highly disciplined network.[66] Manuscript gazettes thus offered a highly various menu, from the simple repetition of printed stories to personalized compilations, based in part on a choice of newsletters from abroad and official information coming from the ministers.[67]

Distributed clandestinely, through the black market, or by subscription, the manuscript newsletters were sought by a well-to-do public of office holders, lawyers, minor nobles, and priests, as we know from the provenance of the collections that have been preserved. These collections also testify to the existence of collective subscriptions, such as the one shared in 1714 by a group of inhabitants of the Gâtinais.[68] Bookseller records indicate similar practices in regard to printed gazettes: in Grenoble at mid-century such collective subscriptions were offered by the bookseller Nicolas, and in Dieppe in 1702, a merchant paper seller and a bookseller offered the same.[69]

Conclusion

The commercial production of manuscript and printed news, as well as of prints, was clearly designed to respond to a demand for political information. This response paralleled the contemporary development of information produced by the monarchy, administrative or ceremonial. These changes depended on the emergence of larger circuits of diffusion that still did not amount to a homogeneous network throughout the kingdom. Major towns constituted the chief nuclei, particularly those that functioned as administrative, commercial, and cultural centres – as demonstrated by the reprint pattern of the *Gazette*. From these, information spread out unequally through the administrative or commercial channels that penetrated as far as the suburbs and surrounding villages.

The various circles of reception of information depended upon this heterogeneous network. For most people, access to official and ceremonial information was limited to attendance at public prayers or participation in rumours whose echo has come down to us only in times of revolt.[70] The Te Deum functioned partially, as I have said, to reveal the 'secret of the prince' and thereby encourage consensus. And it is significant in this regard that in the midst of the troubles of 1709, Louis XIV directly addressed his subjects to assure them that his adversaries were responsible for slowing down the peace negotiations.[71] The more restricted circles of readers of printed information began to expand considerably during the last quarter of the seventeenth century, to include not only servants of the monarchy, but also officers in the middling ranks, clerks, employees in the bureaux, low-level literary figures, and traders, all of whom might share subscriptions to periodicals and read them in groups, or even participate in public readings of news by the 'vocal newsmongers' who frequented the public promenades of Paris.[72]

So inflamed did this appetite for news become during the late seventeenth-century wars that it became an object of satire in itself.[73] Indeed, after Molière's *La Comtesse d'Escarbagnas*, six theatre pieces and five 'moral tableaux' ridiculed the newsmongers, including the *Charactères* of La Bruyère, in the edition of 1689, where he notes, 'the sublime genius of the newsmonger is an empty discourse on politics.'[74] Although La Bruyère's famous comparison between the characters of Démophile and Basilide, as well as the comments of lesser writers, testified to the widespread curiosity about the 'secret of the prince,' their attacks on the newsmongers and their audiences also roughly demonstrate the limits of the permissible field of information at this time. I have proposed the term 'contained opinion'[75] to indicate the restricted circles that I have outlined in this chapter, where judgments might be made concerning news about cabinet affairs, and where public conversation might go on, within spaces controlled by a sovereign who sought, according to his own avowal, to gain 'the applause of the public,' and to do nothing which the public 'might legitimately censure.'[76]

Notes

1 See Jürgen Habermas, *L'Espace public. Archéologie de la Publicité comme dimension constitutive de la société bourgeoise* (Paris, 1986), tr. Marc B. de Launay, p. 42; note the comments of Lucian Hölscher, 'Öffentlichkeit,' in *Geschichtliche Grundbegriffe* (Stuttgart, 1978), vol. 4, eds Otto Brunner, Werner Conze, and Reinhart Koselleck, especially pp. 430–8; as well as the critique of Habermas in Hélène Merlin, *Public et littérature en France au XVIIe siècle* (Paris, 1994), pp. 24–32.

2 Jean-Pierre Vittu, ' "Le peuple est fort curieux de nouvelles": l'information périodique dans la France des années 1690,' *Studies on Voltaire and the Eighteenth Century* 320 (1994), pp. 105–44.

3 Compare Denis Pallier, *Recherches sur l'imprimerie à Paris pendant la Ligue (1585–1594)* (Geneva, 1976). See also Claude Gauvard, 'Rumeur et stéréotypes à la fin du Moyen Âge,' in *La Circulation des nouvelles au Moyen Âge. XXXIVe Congrès de la S.H.M.E.S. (Avignon, juin 1993)* (Paris, 1994), pp. 157–77.

4 For this and the following, see Michèle Fogel, *Les Cérémonies de l'information dans la France du XVIe au XVIIIe siècle* (Paris, 1989).

5 Edmond Esmonin, 'La publication et l'impression des ordonnances royales sous l'Ancien Régime,' *Études sur la France des XVIIe et XVIIIe siècles* (Paris, 1964), pp. 175–82.

6 Nicolas-Claude Fabri de Peiresc, *Lettres de Peiresc* (Paris, 1888–1898), vol. 7, ed. Philippe Tamizey de Larroque; and Robert Mandrou, *Des humanistes aux hommes de science. XVIème et XVIIème siècles* (Paris, 1973), pp. 146–7 and Appendix.

7 Jules Mathorez, *Les Étrangers en France sous l'Ancien Régime. Vol. 2: Les Allemands, les Hollandais, les Scandinaves* (Paris, 1921), pp. 23, 25. Concerning Italian newsletters from 1582 to 1595 in the Lorraine archive of the Bibliothèque Nationale, see François Moureau, 'Les nouvelles à la main dans le système d'information de l'Ancien Régime,' in *De bonne main. La communication manuscrite au XVIIIe siècle* (Paris and Oxford, 1993), ed. François Moureau, p. 118, note 5. On p. 122 note 38 he also notes that between 1644 and 1648, a postmaster of Basle directed manuscript newsletters from Italy to Strasbourg, Metz, and Paris (Archives Nationales, M 757, no. 1).

8 Hippolyte Roy, *La Vie à la cour de Lorraine sous le duc Henri II (1608–1624)* (Paris and Nancy, 1914), p. 149, indicates the provision of manuscript gazettes to Duke Henry II via the Thurm and Taxis post office in 1624.

9 Johannes Kleinpaul, 'Der Nachrichtendienst der Herzogen von Braunschweig im 16. und 17. Jahrhundert,' *Zeitungswissenschaft* 5 (1930): 82–94; and François Moureau, 'Les nouvelles à la main dans le système d'information de l'Ancien Régime,' *op. cit.*, pp. 117–34.

10 Concerning the employment of Jean Epstein by the German Nation of Orleans, see Jules Mathorez, *Les Étrangers en France, op. cit.* Concerning the services rendered by the same to Jean Chapelain, to the marquis de Montausier and to Bernard of Saxe-Weimar, see Jean Chapelain, *Lettres* (Paris, 1880–1883), vol. 1, ed. Philippe Tamizey de Larroque, pp. 521, 602, 628, 639, 640, 666, 711.

11 Gilles Feyel, *L'Annonce et la nouvelle. La presse d'information en France sous l'Ancien Régime (1630–1788)* (Oxford, 2000); and Christian Jouhaud, 'Sur le statut d'homme de lettres au XVIIe siècle. La correspondance de Jean Chapelain (1595–1674),' *Annales HSS* (1994): 311–47.

12 Jean-Pierre Seguin, *L'Information en France avant le périodique, 517 canards imprimés entre 1529 et 1631* (Paris, 1964); and Roger Chartier, 'Lectures populaires et stratégies éditoriales,' *Histoire de l'édition française* (Paris, 1982), eds H.-J. Martin and R. Chartier, pp. 585–603. According to J.-P. Seguin, the production of *canards* developed particularly between the end of the sixteenth century and the beginning of the seventeenth: thirty-nine were produced between 1550 and 1575, 110 between 1575 and 1600, and 323 between 1600 and 1631.

13 See Roger Chartier, 'La pendue miraculeusement sauvée. Étude d'un occasionnel,' in *Les Usages de l'imprimé* (Paris, 1987), ed. R. Chartier, pp. 83–127. In *L'Information en*

France avant le périodique, *op. cit.*, Jean-Pierre Seguin reviews fifty or so canards concerning prodigies and around thirty others concerning the miraculous punishment of sacreligious acts. See also Rudolf Schenda, *Die Französische Prodigienliteratur in der 2. Hälfte des 16. Jahrhundert* (Munich, 1961).

14 Henri Baudrier, *Bibliographie lyonnaise … troisième série* (Lyons and Paris, 1897), pp. 178–182, with accounts of contracts between merchants of Toul, Puy, Saint-Flour, Pau, Montpellier, Aix-en-Provence, and La Grave with clients of the Lyons bookseller Benoît Rigaud.

15 Alfred Soman, 'Press, Pulpit, and Censorship in France before Richelieu,' *Proceedings of the American Philosophical Society* 120 (1976): 439–63. Also, Jules Mathorez, 'À propos d'une campagne de presse contre l'Espagne,' *Bulletin du Bibliophile* (1913): 313–29 and 365–85; and 'Mathurine et les libelles publiés sous son nom,' *Bulletin du Bibliophile* (1922): 64–79.

16 Hélène Duccini, *Histoire de la France au XVIIe siècle* (Paris, 2000), pp. 34–6, and Jeffrey K. Sawyer, *Printed Poison. Pamphlet Propaganda, Faction Politics, and the Public Sphere in Early Seventeenth Century France* (Berkeley, Los Angeles, and Oxford, 1990).

17 Denis Richet, 'Autour des États-Généraux: la polémique politique en France de 1612 à 1615,' *Représentation et vouloirs politiques. Autour des États généraux de 1614* (Paris, 1982), eds Roger Chartier and Denis Richet, pp. 151–94.

18 Hélène Duccini, 'Regard sur la littérature pamphlétaire en France au XVIIe siècle,' *Revue historique* 528 (1978): 313–39; and 'Une campagne de presse sous Louis XIII: l'affaire Concini, 1614–1617,' in *Histoire sociale, sensibilités collectives et mentalités. Mélanges Robert Mandrou* (Paris, 1985), pp. 291–301.

19 Maximin Deloche, *Autour de la plume du cardinal de Richelieu* (Paris, 1920); D. A. Bailey, 'Les pamphlets de Mathieu de Morgues (1582–1670),' *Revue Française d'Histoire du Livre* 18 (1978): 41–86; and 'Les pamphlets des associés polémistes de Mathieu de Morgues: Marie de Médicis, Gaston d'Orléans et Jacques Chanteloube,' *Revue Française d'Histoire du Livre* 27 (1980): 229–70.

20 Paolo Piasenza, 'Opinion publique, identité des institutions, "absolutisme." Le problème de la légalité à Paris entre le XVIIe et le XVIIIe siècle,' *Revue historique* 290 (1994): 97–142, especially pp. 104–6.

21 Hélène Duccini, 'Les auteurs de libelles dans la France de Louis XIII,' *Lendemains* 29 (1983): 81–92; Henri-Jean Martin, *Livres, pouvoirs et société à Paris au XVIIe siècle (1598–1701)* (Geneva, 1969), p. 465; and Howard M. Solomon, *Public Welfare, Science and Propaganda in Seventeenth-Century France: The Innovations of Théophraste Renaudot* (Princeton, 1972).

22 On these strategies of writers, see Christian Jouhaud, *Les Pouvoirs de la littérature. Histoire d'un paradoxe* (Paris, 2000).

23 Christian Jouhaud, 'Imprimer l'événement. La Rochelle à Paris,' in Roger Chartier, ed., *Les Usages de l'imprimé* (Paris, 1987), pp. 381–438.

24 *Dictionnaire de la presse, 1600–1789. I, Dictionnaire des journaux* (Paris and Oxford: 1991), ed. Jean Sgard, no. 937.

25 H. Gachot, 'Relation, le plus ancien journal de Strasbourg (à partir de 1609),' *Annuaire de la Société des Amis du Vieux Strasbourg* (1976): 36–56; Jean-Pierre Kintz, 'Strasbourg, ville de création du premier hebdomadaire du Saint-Empire germanique,' *Saisons d'Alsace* (1988): 9–14, and the chapter here by Thomas Schröder.

26 Gilles Feyel, *L'Annonce et la nouvelle*, *op. cit.*, pp. 137–49; see also 'Gazette [de France],' no. 492 and 'Nouvelles ordinaires de divers endroits,' no. 1052, in *Dictionnaire de la presse, 1600–1789. I, Dictionnaire des journaux*, *op. cit.*

27 Gilles Feyel, *La Gazette en province à travers ses réimpressions, 1631–1752* (Amsterdam and Maarssen, 1982).

28 Jean-Pierre Seguin, 'Les occasionnels au XVIIe siècle et en particulier après l'apparition de la *Gazette*,' in *L'Informazione in Francia nel Seicento* (Bari and Paris, 1983), pp. 33–59.

29 Gilles Feyel, *L'Annonce et la nouvelle*, *op. cit.*, p. 152 ff.
30 See *idem.*, pp. 256–57; also, Henri-Jean Martin and M. Lecocq, *Livres et lecteurs à Grenoble, les registres du libraire Nicolas, 1645–1668* (Paris and Geneva, 1977), pp. 496–501.
31 Robert Descimon and Christian Jouhaud, *La France du premier XVIIe siècle (1594–1661)* (Paris, 1996), pp. 136–49. Concerning the *occasionnels* and the political pamphlets, see Robert O. Lindsay and John Neu, *French Political Pamphlets 1547–1648, a Catalog of Major Collections in American Libraries* (Madison and London, 1969). See also the abundance of booklets, brochures, books, and placards celebrating the surrender of La Rochelle, in Christian Jouhaud, 'Imprimer l'événement. La Rochelle à Paris,' *Les Usages de l'imprimé* (Paris, 1987), ed. R. Chartier, pp. 381–438.
32 Hubert Carrier, *La Presse et la Fronde (1648–1653): les Mazarinades* (Geneva, 1989–1991), 1, p. 84.
33 Christian Jouhaud, *Mazarinades. La Fronde des mots* (Paris, 1985).
34 *Dictionnaire de la presse, 1600–1789. I, Dictionnaire des journaux* (Paris and Oxford, 1991), ed. Jean Sgard.
35 Dubuisson-Aubenay, *Journal des guerres civiles, 1642–1652* (Paris, 1883–1885), vol. 2, ed. Gustave Saige, p. 249; and Robert Descimon, 'Autopsie du massacre de l'Hôtel de Ville du 4 juillet 1652,' *Annales H.S.S.* (1999): 319–51.
36 Jean Vallier, *Journal (1648–1657)* (Paris, 1902–1918), vol. 2, eds. H. Courteault and P. de Vaissière, p. 213.
37 Robert Mandrou, 'Abraham de Wicquefort et le duc August (1646–1653): sur les relations intellectuelles entre France et Allemagne, un siècle avant les Lumières,' *Wolfenbütteler Beiträge* 3 (1978): 191–234; Abraham de Wicquefort, *Chronique discontinue de la Fronde, 1648–1652* (Paris, 1978), ed. R. Mandrou; and Otto von Heinemann, *Die Handschriften der Herzoglichen Bibliothek zu Wolfenbüttel* (Wolfenbüttel, 1890), pp. x–xi and 71–186.
38 Christian Jouhaud, 'Les libelles en France dans le premier XVIIe siècle: lecteurs, auteurs, commenditaires, historiens,' *XVIIe siècle* 195 (1997): 203–17, especially pp. 204–5.
39 Hubert Carrier, *La Presse et la Fronde*, *op. cit.*, 2: 374–80.
40 Henri de Campion, *Mémoires* (Paris, 1967), ed. Marc Fumaroli, p. 236.
41 *Mémoriaux du Conseil de 1661* (Paris, 1905–7), vol 1, ed. Jean de Boislisle, pp. 27 note 14.
42 Henri-Jean Martin, 'Guillaume Desprez, libraire de Pascal et de Port-Royal,' in *Fédération des sociétés historiques et archéologiques de Paris et de l'Ile de France* 2 (1950): 205–28. The Jansenist polemic was pursued in 1657 and 1658 with the *Écrits des curés de Paris*, and later in 1664 and 1665 with the *Imaginaires* and the *Visionnaires* of Nicole.
43 *Mémoriaux du Conseil de 1661*, *op. cit.*, 2, p. 25, note 12.
44 François Ravaisson, *Archives de la Bastille* (Paris, 1866), pp. 126, 149, 181.
45 Frantz Funck-Brentano, *Figaro et ses devanciers* (Paris, 1909), pp. 86, 103, 104, 106; and *Mémoriaux du Conseil de 1661*, *op. cit.*, 1, p. 19.
46 Frantz Funck-Brentano, *Les Lettres de cachet à Paris, étude suivie d'une liste des prisonniers de la Bastille (1659–1789)* (Paris, 1903), pp. 14–15. See also Jean Donneau de Visé, *Les Nouvelles nouvelles* (Paris, 1663), where the frontispiece represents the gallery of the Palace thronged with news writers hawking their works.
47 Archives Nationales, O 14, fol. 176 recto.
48 Arrêt of 9 December 1670, Biblioteque National, Ms. fr. 22087, no. 180, noted in François Moureau's article cited above.
49 Molière, *La Comtesse d'Escarbagnas*, Act I, Scene i.
50 Cited by Frantz Funck-Brentano, in *L'Ancien Régime* (Paris, 1926), p. 496.
51 Henri-Jean Martin, *Livres, pouvoirs et société*, *op. cit.*, 2, pp. 678–98, 757–69; and *Histoire de l'édition française* (Paris, 1984), *op. cit.*, vol. 2, pp. 64–91.

52 Concerning the *Journal des savants*, see Jean-Pierre Vittu, *Le Journal des savants et la République des lettres* (forthcoming); and *Dictionnaire de la presse, 1600–1789. I, Dictionnaire des journaux*, *op. cit.*, n. 710.
53 Although there is as yet no exhaustive study of the *Mercure galant* of Donneau de Visé, see Gilles Feyel, in *La Presse en France des origines à 1944. Histoire politique et matérielle* (Paris, 1999), pp. 23–4. See also Giovanni Dotoli, 'Il *Mercure galant* di Donneau de Visé,' in *L'informazione in Francia nel seicento* (Bari and Paris, 1984), preface by J.-P. Seguin, pp. 219–82.
54 The particular importance of the *Mercure galant* for information on lineages is attested by the existence of manuscript tables, drawn up in the seventeenth century, of names extracted from the periodical, as in Biblioteque National de France Ms. fr. 33048, and Ms. fr. 32688.
55 Michèle Fogel, *Les Cérémonies de l'information*, *op. cit.*, pp. 116–24.
56 Paolo Piasenza, 'Opinion publique, identité des institutions, "absolutisme",' *op. cit.*
57 Michèle Fogel, *Les Cérémonies de l'information*, *op. cit.*, pp. 447–50.
58 La Bruyère, *Les Caractères* (Paris, 1962), ed. Robert Garapon: 'De la ville,' 13: 'C'est son visage que l'on voit aux almanachs représenter le peuple ou l'assistance.' Concerning the almanacs, see Maxime Préaud, *Les Effets du soleil. Almanachs du siècle de Louis XIV* (Paris, 1995). With regard to the notion of public in the seventeenth century, see Hélène Merlin, *Public et littérature en France au XVIIe siècle*, *op. cit.*
59 Michèle Fogel, *Les Cérémonies de l'information*, *op. cit.*, pp. 235–45.
60 Gilles Feyel, *La Gazette en province*, *op. cit.*, p. 44.
61 *Idem.*, pp. 39 ff and 113.
62 Gilles Feyel, *L'Annonce et la nouvelle*, *op. cit.* pp. 504–21.
63 Gilles Feyel, *La Gazette en province*, *op. cit.*, p. 146 ff.
64 For what follows, *De bonne main. La communication manuscrite au XVIIIe siècle* (Paris and Oxford, 1993), ed. François Moureau; and *Répertoire des nouvelles à la main. Dictionnaire de la presse manuscrite clandestine (XVIe-XVIIIe siècle)* (Oxford, 1999), ed. François Moureau.
65 Respectively, Biblioteque National Ms. fr. 21741, fol. 175, and Joseph Klaits, *Printed Propaganda Under Louis XIV. Absolute Monarchy and Public Opinion* (Princeton, 1976), pp. 51–2.
66 Biblioteque National Ms. fr. 23498–510.
67 Concerning the Roman newsletters, see Brendan Dooley, 'De bonne main: les pourvoyeurs de nouvelles à Rome au 17e siècle,' *Annales H.S.S.* (1999): 1317–44.
68 François Moureau, ed., *Répertoire des nouvelles à la main*, *op. cit.*, no. 1714. 1.
69 Henri-Jean Martin and M. Lecocq, *Livres et lecteurs à Grenoble*, p. 520; and Gilles Feyel, *La Gazette en province*, *op. cit.*, p. 96.
70 Yves-Marie Bercé, *Croquants et nu-pieds. Les soulèvements paysans en France du XVIe au XIXe siècle* (Paris, 1974), p. 73, concerning a rumour that circulated in September 1691 in Montauban following the posting of a placard by the town crier, leading to a demonstration, 'quelques artisans ayant leu ce placart et mal conceu ce qui y est porté.'
71 Joseph Klaits, *Printed Propaganda under Louis XIV*, *op. cit.*, pp. 21–220.
72 Pierre Du Camp d'Orgas, *Satires ou réflexions sur les erreurs des hommes et les nouvellistes du temps* (Paris, 1690), pp. 66–74.
73 François Moureau, 'Journaux et journalistes dans la comédie française des 17e et 18e siècles,' in Hans Bots, ed., *La Diffusion et la lecture des journaux de langue française sous l'Ancien Régime* (Amsterdam and Maarssen, 1988), giving a list of these pieces on p. 164; for the works of the moralists, see Frantz Funck-Brentano, *Les Nouvellistes* (Paris, 1905).
74 La Bruyère, *Les Caractères*, *op. cit.*, 'Des ouvrages de l'esprit,' 33.
75 Jean-Pierre Vittu, ' "Le peuple est fort curieux de nouvelles": l'information périodique dans la France des années 1690,' *op. cit.*
76 Louis XIV, *Mémoires* (Paris, 1860), vol. 2, ed. Charles Dreyss, pp. 224, 256–7.

8 Policy and publishing in the Habsburg Netherlands, 1585–1690

Paul Arblaster

After the collapse of royal authority in the Low Countries during the Dutch Revolt, the Prince of Parma's negotiations and campaigns of the early 1580s did much to re-establish the king's power in the southern provinces of the Netherlands. The reconciliation and reconquest of the provinces and cities to the south of the great rivers entailed a restoration, but was in some ways the creation of a new entity. In this area of the Netherlands, public life was emphatically Catholic and loyalist in ways it had never been before, deliberately emphasizing the differences with the Calvinist Republic to the north. Parma was, in the words of Justus Lipsius, the foremost intellectual of the day, the 'founder of Belgium.'[1] The most important provinces of the Habsburg Netherlands were the County of Flanders (where the main towns were Bruges, Ghent, and Ypres), and the Duchy of Brabant (with the chief cities Louvain, Brussels, Antwerp, and 's-Hertogenbosch), but there were large towns in other provinces, and numerous smaller towns throughout the land. In the sixteenth century, the three areas of densest urbanization in Europe were the Po Valley, Naples and its immediate surroundings, and the southern Netherlands.[2]

The towns of the southern Netherlands had for centuries been accustomed to a high degree of internal and local autonomy, and besides merchants, professionals, and the urban nobility, the craft guilds played an unusually strong role in their internal administration.[3] Most town councils had complicated power-sharing arrangements between the patrician-merchant aldermen (latinized as 'senatores') and the craft-guild councillors ('consules').[4] The southern Netherlands in the early modern period had a unique combination of a high degree of urbanization and a socially heterogeneous political class.[5] A third element in the country's political life was the unusually large extent of common privileges and the explicit ideology of government by contract, clearest in the Duchy of Brabant where, before entering into government, each new duke had to swear to uphold the Great Privilege.[6] This charter, dating from 1356, was also known as the Joyous Entry, since the ceremony coincided with the official reception of the prince or his representative, which in turn became a dramatization of contractual political relations.[7] Elsewhere, the privileges of the subject were less clearly codified and constitutional, but the emphasis on a contractual oath to uphold local privileges was still strong, and the power of provincial states to tie conditions to the taxes they voted, and to monitor their use, gave local elites a powerful bargaining position.[8]

The impression that the Habsburg Netherlands were a happy constitutional monarchy should be avoided: the conflicting interests of central government, patricians, and guilds meant that nationally and locally there were often moments of tension and renegotiation between different groups. If the general trend of the seventeenth century was towards greater central authority in the country as a whole, and to greater patrician authority within each town, this general trend was neither uncontested nor uniformly successful.[9] If the history of the Revolt from 1566 onwards encouraged the representatives of royal authority to seek to limit the potential for local resistance, it also showed that this would be no easy task, and that in many situations political realities dictated prudence.[10] Such conflict in itself must have done much to encourage an awareness of political and factional interest in comparatively large circles, and the dynastic, military and economic position of the loyal provinces gave such interest an international dimension. These combined influences meant that in the Habsburg Netherlands the press was very active and very difficult to bring under central control.

This position of the press was not for want of trying. In the course of the sixteenth century a series of enactments on heresy and sedition had gradually established a formidable array of censorship and licensing powers, which again came into effect in the areas reconquered in 1585. Before considering the press as such, I shall examine the legal framework within which printers and official bodies were expected to operate. The key legislative document was the heresy edict of 29 April 1550.[11] It systematically covered every aspect of public communication: preaching, disputation, school-teaching, and the printing, selling, and distributing of books. Ten of the twenty-one articles dealt with the book trade, setting out the law on licensing, preventive censorship and policing, and to the edict was appended the index of forbidden books drawn up by the University of Leuven. The cornerstone of the government's press policy was the system of royal licences. Nobody could set up shop as a printer or book dealer without a licence to do so, and no 'substantial' book could be printed or sold unless it too was licensed by a royal council.[12] In his legislation on the book trade Philip II – who assumed rule in the Netherlands in 1555 – was to try a different tack. Charles V's enactments had increasingly taken the control of the book trade from local magistrates (made responsible for policing the trade in manuscript books by a proclamation of Jacqueline of Bavaria in 1428) and entrusted it to royal councils and officers.[13] Philip II ordered that a guild be founded in Antwerp to regulate the printers and booksellers of that city.[14] Specific details were left to the Antwerp magistracy, who responded in May 1558 with a civic ordinance commanding all printers, booksellers and bookbinders to join the Guild of St Luke, collectively becoming one of the several 'nations' of the guild.[15]

If the preamble to an edict of 1568 is to be believed, the authorities did not rigorously implement the earlier laws, and were moved to introduce new enactments on seditious printing in that year precisely because such leniency had been abused. This law, aimed at Orangist pamphleteering, showed a clear grasp of the propaganda uses of news reports. The particular target was those who printed news in order 'to attempt to stir up and awaken their accomplices who have until now kept themselves hidden or dissimulated, but also, by the aforesaid false inventions and lies ... labour and exert themselves, to frighten or intimidate our good subjects.'[16] Printing news, rather than views, was what made a short-term difference to the decisions and morale of both the disaffected and the 'good subjects.'

The proliferation of war-time legislation, and the incorporation of the decrees of the Council of Trent on diocesan censorship and the Roman Index into the law of the Netherlands in 1570,[17] obscured the clarity achieved in the law of 1550. The cross-purposes of royal, local, episcopal, and apostolic tribunals added nothing to the effectiveness of regulation. Although before 1576 the effectiveness of the laws had been vitiated by the profusion of tribunals, after 1585 fairly clear divisions of concern emerged, in practice if not in theory. Licensed printers and booksellers who broke the law were prosecuted by the royal councils which granted their licences, while individuals not connected to the trade who were found to possess or to have distributed forbidden works were tried by local and diocesan courts. The inquisition proper, a source of great discontent in the Netherlands, had lapsed in 1572 when no replacement was appointed for the deceased Inquisitor General. By 1585, the Privy Council (which in that year relocated from Mons to Brussels) had managed to establish itself as the sole licensing body for the Netherlands as a whole, but books could still be printed and sold within the Duchy of Brabant solely under the licence of the Council of Brabant. If the licensing and policing bodies had to some extent been rationalized, the law itself was a mess, a hotchpotch of licensing laws, the prohibition of specific works, and laws on heresy and sedition only incidentally relating to the book trade. It was not clear exactly what laws a printer was swearing to obey when taking up his licence, and even when the law was clear, it was often out of date (for example, the legal requirement to display mid-sixteenth century indices of forbidden books).

It was not until 1612 that the law was rationalized, and then at the request of the trade itself. The 'nation' of printers and booksellers of Antwerp submitted a request to the Archdukes that anachronistic regulations be suppressed and the laws they were swearing to uphold be clarified, and this resulted in a proclamation which essentially returned the law to the situation of 1550, but with two important differences: there was no mention of heresy, it being taken for granted that the regulation of printing as such was one of the government's legitimate responsibilities; and the severe punishments for printing or possessing heretical works were quietly dropped. At the same time, the 'nation' of booksellers and printers made an attempt to form an autonomous guild, which would have given the book trade an entirely independent standing administratively and corporately, but the deans of the Guild of St Luke took legal action to prevent their secession.[18] In 1616 the regulations promulgated for Antwerp in 1612 were extended first to all the lands under the jurisdiction of the Council of Brabant (Brabant, Limburg, and Overmaas), and a few months later to all the lands ruled by the Archdukes. From 1616, for the first time, the Netherlands had a unified and centralized legal code for the regulation of the book trade, independent of the heresy laws; a code which was absolutist in the only meaningful sense of the term: a claim to unmediated and unchecked central regulation by right. It continued to provide the legal framework for royal regulation until 1764, despite shortcomings that will become clear. The regulation of the book trade was also subject to the problems that beset early modern law enforcement more generally: lack of resources, inefficient methods, over-extended officers (sometimes indolent or corrupt), and almost total reliance on informers and complainants in the notification of crimes and the identification of offenders.[19]

The licensing system worked as follows: anybody intending to become a printer had to provide testimonials of good conduct (from his local magistrates, who might rely on the testimony of neighbours in reaching their decision), of orthodoxy (from his bishop, who in turn relied on the report of his parish priest), and of technical ability (from the guild authorities in Antwerp, who would appoint a senior member to examine candidates). Armed with these documents, he could apply to the Privy Council and, in Brabant, the Council of Brabant for a royal licence, on receipt of which he was administered an oath to uphold the laws on the printing trade and thus became a 'licensed' or 'sworn' printer. The individual in question could then print almanacs, popular romances, pamphlets, and ballads without further government intervention. Although technically even such ephemeral work needed the imprimatur of the diocesan censor, not a single case is known of ecclesiastical courts prosecuting licensed printers.[20] For devotional or theological works, and 'substantial' works on any subject, both the ecclesiastical nihil obstat and a licence (or 'privilege') from the Privy Council and/or the Council of Brabant were required. Such a privilege was an exclusive licence to print the work named in it, and printers were free to apply for such a legally enforceable monopoly on works for which it was not in fact required, in order to enjoy the benefits of exclusivity. This, with the ensuing civil suits brought for breach of privilege, was probably a greater source of government control than was the occasional bringing of criminal charges for unlicensed publication. In one way or another, local and royal officials, the Church, and in Antwerp the guild, were all involved in the regulation of the press.[21]

Let us turn now to the press they were regulating. At the very beginning of his campaign of reconquest, with the court in exile at Mons in Hainaut, Parma had appointed a court printer, Rutger Velpen (or Velpius), a former printer to the university of Leuven. From 1580 to 1585, Velpius was the only printer in the Netherlands systematically to publish the sort of news which Parma wanted made more widely known. Later, with the reconquest of Brussels and Antwerp in 1585, the printing of news which would comfort those loyal to the king and dismay his enemies became more than a one-man industry. These two cities, one the main money market and the other the main seat of administration and diplomacy in the Netherlands, were natural markets for news of all sorts. Numerous current affairs pamphlets and prints were produced there, although on the whole by only a handful of small family businesses, such as those founded by Rutger Velpius (printer to the court) and Jan Mommaert (printer to the city) in Brussels, or in Antwerp the two husbands of Ysabeele Mathys, Mattheus de Rische (active 1585–1590), and Anthoni de Ballo (active 1592–1618). From time to time, however, public curiosity about an event would be so extensive that other printers would risk producing competing pamphlets, while some local stories were only worth printing in provincial towns, such as Leuven, 's-Hertogenbosch, Ghent, or Lille, which were not otherwise remarkable for news publishing.[22]

The main stories that the pamphlets and prints reported or depicted included: successes in the wars against the rebels in the Low Countries and Henry of Navarre in France; the Austrian Habsburgs' Long Turkish War; the peace treaties with France (1598), England (1604), the Ottomans (1606), and the Dutch (1609); the persecution of Catholics in England and Japan and the progress of the Faith in China; Philip II's cession of the Netherlands to his daughter Isabella and her husband Albert of Austria as the 'sovereign Archdukes' (1598–1621), and their arrival and reception in the Low Countries.[23] All tended to suggest that the Habsburg dynasty was the bulwark of orthodoxy and legitimate government against the tyranny, disorder, heterodoxy, and cruelty of Calvinists, Turks, and heathens. The international spread of stories is perhaps deceptive: victories of the House of Burgundy and Austria were the occasion for local ceremonies whether they took place in Hungary, Aragon, or the Indies, and the missionary orders (foremost among them the Society of Jesus) venerated and publicized their foreign achievements and martyrs. However international the news covered in such pamphlets, the events covered were largely those which impinged on local life through official ceremonies, especially Te Deums for victories, royal births and weddings and peace treaties. They should not be seen as propaganda as such, but rather as attempts to profit from the public curiosity aroused by such ceremonies which local gossip networks were unable to satisfy.[24] Not having the networks of regular correspondence available to newspaper editors, news pamphleteers tended to rely on official documents (reports, letters, treaties, notarized copies of depositions) for their information, although some stories, reprinted from pamphlets appearing elsewhere, perhaps reached them through trade connections. Despite the ineffectiveness of regulation, the authorities could largely set the agenda for news publication before the appearance of the newspaper. At the most oppositional, the reception of a new Governor General, or in 1598–1600 of the Sovereign Archdukes, was the occasion for respectful pamphlets extolling the benefits of peace, or the wisdom of the reforms requested by the Estates General which met in 1598 and 1600.

The international information networks on which business correspondents, professional newswriters, and newspaper editors relied were far less dependent on official grace. In the afterglow of its sixteenth-century greatness, Antwerp was, despite the closing of the Scheldt and the fearsome recession of the 1580s, still a powerful centre of international finance, as well as a major centre of craft and industrial production of all sorts, especially luxury artisanship.[25] The city had a high international reputation 'for paynting, and also all sortes of pictures printed in white & black.'[26] It was with a particular genre of printed picture, the current affairs engraving, that Antwerp's first newspaper publisher established his reputation. From 1605 to the ceasefire of 1607, Abraham Verhoeven produced a series of prints depicting the victories of Ambrogio Spínola.[27] In 1609 he brought out a range of copperplate engravings, woodcuts, and pamphlets relating to the Twelve Years' Truce which temporarily ended the war with the Dutch.[28] From 1615 onwards he was printing occasional news pamphlets ever more frequently, reaching a rate of one every ten days in 1619. Late in 1619 or early in 1620, as the military response to the Bohemian crisis began to take off, he applied for an exclusive licence to print news, and after obtaining it he remodelled his frequent but irregular pamphlets as a single, periodically published series: the first newspaper to be printed in what is now Belgium.

The *Nieuwe Tijdinghen* carried general news of miscellaneous military, political, and economic affairs, but primarily of the manoeuvres and negotiations in the Empire. In his application for a licence, Verhoeven had emphasized the propaganda usefulness of his newspaper, but this was far from the full story. The paper's main concern, as expressed in editorials, was to satisfy curiosity and provide matter for conversation. Verhoeven's professional manifesto was prefixed to one of the last issues before the *Nieuwe Tijdinghen* folded:[29]

> The Printer to the Reader.
>
> Dear Reader, as I have exercised myself, and still exercise myself, in giving forth in print such Relations as may come to my knowledge of what happens here and there throughout the world. So I have thought it good, here for the first in the beginning of this present year 1629 to publish, for the contentment of such as do not desire to be ignorant of the occasion of the public affairs of the world, these following Relations which have come to my hands, that hereby the curious lovers of greater knowledge than the blunt ignorant mass, may the better note and observe the causes, reasons and proceedings of the following effects of diverse affairs, which are to take place.
>
> And hoping that I shall herein have done that which will be convenient and agreeable to the benevolent reader, I would hereby refer him to the following Relations and commend him to the Lord.
>
> From Antwerp in the month of March 1629.

The balance between propaganda and information in the *Nieuwe Tijdinghen* was a fine one. Verhoeven used all the stereotypes of Calvinist cruelty, Catholic constancy and Habsburg victory developed in the press since Parma's time and outlined above. He also introduced the novelties of a front-page headline and at least one illustrative woodcut on most issues, and the news singled out for emphasis in this manner was overwhelmingly that of Habsburg military successes.[30] The same was true of the stories on which he, or his collaborators, enlarged with editorial comment. A particularly fine example of the editorial style appeared in the 'Year of Victories' 1625.[31] Nevertheless, a surprising amount of objective reporting was unobtrusively included in the paper, despite the outspoken loyalism of the editorial commentary.[32]

However loyalist the attitudes may have been which Verhoeven expressed, he was not part of the establishment and had no official connection with the authorities. Almost every issue of his newspaper ends with the initials of an ecclesiastical censor – the initials of canon Cornelius De Witte continued to appear for two full months after his death – but Verhoeven apparently never submitted copy to the royal councils for approval.[33] On 7 February 1629 he received an order from the Council of Brabant, dated 29 January, commanding him to cease his daily ('dagelycx') printing of 'various gazettes or news reports most incorrect and without any prior proper visitation.'[34] On 28 April, the Council of Brabant issued Widow Anthoon, the daughter of Rutger Velpius and heir to the position of printer to the court, with a privilege for news publishing, despite Verhoeven's monopoly which dated from 1620.[35] Verhoeven, however, relaunched his newspaper on 27 June as the *Wekelijcke Tijdinghen* (weekly news), which he published for the next two years, before again renaming it the *Courante* and reducing it to a much cheaper format.[36] In 1630, and again in 1631, the Privy Council and the Council of Brabant ordered the seizure and destruction of Verhoeven's almanacs, as contravening the privilege of Jerome Verdussen.[37] Since Verhoeven had in fact obtained a Council of Brabant licence for his 1632 almanac (printed and suppressed in 1631), this seems little short of victimization.[38] He effectively went out of business in 1634, although he managed to stave off his creditors until 1637.[39]

Nor were domestic publications the only concern. From the government's perspective, 1632 was one of the worst years for news in the whole period. Domestic news was bad. The series of military losses which had begun in 1629 with the fall of 's-Hertogenbosch continued, and an abortive noble rising failed to obtain significant support, but led to the loss of Maastricht, Venlo, and Roermond and undermined the government's prestige. The arrival of Don Ferdinand, expected since 1629, was still delayed by Swedish successes in the Empire. These same successes had curtailed the Tassis postal system, since the postmaster of Frankfurt, Johann von der Birghden, had seceded in 1627 to found a rival Swedish postal system. From 1632 this linked Frankfurt, Augsburg, and Nuremberg to the German terminus of the Swedish royal posts at Hamburg and the Swedish military sorting office at Leipzig. At its greatest extent, Von der Birghden's post had sub-offices in Speyer, Strasbourg, Zurich, and Venice.[40] Europe's postal networks, in which Antwerp and Brussels had formerly dominated north of the Alps, and the imperial post office at Frankfurt had been the centre of the German postal system, were thus short-circuited by the Swedes and their German supporters. This facilitated the publication of anti-Habsburg news and prevented effective answers being put into circulation. Isabella's and Philip IV's representatives in London found it necessary to complain about the anti-Habsburg tone of the English press, which now relied on reports from Amsterdam more than Antwerp and showed remarkable animus against a Monarchy with which England was at peace. Their complaints led to a six-year ban on the publication of newspapers in England.[41] The Star Chamber could apparently suppress the work of Nicholas Bourne and Nathaniel Butter far more easily than the Council of Brabant could that of Abraham Verhoeven.

The Widow Anthoon, licensed as a news printer in 1629, printed many news pamphlets in the 1630s, especially in the years 1634, when the Cardinal Infant Don Ferdinand was victorious at Nordlingen and arrived in the Netherlands as Governor General, and 1635, when war broke out with France.[42] But she never managed to produce a regular newspaper, and although Verhoeven's monopoly was broken, a new one was never effectively established. In 1634 and 1635 two Antwerp rivals applied for licences to print newspapers, and both requests were granted.[43] From 1635, Willem Verdussen's *Extraordinarisse Post-tijdinghen* and Martin Binnart's *Ordinarissen Postilioen* both appeared in Antwerp. From 1637, if not before, a newspaper was also published in Bruges: Nicolaes Breyghel's *Nieuwe tydinghen uyt verscheyden gewesten*. This was an unlicensed and hence entirely illegal publication, which apparently enjoyed the patronage of Bruges' city council.

In 1640, Privy Councillor Hovynes, author of a high-absolutist tract on the government of the Netherlands, proposed that a strict prohibition of the bulk importation of French and Dutch gazettes be issued, and that 'a single printer' be granted a monopoly on newspaper publication in the loyal provinces of the Netherlands. It seems likely that he had a particular client of his own in mind, but nobody specific is mentioned in the documents. On 15 June the Privy Council referred the question to the Council of State, which three days later approved Hovynes' proposals: heavy penalties were to be imposed on the 'traffic of gazettes en mass or in large packages' (but not on individual private subscriptions to newspapers printed in enemy territory!), and a monopoly was to be established on two conditions: that the government take no active role in it, and that it be fully self-financing. No steps were taken to establish the monopoly, presumably due to the Council of State's insistence that it be self-financing.[44]

The idea of establishing a newspaper monopoly under tighter government control was again aired in July and August 1642, and this time the proposal apparently came from the Governor General himself, albeit on behalf of Philippe Chifflet, one of his chaplains. Audiencier Verreyken wrote to the Chancellor of Brabant on 13 July asking whether it would be considered desirable to appoint a discreet man to oversee the editors of the Antwerp gazettes, to counter the 'exorbitant' lies published by the French gazettes, tentatively suggesting Chifflet as a possible candidate for the job. On 31 July he wrote again, saying that the Governor General would like to know 'how many in Antwerp are writing gazettes,' and again proposing Chifflet as a suitable man for the job of overseer of the press. On 7 August the Council of State drafted an 'avis' identifying Verdussen and Binnart as the two newspaper publishers in Antwerp and approving the plan in principle, since pre-publication government censorship would prevent the spread of falsities and facilitate the publication of news of victories, but insisting that the newspapers not be 'Gazettes like the French ones' and that all reports be based 'on the truth and not on rumours.' The Council of State apparently also recommended that neither Chifflet nor anyone else be mentioned specifically at this stage (the relevant passage in the draft is heavily scored through), and nobody was mentioned by name in the fair copy of the text, which was accompanied by a Spanish summary for the Governor General's benefit. As in 1640, there is no sign that anything came of the proposals.[45]

Thus far we have considered attempts to regulate the domestic press. But as Hovynes' recommendations make clear, there was also a perceived problem with the bulk importation of newspapers from Holland and France, countries with which the Monarchy was at war (Holland to 1648, France to 1659). Despite the war, a system of passports and exemptions meant that trade and communications were still possible between the belligerents, and indeed for some of the time royal orders from Madrid were carried to Brussels by couriers travelling overland through Paris. On 17 August 1644 the Council of State again involved itself in the business of press regulation, recommending that the Privy Council suppress an *Advis des Interessé aux habitans des pays bas*, 'a very pernicious writing' printed in France. The problem was that the posts from Paris could not be opened, 'in order not to give the French the opportunity to do the same with regard to our orders from Spain regarding the great interest of the service of His Majesty.'[46] Rather than endanger the postal communications through France, the Privy Council could only take measures to have the pamphlet confiscated once it had been distributed in Brussels and Antwerp.[47]

The foreign newspapers which caused Hovynes such concern not only publicized the enemy's perspective, they could also be a vehicle for publicizing internal dissent. The views expressed in the reports from Brussels carried by the Paris *Gazette*, for instance, were of a kind which could not be safely published within the Spanish Monarchy. They culminated in August 1644 with the opinion that if the King of Spain was going to continue to underfund the war with the Dutch, he should not be surprised if the people of the Habsburg Netherlands 'seek, if not to place themselves against their most powerful masters, at least to adopt a position of neutrality, in order to conserve their religion, which is at great risk in this war.'[48] The clear implication was that the King of France would be better able to defend the Catholic Netherlands from Dutch encroachments than would the King of Spain. The attractiveness of France as an alternative guarantor of Catholic orthodoxy was also underlined in a report on the 'recatholicization' of Sedan where, it was emphasized, 'our devotions arise from within our hearts, and not from a servile fear of disobeying the magistrates and the laws, as is practiced in other states, where the people have never tasted Gallican liberty' – a transparent reference to the Spanish Inquisition.[49] Newspapers containing such sentiments were imported into the Habsburg Netherlands both by individual subscription and in bulk.[50]

In other ways, though, the war could be carried to the enemy's gates. Just as the arrival of the Cardinal Infant in the Netherlands coincided with the appearance of two new newspapers, the arrival of the Archduke Leopold-William was soon followed by another new publication, the *Courier véritable des Pays-Bas*, the first newspaper to be printed in Brussels. While earlier newspapers had stressed their informative and entertaining content, the *Courier*'s founder, the Franche-Comté lawyer Pierre Hugonet, specifically founded his paper to oppose the 'lies' of the French *Nouvelles ordinaires* with 'true reports.'[51] In May 1650 he changed the title to *Relations véritables*. The king in Council, judging Hugonet's newspaper 'not useless to our service and the reputation of our arms,' granted a monopoly on French-language news publishing in 1649, a few months after Hugonet had launched his paper. Hugonet was the first editor-proprietor in the Habsburg Netherlands not to print his newspaper himself, the printing being contracted out first to Jan Mommaert and later to Willem Scheybels.

The language in which Hugonet couched his licence application was that of the reputation of the Spanish monarchy, and more particularly of its armies. Like Verhoeven thirty years before, he saw (or wished those in power to see) his primary role as providing news of victories – only the theatre of war had changed. Where Verhoeven relied on news about the war in the Empire from Prague and Vienna as his staple correspondence, Hugonet's focus was Flanders and Italy, and the war against the French. But in his reporting on the war against France he was conducting a personal propaganda war against the Parisian gazetteer Renaudot. Just as there is evidence that Verhoeven consciously opposed the reliability and orthodoxy of his reports to the slipshod Calvinist Broer Janszoon of Amsterdam, so Hugonet publicly declared his purpose to be the independent presentation of more accurate reports on the war than those provided by Mazarin's pensioner.

Although the *Courier véritable* bears every appearance of an officially-sponsored propaganda gazette along the lines of Renaudot's *Nouvelles ordinaires*, this was not in fact the case.[52] There are even signs that Hugonet was more enthusiastic in his assaults on the French than was convenient for royal policy. On 23 December 1656 Philip IV wrote to the Governor General, Don Juan José de Austria, ordering him on no account to consent to the printing of 'manifiesto, paper nor gazette' concerning the government of France or attacking Mazarin.[53] The Cardinal was taking these insults very seriously, especially as he had in the past been assured that orders had been sent to stop them, apparently without effect.[54] Firmly in control of Renaudot's *Nouvelles ordinaires*, Mazarin no doubt found it hard to comprehend that the opinions of the 'gazeta de Bruselas' did not directly reflect the attitude of those in power in Brussels or Madrid. An edict of 1657, expressly reserving the right to licence publication to the Governor General, was perhaps the only tangible result of the King of Spain's letter.[55]

The *Relations*, priced at three stivers an issue, was intended for an up-market and international readership, especially as French was not even the language of the civic elite in Brussels, only of the Governor General's household and the royal councils.[56] The international readership of the *Relations* is further borne out by the survival of copies in Paris, Bohemia, and Oxford. The Antwerp newspapers continued to be sold in Brussels to the end of the century, if not longer.[57] In fact, Brussels does not appear to have had the readership base necessary to support a more popular newspaper printed in the city.

In 1653 Hugonet requested government aid for a newspaper which had shown itself so useful as an organ to 'oppose the injurious writings of the French.' All he asked was that he be granted a full monopoly on news publication, suppressing any competition in the Southern Netherlands. The request was granted on 5 June 1653, with an additional clause that there be appointed 'a person who would see and correct, if necessary, the reports before they are printed.'[58] It is unclear whether any immediate appointment was made, the next reference being in January 1656, when Albert Rubens, secretary to the Privy Council and son of the famous painter, was named 'visiteur' of the gazette – an appointment which did not prevent Hugonet from overstepping the mark with regard to Mazarin.[59]

Concern about public opinion was activated at the highest level in 1655 by the publication and suppression of libellous remarks by a frustrated young cavalry captain critical of the Governor General himself. Hugonet tried to take advantage of the situation by submitting a more ambitious application for government aid.[60] The life of the editor-proprietor, 'continually vexed and importuned by his creditors, without being able to satisfy them,' not to mention 'the notable weakening of his health, deriving from the long and continuous application this occupation entails,' was first sketched.[61] All he asked, having thus ruined his finances and health in unremunerated royal service, was that he be provided with an effective monopoly (his monopoly so far being in name alone), the title of a royal servant without pay or salary as such – the ensuing tax exemptions being sufficient – and a life pension on the income of the titular abbacy of Montbenoit in Burgundy, which had recently fallen vacant: the government would have a subsidized gazette without the treasury having to pay out a penny. The response was disappointing: simply a reaffirmation of his monopoly, now for publication in Dutch as well as French, with no subsidy or pension.

Despite having thrice issued a monopoly in Hugonet's name, the Privy Council in 1663 failed to reject outright an application from Jean Feux la Croix de Belanguet to publish a newspaper in Lille. Instead they solicited the advice of Lille's aldermen, whose reply attempted to take a neutral line while showing a certain distrust of the applicant as a non-native, ultimately leaving it up to the royal councillors to decide whether it would be desirable to have a man with knowledge of 'affairs of state' appointed to make the news public.[62] In the event, no licence was issued, leaving Hugonet's French-language monopoly, at least, intact.

In 1666 Hugonet tried to have this monopoly enforced in Antwerp, not to suppress the newspapers of Willem Verdussen and the widow Binnart outright, but less ambitiously to repress their publication of the English declaration of war on France: the sort of special edition which brought in far more than the average issue of the paper, the greater demand guaranteeing larger sales and perhaps allowing an increase in cover price.[63] Even here he failed, and the following year he sold the *Relations véritables* to the 27-year-old physician, Adrien Foppens, who had the licence renewed in his own name in 1669, after Hugonet's death.[64] The new proprietor soon took steps to have the legal monopoly enforced. The first step was a remonstrance to the Governor General signed simply 'Zeleux,' drawing attention to the on-going illegal composition, publication, and distribution of newspapers 'containing affairs of war and police,' especially in Ghent.[65] The next move was the Privy Council's, a letter being sent to the town councils of Ghent, Bruges, and Antwerp ordering them to investigate the printing of newspapers in their jurisdictions, and particularly to inquire by what licence the printers operated.

The first town council to reply was that of Bruges, the mayor and aldermen of the city writing to the Privy Council on 24 March 1672 that the three newspaper publishers then active in the city were all licensed printers. Although not actually licensed to publish newspapers they had done so without opposition for a long time and had given no reason to be stopped, thus establishing what amounted to a customary right.[66] This despite the edict of 1657 referred to above.

Antwerp's reply, dated five days later, indicated that the widow Binnart published a newspaper licensed to her husband by the Council of Brabant in 1635, renewed in her own name on 9 March 1658 and again in 1668 for a period of ten years, six of which had still to pass. Peter Verdussen's licence, also from the Council of Brabant, was dated 14 July 1661, and was a renewal, 'without limitation of time,' of his father's 1654 licence. The magistrates also pointed out that in 1655 Hugonet had tried to obtain a similar monopoly, but that in 1656 Verdussen and Binnart had jointly appealed to the Council of Brabant and had obtained a continuation of their activities. It would seem that even within Brussels, the provincial council of justice was unwilling to bow to the orders of the Privy Council.

The aldermen of Ghent did not reply until 4 June, when they informed the Privy Council that Maximilian Graet printed a weekly gazette under a Council of Flanders licence dated 16 November 1666 and that on 24 December 1666 alderman Peeters had been appointed the paper's 'visitor,' to be replaced by alderman Claysson when absent. Since Graet had never broken the law and had gone to great expense, 'notably to pay his correspondents, dwelling in diverse Kingdoms & republics of Europe,' it would be unfair to suppress him arbitrarily. Given that his paper only cost one stiver, as against the three charged by Foppens, who only published in French, which was not the common language of the county of Flanders, of which Ghent (in their view) was the chief city, it was also suggested that suppression would be an injustice not just to Graet, but to the citizenry as a whole. It was, they stated, 'convenient' for the citizenry to be informed of 'that which passes in the aforesaid foreign quarters,' i.e. the kingdoms and republics of Europe.

Faced with such clear declarations of support from the corporations under whose jurisdiction the competing newspaper publishers operated, the Privy Council dropped the case, but Foppens was not to be put off. In July 1674 he addressed a remonstrance, this time in his own name, directly to the King of Spain. As a result, the Privy Council was obliged to write to the town councils of Bruges, Ghent, and Antwerp ordering them to take action to suppress the newspapers printed in their cities. The mayor and aldermen of Bruges wrote back that the order would be put into execution at the soonest convenient opportunity, the aldermen of Ghent that the order had been misplaced, but would be put into execution at the earliest convenient opportunity once recovered, while the corporation of Antwerp failed to respond at all.[67] Foppens' second attempt to have his monopoly enforced had come up against as solid a wall of particularist intransigence as had his first, and as Hugonet's less well-documented earlier attempts seem to have done.

Despite this, Foppens did not seem to harbour grudges against his competitors. At Maximilian Graet's death in 1676, widow Graet continued printing the *Ghendtsche Posttijdinghen*, but another printer, Michiel Maes, sought to undermine her position by applying to the Council of Flanders for the news licence, on the grounds that her 'ignorance of French and other foreign languages' made her incapable of publishing a newspaper. Widow Graet appealed to the Privy Council to uphold her position, arguing that it was immemorial custom for the widows of printers to succeed to their businesses in full, including any licences they had obtained while alive, and giving the example of the widow Binnart, who had continued her husband's newspaper in Antwerp until her own death. She enclosed a copy of her husband's 1666 licence from the Council of Flanders, and a document signed by fifteen merchants of the city of Ghent attesting that her newspapers 'soo goedt sijn inden stijl, ende soo curieus inde materie' (are as good in the style and as curious in the matter) as her late husband's had been. The Privy Council solicited the opinion of the official gazetteer, Dr Foppens. He replied that since he had no immediate intention of printing a Flemish gazette, and none had been printed at Antwerp since the death of Peter Verdussen, it would be a shame to deprive the city of Ghent of 'the satisfaction of having the news,' and advised that since the widow Graet already had an established network of correspondents it would be easiest to let her retain the licence.[68]

The widow Graet maintained her position until her death, despite having her licence suspended on 13 November 1681 for printing a news item from the Hague speculating that the English government was more likely to side with France than with Spain. After the widow's plea that the offending item was 'in any case not touching the Spanish monarchy' she was, on 3 December, given permission to resume printing, but only on condition that each edition be approved by a member of the Council of Flanders.[69] This had been a condition of her Council of Flanders licence in the first place, but its reiteration here as though a new stipulation seems to suggest that the practice had rather fallen into disuse. The Privy Council turned to Foppens again in 1682, when the widow Graet herself passed on, requesting his opinion of the application of her children and heirs for a continuation of the licence, and the counter-application of one Jean de Dryvere. The application of the Graet heirs was supported by a letter from the Council of Flanders in their favour, and Foppens advised that since nothing had been done for the general suppression of improperly licensed gazettes, the Graet family may as well retain their licence, especially since Maximilian Graet's original main editor was still 'full of life' and preferred to remain working with the family.[70]

Foppens himself was no more free of legal entanglements than were his competitors, although his tenure of the post first granted him in 1667 was long unchallenged. His attempts to have his monopoly enforced failed, but he enjoyed the support of the central organs of state for almost twenty years, even succeeding, where Hugonet had failed, in obtaining a substantial pension, no less than 480 florins, from the Count of Monterey to subsidize his work as gazetteer. In 1674 the Council of State backed him against the internuncio, who complained that he had published a comment in a report from Rome critical of the Pope. The Council of State insisted that, since the comment had 'slipped in by inadvertence rather than by any premeditated design,' one, and only one, of three fairly lenient sanctions be taken: a private reprimand from the government, a private apology to the internuncio, or recompense in the form of allowing the internuncio to place a piece of his own in a future edition of the gazette. Should the internuncio be unsatisfied with such leniency, it was hinted rather heavily, any more formal apology or punishment would undoubtedly come to the attention of foreign newspaper editors, such as the 'Gazetteer of Holland,' who had so far not picked up the offending story.[71]

In 1680 the Privy Council even intervened to save Foppens' bookseller brother, François Foppens, from the full rigour of the law. François published an edition of Ovid's *Metamorphoses*, the entire print-run of which was immediately confiscated by the Officer Fiscal of Brabant. The Privy Council, however, had his stock returned with orders that no action was to be taken provided that within six months eleven of the plates were corrected according to the guidelines of the Bishop of Bruges ('Tegantur virilia,' 'Tegantur uterus,' 'Tegantur partes inhonestae et utera,' etc.). No copies could be sold in the Habsburg Netherlands until the changes were made, but they could be exported.[72] This makes quite a contrast to the treatment of Verhoeven's almanacs in 1630 and 1631.

Adrien Foppens was clearly considered a useful man, and the action of organs of state both to promote and to defend his interests seem to show a certain degree of highly-placed patronage. His newspaper was everything one would expect of a government gazette on the Renaudot/Richelieu model. In 1685 the Officer Fiscal of Brabant was even to claim that it had shown itself so useful an instrument of communication that in the past some governor generals 'took pains to censor it themselves because of the importance of the matter.'[73] But the context of the Officer Fiscal's remarks was Foppens' disgrace. In 1685 it was discovered that he was abusing his position of trust as gazetteer by using his access to the chanceries to spice up his separate line in manuscript intelligence (for which he received pensions from England, Rome, and Brunswick-Lüneburg), giving a very different picture of affairs from the official line followed in print.[74] The Marquis of Grana revoked his pension, had him tried by a special junta, and replaced him as gazetteer with Claude Antoine Gillard, King of Arms of the County of Burgundy.[75] Foppens, again at liberty, began to take a more active interest in the paper manufactury in which he had long been a partner.[76] But the urge to retaliate soon got the better of him and in 1686 he published a defamatory pamphlet, *Les conquestes du marquis de Grana*, which got him into more trouble.[77] Not until the winter of 1692–3, and through the mediation of Secretary of State Bardé, was Foppens restored to his position, and even then he had to reimburse Gillard for the expenses incurred during his seven years as gazetteer, an amount set at 2,600 guilders.[78] On 6 March 1693, the patent formally reinstating him was issued.[79] After Foppens' death, his heiress, in 1700, auctioned off the furniture (including eighty-six paintings) to cover the debts of the estate.[80] It would not seem that newspaper publishing was a very remunerative business in the seventeenth century.

By the time of Foppens' reinstatement in 1693, his position with regard to his competitors had changed considerably. In 1690 the Privy Council had advised the Council of Namur of a new policy of unofficial toleration. No attempt was to be made to censor gazettes, even the sale of Dutch newspapers being freely allowed, as weekly preventive censorship of the growing number of newspapers was simply too much effort to be worthwhile. Only pamphlets and 'little booklets' were among the news publications still subject to the normal regulations governing bookselling.[81] Henceforth, the sale of individual issues of newspapers might be prohibited (the July 1691 issue of the *Mercure historique et politique*, published in The Hague, was banned for libelling the Pope), but otherwise, with the sole exception of the government's own gazette, the *Relations véritables* (later *Gazette de Bruxelles*), newspapers were free of censorship.[82] The mechanisms of control, already strained, simply could not cope with the flood of information which newspapers brought.

Due to a combination of particularist defiance in the great cities of Antwerp, Bruges, and Ghent, and economizing and lack of manpower at the centre in Brussels, the absolutist ideal of one king, one faith, one version of events was unattainable in the seventeenth-century Habsburg Netherlands. The number of bodies involved in licensing and regulating the book trade – local, central, ecclesiastical, and trade – complemented one another when co-operating. But while all were outspokenly loyal to the Church, the king and the commonweal,[83] they prioritized these loyalties differently when the power to print was at stake, creating a field of tension within which a (limited) range of views could be publicized. It would be foolish to look for truly subversive opinions in war-time newspapers, but the newspapers of Antwerp, Bruges, Ghent, and even Brussels, published private opinions, and news unwelcome to the authorities. The continued printing of uncensored (or self-censored) newspapers, justified in terms of the 'convenience,' 'curiosity,' and 'customary rights' of the subject, was a standing denial of the view that publicity was a prerogative of those in power. At the same time, the ease of communications with France and Holland, and the central government's interest in keeping these communications open, meant that the Habsburg Netherlands were very far from being a 'closed' society in information and intellectual culture, despite the technically strict limits to the public expression of heterodox or anti-Habsburg sentiment.

Appendix

Editorial comment from Abraham Verhoeven's Nieuwe Tijdinghen, *1625, no. 75 (2 August), pp. 13–15*

Dear Reader, here we must note, how much we are obliged to praise and thank God Almighty, for his great favours and beneficence now shown to us in short time and in divers manners.

First we have here in the Netherlands recovered the Town of Breda, where the enemy had the greatest forces, and Foreign Assistance, that they have ever had, or shall have, one may presume.

Secondly, In Italy where the Franch have leagued with the Savoyard, and sailed a little before the wind, There the wind changed suddenly, and went against them, so that the proverb, who laughs last also laughs, was found true.

In Brazil, Bahia was also recovered from the Enemies and Rebels of Holland, whereby they were punished with loss and shame by God who is the lover of justice.

It is not enough for these evil people that they unjustly retain his Hereditary Lands here in the Netherlands from their legitimate Sovereign Lord, but they would prevent and damage him in the East and West Indies, and have wandered so far from justice and natural reason, that they have dared order Days of Prayer to call on God to profit their evil and unjust Intention, for which they have found Wednesday the most fitting day in the week, perhaps because they think that on that day our Dear Lord has the most leisure to give Audience to the Gueux.

But others are of opinion that they have chosen and ordained Wednesday for their Day of Prayer, in honour of the Heathen God Mercury, in whose honour the Heathens kept Wednesday, and it gives some appearance that the Gueux of Holland tend more to this for this Heathen God Mercury was full of falseness and deceit, and they being the same, can do with such a Patron. But God Almighty, the protector of Justice, has shown that he gives little heed to their Wednesday Prayer Days.

Concerning the great Armada of England which is ordered to sail under the Standard of the Palsgrave, Pestilence is striking a blow there, and a short time will give us to understand how it will go with it.

Notes

Thanks are due to Dr M. Thøfner for her generous aid in preparing this article, and to Professor Emeritus Sir John Elliott, and Ms C. Schumann for help with particular points. Much of this material was previously presented, and helpfully commented on, at the Oxford University graduate seminar on Early Modern France organized by Robin Briggs and David Parrott.

1 'Conditor belgii,' Quoted in Geoffrey Parker, *The Dutch Revolt* (London, 1985, revised edn.), p. 215. 'Belgium' meant the whole Netherlandish state, just as did 'The Neth-

erlands,' but each word came eventually to stand for only part of the former territory of the Seventeen Provinces.

2 Wim P. Blockmans, 'Voracious States and Obstructing Cities: An Aspect of State Formation in Preindustrial Europe,' in Charles Tilly and Wim P. Blockmans, eds, *Cities and the Rise of States in Europe, A.D. 1000 to 1800* (Boulder, 1989), p. 219.

3 *Ibid.*, pp. 228–9.

4 See, for example, J. de Conde, ed., *Costuymen ende Rechten der Stadt Brussel* (Brussels, 1657), especially pp. 4–11.

5 See, for example, Robert S. DuPlessis, *Lille and the Dutch Revolt: Urban Stability in an Era of Revolution, 1500–1582* (Cambridge, 1991), p. 21.

6 See G. Griffiths, *Representative Government in Western Europe in the Sixteenth Century* (Oxford, 1968), pp. 346–50.

7 See Margit Thøfner, ' "Domina and Princeps proprietaria." The Ideal of Sovereignty in the Joyous Entries of the Archduke Albert and the Infante Isabella,' in Werner Thomas and Luc Duerloo, eds, *Albert and Isabella, 1598–1621. Essays* (Brepols, 1998), pp. 55–66.

8 Geoffrey Parker, 'The Decision-making Process in the Government of the Catholic Netherlands under the Archdukes, 1596–1621,' in *Spain and the Netherlands, 1559–1659. Ten Studies* (London, 1990), pp. 165–6.

9 See Karin Van Honacker, *Lokaal verzet en oproer in de 17de en 18de eeuw. Collectieve acties tegen het centraal gezag in Brussel, Antwerpen en Leuven* (Standen en Landen 98, 1994), *passim.*

10 Geoffrey Parker, *The Dutch Revolt, op. cit.*, pp. 34–9.

11 L. Kenney, 'The Censorship Edicts of Emperor Charles V in the Low Countries, 1515–1550,' Ph.D. thesis, University of Maryland, 1960 (University Microfilms, Inc., Ann Arbour, Michigan, 1975), pp. 77–181.

12 These were the three 'collateral councils' of the central government (Privy, State, and Finance), the Great Council or Parlement of Mechlin, and the provincial councils of justice. See Parker, 'The Decision-making Process,' *passim.*

13 H. Rousselle, 'Esquisse historique sur la police des livres et sur la législation de la presse, en Belgique,' *Mémoires et publications de la société des sciences, des arts et des lettres du Hainaut* 9 (1851): 190.

14 Algemeen Rijksarchief Brussel (henceforth ARB), Papieren van Staat en Audiëntie, 17092, fol. 47.

15 Antwerp, Koninklijke Academie, Oud Archief Sint-Lucasgilde, XVIII; printed in J. B. Van der Straelen, *Jaerboek der vermaerde en kunstryke Gilde van Sint Lucas binnen de stad Antwerpen, 1434–1793* (Antwerp, 1855), pp. 51–4.

16 *Placcaert ende ordinantie tegens de ghene die eenige fameuse, schandaleuse oft seditieuse boecxkens, artickelen oft scriften maken, versieren, saeyen, divulgeren, drucken, ten voirschijne bringen, oft onder hen houden. Oft quade ende valsche roepen vuytgheven* (Brussels, Michiel van Hamont, 1568), dd. Binche, 11 November 1568.

17 *Philippi II Regis Catholici Edictum De librorum prohibitorum catalogo observando*, dd. Mechlin, 10, 11 and 17 March 1569 (Antwerp, Plantin, 1570).

18 Antwerp, Koninklijke Academie, Archief Oud Sint-Lucasgilde, LVII.

19 See F. Vanhemelrijck, 'Bijdrage tot de studie van het politieapparaat in het ancien regime. De opsporing van het misdrijf in Brabant,' *Belgisch tijdschrift voor filologie en geschiedenis* (*Revue belge de philologie et d'histoire*) 50(2) (1972): 356–94.

20 Jozef De Brouwer, *De kerkelijke rechtspraak en haar evolutie in de bisdommen Antwerpen, Gent en Mechelen tussen 1570 en 1795* (Tielt, 1971–72), 2 vols.

21 In 1662 the system of guild regulation was extended to Brussels, specifically to prevent scandalous and improper publications. See *Placcaeten, ordonnantien, landt-chartres, privilegien, ende instructien By de Princen van dese Neder-landen Uytghegheven* (Brussels, 1724) vol. 4, p. 48.

22 See, for example, M. Hoc, 'Publications anversoises relatives aux campagnes de l'Archiduc Albert, Gouverneur-Général des Pays-Bas (1596–1598),' *Gulden Passer* 3 (1925): 32–50.
23 For a more detailed overview, see the bibliography of my Ph.D. thesis, entitled 'Current-Affairs Publishing in the Habsburg Netherlands, 1620–1660', in *Comparative European Perspective*, Oxford University, 1999.
24 Paul Arblaster, 'The Press Image of the Infanta Isabella,' in Werner Thomas and Luc Duerloo, eds, *Albert and Isabella, 1598–1621. Essays* (Brepols, 1998), pp. 337–8.
25 E. Stols, 'Handel-, geld- en bankwezen in de Zuidelijke Nederlanden,' in *Nieuw Algemeen Geschiedenis der Nederlanden* (Haarlem-Antwerp, 1980), vol. 7, pp. 131–4.
26 M. G. Brennan, ed., *The Travel Diary (1611–1612) of an English Catholic, Sir Charles Somerset, Edited from the Manuscript in the Botherton Collection, University of Leeds* (Leeds, 1993), p. 285. I am very grateful to Ms C. Schumann for this reference.
27 Christiaan Schuckman, *Hollstein's Dutch and Flemish Etchings, Engravings and Woodcuts, ca. 1450–1700* (Roosendaal, 1990), vol. 35, pp. 218–26.
28 Antwerp, Stadsbibliotheek, *Recueil de pieces sur la treve d'Anvers* (1609).
29 *Nieuwe Tijdinghen* (1629), no. 19, p. 2.
30 K. Van Damme and J. Deploige, 'Slecht nieuws geen nieuws.' Abraham Verhoeven (1575–1652) en de Nieuwe Tijdinghen: periodieke pers en propaganda in de Zuidelijke Nederlanden tijdens de vroege zeventiende eeuw,' *Bijdragen en mededelingen betreffende de geschiedenis der Nederlanden* 113(1) (1998): 1–22, especially pp. 9–17. While the comments on Verhoeven's ideological emphasis are useful, the accuracy of the statistical analysis is vitiated by the unwarranted assumption that the headlines are a reliable guide to the contents of each issue, and in general too little emphasis is placed on the primarily informative rather than propagandistic nature of the *Nieuwe Tijdinghen*.
31 See the transcript in the Appendix to this chapter.
32 In January 1624, for instance, a report from Prague appeared which blamed the great dearth in Bohemia on a combination of incompetent monetary policy and indisciplined Habsburg soldiery (*Nieuwe Tijdinghen* [1624], no. 10 [26 January]), while the report from Antwerp in *Nieuwe Tijdinghen* (1625, no. 20), stated that the royal soldiers in the area 'keep house evilly with the Peasants' ('houden met de Boeren drollich huys').
33 The last issue bearing the imprimatur 'V.C.D.W.C.A.' (Vidit Cornelius De Witte Canonicus Antuerpiensis) is that of 9 August 1624; De Witte had died of pestilence on 10 June (P. J. Goetschalckx, *Geschiedenis der Kanunniken van O.L.V. Kapittel te Antwerpen* (1585–1700), ([Antwerp, n.d.], p. 188).
34 'Verscheyden gasetten oft nyeuwe tydingen seer Incorrect ende sonder eenige voorgaende behoorende visitatie.' Order in Council signed Vande Perre, 29 January 1629, and endorsed Cornelis de Claer, messenger of the council, 7 February 1629, in ARB, Officie Fiscal van de Raad van Brabant, liasse 177, dossier 1566.
35 The only surviving evidence is a clerical note on the report (ARB, GRSP, 1278205) of an investigation carried out in 1634 into alleged libels in her pamphlets (see note 42, below).
36 Folke Dahl, *Nouvelles contributions à l'histoire des premiers journaux d'Anvers* (Brussels, 1939; offprint from *La Chronique graphique*, 5 March 1939), pp. 9–10.
37 ARB, GRSP, 1278, no. 200.
38 ARB, OFRB, liasse 632, dossier 5883:190, no. 31.
39 Alfons Goovaerts, *Abraham Verhoeven van Antwerpen de eerste gazettier van Europa. Bio-bibliographische studie* (Antwerp, 1881), tr. E. Van Bergen, p. 215.
40 Wolfgang Behringer, 'Brussel, centrum van het internationale postnet,' in Luc Janssens and Marc Meurrens, eds, *De post van Thurn und Taxis. La poste des Tour et Tassis. 1489–1794* (Brussels, 1992), tr. G. Van Cauwenberge, p. 31.
41 Joad Raymond, *The Invention of the Newspaper* (Oxford, 1996), p. 93.

42 In April 1634 Widow Anthoon was unsuccessfully sued for stating in a 'gazette' or 'libel de nouvelles' that Colonel Koninghe, an associate of the farmer of the royal salt works in the Franche Comté, had received 6,000 ducats from the Duc de Rohan (ARB, GRSP, 1278205). It is not clear that this is a reference to a no-longer extant periodical, and in the Council of State deliberations of 1640 (discussed below) it was taken for granted that newspapers were only printed in Antwerp.

43 Binnart's on 22 November 1635 (ARB, Rekenkamers, 20805 fol. 192v).

44 ARB, Raad van State (henceforth RS), 1843 unnumbered.

45 ARB, RS, 1846 unnumbered.

46 ARB, RS, 1846 unnumbered.

47 ARB, GRSP, 1278223.

48 *Gazette* (Paris, 1644), no. 99, 20 August, p. 679.

49 *Extraordinaire du IX. septemb.* (Paris, 1644), no. 108, p. 748.

50 Conversely, publishers in the Habsburg Netherlands disseminated the views of foreign dissidents throughout the period under consideration: French leaguers, dévots and Frondeurs; Dutch Catholics, Arminians, and (after 1649) Orangists; Irish rebels and confederates; English recusants and royalists.

51 Editorial in first issue.

52 On Renaudot and his newspapers, see Howard M. Solomon, *Public Welfare, Science and Propaganda in Seventeenth Century France: The Innovations of Théophraste Renaudot* (Princeton, 1972) and the chapter here by Vittu.

53 British Library, Additional Manuscript 14000, fol. 241–2v., as communicated by Professor Sir John Elliott, 16 February 1997, for which I am grateful.

54 The article which Mazarini found particularly offensive was presumably that dated Paris, 15 September 1656, in *Relations véritables* (1656, no. 36, 23 September), pp. 426–7, which begins: 'Le Cardinal Mazarin voiant, que tout le monde murmuroit toûjours contre sa conduite, émoignoit plus que jamais de vouloir la paix, fit la semaine passée publier un édit, portant deffences sur peine de la vie de parler ni écrire d'aucunes nouvelles, ni méme en recevoir des païs étrangers, afin que le peuple ne sçache pas le mauvais état des affaires du Roiaume, & la necessité de finir la guerre, que ce Ministre veut rendre perpetuelle …' ('Cardinal Mazarin, seeing that eveyone was constantly complaining about his behaviour and evidently wanted peace more than ever, last week published an edict prohibiting anyone, on pain of life, from speaking or writing of news. Or even from receiving it from foreign countries, so that the people would not know the unfavourable situation of the affairs of the realm, and the need to end the war, which this minister instead wishes to render perpetual …').

55 André Puttemans, *La Censure dans les Pays-Bas autrichiens* (Brussels, 1935), p. 22.

56 Paul De Ridder, 'De Publicatieboeken van de stad Brussel en het taalgebruik ind de "princelycke hoofdstadt van't Nederlandt" (1635–1793),' *Eigen Schoon* 80 (1997): 123–68.

57 ARB, RS, 1846 unnumbered.

58 ARB, GRSP, 1279153.

59 ARB, GRSP, 1279168.

60 On Captain Merode's 'libelles,' see Henri Lonchay, Joseph Cuvelier, and Joseph Lefèvre, eds, *Correspondance de la Cour d'Espagne sur les affaires des Pays-Bas au XVIIe siècle* (Brussels, 1933), vol. 4, pp. 488–95.

61 Letter of application and response both in ARB, GRSP, 1279157.

62 ARB, GRSP, 1279158.

63 ARB, OFRB, liasse 632, dossier 5883: 190, no. 39. According to a manuscript note in Anthony Wood's copy, now in the Bodleian Library at Wood 615(4), the edition of *The Treaty of Peace Between the Crowns of France and Spain*, published in London by Thomas Newcomb in 1660, was priced 8d.

64 ARB, OFRB, liasse 632, dossier 5883: 190, no. 26.

65 A 'zéleux' was an anonymous informer acting out of zeal for justice and without hope of personal reward.
66 The original remonstrance and the replies of the town councils are in ARB, GRSP, 1279185. The Privy Council and Council of State (but not Council of Brabant) documents relating to Foppens' attempts to enforce his monopoly were used by Theo Luyckx, 'De eerste gazettiers en hun kranten in de Spaanse Nederlanden,' *Handelingen van de Koninklijke Zuidnederlandse Maatschappij voor Taal- en Letterkunde en Geschiedenis* 18 (1964): 238–40.
67 ARB, GRSP, 1279187.
68 ARB, GRSP, 128035.
69 ARB, GRSP, 1280114; *Ghendtsche Posttijdinghen* (1681), no. 90 (10 November).
70 ARB, GRSP, 128040.
71 ARB, RS, 1844 unnumbered.
72 ARB, OFRB, liasse 632, dossier 5883: 190, no. 201; GRSP, 1280113bis.
73 Quoted in L. Galesloot, 'Mémoires secrets d'Adrien Foppens sur le gouvernement et les affaires des Pays-Bas, pendant les années 1680–1682,' *Compte rendu des séances de la Commission Royale d'Histoire*, 4th series, 4 (1877): 377.
74 L. Galesloot, *op. cit.*, *passim*.
75 ARB, RS, 1844 unnumbered.
76 Galesloot, *op. cit.*, p. 384.
77 ARB, OFRB, liasse 632, dossier 5883: 190, no. 50.
78 ARB, RS, 1844 unnumbered.
79 ARB, RS, 1844 unnumbered.
80 L. Galesloot, *loc. cit.*
81 ARB, GRSP, 1280130.
82 In 1698, after another unsuccessful attempt to have his monopoly enforced, Foppens was ordered to submit drafts to Privy Councillor Voorspoel (ARB, GRSP, 1280142). The policy of banning specific newspapers by name, seldom for more than a month or two, was continued through the eighteenth century (see André Puttemans, *La Censure dans les Pays-Bas autrichiens* [Brussels, 1935], p. 270 ff).
83 See, for example, Richard Verstegan, *Scherpsinnighe Characteren* (Antwerp, 1622), dedicatory epistle: 'tot den dienst van Godt, van sijn Catholijcke majesteyt ende hun [the dedicatees'] Vaderlant.'

9 Politics and the press in Spain

Henry Ettinghausen

It is only quite recently that students of Spanish history have become aware of the fact that the favourite reading matter of Spaniards in the seventeenth century was the same as that of their twentieth-century descendants. None the less, even in Spain not many people today know that there actually was such a thing as the press in the seventeenth century, let alone that it flourished. In the past fifteen years or so, however, some historians of Spanish culture have begun to wake up to the fact that the press was a major force in both the culture and the politics of the Golden Age. Indeed, the sudden recognition of its importance has started to produce fruits in the form of bibliographies, catalogues, editions, conference papers, articles, and other studies.[1] It is the aim of this chapter to draw on this recent work in order to focus on some of the varied ways in which the press in seventeenth-century Spain was a vehicle for information which – like the press of other places and other times – rarely, if ever, lacked political spin.

The press comes about through a combination of technical developments that are inextricably bound up with changes in behaviour and ways of thinking. This is true to such a degree that it is probably futile to attempt to determine which developments and changes were the chickens, and which the eggs. Thus, to take two essential elements, the opening up and improvement of routes of travel, both on land and by sea, created the means whereby the communication of information could take place and become more rapid and efficient, while the need to improve such communications made it important to improve the means whereby they could take place. To take two others, the urge to disseminate news was one factor which gave impetus to the proliferation of printing shops, while the increasingly ready availability of print technology provided a stimulus to the production of printed news.[2]

Postal services, both regular and special, brought news to cities in which individuals could, in their turn, further disseminate it in their correspondence, while publishers could spread it, near and far, in printed news sheets in prose or in verse which could in turn be reprinted elsewhere, if necessary in translation. In Spain as elsewhere, the Tassis family, connected with the Italian Tassos, had from the beginning of the sixteenth century been instrumental in organizing the postal service as part of the European network. As Correo Mayor (Postmaster General), Juan de Tassis y Acuña, who was made Count of Villamediana by

Philip III, further strengthened Spain's international postal links with France, Italy and Flanders at the end of the century, transforming what had been essentially a royal mail into an efficient public service.[3]

On another level, the increased centralization of power within states provided both the conditions and the need for more efficient and sophisticated modes of information and methods for maintaining internal security, while the availability of appropriate media helped create the conditions for the concentration of power in government. Throughout Western Europe, by the time we reach the seventeenth century the interplay of these factors – and of others, such as the religious, ideological, diplomatic, military, and political divides between Catholic Europe and both Protestant Europe and the Islamic Middle East and North Africa – enables the information and propaganda industries to achieve critical mass. It is from this moment that they become recognizable to us as the forerunners of the worldwide communications business we know today. In the case of Spain and its empire, both in Europe and beyond, all of these factors clearly begin to come into play towards the end of the fifteenth century and they come into their own throughout Spain's so-called Golden Age in the sixteenth and seventeenth centuries.

Seventeenth-century Spain experiences a remarkable rate of mobility, both actual and virtual. Don Quixote is untypical in not roaming further afield from his village in La Mancha than Barcelona. Guzmán de Alfarache, the hero of the best-selling picaresque novel which appeared very shortly before Cervantes' masterpiece, travels extensively in Spain and in Italy. But Cervantes himself, like so many of his contemporaries – in particular, fellow soldiers – knew not only large tracts of Spain and Italy, but also Flanders, the Mediterranean, and North Africa. Indeed, foreign lands (including Italy, Algeria, and England) are the settings for several of his short stories and plays, while his last major novel, *Persiles y Sigismunda*, spans northern Europe, Spain, and Portugal and reaches its climactic end in Rome. Later in the century, Gracián has the main characters in his *Criticón* travel throughout a Europe which is both geographically plausible and politically symbolic, and Quevedo's last great political satire, *La hora de todos*, ranges from the Near East to the New World.

The mental furniture of well-informed seventeenth-century Spaniards derived from the whole of the world as then known, and it did so, to a very large extent, thanks to the influence of the press. It required little effort on the part of literate Spaniards to make themselves as familiar with the martyrdom of Christians in Japan as with the uprisings of indigenous peoples in South America, to become no less *au fait* with political upheavals in Poland or England than with those in Turkey or Ethiopia. Letters from abroad, whether private or official, were often published as newsletters, mingled with autobiographies, both genuine and fictitious, and with diaries, travelogues, and petitions for promotion or transfer, to provide images of far-off lands. With regard to Spain, public events, secular as well as ecclesiastical, in its chief cities provided an important share of the news, with Madrid, the seat of the court and of central government, becoming the main focus of news stories. However, it is not until the beginning of the seventeenth century that we find news pamphlets being printed in Madrid, half a century after it was made Spain's capital and long after other major cities, such as Seville and Barcelona, became well established as centres of news publication. In addition, it is precisely with the start of the century that news publishing really takes off in Spain and the press begins to acquire its role as a shaper of public opinion for the influential literate minority of the population.

If we ask what drives the press in Spain – or, indeed, elsewhere in Europe – in the seventeenth century, it is no less difficult to distinguish then than it would be now where commercial considerations end and political considerations begin, or vice versa. In this respect, too, dialectical processes are at work whereby the availability of the media is exploited by the purveyors of information and propaganda, and the need to inform and control requires the use and development of the media. Some publishers and printers begin to specialize in news pamphlets, although – unlike some of their contemporaries in other countries – none in Spain, until at least the end of the century, do so to the exclusion of other types of production or as the official mouthpieces of government. However, in Spain, too, though in subtler ways than in some other early modern states, the print culture, and especially the press, provide both an expression of, and an indispensable vehicle for, government policy and the dominant ideology.

Throughout most of the seventeenth century Spain is active across almost the entire world stage, not least militarily, at the same time as it has to cope with internal divisions and conflicts which threaten, and even maim, its body politic. While the government of Philip III (who reigned 1598–1621) is rapidly forced by financial constraints to make peace with France and England and to call a halt to Spain's attempts to bring to heel the Protestant Dutch rebels, it ends up being sucked into the maelstrom of the Thirty Years' War. As for the government of Philip IV (who reigned 1621–65), for all that it begins with an ambitious economic and political reform programme, it reaps the whirlwind of war on virtually a world scale while at the same time struggling for a dozen years to hold onto the rebel province of Catalonia and, in 1668, losing Portugal after nearly three decades of warfare. The end of the century, while less disastrous for Spain than has often been thought, was none the less seen by contemporaries as the pathetic prelude to the War of the Spanish Succession, with which the next century was to open.[4]

Not surprisingly, the seventeenth-century Spanish press reflects very clearly her struggles to maintain peace, to wage war, and to keep up political appearances. War reports are, indeed, the staple of the press in seventeenth-century Spain, and, even before the century dawns, it is news of warfare which prompts the press to produce some of its earliest attempts at sustained news coverage.[5] News of Spain's military successes, and those of her allies, dominate the news throughout the period. As for the cessation of hostilities, the illusory prospect of lasting peace with France, represented by the double royal wedding of 1615 whereby Prince Philip and Louis XIII married each other's sister, likewise provoked a spate of news pamphlets, as did the abortive Spanish Match which for nearly a decade thereafter held out the hope of prolonged peace with England. In the middle of the century, after the revolts of the Catalans and the Portuguese in 1640, we can see not only their struggles with the Crown, but the entire panorama of European, and indeed world, conflict both from their points of view, in the Catalan and Portuguese press, and also, in the Spanish press, from that of the government of Philip IV. Both revolts give rise not only to hundreds of news pamphlets which are highly coloured by the standpoint of their authors, their publishers, and their intended readers, but also to dozens of lengthier works in which enemy atrocities reported in the press are exploited as grist to the competing propaganda mills. As well, both give rise to the earliest attempts at periodical publication in the Peninsula: in Portugal, to a monthly gazette which started up in November 1641; in Catalonia, to gazettes translated from French into Catalan whose production, by several different Barcelona printers, appears to have been confined almost entirely to the years 1641 and 1642.[6] War reporting, then as now, was a crucial part of the war effort.

The news in manuscript

As elsewhere in Europe, the press in Spain – in the sense of the information industry – antedates the invention and the proliferation of printing, and even as late as the seventeenth century important manuscript news networks operate alongside those which produce printed news pamphlets. News, after all, has always been one of the driving forces behind private correspondence and behind diplomatic and commercial communication. In seventeenth-century Spain, as elsewhere in Europe, we find writers who, as part of their professional activity, engage in the production of frequent, if not necessarily regular, private or semi-private news services. Two of the best-known Spanish purveyors of such services in the middle of the century – José Pellicer and Jerónimo de Barrionuevo – provided for their patrons in the provinces the news and rumour available at court which they regarded as most significant and/or most likely to interest their readers. These patrons, whose identity is not known, would be likely to disseminate the news both locally in conversation and more widely through their own correspondence. The often highly complex interplay of conversation, private correspondence, and manuscript and printed news pamphlets can be followed in many surviving collections of letters.

The distinction between manuscript and printed news is crucial, not just because it is a question of different media or even because it implies lesser or greater diffusion, but because it involves a difference of kind. As publishers were controlled by a system of censorship which, at least in theory, required all printed works to be licensed prior to publication, the news which appeared in print scarcely ever questioned government policy, or gave anything but good news of wars at home or abroad, or cast the ruling class in a bad light, or indulged in rumour-mongering, or reported civil disorder or crimes as anything but isolated and shockingly untypical incidents. Far less sanitized views of life appear in private correspondence and in the manuscript productions of the private and semi-private newsmen. Thus, if we scan the news services supplied by Pellicer in the 1640s and Barrionuevo in the 1650s, we find a host of items and comments which providers of printed news simply excluded from their productions, either at the insistence of the authorities or, most probably far more often, simply out of a clear awareness that such things were unthinkable in print. At the same time, Pellicer, in particular, is anxious to make his reader(s) aware of his scrupulous concern with sifting out news which is untrue or unreliable, at one point declaring: 'Much of what I have just said may be true, or not; for, as the postal service is unreliable, everyone is adding to or inventing the news as he thinks best. As for me, I leave out much of what I hear and only write what comes from the best sources.'[7]

Pellicer has left us, in his manuscript newsletters, a vivid picture of endemic disorder at the very heart of the Spanish empire: stories of elopements, abductions, muggings, student riots, confidence trickery, sexual promiscuity, sodomy, armed robbery, and assassination. More than once he comes out with such statements as: 'Things have reached such a pretty pass that one cannot venture out at night unless one is well armed and in plenty of company,' or 'not a night goes by but there are four or five murders.' He also gives his correspondent(s) remarkably full and frank accounts of expressions of political dissent, for example the incident in which, during a public procession, a peasant shouted to the king: 'Everyone is deceiving the king! Sire, this country is coming to an end, and those who fail to remedy its ills will burn in hell!' Nor is Pellicer averse to expressing his disapproval of the queen for indulging in catcalling at the theatre, irrespective of whether the plays are good or bad. And he tells of a number of abortive uprisings against the government, of the secret execution of French spies, of disagreements and rivalries between Spanish generals, and of excesses committed by the Spanish troops in Catalonia. Like contemporary private correspondents, but unlike the writers of printed news pamphlets, Pellicer does not shrink from reporting military reverses suffered by Spain and her allies. Indeed, he often comments on their prospects in distinctly pessimistic terms: 'The war in Germany is no less promising'; 'Things are not getting any better in Catalonia'; 'News has arrived from Italy which is far worse than bad.' Unlike his counterparts who wrote news to be printed, Pellicer could clearly afford the luxury of being independent and outspoken.

As for Barrionuevo, we just do not find in the published press such items as these about Philip IV and Queen Mariana: 'Because the queen is said to be jealous, all women have been banned from the church of San Felipe while the king attends Corpus Christi devotions there'; 'On St Matthew's Day there was nothing to eat in the royal palace, and the same is true most other days'; 'At the Escorial the king spent two hours alone kneeling in front of the tomb which is destined for him, emerging with his eyes red from weeping and as large as two fists'; 'The king does not seem to realize that it would be better if he spent his money on sending soldiers to Flanders than on putting on plays with expensive theatrical machinery or on bullfights costing 80,000 ducats apiece'; 'The king has been sleeping with the queen since last Sunday: may God grant them sons.'[8]

Nor do we find in print such comments as these on the nobility and members of the government: 'On Sunday the Count of Rivilla and his son married the Duchess of Frías and her daughter with immense ostentation, although not one of them has a penny to his name'; 'Don Fernando Manuel, who was sworn in yesterday as a member of the Council of Finance, is blind in both eyes, but I think all the members of that council are blind, at least in their greed'; 'The Countess of Benavente died on Sunday night; she used to eat four chickens a day and tell her doctor that she could not sleep if she ate any less'; 'The Duke of Alba is ill, it is said, because he is an inveterate old womanizer; and Don Pedro Pacheco is ill, too, but for the opposite reason.'[9] Printed news pamphlets simply do not contain such comments as these on the general lawlessness of the capital: 'There are a thousand robberies and break-ins a night, with thieves going around in gangs of ten or twenty'; 'Last night they broke into the house of a woman and her three-year-old daughter, slit their throats and made off with everything they owned'; 'On carnival night five men were killed, which did not seem many, seeing how drunk and disorderly people were.'[10] And equally unthinkable in print is criticism of the Church and its ministers, such as: 'Yesterday they arrested a Discalced Carmelite who was living with a handsome woman from Getafe: what a friar will not do the devil will not do either!'[11] Some of Barrionuevo's general comments provide a strong contrast with the pervasive optimism expressed in the printed news. To give just one example: 'The world is in such a state that it is impossible to live without stealing, but it is only petty thieves and pickpockets who are punished. The big fish always manage to slip through the net.'[12]

These negative news stories, and the many others in similar vein which Pellicer and Barrionuevo gleefully or ruefully recount, must have seemed, at the very least, impossibly indecorous and unedifying for public consumption, if not dangerously, even treasonably, lacking in patriotism and support for the Establishment. Yet, obviously, they and their fellow private newsmongers and their readers were not the only people in the know. It is clear from the surviving correspondence of their contemporaries that the optimism which infused the published news was not by any means always shared by the intelligentsia. At the same time as Pellicer was operating his news service, we find the satirist Quevedo, at the end of his life, bitterly disillusioned with Spain's predicament and thoroughly cynical about the upbeat tone maintained in the printed press.[13] And Pellicer himself was capable of expressing the deepest pessimism.[14]

It is by the extent to which manuscript news contrasted with the news appearing in print that we can most easily and precisely gauge the spin that was administered to the latter. At the same time we can be certain that those individuals who were privileged to have access to both forms of news would be clearly, if perhaps not always consciously, aware of the conventions and constraints which separated the two. Far from there being a single or uniform awareness of current affairs or a single collective imagination, nascent public opinion varied from the substantial, if not almost total, ignorance of more or less remote and illiterate peasants to the highly sophisticated awareness of the well-connected and well-informed, especially people who were linked, directly or indirectly, to such vital sources of information as central or local government, the judiciary, the Church, the military, or commerce.

Subscribers to news services such as those of Pellicer and Barrionuevo were obviously interested in more than tittle-tattle, though that evidently interested them a lot. Principal among their concerns was, clearly, the state of the nation and, more particularly, anything that could affect the course of government. Men of consequence in the provinces – whether noblemen or churchmen – needed to know what was going on at court. So, too, did bureaucrats of all grades. In a system of government relying heavily on patronage, anyone who wished to curry or to keep in favour had to make sure he kept abreast of the often subtle, but sometimes abrupt, shifts in fortunes and alliances which could be effected by the promotion, disgrace, illness, engagement, marriage, or death of key players in the political game.

Gazettes and *relations*

Both Pellicer and Barrionuevo make sure they keep their clients well informed of developments, both actual and rumoured, and include, in particular, numerous accounts of the individuals who are on their way up or down. On occasion, however, such matters could also find their way into the printed news. Towards the end of Philip III's reign *provisiones*, or appointments to secular and ecclesiastical posts, in the Americas began to be published annually. The need for the government to publicize appointments to posts at home and abroad, and for those likely to be affected to hear about them as quickly and comprehensively as possible, became particularly pressing on Philip's death. The accession to the throne in 1621 of his teenage son, and the appointment of the Count-Duke of Olivares as the new king's chief minister, set in motion a wholesale change of personnel, a veritable palace revolution, which gave rise to the most important sustained series of printed news pamphlets produced in the first half of the century: the newsletters attributed to Andrés de Almansa y Mendoza.

These pamphlets – a total of seventeen numbered letters – take the form of the type of private or semi-private news service which Pellicer and Barrionuevo were to provide twenty or thirty years later, but with the crucial difference that they appeared in print in series as soon as they were written. Like Pellicer's and Barrionuevo's letters, each of these is (at least until nearly the end of the series) presented as written anonymously to an equally unnamed client. What is more, in the vast majority of contemporary editions they lack the usual details of place and date of publication and the name of the printer. As such, they give an impression of semi-clandestine publications, an impression reinforced by the author's repeated claims, from the fifth letter onwards, that he does not intend his letters to be published and his insistence that his correspondent should take more care to ensure that they do not fall into the hands of printers. Significantly, he claims that there are people intent upon preventing him from disseminating court news, but he counters the charge that his letters are damaging, asserting that, on the contrary, they are laudable, providing, as they do, licit relief for the yearning for news on the part of those who are absent from the court. The anonymous writer of the letters was in fact careful to include extravagantly flattering remarks about key figures in the new regime.

In the first letter, entitled *Copy of a Letter written to a Friend of his by a Gentleman of this Court*, dated barely a fortnight after Philip III's death, the author claims to have been an eye witness of the king's death, and he certainly narrates it in convincingly intimate detail, including supposedly verbatim accounts of the final exchanges between the dying monarch and his closest advisers, most especially the Jesuit preacher Florencia. However, the detail is not there for its own sake. The entire narrative is designed to stress the contrition of the monarch at having derelicted his duty as ruler and to prepare the way for the new reforming government in which critics of the dead king and of his corrupt and self-serving ministers had placed their hopes. Thus, the author holds out the vision of a sea change in which the old order would be removed: 'At this very moment innumerable things are changing everywhere, with some men laying down their power and others arming themselves with it.' Towards the end of this account, Florencia, who has been depicted as skillfully easing the dying king's conscience, is quoted as praising the efficient new style of government set in motion immediately on Philip IV's accession, while Olivares' elevation to grandee is reported as having been greeted at court with general satisfaction.

This letter is in fact a first, consummate, act in what was to become an important part of an extended public relations exercise. Whether this was directly government-inspired or not is impossible to tell. What the letter certainly does is mark off the reign of Philip III as one of inept and corrupt government salvaged, up to a point, by the piteous depiction of the king's last-minute penitence. Just as importantly, it ends by offering the prospect of a new dawn of renewal and reform. It differs, however, from most of the subsequent letters in the series by virtue of concentrating on a single event. While the sixth and the seventh letters are also triggered by and concentrate on deaths – the public execution of Philip III's minister Rodrigo Calderón and the demise of the Count of Benavente – the remainder are written in the form of gazettes packed with hundreds of snippets of news from home and abroad, but most especially with the changes in fortune of the key figures in the government apparatus. The crucial importance of patronage for the smooth running of government is explicitly stated by the author in letter 14: 'As true, practical, reason of state consists in rewarding vassals in order to avoid their wishing to change their lord or their luck, great care must be taken in distributing prizes and punishments, for rewarding the nobility provides the strongest bond [to the Crown].'

This entire series of letters – the first third of which came out in the first six months of the reign – is at least ostensibly concerned to promote the optimistic vision of a new era of just and efficient government. In the second letter the author claims that the entire world has been turned upside down by Spain's new regime, while the brand-new young king is described as being as handsome as an angel. By the fourth letter, readers are being told that the reign of Philip IV heralds a new Golden Age. At the beginning of the eighth they are regaled with a paean which opens thus: 'This is a glorious century for Spain! May our great monarch Philip IV live a thousand years, for, through his Catholic and excellent government, his prudence shines forth in splendour for the common good and universal profit of his subjects!' By the end of the series, however, the brilliant sheen seems to be wearing a little thin. In letter 16, written in late 1624, some three-and-a-half years after the first, we find several references to political, economic, and military setbacks – subjects freely discussed in private correspondence but which only very occasionally found their way into print.

While the numbered newsletters attributed to Almansa y Mendoza were published, almost without exception, with no indication of the author's name, the same is not true of his relations. *Relation* was the name given throughout Western Europe to news pamphlets which, like letters 1, 6 and 7 in the series of numbered newsletters we have just discussed, concentrated typically on a single news story. As such, they constituted a distinct type of journalism, the one which was to remain the overwhelmingly dominant genre in Spain until and even after the founding of the monthly *Gaceta nueva* in 1661. This, the first successful Spanish experiment at regular periodical publication, occurred thirty years after the creation of the thrice-weekly French *Gazette* and more than forty years after the establishment of weeklies – in some instances, even dailies – in the Netherlands, Germany, Switzerland, and England.

Almansa's relations deal with most of the 'serious' topics normally covered by the seventeenth-century Spanish press. These include the activities of the monarchy (for example, Almansa's relation on the birth of an infanta), the nobility (the marriage of the Constable of Castile), and the Church (the auto de fe celebrated in Madrid in 1624), as well, of course, as war (a naval victory off Galicia) and diplomacy (the Constable of Navarre's embassy to Rome). The series of numbered newsletters attributed to Almansa began, as we have seen, in spring 1621, with the death of Philip III; his relations start with no less newsworthy an event: the Prince of Wales' surprise visit to Madrid, two years later, in his bid to clinch his Spanish Match with Philip IV's younger sister.[15] In fact, four out of Almansa's sixteen known relations give accounts of festivities put on to entertain the English, while a fifth relates Charles' departure from Madrid and his journey northwards over land to embark for England. Almansa considered himself an expert at covering public events. Four of his last five relations are accounts of celebrations held in Barcelona prior to Philip IV's official visit to the city in 1626 to raise revenues from the Catalans.

As is the case with most of the authors of published news in seventeenth-century Spain, it is not known whether Almansa was commissioned to write his relations or simply became a self-appointed chronicler. What is known is that he made a point of dedicating most of his relations to members of the aristocracy and the government. Part of his purpose was, no doubt, to curry favour with them, but they also, presumably, were flattered to be publicly associated with prestige public events. Like the many other, mostly anonymous, writers of relations, Almansa was engaged in prolonging such occasions, both in time and in space. Through such relations as his, events which involved very considerable outlay in terms of finance and organization could be made to bring returns to their promoters by virtue of being recorded for posterity and made known far and wide. Thus, Almansa's first relation on Prince Charles' visit, dedicated to the Duchess of Medina de Rioseco, went into at least three editions almost certainly published in Madrid, and it was also printed, under different titles, in both Seville and Valladolid. Two of his accounts of the festivities laid on for Charles, as well as his relation of the Prince's departure, were published in translation in London, and the latter was also published in Italian in Milan.

Like many other examples of the genre, Almansa's accounts of celebrations were ritualized narratives of ritualized events, being remarkably professional in their evident expertise in etiquette, their observation of detail (not least of furnishings and dress), and their elegant style. In his writings, the baroque paraphernalia of triumphant entries, joustings, firework displays, bullfights, balls, and banquets are matched by baroque descriptions of the brilliant improvization and conspicuous extravagance they implied. Hyperbole is, throughout, the order of the day. Like the events they depict, these relations go in for what has nicely been called the aesthetics of excess.[16] Almansa has a special penchant for exotic liveries, and he devotes a large proportion of his accounts of festivities to describing them in minute detail. By doing so he, and other relaters of his ilk, provide a picture of court life which belies the finances of court and country, a picture which no doubt helped sustain morale at home and enhance Spain's reputation abroad.

The brilliance of the Spanish court, as depicted in Almansa's relations of festivities, chimes in well with his flattering references to the king and the government whose arrival in power motivated the series of numbered letters attributed to him. In the very first of those letters the youthful Philip IV is already referred to as a new King Solomon, and in letter 9 he is likened to the 'Spanish' emperors Trajan and Theodosius – the kind of eulogy which is more usually found, even in seventeenth-century Spain, in panegyrics than in the press. Almansa is also unusual in the extent to which he comments on his own practice and on problems involved more generally in journalism. In particular, he defends a journalist's right to use rhetoric and to make moral judgements, on more than one occasion weighing the claims of precision and detail against those of grandiloquence.[17]

The 'popular' press

All of this is a very far cry indeed from what we may call the popular press in seventeenth-century Spain, but the latter is no less heavily tinged with ideology. Both the 'serious' and the 'popular' press – together with the visual arts and architecture, secular and ecclesiastical ceremony and ritual, sermons, the theatre and literature in general – were powerful politico-cultural tools of the Establishment. Although 'serious' news was sometimes written and published in verse, and 'popular' news occasionally appeared in prose, these are the exceptions.

Nine times out of ten, news in verse meant ballad news, and this usually meant particular types of news and particular types of treatment.[18] Whilst most of the verse is doggerel written in the *romance*-metre typical of Spanish ballads, it exploits many of the traditional ballads' oral formulae, which were designed to play on the emotions of listeners or readers. Far more obviously and crudely than relations in prose, verse relations generally make their moral and political messages plain, strongly reinforcing internal consensus by means of sharply depicted stereotype protagonists. Many of them celebrate – and clearly invite their listeners and readers to do likewise – the regal activities of royalty and the noble pursuits of the nobility. These include ritual journeys and visits, such as Philip III's trip to Lisbon in 1619 to present his heir to the Portuguese, as well as the births, marriages, and deaths of members of the royal family.[19]

While the ranks of the Good are packed with royalty, the nobility, churchmen and Spain's Catholic allies, the Bad are well represented by such 'others' as Protestants, Jews, Moors, and Turks – a host of assorted enemies of Spain and Rome. An example typical of many is an account of a naval raid carried out in 1615 on a Turkish fleet in the Peloponnese by a combined force of the galleys of Sicily, Malta, and Florence. Composed by a Lieutenant Manríquez Sarmiento, this ballad relation ends on a note of unmitigated triumph:

> Everyone should know that where invincible Spain sets up her banners, she is always firm. Sword in hand and pike on shoulder, she rules the world to the far-off Indies. Some she commands, others she succours, raising up the fallen and casting down the haughty. Well-born people are the Spaniards: the walls of the faith, the feet of its throne, and – to conclude such well-known facts – lords of the globe and its governance.[20]

The corollary of praise for Spain is, of course, scorn for her enemies, as for example in a verse relation of the burning of two bridges in Paris in 1621 which is blamed on Protestant saboteurs who are described as 'those rabid dogs who scheme to infect the holy body of the Church with poison and venom.'[21]

The popular ballad press creates and consolidates socio-ethical myths in which good, with the help of God, triumphs over evil, while evildoers come to bad ends in this world and to even worse ends in the next. The message is conveyed not simply in terms of victory over Spain's enemies but also, on a more individual scale, in regard to a veritable rogues' gallery of crooks and sinners. Sometimes the latter belong quite clearly to a race or social group which has been consecrated as a national enemy, as in the gory story of the priest who was set upon by a band of gypsies in the Sierra Morena who killed, cooked, and ate him. That relation claims that the gypsies are the cruellest nation on earth and should be banished from Spain, and it ends by telling how the gypsies in question were sentenced to be burnt.[22] On other occasions, however, the malefactor is simply a nasty piece of work. A good instance is the story of a rich man who kept some very large, fierce mastiffs with the sole purpose of scaring beggars off his property in order to avoid giving them alms and of how, one fine day, he was punished by divine providence when his dogs turned on him and tore him to pieces.[23] On other occasions we find shocking stories of sex and violence, such as the case of the monk who became infatuated with a woman, left his order to marry her and then, two nights after the wedding, killed her, her mother, two other female relatives of hers and a little girl.[24]

Although the villains are generally men, that is not by any means always the case. However, women who blaspheme and are sacreligious appear more often than do murderesses. One typical story is that of a beautiful young woman in the town of Yepes who was divinely punished for her blasphemy by being made monstrously ugly.[25] Another tells of the terrible end which befell an ill-tempered woman who cursed her children and sent them to the devil, a ballad which opens by warning imprudent parents of the perils of swearing and cursing.[26] The corollary is, of course, stories of sinful people (especially women) who repent. One such story, which eventually became the source for an opera, tells the tale of a headstrong young woman called La Baltasara who, after leading a notoriously dissolute life with travelling theatrical troupes, saw the error of her ways and retired to live the rest of her life in a hermitage near Malaga. When she died, three years later, she was found kneeling with her arms around a crucifix and was treated like a saint.[27] Closely related to news stories such as these are the many accounts of miracles and martyrdoms, a fair proportion of which were recounted in verse, that were published as news pamphlets throughout the century. It need hardly be emphasized how much both these topics lent themselves to being heavily coloured by ideology.

Natural disasters lent themselves to similar treatment, as did stories of portents and monsters. As regards disasters, these are often presented as divine retribution for sin, with survivors, especially those who escape death by the skin of their teeth, regarded as the beneficiaries of miracles. Thus, in its title, a prose relation of the terrible floods which swept northern Catalonia in the autumn of 1617 highlights not only the numerous deaths but also the miraculous escapes.[28] While portents, like miracles, are generally told in prose, one nice exception is the account of how, in the summer of 1613, no less than thirty-five legions of demons descended upon the town of Castro.[29] As for monsters, these appear especially towards the end of the century in prose accounts, though there are some earlier ones in verse, such as the account of the merman Nicolao, whose origins go back at least as far as the twelfth century, and who appears in a relation published in 1608. Another merman, described as being thought by some also to be Nicolao, appears in 1624 in a broadsheet in which the woodcut illustration of the weird and wonderful monster is explicated in a verse commentary which suggests that this beast is the allegorical secret weapon of a militant Church bent on the destruction of Islam.[30] Yet another curious Counter-Reformation freak is depicted in a verse relation of 1613: a portentous prodigy with thirty-three eyes placed symmetrically all over his person who was born in Bayonne and lived for thirty-three days, speaking out three times in Latin to warn the doubtless bemused populace: *Timete Deum, Vigilate et orate, Quia nescitis hora*.[31] The many reports of strange beings published in prose later in the century include some which are totally fanciful and others which are plausible and even verifiable. One such is the story of a seriously overweight young woman called Eugenia who was taken to the court of Charles II and cared for there as a curiosity. Her two portraits, clothed and nude, by the court painter Juan de Carreño, hang in the Prado. As for the moral or political spin, in the relation she is presented, simply and rather tamely, as an example of God's power to turn tender babes into hefty giants.[32] In the 1640s Pellicer was no doubt voicing the feelings of many of his more serious-minded contemporaries when he repeatedly denounced the kinds of news pamphlets sold in the streets of Madrid by the blind. Though he rarely singles out relations in verse for special censure, it is easy to imagine that these would have been his pet hates. However, not even all his educated contemporaries were as discerning as was Pellicer: Barrionuevo, for instance, had no trouble swallowing reports of such things as armies seen battling in the sky off the Andalusian coast or a seven-headed, seven-armed, half-human, half-goat monster discovered in the mountains of Sardinia.[33]

The 'popular' press differed from the 'serious' not only in terms of tending to be written in verse and in treating its subjects with greater pathos and more explicit moralizing, but also in so far as it made far greater use of illustrative woodcuts. For the most part, these were generic, rather than specific, almost always using blocks chosen from the printer's stock. At the same time as their visual impact attracted potential purchasers, they often also served to inform them instantly of the type of news contained in the relation. Thus, relations of sea battles often have woodcuts of galleys and galleons on their first page, while accounts of military action on land often show a knight on horseback, or a town under siege, or simply a castle. Relations of monsters were among the very few which were illustrated with woodcuts that were obviously purpose-made. At the other extreme, the 'serious' press tended to avoid illustration, though official or semi-official reports often bear a standard coat of arms, which gives them an impressively authoritative look.

The periodical press

The moment in seventeenth-century Spain at which the press becomes most blatantly an instrument of politics is said to be when the *Gaceta Nueva* is founded in 1661. This, the first news pamphlet in Spain to become firmly established as a periodical publication, and the forerunner of numerous subsequent experiments during the following hundred years or more, apparently owed its existence to Philip IV's illegitimate son, the dashing and ambitious general Don Juan José de Austria (1629–79). As commander of the Spanish fleet which blockaded Barcelona at the end of the Catalan revolt, he had been instrumental in forcing the city to capitulate in 1652. It was he, therefore, rather than his father, who took the lead role in press reports of the Catalans' return to Spanish rule and then, as viceroy of Catalonia, in accounts of the campaigns to expel French forces from the province.[34] In 1656 Juan José was made governor of Flanders, returning to Spain in 1661 to take command of the army in Portugal, where initially he achieved considerable success. It was his secretary, the Fleming Francisco Fabro Bremundan, who founded the monthly *Gaceta*, supposedly with a view to publicizing his master's exploits and furthering his political career.[35]

It is worth citing the editorial statement with which the first number of the *Gaceta Nueva* opens, for it recognizes the indebtedness of the enterprise to foreign models, as well as the modesty of its ambition to establish itself as a monthly when compared with them:

> Seeing that in the most populous cities of Italy, Flanders, France and Germany there are printed each week, in addition to the relations of particular events, others which bear the title of gazettes, in which news is given of the most notable things, both political and military, which have happened in the greater part of the globe, it is fitting that this type of publication be introduced [in Spain], if not each week, at least each month, in order that the curious may be informed of such happenings and so that Spaniards should not lack the news in which foreign nations abound.[36]

The *Gaceta Nueva* apparently combined a selection of items culled from foreign gazettes with news gathered by Bremundan's agents. While the war to recover Portugal certainly dominates its news of the Peninsula, Portugal does not, in fact, even merit a mention until the third number. As for Don Juan José de Austria, he does not appear until the sixth and does not get another mention until the ninth.

The *Gaceta Nueva* is, however, typical of the genre, covering, as it does, many parts of Europe, including Italy, France, Austria, Hungary, Germany, Sweden, England, Scotland, Ireland, Poland, and Muscovy and ranging also to North Africa and Turkey. Not least among its achievements was the fact that it was published in several major Spanish cities, sometimes by printers who had been producing relations for many years. One, in particular, Juan Gómez de Blas, who held the title of Chief Printer of Seville, frequently added news which was not contained in the Madrid edition. He also continued to produce the *Gaceta* under his own steam after it suspended publication in Madrid in 1663. Some numbers of the *Gaceta*, at least, were also published in Saragossa, Valencia, Malaga, and Mexico, the main source of the latter edition being, apparently, Gómez de Blas' Seville edition.

In its first incarnation, the *Gaceta* was published in Madrid until 1663, not long before Juan José was relieved of his command in Portugal. From January to September 1676 Bremundan published in Saragossa a periodical entitled *Avisos ordinarios de las cosas del norte*, an outspokenly political paper whose purpose was to counter the anti-Spanish propaganda put out by the *Gazette de Paris*. A sequel to the *Gaceta nueva*, entitled *Gaceta ordinaria de Madrid*, would become Juan José's mouthpiece after his successful *coup d'état* in 1677,[37] and Bremundan would continue publishing several other periodicals: notably, from 1683, the *Nuevas singulares del norte*, which covered the progress of the war against the Turks. Many other regular periodicals, often weeklies, appear in a number of Spanish cities from this date, when a ban on gazettes imposed in 1680 was lifted.[38] Many of the new publications were ephemeral, and they often bore titles which evolved subtly over the months. To give a few examples, Saragossa produced a good half-dozen such publications in the last two decades of the century, including a *Gaceta de Zaragoza*; San Sebastián, at least three, including one entitled *Noticias principales y verdaderas*.[39] An idea of the huge surge in such publications – not only monthlies, but fortnightlies and even weeklies – may be obtained from the numerous titles which came out in Barcelona, many of them printed by two specialists in this field: Vicente Suriá and Rafael Figueró. In 1684 alone we find the following: *Noticias sólidas venidas con el correo de Flandes, Relacion verdadera y noticias generales de Europa venidas a esta corte por el correo de Italia* and *Avisos ciertos y verdaderos de los sucesos de las guerras*.[40] Once again, it is war which stimulates the press, at the end of the century firmly establishing its periodical publication, though by no means to the exclusion of more popular news, which continues to be published well into the nineteenth century in relations written in both prose and verse.

Notes

1 For an up-to-date bibliography, see the University of La Coruña Website at: http://rosalia.dc.fi.udc.es/BORESU/

2 In this connection, it is significant that it was not until the very beginning of the seventeenth century that news pamphlets began to be published in Madrid, which rapidly became one of the main centres of news production, together with Seville, Barcelona, and Lisbon. However, in the course of the century we find news pamphlets being printed in virtually all the cities of Spain, as well as, in some cases doubtless only occasionally, in many small towns.

3 See María Montáñez Matilla, *Ell correo en la España de los Austrias* (Madrid, 1953).

4 See Henry Kamen, *Spain in the Later Seventeenth Century, 1665–1700* (London and New York, 1980).

5 In the mid-1590s the Seville printer Rodrigo de Cabrera produced several newsletters on the war between Transylvania and Turkey, including a remarkable series of at least seven numbered *relaciones*. See Mercedes Agulló y Cobo, *Relaciones de sucesos, I: Años 1477–1619* (Madrid, 1966), nos. 258, 261, 268, 269, 270, 273, 274, 277, 279, 289, 290, 291, 299. At the end of the decade Cabrera also produced *Avisos*: gazette-type pamphlets of news from Rome. See María Dolores Sáiz, *Historia del periodismo en España, I: Los orígenes. El siglo XVIII* (Madrid, 1983), p. 35. In the 1620s two Seville printers, Simón Fajardo and Francisco de Lira, published numerous gazettes translated from the Italian and the Flemish originals.

6 For news pamphlets published by both sides in the Spanish-Catalan war, see Henry Ettinghausen, *La Guerra dels Segadors a través de la premsa de l'època* (Barcelona, 1993), 4 vols.

7 José Pellicer, *Avisos históricos*, 3 vols, in *Semanario Erudito*, ed. Antonio Valladares (Madrid, 1790), vols 31–3, I, 267. In subsequent references I give simply the volume and page number.

8 See Jerónimo de Barrionuevo de Peralta, *Avisos del Madrid de los Austrias y otras noticias*, ed. José María Díez Borque (Madrid, 1996), pp. 62, 83, 85, 87, 90.

9 *Ibid.*, pp. 111, 137, 295, 299.

10 *Ibid.*, pp. 213, 217, 237.

11 *Ibid.*, p. 240.

12 *Ibid.*, p. 254.

13 See Henry Ettinghausen, 'Quevedo y las actualidades de su tiempo,' *Edad de Oro* 13 (1994): 31–45.

14 For instance: 'Things in Catalonia are getting worse by the minute' (Pellicer, I, 232); 'On Corpus Christi Day there was plenty of finery and frippery to be seen in Madrid, as if we did not have war beating at our gates' (Pellicer, II, 72); 'May God succour us, for war is entrenched everywhere' (Pellicer, II, 255).

15 See Henry Ettinghausen, *Prince Charles and the King of Spain's Sister: What the Papers Said* (Southampton, 1985).

16 See Fernando R. de la Flor, *Atenas castellana. Ensayos sobre cultura simbólica y fiestas en la Salamanca del Antiguo Régimen* (Salamanca, 1989), p. 83.

17 For Almansa, see Manuel Borrego, 'El periodismo de Andrés de Almansa y Mendoza: Apuntes biográficos,' in García de Enterría *et al.*, eds, *Las relaciones de sucesos en España (1500–1750): actas del primer coloquio internacional (alcalá de Henares, 8–12 de junio de 1995)* (alcalá de Henares 1996), pp. 9–18; and Henry Ettinghausen, 'La labor "periodística" de Andrés de Almansa y Mendoza: algunas cuestiones bibliográficas,' *ibid.*, pp. 123–55.

18 See Marcial Rubio Árquez, 'Las relaciones en pliegos sueltos poéticos del siglo XVII,' in García de Enterría *et al.*, eds, *Las relaciones de sucesos en España*, pp. 315–30.

19 See Victoria Campo, 'La historia y la política a través de las relaciones en verso en pliegos sueltos del siglo XVII,' in García de Enterría *et al.*, eds, *Las relaciones de sucesos en España*, pp. 19–32, especially pp. 26–8.

20 See *Relacion verdadera de la presa que han hecho las galeras de Cicilia, Malta y Florencia en la Morea, donde hazia el gran Turco una fortaleza...* (Barcelona: Esteban Liberós, 1616), 2 fols.

21 See *Relacion verdadera, en que se da cuenta como en la ciudad de Paris han quemado dos puentes...* (Barcelona: Esteban Liberós, 1621), 2 fols.

22 See *Relacion verdadera de las crueldades, y robos grandes que hazian en Sierra Morena vnos Gitanos salteadores...* (Barcelona: Esteban Liberós, 1618), 2 fols.

23 See *Admirable sucesso, el qual trata como en Eruena vn rico hombre de mala vida tenia en su casa y heredades, grandes y disformes mastines, con intencion que no se atreuiesse a llegar ningun pobre a su puerta...* (Madrid: Antonio Duplastre, 1638), 2 fols.

24 See *Relacion cierta y verdadera del mas estupendo y espantoso caso que se ha oido...* (Cordova: Herederos de Salvador de Cea, n.d. [*c.* 1672]), 2 fols.

25 See *Relacion verdadera, de la mas admirable maravilla, y peregrino asombro, que ha sucedido en la Villa de Yepes...* (Toledo: n.p., n.d. [1678?]), 2 fols.

26 See *Sucesso atroz y espantoso, que ha acontecido a vna mal acondicionada muger, que maldiziendo a sus hijos, les ofrecia al Diablo...* (Barcelona: Sebastian and Jaime Matevat, 1625), 2 fols.

27 See *Relacion verdadera en que se da cuenta, como vna muger llamada la Baltasara ... se boluio a Dios...* (Barcelona: Gabriel Graells and Esteban Liberós, 1615), 2 fols. The opera, by Abbatini (*c.* 1610–*c.* 1679), is entitled, 'La cómica del cielo, overo La Baltasara'.

28 See *Relacion verdadera que truxo Miguel de Valdeosero, Correo de a cauallo de su Magestad, del lastimoso diluuio que vuo el mes de Nouiembre deste año de 1617...* (Seville: Alonso Rodríguez Gamarra, n.d. [1617?]), 2 fols.

29 See *Relacion muy verdadera ... como en la villa de Castro este verano aparecieron treynta y cinco legiones de Demonios...* (Murcia: Augustín Martínez, 1613), 4 fols.

30 See *Verdadero retrato del monstruoso Pescado que se halló en Alemania...* (Seville: Juan Serrano de Vargas, 1614 [in fact, 1624]), 1 fol.

31 See *Admirables prodigios y portentos, que se manifestaron en Bayona de Fra[n]cia...* (Barcelona: Lorenzo Deu, 1613), 4 fols.

32 See *Relacion verdadera en que se da noticia de un gran prodigio de naturaleza que ha llegado a esta Corte...* (Seville: Juan Cabezas, n.d. [1680?]), 2 fols.

33 See Barrionuevo, *Avisos*, pp. 261–2. On marvels and monsters in the sixteenth- and seventeenth-century Spanish press, see Augustín Redondo, 'Los prodigios en las relaciones de sucesos de los siglos XVI y XVII,' in García de Enterría *et al.*, eds, *Las relaciones de sucesos en España*, pp. 287–303.

34 See Ettinghausen, *La guerra dels segadors.*

35 See E. Varela Hervias, *La Gazeta Nueva (1661–1663). Notas sobre la historia del periodismo español en la segunda mitad del siglo XVII* (Murcia, 1960).

36 *Numero I. Relacion o gazeta de algunos casos particulares, assi Politicos, como Militares, sucedidos en la mayor parte del Mundo, hasta fin de Diziembre de 1660* (Madrid: Julián de Paredes, 1661), 4 fols, fol. 1r.

37 Juan José also starred in at least fifteen verse relations published in the 60s and 70s (see Victoria Campo, 'La historia y la política,' p. 27).

38 See Kamen, *Spain in the Later Seventeenth Century*, pp. 318–19.

39 See Varela Hervias, p. lxix.

40 See Henry Ettinghausen, 'La premsa a Catalunya abans de 1792,' in *200 anys de la premsa diària a Catalunya* (Barcelona, 1995), pp. 22–42, 33–4.

10 The war, the news and the curious

Military gazettes in Italy

Mario Infelise

The war against the Turks at the end of the seventeenth century was of particular importance from the point of view of the development of the information media in Italy. Never before had military events continuously held the breath of entire cities, while bands of writers of various sorts sought to satisfy a curiosity that seemed limitless. There had been similar episodes in the past. In the sixteenth century the battle of Lepanto had inflamed popular enthusiasms. The seventeenth century, the Iron Century *par excellence*, had seen experimentation with new information systems that had brought the echo of military events into the centres of every city of Europe. But the war against the Ottoman Empire that followed the liberation of Vienna from 1683 had a far greater resonance in Italy, no doubt at least in part because the news was constantly good, and in part because a broad Christian coalition had been organized against the 'universal enemy.'

This chapter will begin with a short overview of the general characteristics of political information in the seventeenth century, since over the past thirty years it has been much less studied than literary journalism. In fact, the term 'political journal' is far from adequate for describing the heterogeneous miscellany of materials that contained information concerning events. Simpli-fying somewhat, it could be said that at least in the second half of the sixteenth century there existed an organized and rational network for distributing sheets containing information about military and political events on a regular basis, usually once a week, according to a rhythm determined by the postal services. These manu-script sheets were known by various names, such as 'avvisi,' 'reports,' and 'gazettes.' Occasionally, in the case of events that were particularly likely to arouse general interest, they were printed as broadsheets and had a wide distribution. During the 1630s, coinciding with the Thirty Years' War, periodical political news came to be printed regularly in France and Italy – slightly later than elsewhere in Europe.

Certainly, the emergence of printed gazettes by no means signalled the demise of the manuscript news sheets. These continued to circulate throughout the seventeenth century and for much of the eighteenth century. Indeed, the information that really counted – that is, confidential news which was supposedly reserved for the highest spheres in society – long remained in manuscript.

Professionals of the trade and well-organized 'scriptoria' operated full-time to collect and sell information, by means of half-yearly or yearly subscriptions. Princes, courts, ambassadors and cardinals throughout Europe could not avoid making use of these kinds of services. And the individuals involved often lived lives somewhere on the border between espionage and a new *métier* yet to be defined – the reporter. Manuscript information continued to possess certain advantages with respect to its printed counterpart: it was quicker, since it did not have to pass through the various steps of a printing operation; it evaded censorship controls; and it could be kept confidential and adapted to the exigencies of each client.

During the course of the seventeenth century, the increasing diffusion of printed gazettes introduced a new phenomenon in the form of an emerging 'public opinion.' In Italy, what brought about the establishment of new forms of journalism and new expectations among those who used them, were the military events of 1684–1699.

The Siege of Vienna, from July to September 1683, and the fear that the Ottoman troops might spread westward once the city was taken, served to excite interest in military events and inflame the public imagination. The liberation of the Habsburg capital and the surprising revitalization of the Christian forces against the 'Enemy of Europe' attracted an extraordinary amount of attention, in part due to the success of the military campaigns. The general sentiment was one of witnessing a decisive encounter between Western European Catholic civilization and the Empire of the Infidel, a battle between good and evil, which, after centuries of alternation, seemed to be proceeding toward its triumphant conclusion.

In Italy, emotional involvement, already intense during the course of 1683, was further reinforced the following year by the entry of the Venetian Republic into the fray. On 24 May 1684, representatives of the Emperor, the King of Poland and the Republic, in the presence of Pope Innocent XI, formed the Holy League against the sultan. Thus, only fifteen years after the tragic war of Candia, Venice returned to the seas of the Levant in the hope of recovering what it had lost. The results of the military campaigns were unexpected. While the imperial armies won victories along the Danube and in the Balkans, the Venetian troops and fleet made headway along the Dalmatian and Greek coasts. The epic battles of the aging Captain General Francesco Morosini, elected doge during the course of these events, directed the attention of public opinion in Italy and in Venice toward the Levant.[1] In the public imagination, there was an impression of reliving that bygone and glorious period of the Fourth Crusade, when another aging doge had triumphed in the East and planted the flag of St Mark on the tower of Constantinople.

The constant demand for information concerning the course of the military campaign thus forced the news out of the secret manuscript bulletins and into various printed forms, offered, so they claimed, for the 'curiosity' of readers. During the course of the League, bookshops, stalls and hawkers of books and broadsheets were overwhelmed by a multitude of various materials that drew upon the new events to satisfy the needs of the public. During this period, Giovanni Maria Mitelli circulated engravings referring ironically to this situation, depicting 'those impassioned about the wars' as they anxiously await the postmen in order to discover the news, and the 'curious' as they eagerly read or listen to sheets and reports being read.[2]

Two forms of publication were essential for keeping up with what was happening: the reports published on the occasion of military events of particular importance, and the military journals that supplemented the ordinary printed and manuscript gazettes with information on the war situation. Beginning in 1683, hundreds of broadsheets were published, generally consisting of four pages in octavo and illustrating specific military events in a timely fashion. Discovering their origin and sources is no easy matter.[3] A letter or a technical report might be the foundation, and anonymous editors might add further details to this. Frequently, especially for events occurring within the imperial orbit, the basis was an analogous Viennese sheet. In fact, the reprinted sheets often carried the two-headed imperial eagle as their printer's mark. In Italy they had a complicated history. It was entirely usual for reports published in one place to be reprinted unchanged in another. The frontispieces of these works often testified to this practice by the diction 'In Venice and Ferrara,' or, 'In Vienna and Bologna, for Giacomo Monti and Lucca for the Marescandoli family.' Multiple reprints of the same text came out in rapid succession even in the same city, giving evidence of the breadth and speed of their sale. Broadsheets concerning the most insignificant episodes might be produced in four or five editions in a few days. With such titles as, *Distinct relation...*, *New and True Distinct Relation*, *Description of the City and Fortress of...*, *Copy of a Very Curious Letter...*, there was no victorious siege or battle, however tiny and unimportant, that was not recounted in glorious detail for the benefit of the public. Letters written by soldiers involved in the actions and manuscript newsletters picked up by the Viennese gazette writers were immediately printed and diffused, with irregular but constant cadence. Although for the most part these sheets narrated victorious episodes, there were also those of a more descriptive sort, giving complete diagrams of the armies in the field with information about commanders including their names, unusual and portentous episodes, booty and treasure captured, celebrations and demonstrations on the occasion of the victories, and geographical and historical descriptions of places that might excite particular interest. The seizure of Athens in September 1687, during which the Venetian army bombarded the Parthenon, was, for instance, the object of a description of this sort, due not so much to the importance of the military episode as to the suggestiveness of the place. The four pages of the *Report on the Most Curious and Ancient Things that can be Found in the Vicinity of Athens*, published by Antonio Bosio toward the end of 1687, furnish an interesting account of the city, noting the buildings and their present condition, written by a witness. The description, although brief, was accurate, including details about the Acropolis such as its dimensions and the columns still standing: 'Then there is the square tower on which the statue of Minerva was placed; and in front of this was the famous

Temple of Minerva, most of which had survived to our day, and which is now ruined by the bombs that blew up a powder magazine and destroyed everything. It was built upon 56 columns 42 feet high and five in diameter. Its length was 17, but it is now all disfigured. It was called the Parthenon.' There followed an accurate description of the bas reliefs.[4]

The language was simple and effective, intending not to 'delight by poetic dictions' but to expose the facts 'in brief sentences.' Ettore Scala, one of the many compilers of historical-geographical accounts concerning the current wars who used this sort of publication as his primary source, begged pardon from his readers for the appearance of 'words unapproved by the [Accademia della] Crusca,' justifying himself 'not on the basis of any literary daring,' but on the basis of current usage.[5] The topical interest was enhanced by a slightly epic tone. The behaviour of the Christian victors was always noble and glorious; that of the adversary was vile and worthy of scorn. References abounded to the 'Ottoman arrogance' or 'the barbarous Thracian.' Accounts of violent episodes occurring in the Balkans were never lacking. From Knin to Belgrade, from Buda to Valona, there were 'whole hordes of slaughtered Muslims.' Naturally, God's protection was entirely in favour of the Christian troops, so that, as described in a *Very True and Distinct Relation ... of the Important Acquisition of the Piazza of Bagnia in the Vicinity of Sofia* in 1690: 'One can see the Thracian moon eclipsed, and the Ottoman barbarity subdued, which by its most heavy yoke oppressed for so long the followers of the Divine Sun.' Christian generosity is always emphasized. In 1690, during the siege of the castle of Pernick, the imperial troops had attacked to the cry of 'Viva Leopold, the Roman Emperor, our Lord and legitimate King.' The cry had demoralized the Turks to the point of inducing them to surrender: 'during this confusion our troops arrived and cut to pieces anyone who did not cry "Viva Leopoldo"'; naturally, many Turks rushed 'voluntarily' to convert to Christianity, 'and in this brief period 875 have so far been baptized.' The advance of the Venetian troops in Dalmatia involved similar events, described in a similar way. The seizure of Zuppavaz in 1686 elicited the comment that, 'the sword of the barbarous Ottoman, who claimed to be inexorable in the attack, has no courage left for the defence; and, mortified in the Levant, he humbles himself before the valor of the Venetians and forms, with his crescent, a triumphal arch for their immortal glories.' Under pressure from the 'warlike lion,' it was expected that 'those lands will be illuminated by a splendid sun in Leo and no longer by the pallid moon.'

For the most part, the smaller booksellers and printers specialized in this sector, traditionally neglected by the larger firms. As one moved from Piazza San Marco to the Rialto in Venice, one might encounter numerous pedlars, several stalls, and some shops in which material of this sort flourished. Giovanni Francesco Valvasense, Lorenzo Pittoni, Francesco Batti, Giuseppe Prosdocimo, Girolamo Albrizzi, and a few others, engaged in fierce competition for the printed information market, made even fiercer by the immunity of the genre of broadsheets from protection by the usual official government-issued printing privileges. Fist fights over merchandise were not uncommon. As soon as a military notice arrived, it had to be printed up immediately and sold in the piazza. Censorship controls were performed in haste. So as not to lose time, and in order to beat their competitors, printers vying with one another hurried directly to the Riformatori dello Studio di Padova to obtain permission to print, 'by imbroglio,' without passing through the usual secretary, Nicolosi.[6] If another arrived first, one's own miserable investment went up in smoke. In December of 1686, Prosdocimo, a small-time typographer very active in the information business, whose partner, a pedlar named Batti, took responsibility for city-wide distribution, received a knife injury in the face. He revealed to the lawyers who interrogated him a tale of hatred between himself and Girolamo Albrizzi, originating in their competition for the same market. 'Every time news of some interest arrives,' he recounted, 'including daily reports about the Venetian navy as well as about the allied princes, I try to print them myself, utilizing the licence I possess from the magistrates of the Riformatori dello Studio, in order to support myself and my family; then I have them sold in the cities and squares, like everyone else.' This activity had earned him the 'implacable hatred' of Albrizzi. On 23 December, the two had come to blows when Albrizzi, accompanied by his employees, had ordered his competitor to stop selling the reports and threatened him with assassination. The young and daring Albrizzi seemed so sure of himself, and lacking in principles, that many who 'sold histories' throughout the city testified against him in the course of the proceedings.[7]

In 1684 a new genre emerged: the navy journals. Often confused with the already existing battle reports, they soon took their place as a separate type, published periodically and thus not dependent on single salient military actions. They offered a more complete picture of events, joining information together from various places, much like the gazettes.

Vienna was the principal source of information for most of the military journals diffused in Italy between 1684 and 1690. There, news from the theatre of war in the form of letters and reports accumulated very rapidly and was often compiled expressly for eventual publication. Regular manuscript newsletters may well have been a basis.[8] A Flemish-born typographer, Johann Baptist Hacque, published a weekly gazette in Italian and Latin (*Il Corriere ordinario* and *Cursor ordinarius*) from 1671 with a wide diffusion.[9] This was often accompanied by a *Foglietto straordinario* that reported the latest news at mid-week.[10] In 1678 Hacque died and the imperial privilege for printing the Italian gazette went to his brother-in-law from Antwerp, Johann van Ghelen, who remained in the business for several decades. Van Ghelen did not limit himself to recording information gleaned from letters and bulletins in his possession. Sometimes he visited the places in question to collect news, which he then wrote up in weekly sheets, in a correct and succinct Italian without rhetorical flourishes of any sort. These were then submitted to the imperial authorities for censorship and printed.[11] Van Ghelen's Viennese sheets were the most widely distributed, but they were not unique. Also distributed in Italy during this period were the weekly *Ordinariae relationes* in Latin, published by the widow of Pietro Hilden with an imperial privilege.[12]

During the course of 1684, more or less contemporaneously in Milan, Bologna, Lucca, Todi, and Rome, there appeared printed news sheets known as 'military journals.' The name did not necessarily indicate regular periodicity, but rather an intention to provide a day-by-day account of what was happening in the war zones. The periodicity was more a result of protracted military actions that continued to arouse interest because of their favourable outcome. Reconstructing their history is particularly difficult because so few examples have survived, not to mention the confusion caused by broadsheets that also published material in the form of a daily chronicle.[13] Already in 1683, a small printing operation run by Antonio Bossio in Venice and specializing in broadsheets and prints of fortresses published a *Sincere and Distinct Account of the Counsels and Operations of the Imperial and Polish Armies and of the Besieged against the Formidable Ottoman Armies....*[14] The 44-page volume was paginated continuously. The internal titles distinguishing the separate internal fascicles, and the narration of events subsequent to the date of the censor's licence, suggest that all were not issued at the same time.

In the course of 1684 other sheets appeared with more regular periodicity. In summer 1684, a *True Journal of Everything Happening in Hungary* came out in Rome, produced by the bookseller Francesco Leone and the printer Domenico Antonio Ercole. A similar one was circulated by Komarek at the same time.[15] Others with similar content also appeared. In Lucca, the Marescandoli Firm reprinted a weekly *Journal of the Imperial Camp* from June until at least September, which followed the model of the one produced by Giacomo Monti of Bologna that had also been reprinted in Vienna.[16] Similar sheets, not necessarily with identical texts, appeared in Venice, Todi, and Milan.[17]

Closely linked to the military events, these publications naturally ceased in the winter months, when military activity diminished. The twenty-second number of a sheet called *Report* ... concluded with this comment: 'it will be difficult, indeed impossible, to continue the journal now.' The troops were in their quarters and material was, therefore, unavailable. If something occurred, there was no way to confirm it. 'Writing things that have no basis ... is so far from the mind of the person who is proposing this publication, that he has decided to write nothing except what is certain and accredited, as he has done to date and will continue to do in the future.'[18]

These sheets, still uncertain in their structure and in their periodicity, were perfected two years later in Venice by Girolamo Albrizzi. This young and ambitious printer can be called the true inventor of Venetian and Italian journalism, and his dynasty would continue producing periodical sheets of every sort well into the nineteenth century. Born in 1662, he did not originate from a printing family; his father, Giambattista, was a rag collector. On 14 October 1685, Albrizzi entered the printers' guild. At this time, his printing efforts in the field of information were already under way. The year before he had opened a shop with a typographical operation in Campo della Guerra behind the church of San Zulian, which became the centre of his journalistic and printing activities. As in other cases of the sort, it is uncertain whether he operated independently or with some outside financing. The latter is probably the case, but there is no evidence to supprt this.[19] Between 1684 and 1685 he had published a geographical description of the Danube basin with information concerning the history of the Hungarians and the Turks, and concerning all the wars under way, accompanied by some sixty small engravings.[20]

In spring 1686, while the military operations on the Eastern front began to accelerate, Albrizzi started his *Journal from the Imperial Camp at Buda*, the most successful of the many military journals of these years, and the only one that had the structure of a true periodical. It marked a definite evolutionary stage, introducing elements typical of literary journalism into the political gazette genre.[21]

The *Journal* came out in weekly dodicesimo issues for four years. According to the editor, it was not simply a collection of reports, but a complete account of the 'most memorable deeds.' The small format permitted easy binding into small volumes that would form 'a full and perfect history of the current wars.'[22] It was offered for sale at Albrizzi's bookstore or else by a six-month subscription costing a ducat in advance that protected the buyer against possible future price increases. The *Journal* ran from 12 to 64 pages, according to the events. The date of publication is difficult to determine because the reports bore the date of the event in question; but comparison with other sources suggests that the last facts usually occurred some twenty days or so before the journal appeared in Venice.[23]

Albrizzi was both innovative and systematic in his use of the *Journal* for advertising his own products – not only printed ones, but also the 'true and marvellous water of the Queen of Hungary, newly discovered for the health of the human body,' which he sold along with a booklet illustrating its 'miraculous effects.'[24] The list of titles gives some idea of the material that might get into the hands of the 'curious' public. There were brief treatises with summaries of the current wars, and 'instant books,' quickly compiled from gazette material. There were almanacs, works of popular science, other periodicals published by Albrizzi, and above all, many engraved images depicting the war zones.[25] Gazettes in fact were usually sold along with the print showing the fortress being besieged, giving the prospect of the city being conquered and illustrating the battle plans. Though roughly executed, these prints were particularly evocative due to their origin in sketches and drawings actually originating from the zone of operations. The wars of this period furnished material for a highly active printmaking industry, of which the torrential production of Vincenzo Coronelli was merely a salient episode.

Accounts in Albrizzi's *Journal*, rich in detail and reasonably accurate, followed the events day by day. The general impression is that they were edited in Vienna and in the war areas. They shared with the standard war reports a tone expressing active involvement in what was going on. Victories were the only desire proper to a 'Catholic heart,' and furnished 'motives for the most erudite pens of Europe to compile memoirs for all future centuries.'[26] The journal usually began its periodical coverage by focusing on the imperial camp and then extending to all of Europe, with a significant concentration on the Central and

East European area. Military events were the backbone of the periodical, with detailed information concerning troop movements, battles, and the structure and formation of armies. Yet, the point was to elucidate and explain every political and military event in some way related to the war against the Turks. Thus, besides the military events themselves in Hungary, Serbia, and Wallachia, there were regular reports on Poland and Muscovy. To these, somewhat less frequently, was added news from other fronts, originating from Holland or England. On 25 August 1689, the death of the King of Siam was duly noted.

Albrizzi's *Journal from the Imperial Camp* enjoyed a modest success both inside and outside Venice. Occasionally out of print numbers were reprinted. The duke of Modena, who ordered his agent in Venice, Giovanni Francesco Vezzosi, to furnish him with 'the most curious publications,' regularly received it along with information about its compiler.[27] The journal was also reprinted in several places – in Ferrara by the typographer Bernardino Pomatelli.[28] In Rimini, the printer Giovanni Felice Dandi was inspired by Albrizzi's model to produce an analogous paper from 1686 to 1687, entitled, *Military Journal Giving Succinct Reports of What Happens in the Imperial Army Day by Day under the City of Buda and Other Places in Hungary*, with some differences in content.[29]

The extension of military operations to the Mediterranean theatre, of particular interest to the Venetian and Italian public, but not covered by the news from Vienna, induced Albrizzi in 1687 to take up the *Journal of the Venetian Army in the Levant*, entirely devoted to Venetian successes in Dalmatia, Albania, and Morea (Pelponnesus), and based on a source directly connected to the Venetian fleet. The suspicion that Albrizzi might have utilized the very dispatches of the Venetian representatives and high officials themselves, however, is unfounded. A comparison of Albrizzi's text with the official communications demonstrates enough similarities to suggest simultaneous redaction, but also considerable differences in detail.[30]

Unlike the *Journal from the Imperial Camp*, the *Journal of the Venetian Army* came out irregularly.[31] Correspondence arriving in Venice from Vienna by way of regular postal services contributed to determining the frequency of the journal. The arrival of news from Morea on the other hand was subject to the infinite vagaries of maritime transport. For the rest, the formal structure of the periodical differed little from its predecessor. The same format and narrative rhythm accompanied the same chronicle style, although with a slightly greater attention to the geographical details. The journalist was obviously aware of the location of the events in centres with important significance from the standpoint of ancient history; at times he provides accounts of the condition of classical ruins in the area. On 17 August 1687, for instance, concerning Corinth, the writer notes the discovery of 'many antiquities, including the statue of the god Janus'; he goes on to record having seen Mount Parnassus, the fountain of Helicon 'celebrated by the Poets,' and Mount Pindus, 'with everything covered in vegetation, and the greatness of centuries vanished and devoured by time.' The conquest of Athens furnished an occasion for digressions on the surviving classical monuments. As in the report cited earlier, the destruction of the

Parthenon by the Venetian army was an object of an account expressing regret for what had happened. '[One observes] the ruin produced by the munitions in the Temple of Minerva in the fortress, when it caught fire after being hit by a bomb, and we see with horror the collapse of the great colonnade, crushing two hundred bodies, accompanied by a great wealth of marble pieces so large that it will be very difficult if not impossible to move them from there, and in fact, the most beautiful antiquity of the world has been destroyed, a memorial that had never yielded to the injuries of time, adorned with bas reliefs and reliefs on the door mostly made of alabaster, figures that had been preserved intact for so many years and that give a stupendous and marvellous reminiscence of times gone by.'[32]

By way of the Levant there came also information about Constantinople. In 1687 the enthusiasm for the military victories was amplified by the echo of revolts there that were undermining the internal stability of the Ottoman government. 'A tartan arrived from Constantinople three days ago,' it was reported in issue number 9, published toward the end of 1686, 'that had left there ten days ago, with news that the palace there was full of confusion....' 'The king has arrested the Grand Vizir in his own seraglio.... The people of Constantinople were divided into two parties, one of them calling for the coronation of the son of the Grand Turk; the other calling for his brother Sulemein, a ferocious man. All the shops of that great city remained closed, as homicides were occurring every day and people were killing each other.' Frightening news concerning the internal disruptions in the Ottoman capital continued in successive numbers under the title of *Journal of Constantinople.* Homicides, famine, and pestilence were certain to cause the old empire 'quickly to fall into the abyss of its last ruin.'

Inevitably, in Venice, the flood of information served to fire the enthusiasm of the crowds who avidly read it and, when it reported victories, rushed into the streets. Inevitably, too, there were discussions due to disagreements between the stories. The absence of an official state gazette like the ones that had been instituted in other Italian and European states only served to increase the plurality of the voices.

Reports, manuscript and printed gazettes and military journals usually came out anonymously. It is not easy to give names and faces to the authors of these writings, who preferred to operate behind the scenes. When we do discover a name, finding some more significant information about the person in question is difficult. Most of them were obscure figures of a sort rarely covered in the standard repertories or biographical dictionaries. Only occasionally, a fortunate search through police archives makes possible, if not the reconstruction of a biography and a personality, at least a view of the environments in which early journalism emerged.

The military journals, like other works of the kind, came out anonymously, with one interesting exception. This is a reprint – the fourth – of the *Sincere and Distinct Account of the Counsels and Operations* considered above.[33] It carries a dedication by Giacomo Torri to Quintiliano Rezzonico. There is no telling whether Torri was the actual author of this first example of a military gazette. Dedications were frequently signed by an editor or by whoever procured the text to be printed. But in this case the distinction is unimportant. The name of Torri clearly introduces us into the world of the professional gazette writers, of those who practiced full-time the trade of collecting news from different sources and compiling sheets, mainly in manuscript, to be sold by subscription. His biography may therefore be considered exemplary of a late seventeenth-century *reportista*, to use the term then current in Venice. He was born in 1634, most probably in Bologna, a city where the sale of news, if not its actual production, was a good business. Here, for instance, the engraver Mitelli found abundant inspiration for depicting the hunger for information that characterized these years. There is no way of knowing when Torri arrived in Venice. He was certainly there by the 1670s when he was mentioned as the proprietor of a well-established scriptorium at San Moisé, the area where the gazette writers mainly concentrated. For some thirty years he compiled manuscript sheets tailored to the interests of the emperor, whom he called 'my particular lord and patron.' He was manipulated to some extent by the imperial ambassador in Venice, who thought to control the flow of information coming into and out of the city. To his salary from the emperor he added income from the sale of reports. Other contacts of his included German merchants and the city government of Graz.[34] Besides the information he received from the German-speaking world, he had reliable sources in Venice. By way of Carlo Battain, secretary of the patrician Zuanne Corner of San Polo, he might obtain up-to-date news on discussions in the councils.[35]

Employment as an imperial agent procured for Torri numerous difficulties. For years, a sort of secret war went on between the chanceries of the various embassies, with weapons including espionage and the manipulation of information and falsehood.[36] *Reportisti* frequently found themselves involved in a game in which they were only pawns, and in which, despite their total unscrupulousness, they could easily make false moves. In 1679, for instance, the duke of Mantua, Ferdinando Carlo, ordered Torri to retract an article in his Vienna news sheet, which was none the less true, concerning well-advanced negotiations for the delivery of Casale by the duke to the King of France.[37]

Torri's writings also disturbed the French ambassador. And if the latter occasionally complained to the Venetian authorities about the excessive liberty conceded to the *reportisti*, occasionally the tone became more threatening. On 10 March 1681, news circulated that Torri had been assassinated.[38] The information was false but credible. Assassinations of gazette writers were not infrequent. There were reasons why Torri's philo-imperial and anti-French inclinations might incite reprisals. And when the Venetian authorities did not intervene, the diplomats took the matter into their own hands. In March, 1681, Torri apparently was saved only by the French ambassador's sudden decision to go on a pilgrimage to Loreto. Before departure, the ambassador took care to warn Torri to cease and desist or be thrown into the canal. An informant named Castelnuovo, commenting to the State Inquisitors concerning the ambassador's pilgrimage, added that 'this devotion has prevented an evil intention of his, which was to have a *reportista* in San Moisé, one Giacomo Torri, drowned; for there was a report from France suggesting that "it cannot be that the cock will not crow and Peter will not weep," and to this Torri wrote a reply in his Roman newsletter to this effect: "if Peter weeps, Christ will have been denied." The ambassador was told this meant his king would perform the actions of an apostate and against God; and he left with this thought on his mind.'[39] However, the ambassador apparently brought the 'evil intention' back with him from Loreto. In the following June, again according to Castelnuovo's account, 'he showed his capacity to put a just fear into the hearts of the common people in the question of Giacomo Torri the *reportista*.' Three of his men were discovered in the act of 'beating up' the latter 'by someone who commanded them to stop in the name of the Most Excellent Heads of the Council of Ten … but they replied with certain vulgarities, saying they knew neither heads nor councils.' Apparently, the 'cause of the offence was that the *reportista* had written that the king of France had fallen from his horse, and this was a judgment of God, like the previous divine judgment against Fra Paolo [Sarpi], in this case punishing a new persecutor of the Church and enemy of the vicar of Christ.'[40]

Difficulties of the kind were the order of the day in the life of the *reportista*. In March 1685 the duke of Mantua planned to have Torri's 'head smashed' by two thugs because he had written that 'the French are being brought' into the duchy. Such warnings were supposed to serve as an example to others. The duke commanded his agent in Venice to 'make a public spectacle' of the *reportista* so everyone would know that 'thus the duke punishes those who speak ill of his House.'[41]

Torri's biography differs little from those of dozens of other newsletter writers. Several decades previously, these writers had begun seeking positions connected with the various ambassadors. In 1676 a certain Giuliani, well-known in his time for the adventurousness of his news sheets, received an annual stipend of 50 doubloons from the French ambassador. The diffusion of this sheet had forced the ambassador's imperial counterpart to do the same, by 'gaining the confidence of the scribes, so they might be encouraged to write what was desired in return for promises and presents.'[42] In the years of the League the situation of the pro-French gazette writers became riskier, since they had to face a general hostility second only to the hostility to the Turks. Greater rewards were therefore necessary to compensate them for the dangers. Relations between the French embassy and its writers intensified; the writers occasionally were invited inside as guests. Besides Giuliani, there was also Cavalier Giulio Cesare Beaziano, a pompous adventurer, soi-disant marquis, who styled himself as 'a gentleman of Justinopolis, knight of the Royal Order of St. Michel and perpetual commander of Icaria.' He was in fact a 'well-known newsletter writer,' a secret informer of the French and Spanish ambassadors, and had written a tract in favour of the Venetian patriciate in order to better infiltrate the most influential families.[43] Another who frequented the French embassy was Giovanni Francesco Vezzosi, who was also an agent of the duke of Modena in Venice between 1688 and 1693.[44]

The political and military events of the war, and anything connected with them in any way, stimulated an intense production of information of all sorts. Booksellers' stalls were stacked as never before with broadsheets, gazettes, and books that purported to provide complementary information, including geographical descriptions, ancient and modern histories, travel narratives, and imaginative writings set in exotic places.[45]

Closely related to the gazette-type material, and drawing directly upon it, were the annual compendia, mainly published in December and offering a synthetic picture of the main events of the past year. The genre was not new; similar works, varying in length, had appeared throughout the century, some of them published by well-known writers. One of the first had been the *Events of the World of the Year 1636* by Ferrante Pallavicino.[46] Along the same lines were countless works with titles beginning, *Events*, *Successes*, *Information*, and the like, which were nothing but re-workings of journalistic material in book form, hastily collected and presented as complete histories. A typical example was the *Diary of the Events of the Imperial Armies in Hungary after the Seizure of Strigonia*, published at the end of 1684 and 1685 by Combi and Lanoù.[47] Editors behaved with a considerable amount of unscrupulousness. At the end of 1686 Girolamo Albrizzi began selling a *Distinct Report concerning the Glorious Victories and Conquests Obtained by the Armies of the Most Serene Republic of Venice in the Current War Against the Turks*, which was none other than the *Journal of the Levant* with the periodical and journalistic elements left out. Other volumes combined several years. At the beginning of 1686, the editor Giambattista Chiarello, along with the printer Stefano Curti, diffused a *History of the Events of the Imperial Arms … From 1683 to 1687*. The preface to the reader complained about the difficulty of gaining a general understanding of the events by just reading the 'simple and succinct reports' that were constantly in circulation. To supply this need, the editors (so they said) requested the collaboration of an author who however desired to remain anonymous – a tactic these annuals commonly shared with the gazettes and reports on which they were based. Indeed, it is important to remember that the few authors who signed their names to works of this kind usually belonged to the now-familiar world of the newsletters. In 1685 Giovanni Cagnolini and Angiolo Orsetti published a 'historical account' entitled *Diary of the Events of the Imperial Army in Hungary after the Blockade of Nayasel in This Campaign of 1685*. The book was no different, in appearance or content, from so many others of these years, except perhaps in its bombastic, rhetorical tone. The author who appeared on the title page was 'dottor' Pasquale Biondi, a newsletter writer.[48]

Writings clearly derived from gazettes were sold alongside other types that intended to furnish complementary information. Morea was usually the centre of attention, but often the purview extended to the entire Ottoman Empire. Military events were inserted into rapidly delineated historical and geographical contexts, demonstrating the burgeoning interest in the country and its customs, always from a decisively anti-Turkish standpoint. Giambattista Chiarello and Giovanni Domenico Rossi produced *Information Concerning the Current War, Forces and Union of the Christian Princes, and Qualities of the Turkish Army, and its Vices and*

Customs. They began by noting that although 'things concerning the war' were 'sought by everyone,' none the less, that everyone spoke about the events without the proper knowledge, was a fact deserving of 'universal scorn.' In this way, 'the vulgar' received an entirely reductive and defeatist impression of 'the most just' conflict 'that had ever been undertaken.' The two collaborators had therefore persuaded the anonymous author (they claimed), a soldier by profession, to provide a general sketch of the Ottoman Empire. And despite the inevitable anti-Turkish sentiment, the work offered much information about the enemy, including some illustrations of their accoutrements. Along the same lines was a little volume that Leibniz, on a visit to Venice, described as the only new and interesting one in all the city's bookstores. This was the *Report on the Science of the Turks* by Giambattista Donà, former Venetian bailo of Constantinople, and published in a typical low-cost format by Andrea Poletti, one of the most active printers in the field of political and military news. The writing was apparently a letter from the author to a relative, published at the insistence of the printer. It claimed to provide a new interpretation of Ottoman history, inviting the reader to set aside the usual commonplaces. Donà complained that the scarcity of interest in Turkish intellectual life merely reinforced the 'universal opinion, truly erroneous,' that the Turkish nation was entirely dedicated to arms, 'ignorant of good studies and literature, inept in rhetoric and poetry, destitute of knowledge in law, medicine, philosophy and mathematics.'[49]

The variety of material for sale indicates clearly that editors and authors gave careful consideration to the best ways of satisfying the needs of their different audiences. At the end of his edition of the *Description of the Ancient and Modern Kingdom of Negroponte*, mainly dedicated to the ancient history of Euboea, the anonymous writer wondered who his potential reader might be. 'I thought I recognized you. Which are you: learned, curious, plebeian, or among those *quos insignes garrula lingua facit?*' He claimed to give little heed to the first two categories; and went on to say that: 'if you are plebeian, I'm talking to you, since I appreciate and adopt a simple style. If you find something good in it, keep in mind that Agathocles too ate food fit for a king in plates made of the humblest clay.' To this basic simplicity, accompanied by solid substance, he showed a particular attachment; indeed, 'if you are among the last [i.e. *quos insignes* …], you are perfect for me, because your powerful rasp files the rust and roughness off of me.'

That so many different types of information were available, and that many of them were aimed at a popular audience, demonstrates just how much interest these military events aroused. The whole city was involved. In the capital of a state like Venice, in fact, an urban topography of news began to emerge.

Piazza San Marco was obviously the centre of diffusion. This is where the vital organs of the state were located. Letters and dispatches from ambassadors all over Europe as well as from commanders in the military operations came to Palazzo Ducale. We can document the relations between the newsletter writers and the functionaries of the chancery they contacted for secret information. In the piazza, there circulated the broadsheets already mentioned, the popular type of periodical, irregular in publication and variable in appearance.

Even the areas just outside the piazza had a precise role. From the Bocca di Piazza one passed out toward San Moisé and the post office. Not by chance, the street alongside the church of San Moisé, called '*calle* of the scribes,' had the largest concentration of newsletter writers' shops. The scriptoria were among the main meeting places for the 'curious,' i.e., persons interested in the 'news of the world.' This was a complex community, extending from the piazza to the shops. Here minor functionaries bringing secret information from the Palazzo to be sent every Saturday afternoon to Rome or Paris might encounter professionals like Torri or the others mentioned, as well as spies, adventurers of various types, or patricians operating on their own in search of new sources of information and willing to acquire it in return for what they had heard in the councils.

From San Moisé, newsletters spread to the rest of the city – other gathering places, other shops, especially pharmacies and brandy sellers, each with their own regular customers.

Obviously, the many publications concerning the same events encouraged discussion. Reportedly, they caused the formation of 'conventicles and large groups of devotees,' sometimes numbering in the hundreds to discuss matters in Piazza San Marco, accompanied by 'insults, beatings, slaps and fisticuffs.' Such was the outcome on 19 December 1676 between two elderly men, a fruit seller named Berto and another shopkeeper, who 'came to blows concerning the different versions of the taking of Melisso.' The 'liberty of Venice,' one informer wrote to the State Inquisitors, was too permissive. Some Venetian subjects, he added, such as a gentleman named Beaziano, 'exaggerated the glories of His Most Christian Majesty and avowed a desire to see the dominion of the latter extended to Venice.' On that occasion, Beaziano had been reproved by don Giovanni Zisola, a priest of San Marco, who told him to 'go stick it, etc., because I don't give a shit, safe as I am under San Marco.'[50]

During the war years, the 'conventicles' and 'groups' multiplied, where nobles, subjects at every social level, and foreigners joined in heated discussions about the political events taking place. Occasionally, public discussions were announced concerning controversial themes. In summer 1687, a 'public academy' was held in the palace at Santa Sofa of the 'new nobleman' Quintilino Rezzonico, an associate of Torri and the object of the fulsome dedications often given to the various war writings; the theme proposed was 'whether losing or winning has been more advantageous for this Republic.' In spite of 'the state's pressing concerns,' advertisements were posted 'on the walls of the shops and on the bridges,' inviting everyone to attend. At the meeting, the patrician Orazio Angaran scandalized everyone by provocatively stating that 'losses are more advantageous ... than victories,' before an audience including 'a great number of people of all nations and all parties, including the French, the Austrians and others.'[51]

Though Rezzonico's 'public academy' was an unusual occasion, the usual gathering places were available every evening for the reading and discussion of publicly displayed gazettes in manuscript or print. Pharmacies, brandy shops and barber shops became particularly important places for the exchange of opinions. There persons of various social levels might meet, and 'everyone plays the statesman.'[52]

Colonel Castelnuovo, a frequenter of these places and an acute observer of what went on there, reported to the State Inquisitors that 'many gentlemen meet there, along with persons of other conditions; they sit together as in a private consultation, and each one talks about everything he has heard and observed that day. They speak of the kingdoms, the wars, the treaties; and these days they sometimes go on until two or more hours of the night.'[53]

Every pharmacy had its regular crowd. At the Maltese Cross in San Giorgio dei Greci it was 'the crowd hanging around the nobleman Ludovico Widman....' At Sturion in San Boldo, numerous noblemen talked about deals being made and wars being fought. At San Cassiano many merchants, priests and others formed a 'regular circle, where everything was discussed'; they had even organized a 'little council room with some benches, and talk in secret about whatever is going on with this Republic as well as with France and elsewhere, and every evening this sect arranges for one or another of their members to bring news of this or that sort.'[54] In the pharmacy in Fondamenta di S. Marcilian 'there was a great assembly of people who speak openly about these serious matters.' The same went on at the pharmacies in Campo Santa Marina and at the Morion at S. Francesco della Vigna. Other 'assemblies' with similar characteristics, made up 'of various sorts of people' were held in many barber shops.

The image of these groups of people discussing war and politics can be filled out by the satirical comments of Bartolomeo Dotti, a writer and adventurer from Brescia who had been to Greece with the Venetian fleet and came back an assiduous devotee of the main gathering places. Passionately interested in the news, when he was imprisoned in 1685 in the fortress of Tortona, he had implored a friend to send 'the news of the armadas' to him 'by every post.'[55] A few years later, in Venice, he composed a long and lively satire entitled, 'To the News writers,' that adds some colourful details to the information gleaned from the archives of the State Inquisitors.[56] Although the military events to which he referred were probably not those in Morea but those connected with the Spanish Succession war, the situations and the attitudes of the public concerning what was going on must have been similar. Dotti frequently alluded to real persons, using their real names. The 'shop of Minummi' actually existed, and was one of the best-known newsletter producers. Therein 'the indolent pupils' 'of idleness' 'sweated.' Most of the composition dwelt upon the circles where politics was discussed and the persons who participated, showing their 'passionate obsession' with 'the order of the world.' See the pharmacist (as the poem states) 'in the shop of our Grappiglia / a big discussion's under way, / all the news is picked apart.'

Those who say, besides the secrets,
What is true and what is false,
Priests and monks they mostly are,
And what they know is mostly nought.

These 'Priests and monks, so ignorant / with brains reversed, extravagant' are particularly taken to task. Their discourses in favour of France or Austria are mercilessly and uninhibitedly ridiculed. A certain Viotti 'raises his voice' 'with words of bitterness and anger,' showing 'chimerical messages'; another priest, Mea, trying to speak an educated Tuscan Italian, confuses Italian words with Venetian dialect. 'Buranello,' a priest from Burano, would be better off speaking in 'a bordello.' A priest from Abruzzo would like to see the French all dead; he is opposed by Padre Grissi, who 'says the opposite.' Elsewhere, another priest, an 'Illyrian beast,' just having left the sacristy, goes about 'peddling philosophy' in 'Morione's shop.' Others besides ecclesiastics are the butt of Dotti's witticisms. In other places around the city, he commented, it was possible to encounter 'a gentleman of great politics,' 'erudite' and thoughtful, who after long meditation 'says believing has no point; / truth being what one would.' There is 'Teodori the physician,' dressed in the Parisian fashion, 'who sneers at everything and hankers only after honors.'

Discussions often ended in fights. In the collective enthusiasm that characterized the arrival of every notice concerning a victory, public order was put at risk, especially since the popular celebrations that occurred regularly on such occasions sometimes involved exaggerated or abnormal mass behaviour. With deeds done at sea and on the fields of battle echoing through the broadsheets and gazettes, celebrations of the victories of Christian forces were a constant in all of Italy. News of the end of the siege of Vienna in September 1683 was accompanied in Venice by the announcement of three holidays, with public performances and fireworks. Similar celebrations were reported also in Bologna. In Rome, shops closed for three days. In Lucca a parade was organized, with triumphal floats. Everywhere, dances, songs, and cries of enthusiasm were the reaction of a population that, as a manuscript newsletter noted, 'had not experienced such joy in many years.'[57]

This was only the first occasion. The following years saw a continuous series of similar celebrations, often accompanied by complicated scenographical apparatus, described with some exaggeration in broadsheets. In 1686, for the conquest of Nauphia in Greece, there were fireworks in Venice in Piazza San Marco and celebrations in all the main squares. At Santa Maria Formosa an artificial fortress was erected to represent that of the capital of Morea, and a simulated battle was staged. At San Lio a Te Deum was performed. At Santi Apostoli there 'all the deeds' of Morosini, 'the true Mars of our times,' were represented. Decorations and ornaments were put up even in the peripheral zones of the Giudecca and the ghetto.[58] Outside Venice the same behaviour was registered. For the taking of Corone in 1685, fireworks were organized in Padua, while the local poet Bottazzo Tombolon 'with his heart rising in his breast …

cried out for joy.' Two years later, on the occasion of another fortunate event, the whole city en masse witnessed a complex theatrical piece with a 'lion,' 'vomiting bombs,' 'falling crescent moons,' 'burning cornucopias; and a great book of their false prophecies written in Turkish characters, to everyone's astonishment, and labelled Alcoranum.' Meanwhile, there were 'fires forming huge letters' 'saying viva Venezia.'[59] In Ferrara the previous year, festivities concerning the taking of Buda had gone on for fifteen days.[60] In 1690, for the Venetian conquest of Vallona, great celebrations were reported as far as Puglia and Sicily.[61]

While these celebrations and discussions were going on, there were also civil disturbances, caused for the most part by cries and demonstrations against the French and the Turks. 'Kill any Frenchman you meet,' was heard in Venice. On the occasion of the celebrations for the liberation of Vienna, some subjects of the Most Christian King were mistreated for daring to affirm that 'the victory was not so great.' During the same period, for security purposes merchants coming from the Ottoman lands were kept inside the Fondaco dei Turchi.[62] In Bologna a Frenchman thrown into a fire in connection with contemporary events escaped with his life only by a miracle.[63] In Rome, in Piazza Navona, Turks were impaled and hung in effigy, then carried around the city by a great multitude of people.[64]

The entry of the Republic into the Holy League increased the tension. 'On hearing this,' Castelnuovo wrote, 'people began meeting in such large numbers that groups of up to a hundred were said to be forming, and instigators began to plot a rebellion.'[65] Not surprisingly, the people's agitation was vented on the Jews, whom some viewed as 'spies and supporters of the Turks, and great enemies of Christianity.'[66] On 21 August 1684 in Padua, some 4,000 persons set about sacking and burning the ghetto. In the shop of the scribe Zanette at the Rialto bridge, where news was registered, it was rumoured that something similar was about to happen in Venice. A few days later, following the news of the taking of Buda, which proved false, 200 Venetians from Castello attempted to burn down the portal of the ghetto.[67] In the same period a newsletter from Rome arrived in Venice, with lines censored out in the copy, calling for 'the expulsion of the Jews,' who, it said, were 'worse than the Turks.'[68]

Tensions of this nature continued throughout the years of the war. The impact that the diffusion of information appeared to have upon public order induced the Venetian authorities to put greater controls in place; and the traditional Venetian prohibition of all printed weekly gazettes was reinstated. In August 1688, all journals were prohibited for the first time; although the following month the prohibition was lifted. The following year, Girolamo Albrizzi was thrown into the dungeons of the Ducal Palace for publishing a letter from the Pope to the Senate which he had managed to obtain by way of clandestine channels. And tacitly, without any public decree, on 30 September 1690, the publication of all military journals was definitively prohibited.[69] In such a difficult moment from a military standpoint, someone must have recalled what Paolo Sarpi, counsellor to the Venetian Senate, had said back in 1613, in one of the first definitions of public opinion and its weight in political matters:

that books and printed matter were made only of words, 'but from those words are formed the opinions of the world that bring about parties, seditions, and eventually wars. Yes, they are words; but they are words that draw armies behind them.'[70]

Notes

1 Concerning the military events, see Kenneth M. Setton, *Venice, Austria, and the Turks in the Seventeenth Century* (Philadelphia, PA, 1991).
2 F. Varignana, *Le collezioni d'arte della Cassa di Risparmio in Bologna. Le incisioni. Giovanni Maria Mitelli* (Bologna, 1978), plates 122, 124, 131, 136, 141.
3 The journalistic material on which this article is based has mostly been lost. Surviving examples of printed gazettes are rare and exist mainly in diplomatic archives; and some reports have survived by chance. The observations here are based for the most part on the reports conserved in the following collections of miscellanies in the Biblioteca Marciana in Venice (henceforth, BMV): 167 (contains forty-one reports between 1668 and 1717, and twenty-seven reports concerning the war in Morea), 449 (eighty-four reports, all relating to the battles between the imperial army and the Turks during the Holy League war), 2707 (forty-seven military reports, of which twenty refer to the same war), 2871 (seventy-one broadsides, of which forty-eight refer to the events in the Levant with which Venice was concerned during the Morea war). Other titles of sheets referring to the war of the Holy League are indicated in Sandro Bulgarelli and Tullio Bulgarelli, *Il giornalismo a Roma nel Seicento. Avvisi a stampa e periodici italiani conservati nelle biblioteche romane* (Rome, 1988).
4 Concerning the conquest of Athens and the bombardment of the Parthenon, see L. de Laborde, *Athénes aux XVe, XVIe et XVIIe siècles* (Paris, 1854), which, however, is inspired by a ferocious anti-Venetian sentiment. Also see, J. M. Paton, *The Venetians in Athens 1687–1688. From the 'Istoria' of Cristoforo Ivanovic* (Cambridge, MA, 1940); M. Pavan, *L'avventura del Partenone. Un monumento nella storia* (Florence, 1983), pp. 169–81.
5 Ettore Scala, *L'Ungheria compendiata*... (Venice: Leonardo Pittoni, 1687 [I ed. Modena 1685]).
6 Venice, Archivio di Stato (henceforth, ASV), *Inquisitori di Stato*, b. 548, riferta del confidente Castelnuovo, 30 August 1686.
7 ASV, *Avogaria di Comun. Miscellanea penale*, b. 220, fasc. 3.
8 Rome, Archivio Segreto Vaticano (henceforth, ASVAT), *Segreteria di Stato. Avvisi*, f. 49, fols 195–215 contains a series of manuscript sheets entitled, 'Dal campo elettorale sotto di Buda,' dated 27 June 1687, with the same characteristics as the printed sheets. It is difficult to say whether they were the basis for the printed *Giornali*, since it is not infrequent to find manuscript sheets that derive from printed ones.
9 H. W. Lang, *Bibliographie der Österreichischen Zeitungen 1492–1800* (Vienna, 1981).
10 Various copies of the 'Foglietto straordinario' of Johann Van Ghelen from the year 1687 can be found in ASVAT, *Segreteria di Stato. Avvisi*, f. 50.
11 See, for example, Johann van Ghelen's *Relazione compediosa, ma veridica di quanto è passato nel famoso assedio dell'imperial residenza di Vienna attaccata da i Turchi li 14 di luglio e liberata li 12 di settembre 1683. Aggiuntava la segnalata vittoria ottenuta dall'armi christiane nel liberare la medesima città dalle forze ottomane* (Vienna: Van Ghelen stampator accademico, n.d. [1683]). The same report was printed at the beginning of 1684 in Venice by Andrea Poletti. Concerning Hacque and van Ghelen, see H. W. Lang, *Die Buchdrucker des 15. bis 17. Jahrhunderts in Österreich* (Baden-Baden, 1972), pp. 62–3, 65–7; A. Dresler, 'Italienische Wochenblätter in Wien,' in *Zeitungswissenschaft* 11, no. 78 (1936): 327–8; G. Wacha, '*Il Corriere ordinario*. Eine vergessene Quelle zur Kulturgeschichte des Späten 17. Jhdts,' in *Oberösterreichische Heimatblätter* 19, 12 (1965): 27–35. There is also some information in A. Dresler, *Geschichte der italienischen Presse, I: Von den Anfängen bis 1815* (Munich, 1931), pp. 66–7.

12 A sheet dated 15 October 1686 exists in Parma, Archivio di Stato, *Carteggio Farnesiano*, Venezia, b. 520, 2 November 1686.

13 For example, in 1683 from Vienna there came the *Diario del seguito di giorno in giorno durante l'assedio della città di Vienna tra gli assediati e il nemico descritta con singolar diligenza e fatta stampare in questa città da un della cancelleria della corte che si trovò in essa presente* (Vienna, n.d. [Florence, Biblioteca Nazionale Centrale, henceforth, BNCF: 268.5]), following the siege of the city from 12 July to 14 September 1683.

14 Rome, Biblioteca Casanatense (henceforth, BCR), Misc. 2472.34.

15 BCR, Misc. 2472.6 and following.

16 BNCF, *Magl.* 9.5.474.

17 In Milan, Pandolfo Malatesta published the *Giornale III dal campo cesareo a Pest in data de' 3 luglio 1684*. It is not clear whether this is a once only publication. Modena, Archivio di Stato (henceforth ASMO), *Cancelleria Ducale, avvisi e notizie dall'estero*, b. 142.

18 The sheet had the following colophon: 'In Venezia e in Todi per il Galani, si vende a Roma da Leoni,' BCR, Misc. 2472.22. The sheet continued by referring to the only information that, according to the compiler, needed verification.

19 Information concerning the Albrizzi family is in the 1759 citizenship petition: ASV, *Avogaria di Comun*, b. 416, fasc. 24.

20 *Origine del Danubio, con li nomi antichi e moderni di tutti li fiumi & acque che in esso concorrono, come anco delli regni, provincie, signorie e città irrigate dal detto fiume, fino dove sbocca nel mare Eusino. Nuovamente corretto con succinta relazione di quanto é seguito sotto dette città nelle due campagne del 1684 e 1685* (Venice: all'insegna del nome di Dio, dietro la chiesa di San Zulian, [Albrizzi] 1684–1685). Since Albrizzi had not yet been admitted to the printers' guild, he procured the licence for the first volume on 22 August 1684, in the name of 'Lorenzo Baseggio and Girolamo Albrizzi.' The following year, for the second volume the first was reprinted under the name of Albrizzi alone.

21 A collection in sixteen volumes of the *Giornale dal campo cesareo di Buda* is in BMV, with the indication 135 D 195–210 (lacking, however, the first volume containing the first eleven numbers). In 1687 Albrizzi accompanied the military journal with two other periodicals: the *Giornale veneto de' letterati* compiled by Pietro Maria Moretti and the *Pallade veneta*, on the model of the Parisian *Mercure galant*.

22 *Giornale dal campo cesareo…*, no. 158, 16 June 1689.

23 The foreign ambassadors stationed in Venice often included numbers of the *Giornale* in their weekly dispatches.

24 This was no doubt the pamphlet by Marco Antonio Fratta et Montalbano, *Dell'acque minerali del regno d'Ungaria, relatione* (Venice: Albrizzi, 1687), mentioned in the catalogue of the British Library.

25 Many of the titles mentioned in the *Giornale* cannot be found in any of the main libraries. Almanacs and prognostications especially are impossible to find, and are not mentioned in any of the main bibliographies. They usually came out at the end of the year. In December 1686, for instance, there were published titles like: *Villano accorto, Dragomano delle stelle, Tartana, Contra Tartana, Il Maggiordomo de' pianeti del cielo, Almanacco del pescatore di Chiaravalle* (noted as a 'true' reprint from Milan), *Il Rossignolo, Protogiornale veneto, L'Indovina tutto, Il folletto indovino*, previously printed in Modena, *Il pronostico perpetuo, Rete dei matti*, and *Contrarete dei matti*.

26 *Giornale dal campo cesareo…*, no. 30, 5 January 1686 (1687).

27 ASMO, *Cancelleria. Estero. Ambasciatori, agenti e corrispondenti dall'estero*, b. 125.

28 An example of no. 115 of the Ferrara edition is in the Marciana collection.

29 Rimini, Biblioteca Gambalunga, 4 N IV 24. There is some information in P. Bellettini, 'Publishing in the Provinces. Printing Houses in Romagna in the 17th century,' in *The Italian Book*, ed. D. V. Reidy (London, 1993), pp. 315, 322, indicating an example from 1687 in the Biblioteca Comunale of Forlì.

30 See ASV, *Provveditori da terra e da mar*, f. 1120, the dispatches of Francesco Morosini from 20 September 1687 to May 1688: there the same questions are discussed, a sign

that the gazette writer was actually serving in the army. From the Levant, letters continued to arrive, addressed mainly to merchants; the list of addressees of recipients is in ASV, *Inquisitori di Stato*, b. 700.

31 The *Giornale dell'armata veneta in Levante* from no. 24 onward is in BMV, Incompleti 331. It is missing the first volume, which, however, is listed with the call no. 135 D 214 under the title of *Ragguaglio giornaliero delle invittissime armate venete maritime e terrestri co' suoi acquisti a pontino distinti contro la potenza ottomana*, (Venice: Albrizzi, 1687), containing numbers 1–20.

32 The accounts of Athens are in nos 6 (29 September 1687) and 8 (27 October 1687).

33 BCR, Misc. 2472.34.

34 This information is from his last will, dated 1 March 1706: ASV, *Notarile Testamenti*, Cristoforo Brambilla, b. 167, n. 215. Torri died at the age of 72 on 12 March 1706: ASV, *Provveditori alla Sanità, Necrologi*, reg. 906.

35 ASV, *Inquisitori di Stato*, b. 566, referral by the confidant Castelnuovo, 22 February 1679.

36 On this problem, see P. Preto, *I servizi segreti di Venezia* (Milan, 1994).

37 ASV, *Inquisitori di Stato*, b. 566, referral by the confidant Castelnuovo, 10 March 1679.

38 *Ibid.*, b. 567, 10 March 1681.

39 *Ibid..*, b. 567, 30 March 1681.

40 *Ibid.*, b. 567, 25 June 1681.

41 *Ibid.*, b. 547, 3 March 1685.

42 *Ibid.*, b. 566, 19 December 1676.

43 *Ibid.*, b. 547, 15 October 1683; b. 650, referral by the confidant posted with the nuncio, March 1682. Giulio Cesare de Beaziano, *L'araldo veneto overo universale armerista mettodico di tutta la scienza araldica. Trattato in cui si rappresentano le figure e simboli di tutti gl'armeggi nobili, usitati da qualunque natione del mondo con le maggiori e più esaminate definitioni et altre materie utili e necessarie non solo a cavalieri ma ad ogni stato di persone* (Venice: Nicolò Pezzana, 1680). Concerning Beaziano, see G. Mazzucchelli, *Gli scrittori d'Italia cioè notizie storiche e critiche intorno alla vita e agli scritti dei letterati italiani* (Brescia: Bossini, 1760), vol. 2, pt. 2, p. 571.

44 His dispatches are in ASMO, *Cancelleria. Estero. Ambasciatori, agenti e corrispondenti dall'estero*, b. 125.

45 Besides the indicated titles in Albrizzi's journals, war books are touted also in the broadsheets. In ASV, *Arti*, b. 166, there are lists of books for which a permission to print had been obtained. The most active printers were the same ones already mentioned in connection with broadsheets: Albrizzi, Stefano Curti, and Andrea Poletti.

46 The book, a translation of a German work, had been published in Venice in 1638 by Cristoforo Tommasini.

47 The two volumes that came out each year were later bound in a single volume with a new frontispiece.

48 In 1702 Biondi was jailed for fifteen days in the famous Piombi for not having censored himself 'in the way that has been commanded concerning affairs of princes or their ministers.' ASV, *Inquisitori di Stato*, b. 529, 20 June 1702.

49 Gio. Battista Donado, *Della letteratura de' Turchi* (Venice: Andrea Poletti, 1688). The revaluation of Turkish culture was later proposed again by Donà, who ordered a translation from Gian Rinaldo Carli of the Turkish chronology by Hazi Halifè Mustafà (*Cronologia historica scritta in lingua turca, persiana & araba …* [Venice: Andrea Poletti, 1697], published by his brother Pietro, who added an important introductory note). Concerning Giambattista Donà, see P. Preto, *Venezia e i Turchi* (Florence, Sansoni, 1975), pp. 345–49.

50 ASV, *Inquisitori di Stato*, b. 566, referral by the confidant Castelnuovo 19 December 1676.

51 *Ibid.*, b. 547, 30 July 1687.

52 *Ibid.*, b. 547, 4 June 1684.
53 *Ibid.*, b. 547, 28 May 1683.
54 *Ibid.*, b. 547, 28 May 1683.
55 Concerning Dotti, see A. Pellegrino, entry in *Dizionario Biografico degli Italiani* 41 (Rome, 1992), pp. 532–4. With regard to Dotti's letters, I referred to the forthcoming book by C. Vovelle, *Il fascino discreto della nobiltà: Bartolomeo Dotti tra esilio e compromesso.*
56 Bartolomeo Dotti, *Satire del cavalier Dotti* (Geneva: Cramer, 1757), pp. 187–99.
57 Descriptions of celebrations held on the occasion of the liberation of Vienna are in the newsletters of Venice and Rome in BMV, ms. it., VI 460 (12104), dated 25 September and 2 October 1683. Information concerning other narratives of the event is in E. Bordignon Favero, 'La "Santa Lega" contro il turco e il rinnovamento del duomo di Bassano: Volpato, Meyering e la "Madonna del Rosario",' *Studi veneziani* 11 (1986): 216.
58 *Verissima e distinta relazione delle feste seguite nella gloriosa città di Venezia per la presa di Napoli di Romania* (Venice: Tramontin, 1686); *Distinta relazione del solenne apparato ... 27 ottobre nella parocchia di S. Eufemia della Giudeca per la Presa di Napoli di Romania* (Venice: Leonardo Pittoni, 1686).
59 Bottazzo Tombolon, *La fontega boggiente dell'affetto de i pavani fedeli suggiti della nuostra serenissima Republica di Venezia* (Padua: Sardi, 1685); *Vera e distinta relatione delle solenni allegrezze e fuochi fatti dalla magnifica città di Padova ... la notte 26 novembre 1687* (Padua: Sardi, n.d. [1687]).
60 *Descritione delle feste fatte in Ferrara ... per le gloriose vittorie ottenute dall'armi imperiali e venete contro il Turco* (Ferrara: Bernardino Pomatelli, n.d. [1686]).
61 *Nova e distinta relazione delle feste & allegrezze fatte ... Venetia ... Roma, con tutte le città di Terra ferma ..., per l'acquisto di Valona e Canina...* (Venice: Batti, 1690).
62 BMV, ms. it., VI 460 (12104), avvisi da Venezia, 25 September 1683.
63 *Ibid.*, avvisi da Venezia, 2 October 1683.
64 *Ibid.*, avvisi da Roma, 25 September 1683.
65 ASV, *Inquisitori di Stato*, b. 547, referral by Castelnuovo 4 June 1684.
66 *Ibid.*, b. 548, 7 June 1686.
67 *Ibid.*, b. 547, 21 August 1684.
68 BMV, ms. it., VI 461 (12105), Rome, 19 August 1684.
69 None of this information can be confirmed in Venetian archives; the indication was by Giovanni Francesco Vezzosi, a newsletter writer and agent of Modena in a message to his Duke. (ASMO, *Cancelleria. Estero. Ambasciatori, agenti e corrispondenti dall'estero*, b. 125, dispacci di Giovanni Francesco Vezzosi, 28 August, 2 October 1688, 22 October 1689, 30 September 1690). The *Giornale dal campo cesareo* ended with no. 219 of 17 August 1690, which came out in the beginning of September; the *Giornale dell'armata veneta in Levante* ended with no. 53, dated 12 August 1690, also published in the beginning of September.
70 Paolo Sarpi, *Scritti giurisdizionalistici*, ed. G. Gambarin (Bari, 1958), p. 190.

11 The politics of information in seventeenth-century Scandinavia

Paul Ries

There were many similarities between the dual monarchies of Denmark-Norway and Sweden-Finland other than their shared desire to dominate the Baltic region and thereby play an important role in European politics. Constitutionally, both were in the process of changing from elective into absolutist monarchies, as successive monarchs strove to liberate themselves from domination by the nobility. While the transition from oligarchy towards an increasingly powerful monarchic rule moved with speed and direction determined by the skills, attitudes, and good luck of princes and politicians, the bedrock of society remained the same, as no authority claimed or power wielded was legitimate without the divine sanction. The power to confer this status had changed hands at the Reformation, when those princes who broke with Rome had to look to their own clergy to supply Scriptural sanction for their powers. The Lutheran clergy found itself in a position that was both more and less secure than that of their Catholic predecessors: less secure because they could no longer appeal to a higher authority outside the realm in which they resided; but more secure because they alone now held the ideological keys to the political power exercised by their rulers and, though their obedient servants like all other subjects, were ultimately only answerable to God for the maintenance of His Word against all His enemies.

The Lutheran clergy defended their position of responsibility and power fiercely and successfully against all comers, be they Catholics or fellow Protestants, to say nothing of the followers of other belief systems, or none. From now on, they were the defenders of the faith, but as before, defending the faith continued to be a task shared with the state, which in practice meant that it remained the duty of the Church to ferret out dissent, and the duty of the state to destroy it.

One of the weapons – but unfortunately not the only one – in the battle for the right to control people's minds and create a 'public opinion' was the printing press, and as in the rest of Europe it had played a crucial role in Scandinavia. No book could be printed in either country, nor bought or imported from abroad, whose contents had not previously been checked and approved by a high official of the Church. As this involved reading the publication in manuscript, making corrections where necessary, and ensuring that the amended and censored version was in fact the only one printed, censorship was a lengthy and laborious process; and as the production of books increased year on year, the Swedish government handed over this responsibility to the office of a specially appointed member of the chancellery with the title of *censor librorum*.[1] The guidelines for the censor and his appointees remained the same, namely prohibiting anything which could be construed not to be consonant with the teachings of Church and state, and they applied not only to books, but to any printed matter, including single sheet pamphlets and, from 1645, newspapers.

In Denmark, the situation was similar but less clear. Here the officially appointed censor of books – in 1661, for example, the professor of history at the University of Copenhagen – was in overall control, but he could delegate the censorship of books about particular subjects to those colleagues who were specialists in that field, though he must always leave the censorship of religious books to the clergy.[2] This practice was confirmed by Royal Ordinance in 1667 and eventually codified in 1683[3] in words clearly intended to cover all manner of publications. As in Sweden, any work not conforming to the Augsburg Confession was prohibited, but in addition certain kinds of publication were singled out for special scrutiny, such as calendars, almanacs, and prognostica, because they often contained predictions about or interpretations of 'war, times of dearth, pestilence or other such incidents.' But unlike in Sweden, there is no reference to newspapers, and as far as can be ascertained no specific regulations for the censoring of newspapers were issued in Denmark during the seventeenth century.

Through its monopoly on education and religious instruction, its state-supported control of the press, and its unrivalled influence upon every aspect of the daily lives of the population, the clergy had been able to create a 'public opinion' at home, without which it was believed that both Church and state and all its members would perish, body and soul. Henceforth, it was its principal task before God and His lieutenant the king to keep that belief inviolate and protect it against any religious and political notions from whatever quarter, domestic or foreign, which might question or challenge the prevailing politico-religious ideology. Celebrating its success in 1687, but at the same time warning the temporal powers against the slightest relaxation of control, Hector Gottfried Masius, a leading Lutheran ideologue, explained – in Latin, for the argument was also intended for foreign consumption – that 'Illa est optima omnium Religio qvae nexum inter parentes ac Imperantes sanctum ac inviolatum servat'; and being court preacher in Copenhagen, he concluded more specifically: 'Erit in Dania Summa et Absoluta Majestas, quamdiu Lutherana Religio manserit.'[4] Robert Molesworth, William III's ambassador to Denmark and one of the severest of critics of the Scandinavian way of life, was prepared to concede that by the end of the seventeenth century 'in Denmark, as well as other Protestant Countries of the North, through the entire and sole dependence of the Clergy upon the Prince, without the interfering of the Authority of any Spiritual Superior, such as the Pope among the Romanists; through their Principles and Doctrine, which are those of unlimited Obedience; through the Authority they have with the Common People, etc., slavery seems more absolutely established than it is in France.'[5]

While the ideological control described by Masius and Molesworth was undoubtedly well founded as far as the 'common people' were concerned, it was not as complete as either of the two men believed or feared, for in Scandinavia as elsewhere there were social groups who for professional reasons had long been in a position to go beyond the geographical and ideological boundaries established by Church and state: aristocrats seeking fame through service in foreign armies, ambassadors lying abroad for their countries, students and others on educational travels throughout Europe, and merchants seeking their fortune anywhere. Moreover, when not being able to travel in person, members of those groups had long maintained a two-way system of communication by employing couriers and carriers as and when the need arose, and in Scandinavia, as in other parts of Europe, this system of private postal services was supplemented during the seventeenth century by the establishment of nation-wide postal networks under state control.

With the establishment of separate Danish and Swedish post offices in Hamburg (in 1618), the Scandinavian national networks of postal routes became connected directly and regularly – initially once per week – to the several European networks, which served that city. Severely disrupted from time to time during the Thirty Years' War and the subsequent wars between Denmark and Sweden (between 1657–60 and 1675–79), the link to Hamburg, an important European market for goods and money transactions, as well as a staple of news about Europe and beyond, nevertheless remained sufficiently intact to enable both nations to increase the efficiency of their postal services, and so provide the essential means to develop a way of looking at the world and understand the events in it, very different from that conveyed by the Lutheran clergy or Absolutist politicians, namely a newspaper industry. However, because of the disruptions created by armed hostilities, when flysheets and other forms of single-leaf publications re-emerged as an additional rather than an alternative activity for the newsmen, the early history of regular Scandinavian newspapers looks like a chronicle of several beginnings; on the other hand, there exists, for both countries, enough material from certain periods during the last four decades of the century to make detailed contents analysis of individual newspapers, and comparisons between them, possible, and therefore indicate what kind of information service was envisaged and provided, both by those who wanted to disseminate the news and those who wanted to control it.

Scandinavian newspapers before 1700[6]

Though organized newscasting in both countries had served the political, religious, and economic elites since the Middle Ages, it was the pamphlets and flysheets of the Reformation, Counter-Reformation and ultimately the Thirty Years' War which put news into the public domain to an extent which made its subsequent prohibition impossible and its control equally imperative in both countries. There was, however, at least initially, a significant difference between the Danish and Swedish solutions to this problem, for whereas the two groups – the purveyors and the controllers – remained separate in Denmark, and it took a good while for the latter to control the former through legislation (see below), in Sweden the two groups merged, as all newscasting was monopolized in the editorial hands of the government official in control of communications within the realm and beyond it, i.e. the Stockholm postmaster. In other words, the first Swedish newspaper was published, not only by authority, but by order of, indeed at the expense of, and under the complete control of the government.

The Stockholm Ordinari Post-Tijdender *for 1667 and 1673*

Within this system of control, the constraints of which were unlikely to worry a loyal and well-paid government official keen to follow the instruction to suppress any news deemed to be prejudicial to Church and state, the Stockholm postmaster was free to draw on the national and international sources best suited to making the official vehicle for news, the *Ordinari Post-Tijdender*, as informative and useful as possible. And an early, undated list or *Taxa*[7] of foreign newspapers available to him shows that in his capacity as postmaster he was able to procure a great number of foreign publications, from which as newspaper editor and censor he was in a position to provide 'persons interested in the affairs of state and the way of the world' with his own selections from them, that is, the weekly *Ordinari Post-Tijdender*, against an annual subscription of 2 daler and 8 öre in silver or 5 daler and 20 öre in copper.[8] He also announced that he would be able to supply 'both printed Hamburg papers'[9] at the annual cost of 5 daler and 8 öre in silver, or 13 daler and 4 öre in copper. Other publications on offer were 8 'Aviser eller Couranter' from Amsterdam by three different 'Autorer,' of which three were published on Tuesdays, two on Thursdays and a further three on Saturdays, the price of each paper set at 3 daler and 24 öre in silver, or 9 daler and 12 öre copper (including postage), and of which he particularly recommended the Saturday paper as carrying the latest news, because they appeared in the evening just before the departure of the post from Amsterdam. On similar terms, he also offered to provide the weekly printed 'Aviser' from Antwerp, Cologne (in German and Latin), Leipzig, Frankfurt, and Danzig, as well as Italian and French 'gazettes' and English 'diurnals,' as well as the commodity price currents from Amsterdam, Hamburg, Danzig, and other important trading centres. He would also undertake to procure copies of 'nya Discourser och Skrifter' (new discourses and publications) in foreign languages as requested by customers on payment of the cost of the publication and the postage. And finally, he offered to furnish weekly written extracts from the above mentioned printed papers, as well as from letters and correspondence received at the post office, always on condition that they contain nothing 'prejudicial,' and only on payment annually to the copiers of such sums as had been agreed between the customer and the postmaster. The material subscribed to would be delivered not only in Stockholm, but throughout the kingdom, including Finland and Livonia, and the service was available to anyone, whether a regular subscriber or not, though annual subscribers would receive preferential treatment if or when there was a shortage of stock.

However, it would be wrong to assume that the sources of information mentioned in the *Taxa* played an important part in the formation of public opinion in general in seventeenth-century Sweden, for many of the sources of information mentioned were single publications rather than serial newspapers; English 'diurnals' were not serial, let alone daily publications, and their coverage was as restricted, geographically and politically, as many printed 'Advices' were in terms of their contents. Even the title 'Coranto' might merely mean that the news was current, as was certainly the case with price corantos. On the other hand, as we have already seen, the German publications mentioned were proper newspapers, and research in Swedish archives has shown the presence of copies from 1645–46 of a considerable number of Dutch corantos, of which one appeared on Thursdays without an imprint,[10] those published by Jan van Hilten on Saturdays,[11] by Mathijs van Meininga on Tuesdays, Thursday and Saturdays,[12] by Broer Jansz's on Saturdays,[13] by his son Joost Broersz's on Tuesdays and Saturdays,[14] and by his son-in-law on Thursdays and Sundays.[15]

Nevertheless, any attempt at assessing the significance of the wealth of information offered in the *Taxa* must be seen against the fact that the supply of foreign news would have reached a particularly high point at this stage of the endgame of the Thirty Years' War, partly due to Sweden's prominent role, and partly because her victorious troops had taken over or at least controlled the postal services in the conquered areas. In other words, what the *Taxa* reflects is the amount of news material potentially available in Stockholm at this point in time, but only to those who could afford it, and if the cost in 1645–6 was anything like that in 1685, when the annual postage charge alone amounted to 1,570 daler for the stretch between Hamburg and Stockholm, those sources of information would have been well beyond the reach of most citizens. There is evidence that very wealthy individuals[16] continued to be prepared to pay the price, either on their own or with others, and that in 1685 about twenty copies of foreign newspapers arrived by post at the Stockholm post office every week.[17] But we may safely assume that for the majority of the city's 40,000 inhabitants this wealth of information would only have been available in one of two ways: through the 'unprejudicial' handwritten excerpts copied by clerks in the postmaster's office, or through the equally censored selections printed under his auspices in his new and official capacity as editor of the *Ordinari Post-Tijdender*.[18]

More specifically, the postmaster was ordered to select reports about national and international affairs, in particular those dealing with trade, remove any 'prejudicial' passages or phrases, translate them into Swedish, submit the extracts to the censor for further correction as necessary, and then arrange for their printing and sale. Other material to be published, either as part of the paper or as a supplement to it, included official government announcements, and publications of particular interest to the merchant community, such as lists of prices of Swedish goods abroad and of foreign goods obtainable at home, price corantos, etc.[19]

Though the *Ordinari Post-Tijdender* changed its name several times between its inception in 1645 and the end of the century, an efficient and bureaucratic system of censorship ensured that its contents remained the same, that is, the news which the government at any given time wanted its subjects to receive. The system also secured the postmaster a monopoly[20] on newscasting, which not only made his new office more lucrative, but also that of the censor more simple. The appointment of a second censor with sole responsibility for the newspaper on 10 February 1676[21] would have made it even more of a sinecure, as the editor was still the one who had to do all the necessary work.

By attaching the editorship of the *Ordinari Post-Tijdender* to the office of the Stockholm postmaster, the authorities underlined the importance of the link between the two services, just as they emphasized the connection between both services and the trading community, when they appointed postmaster Johan Beier as the first holder of the editorship, for he had been secretary to the chamber of commerce since 1637 and was after 1645 its leading member. On his death in 1669, his widow retained the Stockholm post office, while the chancellor, Magnus Gabriel de la Gardie, temporarily appointed one of his own secretaries, J. Bergenhielm, as editor until J. G. von Beier 1673 succeeded his father in both offices. In 1685 the two offices were again separated, following complaints about administrative irregularities within the post office, but in practice this made little difference, as the first man appointed editor under the new arrangement, S. Åkerhielm, was already chief postmaster. What did make a difference was the clamp down on the practices which had been the reason for the complaints in the first place, namely that some officials at the post offices had spent so much time collecting, distributing, and selling their own gazettes, that they not only neglected their proper duties,[22] but also infringed censorship regulations and cut into the postmaster-editor's profits.[23]

However, the profits from the sale of the material advertised in the *Taxa* was only an additional source of income. Thus, in 1669, Johan Beier received a total subsidy for the newspaper of 1,000 daler in silver, of which 400 was his salary as editor, while the remaining sum covered the cost of subscribing to the foreign gazettes and printing of the *Ordinari Post-Tijdender*, but not the postage, as this was free. Both of his successors, J. Bergenhielm and, from 1673, his son J. G. von Beier were similarly remunerated. By 1685 the value of the editorship alone had increased to 450 daler,[24] and the office became hugely more lucrative when the right to print and sell the newspaper was opened to tender among the Stockholm printers, and applicants competed by offering the editor substantial annual payments for the privilege.[25] Furthermore, the office of editor was, like that of the censor, something of a sinecure, for it was accepted by the chancellery that the actual editorial work – that is, the selection of the relatively small number of news items to be included in the *Ordinari Post-Tijdender* from the total number available in the editorial office – would be delegated to more lowly functionaries already working in the chancery who had a good knowledge of domestic and foreign affairs, and who like their superiors held other posts relevant to their activities as newsmen.[26] The 'sub-editors', of course, had to confer with their superiors, and must always abide by their ruling,[27] but once their selection had been approved by the editor and censor, it was they who were in charge of the rest of the proceedings, and their influence on the daily business contents of the newspaper and the way in which it was run was considerable. For example, in 1685 it was decided by Schantz's superiors to put the newspaper licence out to tender and shift some of the expenses from the editor to the printer by making the latter pay the censor, editor, sub-editor as well as his own staff.[28] But it would have been Schantz who negotiated the details and concluded the agreements, which in 1686 led to the transfer of the printing privilege[29] to the printer recommended by him, Henrik III Keyser, who had been the Royal Printer since 1678, and who retained both offices until his death on 1 August 1699, despite frequent and severe criticism of the poor quality of the print and lay-out of the newspaper.[30] Similarly when, after 1700, the authorities contemplated allowing a second newspaper to appear, the chancellery ruled that no newspaper could be published unless Schantz had examined its contents and agreed that it could be printed.[31]

It is not known how many copies of the *Ordinari Post-Tijdender* were printed and sold at this time. The post from Hamburg arrived on Fridays, and the paper came out on Wednesdays, so there would be ample time in which to complete the entire elaborate editing process – selection, translation, censorship, and printing.[32] There is, however, no evidence that large numbers of copies or wide dissemination were a priority for the authorities; on the contrary, when the Swedish post between Hamburg and Stockholm was doubled in 1662, there was no attempt at doubling the number of issues printed until 1684, and that experiment was abandoned later the same year.[33] The market for pirated copies of the *Ordinari Post-Tijdender*, and the fact that no second official newspaper came out until 1731, also suggest that the chief concern of the authorities was to control the flow of information and the contents of the *Ordinari Post-Tijdender* through the employment of a hierarchical network of trusted servants.

Analysis of the contents of the *Ordinari Post-Tijdender* is problematic as only a few issues are extant from a period whence potential sources have also survived. But even where they are to hand, it is not possible, as it is with some Danish papers, to identify precisely which one was used, since all reports taken from foreign-language sources were translated into Swedish. Parallels can be found because the layout in the *Ordinari Post-Tijdender* and its sources was the same, with each report headed by the place and date of composition, but as they were in effect re-written, we cannot tell which reports were adopted verbatim, nor assess the significance of differences from the original such as abbreviations, omissions, or additions. In short, we cannot study the editing process, only its outcome, though we may conclude that nothing 'prejudicial' is likely to have survived the meticulous censorship procedure.

Nevertheless, it is possible to use contents analysis as a rough guide to the way the editor worked in 1667 and 1673. During May, June, July, and August 1667 he fulfilled his obligation to publish Swedish news with reports sent from Gothenburg, Hälsingborg, Jönköping, and Kalmar (one report from each), while at least some of the forty-six reports from abroad came from places named in the *Taxa*: Hamburg (sixteen), Breda (six), Amsterdam (three), Elsinore (three), London (three), Warsaw (three), Rome (two), and one each from Antwerp, Besançon, Bremen, Copenhagen, Danzig, Lübeck, Paris, Stettin, The Hague, and Venice. All reports are written in plain, colloquial Swedish, cover a wide variety of everyday events in a factual manner, and avoid sensationalist language and value judgements. Even so, among the foreign reports those from Hamburg differ from the rest in several respects: they are usually longer; they carry news from all over Europe; and no printed source covering all items in these composite reports has been found in other newspapers, which suggests that the editor may either have had his own Hamburg correspondent, or received handwritten excerpts from the papers published there by a resident merchant or some other agent.

By contrast, the contents of all other foreign reports can be found under the same headings (date and place name) in one of two printed Hamburg papers, those from Stettin and Besançon in Schumacher's thrice weekly *Wochentliche Zeitung*, and the rest in Greflinger's twice weekly *Nordischer Mercurius*. They may therefore be translations from those papers, but comparison with the contents of a Copenhagen paper published in German by Henrik Gøde, the twice weekly *Ordinaire Post-Zeitung*, shows that the reports from Amsterdam, Breda, London, Paris, and Venice had already been copied verbatim in his paper and printed only four to five days later than the Hamburg originals. This makes that paper another potential source, particularly because some of Gøde's reports were shorter than Greflinger's and the version in the *Ordinari Post-Tijdender* is closer to the former than the latter.

Contents analysis of the only two issues of the *Ordinari Post-Tijdender* extant from January 1673 – the only month from which a sufficient number of copies of the original German papers and their Danish derivatives (*Ordinari Post-Zeitung* and *Extraordinaires Relationes aus Allerley Orten*) has survived to make comparisons possible – suggest a similar practice and leaves the same degree of uncertainty. The contents of the ten reports, i.e. forty different news items, is similar to that found in other papers, but once again it is not possible to find the sources for the composite reports from Hamburg; three of the eight items in one such report about troop movements along the Weser *could* be translations from *two* items printed in the *Nordischer Mercurius* under 'Niederelbe 1. Januar,' but the remaining five items are not in that source, and they cover events in various other parts of Europe (the Netherlands, Poland, and Turkey), so once again an independent Hamburg agency report is the most likely source for them all. Some of the other reports, for example from Vienna, are simple in the sense that near 'matches' can be found in other papers, but the length and composition of those from The Hague also look like composite agency reports. And in the case of one long report from Paris with seven items, three read like translations of two printed earlier in the *Nordischer Mercurius*, while near matches for the remaining four items had previously appeared in several newspapers published in Copenhagen (see below).

The above characteristics of the contents of the *Ordinari Post-Tijdender* makes it very difficult to draw conclusions about the way in which this paper, the only officially approved newspaper in seventeenth-century Sweden, may have influenced public opinion.[34] Obviously, straight reporting of facts about events otherwise unknown to the readers would have enabled them to learn something about 'the affairs of state and the way of the world,' over and above the preachings of the Church and the edicts of the state; but the tight government grip at every stage of newspaper production, together with the paucity of extant material, must leave it an open question whether or not a Swedish editor *could* have produced, from all the news available to him, a newspaper with a different selection of news, i.e. with a potentially different impact on the formation of public opinion at the time.

The Copenhagen **Ordinari Post-Zeitung,** *1669*

As in Sweden, the people engaged in newscasting in Denmark were working under the dual stewardship of religious and political ideology, and they too were not only controlled by the authorities, but also employed and paid as government officials, whether in cash, or in kind, or by occupying some additional office, often within the postal services, or the world of printing, or a combination of these. However, there was an important difference in the way the newspapers came into existence in the two countries, for whereas the first Swedish newsmen had been *instructed* by the chancellery to publish an official newspaper in accordance with specific regulations laid down for the post and the press, the first regular Danish newspaper was launched ten years after the reorganization of the postal services, and because two enterprising individuals, a printer, Melchior Martzan, and a bookseller, Joachim Moltke, had applied for and been granted a royal licence *permitting* them to subscribe to foreign newspapers through the post and print and sell extracts from them in Danish and German.[35]

Both Martzan and Moltke were well placed to make a success of this attempt at expanding their already existing businesses. At the time of their application Martzan, who had left his native Germany in 1626 to work for the First University Printer in Copenhagen, had been Second Printer to the University since 1631 and, having married his master's widow in 1644, became First Printer. Joachim Moltke had left his native Rostock, also in 1626, to manage the Copenhagen branch of the Hallerfort firm of booksellers (with other branches in Lübeck and Königsberg), had held the office of University bookseller since 1627, and also bought and sold books and other publications for firms in Amsterdam (Elsevier), Antwerp, London, Padua, and Venice. In addition to their own international contacts and those established through and on behalf of the University, they had rooms at the newly built Royal Exchange and links with the general postmaster, who was a government employee, but elected by four merchant members of the city magistracy, one each from the Icelandic, the East India, the Cloth, and the Silk companies.

Though their University appointments put both men in a privileged position, they also involved them in considerable cost. Between them, they were obliged to keep a workshop with good presses, including one for the printing of copperplate, as well as the types and styles needed for the printing of the books required by the university. They were also required to maintain a book-binding department, deliver one free copy to the royal library of all books printed, and maintain a bookshop 'in the French and Dutch manner,' at which books needed by the University could be bought at prices controlled by their employer. In return, they enjoyed exemption from duty and tax levied on materials connected with their trade, as well as privileges protecting their products, including their newspapers. But as holders of university offices they were barred from engaging in other business or trade which would put them at a financial disadvantage *vis-à-vis* their 'freelance' competitors. Martzan, and his successors, therefore tried to acquire exclusive rights to publish printed matter for 'popular' use, such as almanacs, hymn books, devotional tracts, and so forth. For his part, Moltke established himself as the city's leading publisher and developed his bookshop into an establishment unrivalled for the quality of its products until well into the next century, which not only enabled him to support Martzan financially as necessary, but also to play a major role in the business and private affairs of his successors (see below).[36]

The licence of 29 June 1634 contained no specific regulations regarding the censorship of newspapers, but Moltke and Martzan must have established an *ad hoc* procedure for pre-publication examination of its contents, since when in 1644 they and another bookseller were charged with having published 'implausible and false news,' Moltke explained that he had on occasion submitted material for publication to the tutor of the chancellor's children, who had simply struck out what in his opinion ought not to be printed.[37] Their transgression, which included the publication of an uncensored religious tract, earned the two printers a severe reprimand, but it did not prevent Moltke from being appointed First University Printer the same year, and no action was taken against Martzan, the magistrate declaring that he had published 'nothing other than the ordinary corantos and such other matter as the authorities forwarded to him.'[38] Nevertheless, to prevent a repetition of these events, the university decided that henceforth all news must be approved by the professor of history prior to publication, but added that as a 'politicum negotium' the newspaper had best be censored by someone in the chancellery, 'because they know best how to tell true from false.'[39]

The censorship procedure, like that prescribed in the Swedish regulation of 1643 and the Danish regulation of 1701,[40] was a cumbersome one. First, the editor must scrutinize the extracts from his sources (see below) to ensure that they contained no 'prejudicial' matter, before submitting two identical handwritten copies of them to the censor, who amended them as necessary and then signed both copies. Leaving one copy of the approved text with the censor, the editor must then have two copies of it printed and submit them to the censor who, having checked that they both corresponded in every detail to the approved copy, would again sign both copies and retain one, while the editor was now free to hand the second copy to the printer, who must print it without either adding or deleting or in other way changing the censored and approved text.

The instructions were equally detailed concerning the material to be excluded: any remarks questioning the foundations or splendour of the realm or prejudicial to the interest of the king, ministers and officials; information about size or strength of the nation's army or navy; details of negotiations with foreign powers and 'sceptical, scornful or offensive' remarks about foreign princes or their representative; [41] and comments on, speculations about, or interpretations of any of the events mentioned, whether they were part of the original material or not. By contrast, what must be included: detailed and respectful descriptions of grand occasions, such as processions, feasts, etc., to ensure that no fault could be found by others in the ceremonies of the Danish court; official announcements and royal proclamations; information about shipping and other forms of trade; and advertisements of important auctions or the loss of valuable property. All information must be written in plain language and seemly terms and published as soon as possible after the arrival of the post, except in the case of monthly newspapers, which must contain the most important and recent reports already published during the preceding month and nothing else.

When followed to the letter, this procedure reduced the speed with which the editors of weekly newspapers could make the extracts of their Hamburg, Altona, and possible other sources available to their readers. Copies of those sources ready in time to catch the Hamburg post for Copenhagen, which left from the post office opposite the Exchange on Tuesdays and Fridays after 6 p.m.,[42] would usually be in the hands of the editors three days later, but normally not be available to their readers until the following Saturday and Wednesday respectively. On the other hand, if the censorship procedure was not followed, editors could get into the kind of trouble we will soon see experienced by Moltke and Martzan and their successors.

During the war with Sweden between 1657 and 1660, the sober weekly newspaper based on extracts from Hamburg sources, the *Ordinari Post-Zeitung*, nearly disappeared under the flood of more than 200 single publications of sensationalist and nationalistic contents.[43] Nor was it involved in any way during the *coup d'état* in 1660 which, unlike the overthrow of the monarchy in England in 1649, was indeed 'something done in a corner,' the only display of 'public opinion' being that orchestrated by the new hereditary and absolutist regime and celebrated by among others the poet and future newspaperman Anders Bording (see below), as representatives of the estates gathered in front of the castle and solemnly swore an oath of allegiance to the king on the nation's behalf.[44]

However, once the war was over and the new regime in place, problems about the right to publish newspapers arose as some of the many Copenhagen printers who had shown their ability as publishers of news flysheets applied for the newspaper licence which had become available because the previous holder,

Peder Morsing, who was also Royal and First University Printer, had been killed by a Swedish canon ball in September 1658 on his way home from the castle. An interim ruling by the university permitted his widow, Sophie, to succeed her husband, as long as she employed good journeymen and maintained the standard of work expected. With Joachim Moltke as financial guarantor and Henrik Gøde[45] as chief printer, she promised to do just this, and indeed did until Moltke, as her best man, arranged a marriage between her and Henrik in 1660, whereupon he was granted the privileges and offices held by Morsing seeing that he had now, as one professor put it, succeeded his predecessor 'in officio juxta ac thoro.'[46]

Few issues of the *Ordinari Post-Zeitung*[47] have survived from the early years, when the paper came out only once in the week, but by 1669 Gøde had for several years published it twice weekly, offering its readers approximately 800 reports each year consisting of around 2,000 individual news items about events in Europe and beyond. Reporting in 1669 on the events of the day *outside* Denmark only, the paper covered the affairs of Germany, the Netherlands (Dutch and Spanish), France, Italy, Spain, the Mediterranean and North Africa, Poland and Russia, as well as the relations between those nations and the Ottoman Empire. With a monthly output in the region of 180 news items – the number of items in each report was variable – the paper reported on a wide variety of matters: diplomatic negotiations and treaties; domestic politics in the foreign countries, including promotions or sackings of military and civilian personnel; the splendours of life at court and the birth and death of its most prominent members; crimes and misdemeanours and their deserved punishment; natural and supernatural occurrences, usually with some religious admonition or interpretation attached. It also covered information of particular interest to the merchant community: prices of commodities locally and at different exchanges; dates of markets; exchange rates; colonial expansion; and, in a century of near constant warfare, whether as full-scale battles or minor skirmishes, the provision of supplies and money needed to support the large armies and navies.

The state of preservation of the *Ordinari Post-Zeitung* and its sources for 1669 makes it possible to learn a little more about the publisher's editorial practice than is the case with the Swedish *Ordinari Post-Tijdender.* Thus, analysis of the 1669 contents of the *Ordinari Post-Zeitung* shows that it consisted of nothing other than 46 per cent of the 713 reports printed earlier in Georg Greflinger's twice weekly *Nordischer Mercurius*, 25 per cent of the 713 printed in the twice weekly *Europaeische Mitwochentliche Sambstätige Zeitung* published under the auspices of the Thurn und Taxis postmaster, Johannes Vrints, and 4 per cent of the 1647 reports printed in the *Ordinari Wochentliche … Zeitung*, which appeared on Tuesdays and Thursdays with an appendix on Saturdays.[48] In other words, of 3,073 reports available to him, some 700[49] went into the paper, the rest into his waste paper bin. He could, of course, have chosen any of the reports available to him, so by the selection process alone the editor made the *Ordinari Post-Zeitung* his very own paper, and in that sense also *his* contribution to the formation of public opinion.

Moreover, as 60 per cent of his reports were copied from Greflinger's paper, but only 29 per cent from Vrints' and 10 per cent from Schumacher's, Gøde's choice also shows his assessment of the relative value, for his particular purpose, of those papers.

In other words, through the selection process alone, Gøde's paper came to express to his readers a particular view of European politics. That view was one in which the emphasis was on the importance of political and economic stability, and on the measures taken by politicians to curb unrest within their countries, and by diplomats to prevent war among the 'Christian' nations. 1669 was one of the few years in the seventeenth century in which there was peace, or at least a hiatus in the French designs on the Netherlands and Spain brought about by the Triple Alliance and the peace of Aachen of 2 May 1668, but the paper's many reports on supplies to the army and the navy underscored the feeling that peace would not last, despite the equally frequently reported attempts by the diplomats of all nations to secure it. That was the view of Europe presented twice weekly by the *Ordinari Post-Zeitung* in 1669, and as no government action was taken against it in that year, we may conclude that it was a view which the authorities shared, or at least tolerated as an influence on public opinion.[50]

Extraordinaires Relationes aus Allerley Orten *versus the* Ordinaire Post-Zeitung, *1672 to 1673*[51]

Thanks to their official positions and various printing licences, Henrik Gøde and his brother Jørgen built up a substantial business, and they seem to have satisfied the Copenhagen readership well until 1672, when the Royal Bookseller Daniel Paulli[52] claimed that that was no longer the case. With Europe once again embroiled in war, he argued in his application to the king of 11 June, no single newspaper appearing only on ordinary post days could possibly carry enough information to benefit those engaged in trade. He therefore proposed to publish not only what he termed *extraordinary* relations on *all* post days from *all* sorts of places, but also to print and sell supplements and separate publications containing information about exchange rates, the price of goods at home and abroad, etc. He also argued, in a vein likely to appeal to the pride of king, government, and city fathers, that other important European cities already had two or more regular newspapers. The king referred the matter to the commissioners for trade, who approved the application on 31 August, and on 22 October 1672 Paulli's licence received the king's signature.[53] This was a remarkable licence because it not only allowed Paulli to breach Gøde's clearly formulated exclusive licence to publish newspapers in German and Danish, but it also was backdated to 6 July, thereby retrospectively covering the extraordinary relations and appendices which Paulli had in fact been publishing periodically since 3 August, indeed using the title *Extraordinaires Relationes aus Allerley Orten* as early as 10 August.

Unable or unwilling to challenge Paulli's licence in the courts – the Paulli family had powerful allies at court and had a reputation as ferocious litigants – Jørgen Gøde,[54] (to whom Henrik had handed over the office of Royal Printer with the newspaper licence on 20 December 1670, allegedly for health reasons[55]) decided to meet the challenge from Paulli in two other ways. First, he doubled the amount of news carried by the *Ordinari Post-Zeitung* by publishing an *Anhang*, which appeared later the same day as the main paper or on the following day; and second, he increased his service to the Danish readership, already provided with a monthly survey of events in his *Danske Mercurius* (see below), by launching a weekly Danish version of his German paper, entitled the *Ordinarie Post-Tidende*, the first eight pages of which appeared on Wednesday 13 November, that is, three weeks after Paulli's licence had received the royal signature. However, as the reports in the Danish weekly had appeared in his German weekly the day before or earlier, the parent paper was both a resource and a competitor, and the Danish weekly was not a success.[56] In any case, any initial advantage gained over Paulli by publishing news in the Danish language was soon lost, for within a fortnight of the publication of the first number of Gøde's *Ordinarie Post-Tidende*, Paulli offered the Copenhagen Danish readership the first number of his survey of the events of the past month entitled *Extraordinaires Maanedlige Relationer* (see below).

By the very wording of the title of his newspaper – *Extraordinaires Relationes aus Allerley Orten* – Paulli announced to potential readers the point made earlier in his application to the authorities, namely that the Copenhagen readership deserved something bigger and better than the Gøde papers, and the fact that it contained, during January 1673, 121 reports with 383 news items from 122 different correspondents seems to prove this point, for the monthly number of items printed in Gøde's *Ordinaire Post-Zeitung* prior to the challenge from Paulli, had been less than 200.[57] Moreover, by publishing the eight pages of his paper on Tuesdays and Saturdays, i.e. one day before Gøde, and an eight-page *Appendix* either later the same day or on Wednesdays and Sundays, i.e. Gøde's usual days, Paulli poised himself not only to inform the Copenhagen readership more fully and better, but also earlier than Gøde.

Comparisons between the output of the two weeklies in German over longer periods of time are difficult because of their fragmentary state of preservation, and they are further complicated by the fact that where periods of overlap between the two papers can be found, their sources are often lost or have survived in insufficient quantity to support comparisons. Despite these limitations, however, a closer look at the news available to the Copenhagen readership during even a brief period of such overlaps, such as the month of January 1673, gives an indication of the nature and extent of the competition between the two enterprises and what effect, if any, it might have had on public opinion at the time.

During that month, the three Hamburg papers published 389 reports, and contents analysis of the two Copenhagen papers shows that many of those reports can be found, either verbatim or edited, among the 141 reports which made up Gøde *Ordinari Post-Zeitung*, and the 111 published in Paulli's *Extraordinaires Relationes aus Allerley Orten*. As was the case in 1669, the *Nordischer Mercurius* remained Gøde's preferred source, and so it was for Paulli, almost to the exclusion of the other two Hamburg papers. Moreover, in his address to the reader at the beginning of January 1673, Paulli made his respect for and reliance on Greflinger explicit; for having stressed the value of newspapers to those engaged in trade, and to the young generation interested in contemporary events, he went on to answer the important question about how, in a world of often conflicting news reports, these noble aims could best be achieved, with the following reference to Greflinger:

> The renowned Celadon once wrote: 'I do not make up the news myself but communicate it unchanged as it is related to me now by one, now by another [person] and present it to the public as a naked girl so that everybody can dress her the way he wishes and believe as much of it as he thinks fit.'[58]

Furthermore, to attract the attention of potential buyers already familiar with the appearance of the *Nordischer Mercurius*, Paulli also used a figure of Mercury on the front page of each number – in all but the smallest detail identical to that used by Greflinger[59] – and adopted his layout and presentation of the news, including the pagination of the newspaper throughout the year, which made cross-referencing useful and educationally rewarding.

Though the dependence on the three traditional Hamburg newspapers is clear in both Copenhagen weeklies, they also contained a considerable number of reports – sixty-six in Gøde's paper and seventy-nine in Paulli's – with no obvious basis in the usual sources. Some of these cannot be accounted for today because the potential sources are no longer extant, others need no basis, such as advertisements for their own products or official announcements; in other cases, their reports read as if several sources may have been conflated into single reports as part of the editing process in Gøde's and Paulli's offices. However, the fact that thirty-three unsourced reports appeared in both Copenhagen papers suggests that both publishers used one or more shared sources, and because Paulli, as well as an Altona newspaper publisher, fell foul of the authorities in October 1672, it has been possible to identify one of those sources: an untitled newspaper published in German thrice weekly in Altona, commonly referred to as the *Altonaische Relation* and published by the Dutch printer Victor de Loew.[60]

The incident which led to the prosecution of both Paulli and de Loew is significant for several reasons. First, it highlights the important link between Copenhagen and the important Danish city Altona on German soil, close enough, indeed according to local wits 'allzunah,' to Hamburg to benefit from its postal services and its newspaper industry. In 1664, to attract wealthy merchants from outside Denmark and so strengthen the city's ability to encroach on Hamburg's national and international trade, it had received a royal charter allowing non-Lutheran religious practices, and on 6 July 1672 the Dutchman Victor de Loew had been granted permission by the city council to publish a newspaper.[61] Second, it confirms that even traditional, non-committal reporting could be read, at least by some but probably by many, as revealing a bias, for it was no report in particular but its general 'line' that had convinced the French ambassador in Copenhagen, Terlon (according to Molesworth one of the most obnoxious proponents of the doctrine of blind obedience[62]), that the Danish press was anti-French. Writing on 4 October to thank the Danish king for having acted upon an earlier complaint against 'le gazetier de sa uille de Coppenhaguen' and put the unnamed culprit under arrest, Terlon now asked His Majesty to proceed in a similar way against 'l'êcrivain de sa uille d'Altena qui est l'auteur de toutes les nouelles que la gazete a icy publiées contre la reputation du Roy mon Maistre,' adding that the latter had even had the temerity to announce the death of His Most Christian Majesty, Louis XIV, an offence, which earned de Loew three months' house arrest.[63] And third, it confirms that the Altona printer was indeed Victor de Loew, whose *Altonaische Relation* in a subsequent analysis turned out to have carried twenty-seven previously unsourced reports in Gøde's and Paulli's papers.

Whether Gøde and Paulli had yet another common source, whose reports could produce a basis for the remaining sixty-six unsourced reports in their papers, is a possibility, but not a certainty. If the seven lost issues of the *Altonaische Relation* from January 1673 contained a number of reports similar to that in the five extant, and if Gøde and Paulli had made similar use of them, then they would, for the whole month, have had a further 125 de Loew reports from which to choose. Assuming this to have been the case, both Gøde and Paulli would during the month of January 1673 have had 437 reports from which to make their selections; that is, seventy-seven in Greflinger's paper, 138 in Schumacher's, ninety-seven in Vrints', and 157 in de Loew's, for the latter's house arrest had been lifted by then, which enabled him to provide his customers with reports from – in descending order of frequency – Altona, The Hague, Vienna, Amsterdam, Lipstadt, Warsaw, Antwerp, Bielefeld, Gouda, Hildesheim, Paris and Utrecht, as well as from other European capitals and minor towns in Germany and the Netherlands.

As mentioned above, one of the differences between Gøde's and Paulli's use of their shared sources was, that Gøde copied his verbatim reports from all four, while Paulli mostly used only two. Analysis of the contents of edited reports in both papers shows a similar distribution.

Table 1 Sources used in Gøde's and Paulli's papers

	Greflinger	Schumacher	Vrints	de Loew	Total
Gøde	28	11	18	14	71
Paulli	19	2	1	13	35

They also differed in the way they presented the news. Gøde continued the traditional layout, heading each report with the place and date of its composition, a method which focuses the reader's attention on what the news *from* a particular place happened to be; also, because the reports were not linked by subject or followed one another in a particular order, this style of 'staccato' reporting conveys a disjointed picture of events. Paulli also used the traditional method, but in addition he used fourteen rubrics not found in Gøde's paper, all headed by the names of countries, but undated and without any indication of where they came from.[64] This method of presentation turned the reports into the news *about* a particular country or region, and the fact that 139 of all 389 news items were linked together in this way means that more than one-third of his reports present a coherent, contextual picture of events very different from that conveyed by Gøde's traditional staccato style of simple reporting. In other words, because of competition between the two enterprises, there were now two different ways of dressing Celadon's naked lady, i.e. of influencing public opinion in Copenhagen. And once again it may be concluded that this had come about without either editor uttering a word of his own, but purely by their selection of the words of their sources and the practices of their editors.

The making and breaking of images

Paulli's Extraordinaires Maanedlige Relationer *versus* *Gøde's* Den Danske Mercurius, *January 1673*

A further effect of the rivalry between the two enterprises was the launching of two new newspapers in the Danish language, of which, as we have already seen, Gøde's weekly *Ordinarie Post-Tidende* met with little success. By contrast, Paulli's Danish monthly, *Extraordinaires Maanedlige Relationer*, went from strength to strength, and it was indeed extraordinary in other respects as well. First, because Paulli had not mentioned in his application to the king that he also intended to publish a monthly newspaper in Danish, nor did his licence say that he could do so; indeed, it seems that this publication never received a licence. Second, because its contents in January 1673 consisted of forty-seven news items, of which forty-three were translations into Danish of the 389 reports already used for his weekly *Extraordinaires Relationes aus Allerley Orten*, their re-selection confirming them as being considered of particular importance by the editor. Third, because twenty-two of those news items are literal translations, whereas the remaining twenty-one are reformulations, updates, extensions, or summaries of between three and thirteen items about important events covered at various stages during the past month and, most important, because it has been possible to identify his sources for all of them. In other words, we are in a position to follow each of the forty-three reports in the *Extraordinaires Maanedlige Relationer* for January 1673 back through its previous incarnations to its source, to see how the editor decided to dress the 'nudam puellam' of the original Hamburg report, first in his own German version in the *Extraordinaires Relationes aus Allerley Orten* and then in Danish, processes which involved personal judgement, decision, and action by the editor, and which contributed to the creation of images of persons or nations in the minds of his readers.

Of course, making or breaking of images was not what Copenhagen editors were either allowed or supposed to do. Their licences permitted them to extract, copy, and sometimes translate objective information and present it to the reading public, and as we have seen the editors themselves set great store by meeting the high standard set by the great Celadon. On the other hand, we have also seen, that the straight, 'staccato' reporting in their sources carried a bias implicitly, as did their different uses of them, for that alone explains why Gøde's paper was, indeed had to be, different from Paulli's. With the publication of their monthly summaries, Paulli's *Extraordinaires Maanedlige Relationer* and Gøde's *Den Danske Mercurius*, both editors took this process one step further.

In order to be able to publish his *Extraordinaires Maanedlige Relationer* for January 1673, Paulli had to go through this selection process once more, as he decided at the end of the month which of the 389 items in his weekly paper were important enough to merit inclusion in a monthly summary of world events. As there had been no complaints from the authorities during the month, he was entitled to assume – as we are today – that the reports already published were acceptable to the authorities as a potential influence on public opinion, and thus he was free to translate those items which would sell most copies of his paper. One consideration was that with the monthly paper he was addressing for the first time the merchants and young people interested in politics whose usual, or perhaps only, language was Danish,[65] and he clearly judged that some extra assistance would be required. Thus he used and also translated the Latin and other foreign words of his sources, added place names to locate a particular event and explain its particular historical or political significance (Charleroi, Stockholm), and converted foreign currencies (Lübeck mark, Spanish patacon, English pound sterling, German reichthaler, Dutch stuiver) into Danish rigsdaler or their equivalent value in gold. In two cases, he even referred his readers to publications by the learned scholars Cluverus[66] and Schottus,[67] which would further elucidate his reports on strange 'natural' occurrences – for example, the harsh landowner near Nürnberg who was turned into a dog by God, and the rain storm which left thousands of warring yellow and black worms covering the fields near Neusol in Hungary.

In the reporting of diplomatic matters, Paulli's readers' service consisted primarily in linking related events and providing the context which could help a reader make a coherent whole out of the complex and, in the disparate 'staccato' reports of the weekly papers, near incomprehensible facts and events. He explained that the reason why France in 1673 charged Spain with breach of the 1668 treaty of Aix-la-Chapelle was that Spanish soldiers had taken part in the Dutch attack on the French fortress Charleroi in 1672; and he went on to say that although Spain had denied the charge, Britain agreed with France and had used this opportunity to terminate her treaty of mutual defence with Spain. Similarly, weekly reports about the arrivals of Papal, Polish, and Russian envoys at various European courts were brought together as moves in an Eastern European grand plan against Turkey, an enterprise supported by Rome's appeal to all Christian nations to stop fighting among themselves and face the common enemy. On the other hand – and here he clearly expressed a particular, though not necessarily personal, view – he also pointed out that the desired peace in Europe was not imminent because the German emperor had instructed his councillors at Regensburg not to allow a settlement between France and Brandenburg which did not include the Empire. Indeed, using the colloquial Danish equivalent to 'and pigs might fly'[68] he gave vent to the frustration felt by those who, as reported throughout the papers at the time, suffered most from the European war – the peasants, the citizenry, the merchants, as well as those politicians who wanted Europe to produce, trade, and prosper.

However, as Paulli (and de Loew) had recently experienced, comments on foreign potentates could be a precarious business, and in January 1673 there were many occasions when Paulli seems to have been overcautious, in the sense that he failed to include negative comments about policies, though they were known to be anathema in Lutheran, Absolutist Denmark. The (abdicated) Queen Christina's application for permission to practice her (Catholic) religion in Sweden went without political or religious comment, as did Louis XIV's distribution of the enormous French assets of the deceased Polish king Casimir,[69] though Paulli also reported that the main beneficiaries were two groups particularly odious to the Danish ideologues, namely the (perfidious) Jesuits and the (disloyal) German princes along the Rhine, who supported Louis XIV and so were guilty of treason. Similarly, when reporting that Charles II of England had put his seal to an act allowing freedom of practice for several religious persuasions, Paulli did not echo the oft-repeated warning from the Danish clergy that precisely this kind of 'mixed religion' was bound to undermine both Church and state, but instead tried to exonerate the English monarch, when in the number for February he played down the significance of that seemingly reckless act.

In fact, all foreign kings, queens, princes and other persons in high authority, whether Lutheran or not, were treated with the utmost respect, which made the *Extraordinaires Maanedlige Relationer* a better champion of politics than of religion. The one exception to this rule was the Ottoman emperor, 'the arch enemy of all Christendom.' His raids into Poland and Russia, and his duplicitous support for the Hungarian rebels against their Holy Roman emperor, were condemned as a serious attack on Europe as a whole, and the paper was delighted to report that 'the Turk' might not be able to attack the following Spring, because he was, thankfully, preoccupied with suppressing a rebellion in Persia. Otherwise, when things went wrong, it was not the rulers who were at fault but their appointees, and their fall from power followed as night follows day.

Nevertheless, in January 1673 there were two reports which may even have raised doubts about two foreign rulers, the kings of Sweden and France. The first case may be due to no more than a typographical error. However, it could be seen as significant that a report from Stockholm about how very pleased 'all (!)

the king's subjects' were at his assumption of absolute power, in the Danish translation acquired an exclamation mark after the word 'all.' Certainly, in the previous number an exclamation point had been used by Paulli to express ridicule at the 'martyrdom (!) of Jesuits,' so it could have been used on this occasion for the same purpose. If indeed this was the case, its use – whether it was intentional or not, or a Freudian slip – could well have raised questions in the reader's mind about the state of absolutism in Sweden. It could also, and this would have been even more dangerous to the printer, have been interpreted as a comment on absolutism itself and its enforced blind obedience anywhere. The other instance is a similarly trivial report about the death of a tightrope artist, which ran in all the Hamburg and Copenhagen papers at the time. This time, however, it is Paulli's meticulous reporting in both his papers that suggests why that incident might have warranted selection for the second time in a monthly review of the state of Europe. The report came from Regensburg, the permanent seat of the German Diet since 1663, and concerned the fatal fall of a French tightrope artist who attempted a descent from the highest tower of Regensburg castle into the central court yard, but who lost his balance because he insisted on firing rockets in all directions from his arms and legs. Once again, many may simply have marvelled at the tale, but an alert reader familiar with the numerous illustrations in flysheets of rulers or their emblematic representations trying to keep their balance in the European struggle for power, might well have seen more in it, and one cannot exclude the possibility that a particularly suspicious and emblematically sensitive French ambassador might have taken umbrage at the report.

Much more explosive than the intricacies of diplomatic balancing acts were the reports on the military activities of Louis XIV and his generals, Turenne and Luxembourg, as they began what looked to become the final push in a three-pronged attack on William of Orange, his commanders in the field, Wurtz, Waldek, Hoorn, Rabenhaupt, and Königsmarck, and his ally the Elector of Brandenburg.

A constant theme in the reports under the headings 'From the German army' and 'From the French army and the conquered towns' was the huge imbalance in manpower between the two armies, aggravated by the fact that the imperial forces were doing nothing at all, and Brandenburg's chief objective clearly was to protect his own lands. Still in their winter quarters near Hildesheim far from the theatre of war, the Imperials left the fighting to Brandenburg, whose only reported contribution amounted to two failed attempts at taking a suburb of Marburg, the fortified town of Werle, and the loss of Duisburg to the French. This left the vastly outnumbered but brave Dutch to fend for themselves.[70]

Had Paulli wished to balance his reporting, he could have re-selected a similar French exploit, for example the raising of the siege of Charleroi by Colonel Montal ahead of 180 French soldiers, for which he and his family had been rewarded even more richly by Louis XIV. All the details about it had already been reported by Paulli in his weekly paper, but in the monthly, Montal's action was merely listed as a Dutch defeat, followed by a description of Charleroi's impenetrable defences, and the comment that it actually belonged to Spain. Instead, Paulli chose to report, both under the headings 'From the French army' and 'Holland,' on the atrocities committed against the civilian population by the French conquerors of the Dutch towns of Bodegrave and Zwammerdam, where they had hanged the men by their genitals, raped the women, murdered the children, and maltreated the clergy. Indeed, as was also reported under 'Holland,' it was the fear of similar reprisals which caused the women of The Hague to rebel so violently that the duke of Plön, appointed military governor of the city, had to threaten to use his troops against them to re-establish law and order,[71] after which the Dutch authorities banned all public meetings of women anywhere. And finally, as an illustration that French atrocities also stiffened the resolve elsewhere, Paulli ended the 'Holland' section with a report about some unarmed Dutch peasants who, with no military protection in sight, attacked and killed all 200 soldiers in a French party attempting to cross the river near Gouda.

While Paulli's reports clearly created a favourable image of the Dutch and demonized the French, they would have had an additional effect on the Copenhagen readers old or knowledgeable enough to recall the Swedish attack on Denmark only twelve years previously. Stories about atrocities perpetrated by an invading superior power would have stirred up memories, the heroic Dutch defence would have reminded many of the bravery of Danish peasants in the countryside and the burghers and students of Copenhagen. In short their own recent history would have increased their sympathy for the Dutch, whose navy had finally broken the siege of Copenhagen in 1660 and so saved the nation from defeat.

The reports on military exploits, as did those on political and diplomatic affairs, also create another kind of image: that heads of state were personally responsible for successes, others for defeat, and that within the military hierarchy, the high command were like kings. When things went well, it was the generals who wrote, or at least signed, the final reports submitted to the authorities, and their rewards were usually higher than that of their officers in the field, to say nothing of the rank and file; and it was Rabenhaupt's report which found its way into the newspapers. When disaster struck, the blame would fall upon the officers in the field, as in the case of Colonel Pain-et-Vin, though there must have been another view current about that particular event, or Königsmarck would not have found it necessary to threaten with the death penalty anyone suggesting that he was really to blame! Nor were generals considered to be in any way responsible for the fact that there was a war at all, though there was plenty of evidence to show that these military and mercenary entrepreneurs did extremely well in wartime, but incurred huge expenses when peace broke out, unless they quickly disbanded their armies and sent marauding, out-of-work soldiers by their thousands in among the civilian population once again. According to the Scandinavian newspapers, at least, the generals were no more to blame for the wars they conducted than were the princes who declared them. Like showers of yellow and black worms from the heavens, inundations in Cambridgeshire, Brabant, or Silesia, or the dense clouds of birds darkening the sky, an omen which had not been seen since 1628 when a war broke out, war was a natural disaster visited upon man for reasons beyond his comprehension.

All the same, and precisely because commenting on those fundamental issues was taboo, their reporting without reference to the religious foundation of the political system reminded the newspaper reader several times per week of the reality and importance of a non-religious view, a secular understanding of the way of the world. That was, of course, an additional rather than an alternative view for most people at the time. Nevertheless, it was a contribution, however slight and inadvertent, to the formation of a secular view of the world similar to that for which Molesworth yearned, when he looked forward to an end to a world 'in which men fall down and worship the work of their own Hands, as if it dropped from Heaven.'[72]

Den Danske Mercurius, *1666 to 1677*

The original licence of 1634 had permitted Martzan and Moltke to publish regular newspapers in German and Danish, and when Paulli in 1672 decided to challenge the position of the Gøde brothers, they had for the past seven years already catered for the Danish readership with *Den Danske Mercurius*, the first regular newspaper to be published in the Danish language. A monthly paper, whose four pages of text were written in alexandrines by Anders Bording, the most felicitous of Danish poets of the period, it has traditionally been considered a poetic bagatelle similar to, and possibly imitative of, a Paris gossip newspaper writer by Jean Loret in verse for the delectation of the ladies and gentlemen in court circles.[73] According to the latest version of that view, for which there is no more documentary evidence than before, the idea may even have been brought back to Copenhagen in 1663 by the crown prince himself or some other courtier and discussed in a conversation between Bording and King Frederik III.[74] If that were the case, there is ample circumstantial evidence to show that the idea of a newspaper in verse would have been approved by the highest authority of all.

It is, however, not its form but its contents which determines whether or not *Den Danske Mercurius* was a proper newspaper rather than a monthly dose of 'royal incense' to celebrate all the righteous deeds of the monarch and entertain his court. The fact that the reports in *Den Danske Mercurius* under the rubric 'Denmark' contained passages of fulsome praise of all the members of the Danish royal family supports the traditional view, but close analysis of them also shows that there was much more to them than that. In any case, contents analysis of all 14,700 alexandrines published between 1666 and 1677 shows, first, that two-thirds of its reports appeared under the headings other than 'Denmark,'. These were: Germany (2,776 lines), France (1,522), Holland (1,318), England (1,028), Poland (762), Italy (450), Spain (388), Sweden (348), and so forth. And second, that all those reports prior to being 'dressed in poetry' by Anders Bording, had appeared in prose in the corresponding numbers of the newspapers known to have been available in the Gøde workshop, that is the three Hamburg papers, his weekly excerpts from them, the *Ordinari Post-Zeitung*, as well as Paulli's *Extraordinaires Relationes aus Allerley Orten*. As the *Mercurius* reports were not only translated from German, like those in the Swedish *Ordinari Post-Tijdender*, but also transposed into poetry, it is not possible to identify the precise source for each news item in all cases, also because like Paulli in his monthly, Bording conflated many reports and presented them as *news about*, not *news from* a particular place. Nevertheless, using the entire corpus of reports available to the editor of *Den Danske Mercurius* in Gøde's workshop, it is possible to identify prose versions of all the news items printed in *Den Danske Mercurius* – with the exception of those printed under the heading of 'Denmark.'

The fact that more than one-third of its contents (5,676 lines) appeared under the heading 'Denmark' is a feature as unique to the *Den Danske Mercurius* as its metrical form – and more significant. Whereas its form has been a principal reason for *not* considering it a proper regular newspaper, analysis of its contents confirms that it *was* one, though a very special one; for whereas Gøde's prose paper only carried three reports under the heading of 'Denmark' between 1664 and 1669, every issue except one of *Den Danske Mercurius* opened with it in 1666 and 1677. In fact, it would be difficult, if not impossible, to find another regular newspaper anywhere in Europe at the time which carried a similar proportion of national news so prominently.

Moreover, the national news covered as wide a variety of events as those under other headings, or in the prose papers. What separates those reports from their prose counterparts is not their poetic garb, but the fact that the editor invariably and explicitly ascribed all good things, great or small, to the personal actions or interventions of the great, pious, just, wise, courageous, etc., King of Denmark, be he Frederik III or Christian V. With the skill and decorum of a well-schooled baroque poet, Bording compared the monarch to the eternal sun, a brave lion, the ever-vigilant cock, etc., and drew on other literary devices such as simple proverbs illustrating homely truths, complex similes from classical literature, and parallels with the fables of Aesop, to bring home to his readers how fortunate they were to live under a regime whose head can do no wrong. It was to the Bible, however, that he would turn for the ultimate reason why that was so, namely that the king was set by God and anointed by His clergy to rule his people, or as some even maintained, His people. His appointees, such as generals, admirals, diplomats, and politicians could err, though responsibility for failure was usually placed much further down the ranks, while Christ-like, the good shepherd king watched over his flock, or, like Moses or Joshua led his people or, with God's hand on the tiller, steered the ship of state through troubled political waters and saved the crew, all of whom were bound to him in gratitude and total obedience. All those images, like the beliefs expressed by them, abounded in Scandinavian baroque hymns and sermons and were part of the common language in which Bording and his contemporaries communicated. Their poetic garb, though perhaps alien to some then and now, made their contents more powerful as an instrument of communication and set *Den Danske*

Mercurius apart from other newspapers, not as obsequious deference to Danish royalty, but as a unique attempt at employing Pegasus as a means of influencing public opinion.

And in that respect, there was no difference between the national and international news carried in *Den Danske Mercurius.* Reporting on an emblematic theatrical performance at a German court, Bording reminded his readers, that 'all the world is a stage,' and that not only news, but lessons could be learnt from observing the actions of all the players on it.[75] Accordingly, the news about foreign countries also reflect Bording's views of the events reported upon, or at least the 'spin' put upon it or desired by his masters. Thus he pointedly commented on the many occasions elsewhere in Europe on which the hydra of insubordination raised its many heads: the numerous nobles in the elective, Catholic monarchy of Poland; the lower nobility and even peasants in 'semi-Christian,' i.e. Orthodox Russia; the shifty Hungarian grandees constantly plotting with the Turk against the Emperor; self-appointed leaders of rebellious commoners, in France and Holland.

As a result, all Europe was torn apart by Mars, when she should be ruled by Mercury. Indeed, to the Danish Mercury, the guardian of trade and communications, the word war meant 'all evils imaginable,' though like most of his contemporaries he excepted the colonial efforts of the Christian nations individually anywhere in the world, and their much hoped for joint action against the Ottoman Empire. Naturally, in the war 'forced upon' Denmark by Sweden in 1675, *Den Danske Mercurius* prays that God will send His Danish king victorious, and he knows how to describe even the most appalling defeats as victories. But his rage at a world out of joint pervades his anguished depictions of the loss of life and the visitations upon the civil population of a war, which neither Bording as writer of *Den Danske Mercurius*, nor chancellor Griffenfeld wanted. For until chauvinism became the order of the day, the constant theme in *Den Danske Mercurius* was the search for a peaceful Europe driven by Mercury, not destroyed by the dreadful 'gradivus' Mars.

The state of Europe desired by *Den Danske Mercurius* is described as one in which peaceful nations compete to increase their national wealth through trade, and in that respect Holland – her occasional constitutional difficulties and her non-Lutheran religion notwithstanding – stands out in the paper as the most successful state, indeed as an economic model to be imitated. To achieve 'Dutch success' – but without following her in respect of politics or religion – *Den Danske Mercurius* advised that Denmark must increase the yield from her own 'beehive,' i.e. increase domestic production of as many goods as possible to avoid costly imports. The paper, therefore, reported with approval on the ban on import of corn, cloth, salt, fish, timber, meat, etc. and saluted the brave Danish sailors who brought their ships safely home with the spices of the East, which would otherwise have had to be imported from Holland. And it urged its readers in 1669 to continue to drink good Danish beer and other established national drinks (among which he manages to include the foreign wines much beloved and drunk by himself, and imported by successful merchants, among them

Schumacher senior) and not to succumb to the temptations of foreign exotic drinks such as chocolate, tea, and coffee, but leave their consumption to 'Indians and Turks.'

Together with the reports eulogizing the politico-religious foundation of the realm, the many economic, largely mercantilist, observations on the events of the day, constitute the main powerful message of *Den Danske Mercurius*, a message unerringly expressed in a rich language peppered with colloquialisms and homely proverbs, and couched in a metre which faultlessly trips along, memorable, educative, and entertaining at the same time.[76] In short, where other newspapers relied on the editor's selection of news for their impact, *Den Danske Mercurius* not only told its readers what was happening around them, but also how to understand it.[77]

The regular publication of a politically correct interpretation of the main events of the preceding month to accompany[78] the weekly supplies of factual reports about those events was, of course, no accident, let alone the product of some fashion-conscious poetaster. On the other hand, the precise circumstances surrounding its inception are harder to establish than was the case with the Swedish newspaper, for no single document has survived instructing named persons in official positions to publish *Den Danske Mercurius* and how to go about it. Nevertheless, as we have seen, there is circumstantial evidence to suggest that the king or the crown prince may in some way have been involved, while a look at the recipient of Bording's political poems before 1666 may suggest why he was eventually chosen to write the paper. Important in that connection is, of course, Bording's enthusiastic address to the king celebrating his assumption of absolute power (1660), as are the poems addressed to influential politicians and other members of the new regime, including another member of the royal family, General U. F. Gyldenløve (1663), Chancellor Christopher Gabel (twice in 1663), General Paul Würtz (1664), Chief Army Prosecutor Paul Tscherning (1664), and Major General Ejler Holck (1665). With his virulent attack (1663) on the 'bloodthirsty' traitor Korfitz Ulfeldt, former leader of the aristocracy and now condemned to death in absentia for having opposed the establishment of the new regime,[79] Bording further demonstrated his devotion to the new rulers, while in the same year he appealed to the chancellor for preferment at court, and directly to the king in a poem in which he asked to be employed, as he put it, as 'the king's poet.'[80]

It may also be significant that precisely at the time when Bording was looking for employment in the king's service, the regime found itself to be under renewed pressure because the citizens of Copenhagen, without whose support the coup would have failed, were becoming disaffected because they realized that promises made to them in return for their participation would not now be honoured. Indeed, someone was reported to have stated that 'we are the people who kept the crown on the king's head, and we can remove it whenever we want,' and the situation was certainly considered by one of Bording's addressees, Paul Tscherning, to be serious enough to warn the king that it might be necessary to secure the future of the regime with the army alone.[81] There is no evidence to suggest that Tscherning was involved in the newspaper project, but the fact that Georg Greflinger dedicated his latest volume of poems to him in the same year (1664) in which Bording also paid him a poetic compliment adds a further string to the web of the 'Hamburg connection' and its importance for the Scandinavian newspaper industry, for that was also the year in which Greflinger began his *Nordischer Mercurius*. By that time Gøde had already been publishing the *Ordinari Post-Zeitung* from extracts from the other two Hamburg newspapers mentioned above, but as we have seen, Greflinger's paper soon became his preferred source of information, and it is worth mentioning that the *Nordischer Mercurius* had also on occasion summed up events in alexandrines. In any case, that was the metre in which Bording, having waited impatiently until June 1666 for the go-ahead from the authorities, submitted a specimen copy for their inspection, and they must have been pleased with what they saw, for on 30 June 1666 the king signed an order allocating to Bording until further notice the royal corn tithes from a Norwegian shire, an income which was converted into an annual remuneration of 200 Rdl. in 1670, and increased to 250 in 1672. That year Bording opens with the proud declaration that writing *Den Danske Mercurius* is his way of serving his king.

However, while the political situation in Copenhagen, the launching of an additional newspaper in Hamburg, and the royal financing of *Den Danske Mercurius* to a large extent account for its origin, form, and excellent coverage of events, the question of who was responsible for its political message remains open. Gøde was certainly able to deliver the information, and Bording was clearly able to turn it into alexandrines, but did either man possess the knowledge, not just about Danish politics but about the politics of all the nations commented upon in *Den Danske Mercurius*, to be able to attach, where necessary, a politically correct value judgement on, or a valid interpretation of, the complex issues in European politics at the time? That question may be unanswerable, in the sense that no named person can be proved to have played this vital role. On the other hand, we know where he must have worked, for the Statute of 1644 had ruled that newspapers were a 'negotium politicum' and should therefore be censored by someone employed in the chancellery, 'because they know best how to tell true from false.' This makes it particularly significant that the printed Ordinance banning all other Copenhagen printers from printing or selling pirated copies of *Den Danske Mercurius* in manuscript form bore the annotation 'by order of secretary Schumacher,'[82] the man, whose understanding of politics at home and abroad was unrivalled, and who determined the course of Danish politics until his spectacular fall in 1676. As one of the most astute politicians of the age, he would have valued journalists who not only published reports, but who gave the news sufficient 'spin' to point public opinion in the direction he desired. He may not have had a direct hand in the monthly affairs of *Den Danske Mercurius*, but his deputies would have been briefed well enough to guide Anders Bording, not only in his choice of subject for his 5,676 lines of Danish news, but also about the political line in accordance with which all the news should be presented and commented upon.

If Peder Griffenfeld did play an important part in the launching of *Den Danske Mercurius* as a government mouthpiece, there would seem to have been an ironical twist to that connection, for when the mighty politician suddenly fell from power, the task of feeding an explanation into the public opinion at the time fell to the writer of the only newspaper allowed to speculate on such events. But that is not the way Bording would have seen it. For him, it was the cause of Griffenfeld's fall which was significant, and which he managed to convey most skilfully. On nine previous occasions in eleven years he had reported the fall of other great European politicians, likening the steps leading to high position to a bridge of ice, which might at any time melt under their feet. In 1676, he chose a very different simile as he likened Griffenfeld – accused by his opponents of having made the king himself into an instrument for his policies – to Phaëton, who attempted to ride the sun's chariot, but was blinded by the light of its rays and fell to his death.

Griffenfeld's fall brought about a radical change in Danish politics, while Bording and those advising him deftly and immediately brought *Den Danske Mercurius* into line with the new political order of the day, thus continuing the purpose for which it had been created in the first place.

Conclusion

The opening of the 'Hamburg connection' provided the means needed for the production of newspapers, but it also raised serious questions about how to control this flow of information which the authorities in the two Scandinavian areas answered differently. In Sweden, pre-publication censorship determined the contents of the newspaper from the start, with the result that only one official newspaper was published during the seventeenth century. In Denmark, a number of *ad hoc* measures with a similar intent developed as printers competed for their corner of the market in news, and no official newspaper was published, though one was entirely financed and controlled by the authorities.

Under those conditions, editors and their backers set out to serve a particular and new portion of the literate population, above all those engaged in commerce, but also anyone else with enough interest in the world and who had the means to avail themselves of that information. We cannot say how large that portion of readers was at the time, though it is clear from the time available to editors between the arrival of the post and the time of publication – usually between three and five days – that the cumbersome censorship procedure when followed to the letter would have prevented the production of large numbers of copies. The selection of reports to be used was clearly not a haphazard affair, but one which involved personal judgement and would have taken considerable time, and so would the necessary visits to the censor or such deputies as were available. Where translation was involved, those initial steps would have taken even longer. Typesetting the forms for a four-page publication in small quarto, a frequently used format, would have taken several hours, proof-reading a further thirty minutes at least, and dressing the press thirty minutes after that. Providing the paper had been made ready beforehand and was moist enough to take the printing ink, and allowing further time for the meticulous inking of the forms, printing could now commence. Two experienced printers working one press would have been able to print one side of 100 folio sheets per hour with little loss of faulty sheets but would need a further hour to complete the printing process. And finally, the sheets must be dried, folded, and cut, ready for delivery or sale.[83]

On the other hand, one copy could be read by many, particularly if readers met at coffee houses, wine and beer cellars, or in private residences to discuss its contents and the way of the world in general. In 1658, one such group had been founded near Hamburg by Johann Rist (1603–1667), and judging from its deliberations the topics discussed were a good deal wider than those of the earlier *Sprachgesellschaften* and rather similar to the spectator clubs, real or imaginary, which came to play such a prominent role in the intellectual life of the following century. Thus, in one of the 1663 sessions of the *Elbschwaneorden*,[84] when its members were discussing why living in or near a great city like Hamburg was the most valuable lifestyle of all, it was agreed that what made the big difference was not only the rapid supply of information about the world received through the postal services, but access to newspapers. He who did not possess that information was no better than the 'village idiots' who knew nothing about the rest of the world; such people only exist, they do not live in the world, for 'He who wishes to live in this world in the right way must also understand the way of the world its nature its changes its management.'[85] From 1665 onwards, another member of the *Elbschwaneorden*, Georg Greflinger, advised schoolmasters and others charged with the education of the young to use the *Nordischer Mercurius* to make them, as he put it, 'good politicians.' Similarly, from 1676 the *Altonaische Relation* published, as a weekly supplement, the debates between the members of a club invented by the Altona preacher Johann Frisch (1636–1692) for the same purpose, making explicit an implicit point in the statements of Rist and Greflinger, namely that regular reading of newspapers not only brings factual information, but over time builds up in the reader a fund of knowledge which equips him to understand and interpret new information in context. Without such a fund of political and historical knowledge, which Frisch called 'the inexhaustible source of all necessary and useful knowledge,' a recipient of news was like a man led through a city covered in dense fog, and the learned professor and publicist Christian Weise (1641–1708) agreed, describing the usefulness of the newspapers to members of the learned republic in a Latin treatise from 1676, which with an attached geographical and genealogical compendium was translated into German for the benefit of all newspaper readers in 1703, the year before Johannes Hübner published his *Reales Staats- und Zeitungs-Lexicon*.

It is difficult to judge the impact of a secular view of the world based on the high degree of familiarity with it created by newspaper editors and their supporters, not least in societies like Denmark and Sweden in which the control of public opinion and all aspects of daily life lay in the hands of the all powerful indoctrinators within the Church and state. Certainly, none of the newspapers discussed here were revolutionary in the sense that they deliberately set out to challenge the prevailing ideology; yet, as was the case with the hypersensitive censors mentioned above, there were those who saw them as a serious threat to law and order. Attacking the newspapers as endangering the political order, the court official Ahasver Fritsch (1629–1701) in 1676 advised his prince to exercise the kind of complete control that we have seen was established in Sweden from the start, and in Denmark by degrees. In the same year Johann Ludwig Hartmann (1640–84) preached a sermon in which he explained why reading newspapers was a sin.

> The pleasure/ which many people derive/ from relishing to hear something new/ and to speak of or hear others narrate with pleasure of other people's matters/ which in fact are nothing to do with them/ that is a sinful pleasure/ because much of our allotted time is wasted in this manner/ and important matters which should concern us are neglected.[86]

What the preacher feared would be neglected by all this information about the troubles of the world and discussions about them was the true value and meaning of those events, that is to say God's hand in the history of a world without end.

> It is by no means enough/ that we notice and feel our ravages and misery/ we must also know and understand/ whence all this comes/ and why we have deserved that our pious God/ should punish and chastise thus;/ only then will we truly be able to understand/ how we might free ourselves from our misery, our wretchedness, and the well deserved divine punishments/ which have been visited upon us; and [understand] how to accept this in a truly Christian way/ so that not only the present [lesser] evil may be restrained, but that we may also escape future affliction, indeed the everlasting punishment of Hell.[87]

No similar clerical attacks were levelled at the Scandinavian press at the time, and bearing in mind the control of peoples' minds in those Protestant countries as described by both Masius and Molesworth, it is not difficult to see that there was no need. Of course, newspapers had their critics and were often accused of telling lies (a charge which Greflinger countered by saying that he wished they were!), but when, after the end of the century, a more concerted attack was launched, it was directed at the possible political damage that newspapers could inflict on the established order. And once again, it was Ludwig Holberg who put the matter centre stage, with his comedies about the inability of ordinary citizens to understand, let alone order their lives. All manner of Copenhagen citizens could see themselves represented on stage during the 1720s, making a mess of their language, the sciences, history, geography, their love lives, justice, etc., though curiously not of the dogmas of the Lutheran Church. Puffed up lower clergy without a university education and rapacious lawyers of the lower orders were pilloried, but bishops, judges and rich landowners were not called to account. The culprits, if that is not too strong a word to use in connection with Holberg's gentle and complacent satires, were the burghers who tried to rise above their station and run society. The artisans and other would-be politicians who populate Holberg's satire *Den politiske Kandestøber* have nothing in common with the cogent magistrates and burghers who in 1660 helped bring to power the regime which was now lavishing its support on its witty, but trusted and eventually ennobled man of letters. Having for a while played the part of a bulwark around the monarchy against the aristocracy, the citizens of the capital were now perceived as a threat, albeit a comical and unrealistic one, to the way things should be, and remain. What Holberg wanted instead, and what he most excellently produced in his last years, were deliberations about the way of the world among educated people of the right sort, with the right sort of outcome, which he ensured was the case as his club had no other members and all his essays and moral cogitations no other addressee than Ludwig Holberg, writing and talking to himself about the best of all possible worlds.

Notes

1 For documents relating to the history and development of this office, see E. Key, *Försök till Svenska tidningspressens historia 1634–1719* (Stockholm, 1883), p. 96.
2 For an example of this oft-repeated injunction printed in a newspaper, see, for example, *Extraordinaires Maanedlige Relationer*, November 1672.
3 Censorship regulation of 6 May 1667; *Kong Christian Den Femtis Danske Lov* (1683), vol. 2, chap. 21, paras. 1–6.
4 Hector Gottfried Masius in *Interesse Principum circa Religionem Evangelicam* (Copenhagen, 1687), section 6, pp. 168–9.
5 Robert Molesworth, *An Account of Denmark As It Was in the Year 1692* (London, 1694), pp. 235–6.
6 As in my other studies in this field the emphasis is on the fully-fledged newspaper, i.e. 'a publication which was, or was intended to be, one of a series planned to appear at regular intervals, recording everyday events and matters with as high degree of topicality as the anonymous writers could manage and from as far-flung parts of the world as it was then known to be of interest to men' (P. Ries, 'The Anatomy of a Seventeenth Century Newspaper. A contribution towards a re-definition of the methods employed in newspaper research, by way of an analytical and comparative study of four German-language newspapers, published in Hamburg and Copenhagen in the year 1669,' *Daphnis* 6 [1977]: 178).
7 The 'Taxa,' found and reprinted by Klemming (1873), pp. 241–3, is undated. Klemming believed it was published shortly after 1645, but offered no evidence. As it mentions 'both Hamburg papers,' 1665 is the latest possible date, as there were by then at least three Hamburg papers, all of which were regularly excerpted by the newsmen in Copenhagen, and some of which were also used by the publisher of the *Ordinari Post-Tijdender* (see below).
8 At the time, a barrel of rye cost 2 daler silver (20 Mark copper), while a miner's daily pay was 3 Mark copper (Sven Carlsson and Jerker Rosen, *Den Svenska Historien* [Stockholm, 1966–68], 10 vols, 4, p. 189; henceforth *DSH*).
9 The two Hamburg papers at the time were the *Europaeische Mitwochentliche/Sambstägige Zeitung*, published 1640–46 by Abondio Somigliano, the resident Imperial Postmaster, and his successor Johann Baptista Vrints, 1646–75, and the *Wöchentliche Zeitung* published three times a week by the carrier Johann Meyer and his widow (1618–1656)

and her second husband, the public notary Martin Schumacher (1656 ff.). For both papers, see below and Ries, 'The Anatomy of a Seventeenth Century Newspaper,' *passim.*

10 *Extraordinairie Advijsen op Dondersdagh.* Folke Dahl, *Dutch Corantos 1618–1650. A Bibliography* (The Hague, 1946), pp. 52–3.

11 *Courante uyt Italien, Duytslandt, &c.* This also appeared in French and English. Folke Dahl, *Dutch Corantos 1618–1650. A Bibliography*, pp. 33–52.

12 *Europische Dingstdaegh/Donderdaeghs/Saterdaeghs Courant.* Folke Dahl, *Dutch Corantos 1618–1650. A Bibliography*, pp. 70–4.

13 *Tijdinghen uyt verscheyde Quartieren.* The French edition came out on the following Monday. Folke Dahl, *Dutch Corantos 1618–1650. A Bibliography*, pp. 55–69.

14 *Ordinaris Dingsdaegsche/Saterdaegsche/Courante.* Folke Dahl, *Dutch Corantos 1618–1650. A Bibliography*, pp. 75–8.

15 *Extra Europische tijdingen uyt verscheyde Quartieren.* Folke Dahl, *Dutch Corantos 1618–1650. A Bibliography*, p. 83.

16 See A. Losman, 'The European Communications Network of Carl Gustaf Wrangel and Magnus Gabriel de la Gardie,' in G. Rystad, ed., *Europe and Scandinavia. Aspects of the Process of Integration in the Seventeenth Century* (Lund, 1983), pp. 199–207. In 1639 the aristocrat Per Brahe the Younger ordered his paymaster to give the postmaster's widow 'a good ox' for dealing with his letters and providing him with newspapers from abroad, an unusual form of payment, but one which gives some idea of the value of the services rendered. P. G. Heugren, *Post och Press i Sverige 1643–1791* (Stockholm, 1929), p. 31.

17 Heurgren, *Post och Press*, pp. 31, 33.

18 The newspaper or its various supplements, also simply referred to as 'dhe Swenske Post-Tijender' (no. 29, 16 July 1678), appeared under the original (1645) title *Ordinari Post-Tijdender* (1663–73), *Svenska Mercurius* (1674–78), *Svenska Ordinarie Post-Tijender* (1680–81), *Svenska Mercurius* (1681–86), *Svenska Post-Ryttaren* (1683–86), and *Ordinarie Stockholmiske Post-Tijdingar.*

19 Instruction of 2 January 1643, republished in 1645 and 1673 (Key, *Försök till Svenska tidningspressens*, pp. 63–5) and again in 1686, when the responsibility for the newspaper was transferred from the postmaster to the secretary to the chancellery. See Nils Forssell, *Svenska postverkats historia* (Stockholm, 1936), pp. 274–85.

20 Even after other newspapers were allowed, a ruling in 1702 confirmed that no one could publish any newspaper unless it had been censored by secretary von Schantz, then editor of the *Ordinari Post-Tijdender.*

21 O. Sylwan, *Svenska pressans historia till statshvälfningen 1772* (Lund, 1896), p. 37; cf. note 6 above.

22 According to a Resolution of 17 March 1685, the reason for the separation was that 'Betjenterna på Posthuset låta sitt arbete mere bestå uti införskrivande och utdelande af Gazetter, så skrifna som tryckta, än uti deres egentliga embetes sysslor,' (Key, *Försök till Svenska tidningspressens*, p. 65; cf. P. G. Heugren, *Post och Press*, pp. 13–14).

23 A further infringement frequently occurred because Swedish printers worked in accordance with the 'German method,' which among other things allowed each worker to print for his own use three copies on the master's paper and three on his own. Gustaf Klemming and Johan Nordin, *Svensk boktryckeri-historia 1483–1883* (Stockholm, 1883), p. 278.

24 Sylwan, *Svenska pressans historia*, pp. 36–7; Heugren, *Post och Press*, pp. 10–11.

25 The practice continued in the eighteenth century. One printer paid the editor 1,200 daler in silver (1715), another 700 (1740), in 1786 another 944 rixdaler for the newspaper licence (Nils Forssell, *Svenska postverkats historia* [Stockholm, 1936], p. 285).

26 Daniel von Möller, employed by J. G. von Beier from 1673, was also deputy postmaster in Stockholm. Johan Fredrik von Schantz, employed by Åkerhielm from

1686 (and ennobled in 1693), was also secretary to the national bank and to the royal archives. Heugren, *Post och Press*, pp. 26–7; Sylwan, *Svenska pressans historia*, p. 37.

27 One of the manuscript copies in Schantz's hand bears the following note: 'Detta har Secret. Åkerhielm extraherat ur bref och är således af mig infördt i gazetten, som det där finnes' ('This secretary Åkerhielm has extracted from letters and has therefore been included in the gazette, where it can be found'). Sylwan, *Svenska pressans historia*, pp. 38–9.

28 To make his tender of 29 September 1685 as low as possible, one printer, Olof Skragge-Hermelin, suggested that he himself be appointed censor, but though he offered the postmaster and editor-in-chief Åkerhielm 600 daler annually for the licence to print the newspaper, his 'offer' was turned down (Sylwan, *Svenska pressans historia*, p. 39, footnote 2).

29 Initially and until his death in 1672, Ignatius Meurer held the licence to print *Ordinari Post-Tijdender*, when it was transferred to N. Wankijf who had married the widow of the previous royal printer. For the role of widows in Copenhagen see below.

30 For the history of the Keyser printing dynasty, see Klemming and Nordin, *Svensk boktryckeri-historia*, pp. 164–73 and Henrik Schück and Karl Warburg, *Illustrerad Svensk Litteraturhistoria* (Stockholm, 1927), 2 vols, 2: 177–9; the latter also reproduces a 1691 illustration of their famous printing works. See also Sten Lindroth, *Svensk Lärdomshistoria. Stormaktstiden* (Stockholm, 1975), pp. 69–71.

31 No second official paper was in fact printed until 1731. Heugren, *Post och Press*, p. 27.

32 Analysis of the reports in the *Ordinari Post-Tijdender* taken from the *Nordischer Mercurius* and also used in the Copenhagen paper *Ordinari Post-Zeitung* shows that they were printed in Copenhagen less than a week after their composition in Hamburg, and ten to twelve days after that in Stockholm. These calculations tally with an earlier suggestion that the entire procedure could have been completed within three to four days (Forssell, *Svenska postverkats historia*, p.280).

33 Sylwan, *Svenska pressans historia*, 1896 p. 41, footnote. The need for pirated copies mentioned above also suggests that the potential readership was larger than the number of copies printed.

34 No copies are extant from the year in which Queen Christina abdicated and converted to Catholicism, but it would not have been considered an item for newspaper comment, any more than the equally unreported *coup d'état* in Denmark in 1660 (see below).

35 Licence of 29 June 1634, reprinted in P. M. Stolpe, *Dagspressen i Danmark, dens Vilkaar og Personer indtil Midten af det attende Aarhundrede* (Copenhagen, 1878–82), 4 vols, 1: 233.

36 Stolpe, *Dagspressen i Danmark*, 1: 158–68; Camillus Nyrop, *Bidrag til den danske Boghandels Historie* (Copenhagen, 1870), 2 vols, 1: 160–87; *Nordisk Leksikon for Bogvæsen* (Copenhagen, Oslo, Stockholm, 1951), 2 vols, eds Palle Birkelund, Esli Dansten, and Lauritz Nielsen, 2: 97–8.

37 Stolpe, *Dagspressen i Danmark*, 1: 129.

38 'Jocum oc Jørgen befantis heruid meest Skyldige, the Melchior trycker intet andet end de ordinairi Curranter, oc huis ham *ellers* af Øffrigheden bliffuer tilstillet,' in Stolpe, *Dagspressen i Danmark*, 1: 234. This wording would support the interpretation that the ordinary corantos were also forwarded by the authorities.

39 Statute of 13 July 1644 (Stolpe, *Dagspressen i Danmark*, 1: 130).

40 See Stolpe, *Dagspressen i Danmark*, 2: 293–95. Though an instruction for the chief of Copenhagen police, to whom the 1701 regulation handed over the censorship of newspapers, they were not only a guide for the future, but a reiteration of the policies in force since 1644.

41 Summary of all paragraphs in the licence of 29 January 1701 as reprinted in Stolpe, *Dagspressen i Danmark*, 2: 350–5.

42 Georg Greflinger, ed., *Des Nordischen Mercurij Verbesserter VVegvveiser von Zehen Haupt-Reisen aus der Stadt Hamburg, Gedruckt daselbst, Annp 1674, und vvird bey ihm allein, gegen der Börsche über, verkaufft* (Hamburg, 1674), pp. 90–1.

43 Bibliography in Stolpe, *Dagspressen i Danmark*, 1: iii–xcii.

44 The title of Bording's poem specifically states that the hereditary monarchy was established in response to the unanimous wish and desire of all estates. Anders Bording, *Den Danske Mercurius* (Copenhagen: 1984), vol. 1, ed. P. Ries, pp. 88–91.

45 Henrik Gøde had worked as Second University Printer since 1654.

46 Marrying an incumbent widow was not only common practice among young clergymen seeking a living. Before Gøde, Martzan had married the twice widowed Catherine; similarly, when Henrik's brother Jørgen died in 1676, his widow Dorothea Cassube, the daughter of a Mecklenburg bookseller, was confirmed in his offices and occupied them until her marriage, first to Korfitz Luft and after his death to Johan Bockenhoffer (Stolpe, *Dagspressen i Danmark*, 1: 202; Nyrop, *Bidrag til den danske Boghandels Historie*, 1: 214–15).

47 The title before 1663 was *Wochentliche Zeitung*, then *Europäische Wochentliche Zeitung* until 1666, when the title *Ordinaire Post-Zeitung* (*OPZ*) was adopted and also appeared on most of the additional material published with it.

48 For details about the Hamburg and Copenhagen papers, see Elger Blühm and Ilse Bogel, *Die Deutschen Zeitungen des 17. Jahrhunderts. Ein Bestandsverzeichnis mit historischen und bibliographischen Angaben* (Bremen, 1971–1985), 3 vols, vol. 1; and Ries, 'The Anatomy of a Seventeenth Century Newspaper.'

49 The seventy-seven extant copies of the *Ordinari Post-Zeitung* from 1669 contain 582 reports, suggesting that each of the now lost twenty-seven copies would also have carried an average of seven or eight reports.

50 For a detailed analysis of the contents of the *Ordinari Post-Zeitung* and its German sources, see Ries, 'The Anatomy of a Seventeenth Century Newspaper,' *passim.*

51 I wish to express my gratitude to Dr Weber of the Institut für Deutsche Presseforschung, Bremen, for providing me with Xerox copies of all the German-language papers from January 1673 requested by me, with the exception of the *Extraordinaires Relationes aus Allerley Orten*, of which I possess a microfilm.

52 Daniel Paulli (1640[?]–1684) a son of the king's physician had, like his older brother in Strasbourg, worked in the book trade in Nürnberg until 1665, when he was invited by the widows of Joachim Moltke and of his son Johan to administer the business on their behalf. After his return to Copenhagen he was duly appointed Royal Bookseller, but due to a prolonged legal battle between the two widows, which prevented him from taking over the Copenhagen bookshop in its entirety, he opened his own shop in 1667 and, from 1672, a booth at the Exchange.

53 Application, deliberations, and licenses in Stolpe, *Dagspressen i Danmark*, 2: 338–41.

54 Jørgen Gøde married Dorothea Cassube, the daughter of a Mecklenburg bookseller, in 1671. On his brother's death he was also appointed University Printer, but he died later the same year.

55 Henrik was not only in poor health but also in mortal danger of his life, since he had been found guilty for the second time, the prosecutor claimed, of printing uncensored German and Danish almanacs in 1669–71, and he was sentenced to life imprisonment in chains at the naval dockyard and forfeiture of all rights, licences, etc. Henrik appealed to the High Court, arguing that as he had not been prosecuted the first time (1667) but pardoned by the king, he had been right to assume that printing Danish almanacs uncensored was covered by his licence; he also claimed that the re-printing of foreign almanacs did not constitute a crime under Danish law. The case was finally dismissed on 31 August 1672. Stolpe, *Dagspressen i Danmark*, 1: 206–10.

56 Assessments of the quality of the *Ordinarie Post-Tidende* and comparisons with other papers are severely hampered by the fact that few issues of the paper are extant. The

first fifteen are lost, only six are extant from the period when it came out twice weekly, and none after 1681.

57 January 1669; no issues extant from 1670–72. Those extant from 1669 show that the highest monthly output was 203 items (November), the lowest 174 (September).

58 *Extraordinaires Relationes aus Allerley Orten* 1673 p. [II]. Celadon was the name adopted by Greflinger as member of the *Elbschwaneorden.*

59 In the *Nordischer Mercurius*, Mercury walks from left to right carrying Greflinger's motto 'sine mora' in his right hand and the caduceus in his left. In the head of the *Extraordinaires Relationes aus Allerley Orten*, Mercury appears to the right of the full title and with Greflinger's motto replaced by the word *Relationes*. In the *Appendix* head, the Mercury figure is reversed, now carrying the word *Appendix* in his left hand.

60 See Blühm and Bogel, *Die Deutschen Zeitungen des 17. Jahrhunderts*, 1: 206–12.

61 At the time, De Loew's paper usually appeared without a title, date of publication or printer identification, often without a number. The pagination, obviously intended to be consecutive for the whole year, is wrong.

62 In his preface, Molesworth relates how Terlon had torn out of the Royal Library's visitors' book the words previously entered by the English Republican ambassador, Algernon Sydney, claiming that they constituted an affront to the king of France. R. Molesworth, *An Account of Denmark, as it was in the year 1692* (London, 1694), p. xxxiv–xxxv.

63 Documentation in Stolpe, *Dagspressen i Danmark*, 2: 304–5, 357–8.

64 Of thirty-eight reports, containing 139 individual news items, eight appeared under Italy (twenty-five news items), six under Hungary and Austria (sixteen items), five under Holland (fifty-one items), three under Barbary and Turkey (eight items), three under France (seven items), three under Spain (five items), two under Poland (nine items), two under Poland and Prussia (eight items), and one under Switzerland (three items), England (two items), Sweden (two items), Germany (one item), Portugal (one item), and Sicily (one item),

65 Of an estimated population of 40,000 (1670) about 20 per cent of Copenhageners were Germans or of German extraction (Gunnar Olsen, 'Den unge Enevælde 1660–1721,' *Politikens Danmarks Historie* (Copenhagen, 1964), vol. 1, pp. 106–7). German was the official language at court and in the upper echelons of the administration and the military, and to be bilingual (High or Low German, and Danish) was a necessity for the lower orders. Merchants, printers, booksellers, and others with connections abroad would, if they added a third language, have chosen French, which was the natural choice after Latin for diplomats, some of whom also spoke Spanish and Italian. Those who like Griffenfeld had studied at Oxford also spoke English. In addition, those with a University education wrote and spoke Latin, and among the clergy many were familiar with ancient Greek and Hebrew. Peter Skautrup, *Det danske Sprogs Historie, vol. II: Fra Unionsbrevet til Danske Lov* (Copenhagen, 1947), 2: 301–9.

66 Paulli's reference is to the *Historiarum III epitome* ('qvidem in append. lib. X, p. m. 706, 707') by the German geographer and historian Johann Clüver (1580–1622). He says that Cluverus had not himself seen the harsh Russian landowner Albertus Pericoscius, who in 1632 was also turned into a dog, but adds that Cluverus is a trustworthy person who had the story from an eyewitness.

67 Paulli's reference in connection with the worms is to the *Physica curiosa* lib. 7 cap. 7 by the geographer Gaspar Schott, who also mentions mouse rain in Norway, fish rain elsewhere, and other similar incidents.

68 'Men hvor om alting er; da siunes dette Græs at groe saa langsomt at den Koe som der af skulle fødes kand nok døe førend det faar sin Grøde och Fremvext' ('When all is said, the cow will have died before the grass with which to feed it has grown'), December 1672, p. 24.

69 After twenty difficult years on the Polish throne, Jan Kazimierz abdicated in 1668, supported a French candidate as his successor, and was rewarded with a string of

monasteries in France by Louis XIV. *Den Danske Mercurius* also ignored that Jan was a zealous Jesuit, who as king had introduced the death penalty for Catholics converting to Protestantism, using instead his abdication as a sorry example of what happens to royal power in elective monarchies.

70 On the scaffold the colonel himself expressed this view and expressed the hope that his execution would strengthen the resolve of others not to make a similar mistake. Gøde, who copied a detailed report on the speech from the scaffold and the execution from the *Nordischer Mercurius*, shared that view, as did Bording in *Den Danske Mercurius*.

71 The report is translated from Paulli's German paper in a report from Amsterdam dated 10 December (i. e., 30 December 1672). The incident may have been even more complex, because in Gøde's German report under the same date, but sent from The Hague, it is clear that it was the poor women who objected to the rich women fleeing with all their goods, arguing that they should stay and share the bad as well as the good times. Gøde dropped this explanation in his Danish paper.

72 Molesworth, *An Account of Denmark*, p. xx.

73 R. Nyerup, 'Bidrag til de Kjøbenhavnske Bogtrykkeriers Historie,' *Det skandinaviske Litteraturselskabs Skrifter* 1 (1805): 228–55; Stolpe, *Dagspressen i Danmark*, 2: 31–63; C. Kirchoff-Larsen, *Den danske Presses Historie* (Copenhagen, 1942), 3 vols, 1: 49–77; *Politikens Dansk litteratur historie I–IV* (Copenhagen, 1964), pp. 217–22; *Politikens Dansk Litteratur Histoire* (Copenhagen, 1964), 4 vols, 1976, pp. 316–21. For the impact of the different, and at the time controversial, view based on contents analysis first presented in Anders Bording, *Den danske Mercurius 1666–1677*, ed., with commentary by Paul Ries (Copenhagen, 1973), pp. 200–26, see the latest standard history of Danish literature (*Gyldendals Dansk litteraturhistorie I–XI* [Copenhagen, 1983], pp. 198–205).

74 See Bording, *Den danske Mercurius* vol. 2, ed. P. Ries, pp. 29 and 144–5.

75 A popular comparison at the time and famously used by Shakespeare's Jacques, it was probably made a European stock phrase by the French historian Etienne Pasquier (1560–1621), from whom Christian Weise adopted it as the introduction to his chapter on the usefulness of reading newspapers. See Elger Blühm und Rolf Engelsing, eds, *Die Zeitung. Deutsche Urteile und Dokumente von den Anfängen bis zur Gegenwart* (Bremen, 1967), p. 56. Shakespeare's play was unknown in Scandinavia at the time.

76 Keeping his language simple and clear, indeed colloquial and with occasional humorous asides, Bording also managed to use 177 references to biblical and classical literature and 629 proverbs of classical and domestic origin to drive home his interpretations of contemporary politics.

77 For details of all references to *Den Danske Mercurius*, see *Den Danske Mercurius 1666–1677*, ed., with commentary by Paul Ries, Postscript pp. 200–26.

78 According to advertisements in his German weekly, Gøde offered to supply subscribers, for the annual price of 2 Rdl., the *Ordinari Post-Zeitung*, *Den Danske Mercurius*, government ordinances, and other 'particular relations' he might publish.

79 Bording, *Den danske Mercurius*, 1: 86–140.

80 *Forhaabnings och forhalings Griller*. *Den Danske Mercurius*, 1: 99.

81 Gunnar Olsen, 'Den unge Enevælde 1660–1721,' *Politikens Danmarks Historie*, (Copenhagen, 1964), vol. 8, pp. 62 and 118.

82 Sjaellandske Missive no. 155, 23 March 1667, Royal Archives, Copenhagen.

83 These calculations are based on research done by the author at the Plantin-Moretus Museum in Antwerp in 1976 and on work carried out with replica seventeenth-century presses and material at the university library in Cambridge the following year.

84 A *Sprachgesellschaft*, i.e., a society for the study of language and poetic diction, founded by Johann Rist in 1658 in imitation of similar societies in Weimar, Heidelberg, Strasbourg, Nürnberg, etc., whose members set standards adopted by Scandinavian

poets throughout the seventeenth century. At its height the membership reached forty-five, among them poets, historiographers, linguists, geographers, novelists, satirists, composers, and at least two with an interest in news (Rist himself and Georg Greflinger).

85 Johann Rist, 'Das alleredelste Leben der gantzen Welt' (Hamburg, 1663); *Sämtliche Werke*, ed. E. Mannack (Berlin, 1972) 2: 240 ff.

86 Johann Ludwig Hartmann, *Unzeitige Neue-Zeitungs-Sucht und Vorwitziger Kriegs-Discoursen Flucht Nebst beygefügten Theologischen Gedanken von heutigen unnöthigen Rechts-Processen auch un-Christlichen Retorsionibus* (Rotenburg, 1679), p. 41 (quoted from Blühm & Engelsing, *Die Zeitung*, p. 53).

87 Hartmann, *Unzeitige Neue-Zeitungs-Sucht*, pp. 40–1 (quoted from Blühm & Engelsing, *Die Zeitung*, pp. 52–3. By contrast, see Kaspar Stieler, *Zeitungs Lust und Nutz 1695. Vollständiger Neudruck der Originalausgabe von 1695*, ed. Gert Hagelweide (Bremen, 1969) for a full, positive introduction to the proper use of newspapers.

Part III

Pan-European trajectories

The final chapter, by Brendan Dooley, attempts to take stock of political information in the whole of Europe by looking at it from a special point of view: namely, the recorded impressions of a small group of elite readers in the upper echelons of European intellectual life. These readers found much to criticize in what they read. They saw their new hopes for a better knowledge of their world more often disappointed than satisfied. And considering the inaccuracies and manipulations they observed, they raised serious questions not only about the intentions of the writers, but concerning the very nature of political reality itself. This chapter considers some of the most incisive criticisms in the context of the news they criticized. It then evaluates the significance of this criticism from the standpoint of the political culture of the time. How could a meaningful discussion about the political realm be carried on in the midst of scepticism and uncertainty? In fact, discussions about the media and its masters may well have played an important role in the sphere of public reasoning that began to emerge among certain sectors of the populations of the European states in this period, with significant consequences for the future.

12 News and doubt in early modern culture

Or, are we having a public sphere yet?

Brendan Dooley

'What a great invention is this one, of sending the news about events, especially concerning the princes of the whole world, around to every place, and making known what is going on in Rome, in France, in Spain, in Germany and elsewhere, without spending a fortune.'[1] For Secondo Lancellotti, an Olivetan monk writing in Rome in the 1620s, there could be no mistaking that the publication of political information was one of the wonders of the age. His feelings were shared by many, as political information became part of everyday life for growing numbers of Europeans in the seventeenth century. No wonder that, in the same period, two English proclamations began with the declaration that news did 'dayly more and more increase.'[2] And later in the century Ahasver Fritsch, writing in Germany, noted that printed newspapers, in his words, 'get in the hands of everyone.' Such testimonies about a revolutionary change in the means of political communication have been accompanied, in recent research, by impressive statistics showing that newsletters, newspapers, reports on events, and works of contemporary history left an increasingly voluminous paper trail.

But what the newly news-conscious readers of the early modern period may have made of what they read is still shrouded in uncertainty.[3] Formidable methodological difficulties face anyone intending to reach inside the minds of seventeenth-century people. What sources could possibly be representative enough to give more than a suggestive impression? What evidence concerning how readers read political information is likely to be reliable enough to reveal some of the basic tendencies? How do we account for the varying effects of information on the minds of readers in different geographical locations, following the pattern of the spread of information itself? And, how to account for variations in impact from social category to social category?

The public sphere of the seventeenth century, wherever it may have emerged, was compounded of a myriad of individual readers, differing perhaps as much from one another as from place to place. Readers made effective the uses of political information in this period. In times of peace they determined the emancipatory potential of the press. And in periods of civil strife, during the English Civil War, during the French Fronde, during the revolts of Naples and Messina, they decided the disruptive effectiveness of the press. We must distinguish their actions as readers from their actions due to other causes. In order to do so, we have to know more about how they experienced what they read.

In this chapter I would like to focus on one kind of reader – not the fruit sellers of Naples, nor the yeomen farmers of England, but the members of the intellectual elite in both of those places, as well as in France, Holland, and elsewhere in Italy. And the reading experiences I want to study are not those tending to question or subvert an established order. I am concerned to probe a bit deeper, and ask some questions that are perhaps even more fundamental to the press's overall effectiveness. How much did seventeenth-century people believe of the news they read? How critical were the most discerning readers, and how trusting were the rest? A medium purporting to convey information must, after all, persuade readers that it is worthy of the name. The study of a few cases may bring us a little closer to the reception history of news.

To find meaningful answers to such questions does not promise to be easy. Nevertheless, we know enough about the cultural history of the period to suggest a few tantalizing hypotheses. In a century that began with Francis Bacon and ended with John Locke, where speculations about the nature of reality provoked the reflections of Descartes and addled the consciences of Lorenzo Magalotti and Pierre Bayle, we should not be too surprised to find a common thread of doubt. In an age when the discipline of history, a category comprising all sorts of news, was shaken to its foundations by the onslaught of Pyrrhonism, and finally restored, at the end of the century, by a movement for methodological reform, we might expect that political information of all sorts would be scrutinized with a particularly critical eye.

To be sure, many readers, writers, thinkers, and theorists in the period may well have found the inaccuracy of information was no more than a minor inconvenience; a curious artefact of the explosion of news. They could live their lives as conveniently, knowing that a rain of blood probably did not really occur in Argentina, as one paper said, or that a screaming foetus had probably not really been heard in its mother's womb in Cologne, as another avowed, or any number of other accounts designed to spice up the otherwise rather dreary fare.[4] The same went for stories about battles never fought, celebrations that never occurred, or rulers who never ruled quite in the way the press described.

The readers discussed in this chapter, however, shared a radical scepticism about political information. In spite of their differences, they all agreed that the unreliability of the stories they were being told raised deeply troubling questions about human nature and existence. They worried that inaccuracy and fraud added to a growing cultural malaise. The more the fabric of political reality came under scrutiny, the more its precise texture seemed to fade from view. The more accurate pictures of the civic world were promised, the more these were overshadowed by convictions that the construction of events was just another negotiable aspect of the discourse about power. They began to wonder about the possibility of gaining any knowledge at all, about the past or the present. Their ideas formed a subtle counter-current beneath the more or less complacent utilization of the new medium by so many other readers. And they remind us that new media do not always aid in the formation of a public sphere.

What is more, the readers we will be studying viewed everyday social and political reality as forming part of the same world of experience in which the new science and cosmology had induced a new feeling of uncertainty – a feeling of abandonment in uncontrollable currents whose exact nature the best minds seemed incapable of understanding. The disquiet produced by confessional disputes only made things worse, suggesting that truth might be beyond human capacity to grasp.[5] Throughout Europe in the late seventeenth century, such readers submitted existing methods of ascertaining facts in political and military affairs both in the present and in past times to a new sort of scrutiny. They contributed to what some scholarship has regarded as no less than a wide-ranging 'crisis of consciousness' at the threshold of the Enlightenment.

And indeed, Secondo Lancellotti himself, whose effusions about the new media of political information began this chapter, went on to note that, 'I know that some people, especially the today-haters, shake their heads, saying that [the news] is full of lies.' The other chapters in this book have shown that, almost as soon as the new quantities made information impossible to ignore, questions arose concerning the quality of what was being said. A celebrated press debate opened up in Germany, as Thomas Schröder has shown. It was echoed in Scandinavia, as we have seen from the account by Paul Ries.

At times, suspicions about the defects of the press extended to the sinister political influences that might have tainted the news. 'Now, what difference does it make to the people of France to know that the emperor held a dance for the dames?' complained Gregorio Leti, a Milanese expatriate living in Switzerland, citing a typical story. Furthermore,

> What need do the Germans have to know that the Most Christian King was or was not at the hunt? What effect will it make upon the Roman people, to know that the king of Spain went to see a bull fight? What profit may the English people gain from hearing that the pope went to Sant' Andrea della Valle?

According to Leti, intelligent readers could see through stories that were evidently intended to busy their minds with matters of little importance while more sinister dealings were going on behind their backs. 'Such bagatelles … serve for nothing but for making everyone laugh who reads them.' And when the news media were not peddling useless bagatelles, they were peddling false news, often planted by governments. Yet, Leti continued, 'everyone knows that very frequently princes turn losses into victories in order to terrify the people.' Consequently, 'The people, so frequently hoodwinked, always turn victories into losses, forming squadrons at their pleasure and princes to their tastes.'[6] Leti hoped inaccuracy would encourage the more discerning readers to be sceptical about what they read and critical of the governments behind it. Other media critics were less confident.

In case readers did not already guess that the sources for news reports were notoriously unreliable, they were continuously told this, occasionally in so many words, by the writers themselves. When stories began by the customary diction, 'it is said that,' and variations thereof, most readers knew exactly what was meant. Except for a tiny number who had direct access to privileged sources, news writers depended for their information for the most part upon rumour and hearsay. Even those who frequented the palaces of the great were not necessarily able to procure anything more reliable than what was heard throughout the streets and squares.

That information was often modified for pure entertainment purposes was well known. In an age of literary experimentation and exquisite taste, nothing else could be expected – especially in the more discursive kinds of narrative about contemporary events. Gabriele Tontoli offered his account of the events of the Masaniello Revolt in Naples as a 'combined historical, poetical, declamatory and familiar discourse.' Let pedantic critics object all they wished, he went on. Sooner or later, they would have to admit that 'modern intellects cannot be prevented from inventing,' and that the capricious events he had to relate demanded for their exposition a capricious style of writing.[7] Readers could expect him 'to be unfailingly more truthful in praise than in narration.' Let not the critics complain, he continued, about finding encomiums where they expected facts. After all, there were already too many writers in town trying to write simple history. 'Therefore,' he said, 'I had to resort to invention, and turn my pen into the lance of Achilles; so that, by injuring history it should save discourse.' It was only a matter of time before the straightforward concept of 'history' in itself was viewed as being far too dull. Accordingly, the anonymous writer of a work on recent Venetian conquests preferred to refer to 'episodes that could be history' rather than history *per se.* He told his readers, 'I know you do not like foods unless they are very delectable.' Anyway, 'in these times, fables are histories and histories are fables.'[8]

That governments financed favourable versions of events to enhance their prestige was impossible to ignore. Professional writers hired themselves out to provide the necessary accounts: Raffaelle Della Torre to Naples; Luca Assarino to Rome, Genoa and Venice; Agostino Mascardi to Genoa; Pietro Gazzotti to Genoa and Modena; Galeazzo Gualdo Priorato to France; Pier Giovanni Capriata to Genoa, France, and Spain; Vittorio Siri and Giovanni Birago Avogadro to Florence; Giovanni Francesco Fossati to Venice and Spain; and a host of others to all the major governments of the time.[9] The historians themselves were the first to admit the dangerous consequences of such practices. Siri referred to the Venetian historians as 'murderers of the public' because of their application of the historian's craft to the adulator's task.[10] Others offered their own works as containing 'more truth' (in Capriata's words) than any one else's.[11] With ostensible sincerity, Luca Assarino claimed that 'seeing not only the variations but also the manifest contradictions in accounts of the same event, with too much damage to posterity, has persuaded me to enter the fray.'[12] And this claim was no more extravagant than that of Maiolino Bisaccioni, who recommended his account of the Neapolitan revolution as a 'foreign' work, i.e. not Neapolitan, and therefore more likely to be 'dispassionate.'[13] And the anonymous writer who uttered, 'those who are too accustomed to lies will never believe or heed the truth,' was far more accurate than even he himself could have imagined.[14]

Newspapers run by governments in order to, in Gregorio Leti's words, 'remind the people about the majesty of the prince,'[15] could scarcely hope to maintain a reputation for strict accuracy. And after the English royal government established the *Mercurius Aulicus* and that of France put Théophraste Renaudot on the payroll, the Milanese government and that of Piedmont eventually gave the official print shop exclusive rights to publish the local newspaper. The latter government gave the journalist a 1,000 lire pension; while the government of France, thoroughly outdone, was giving the same journalist half as much. And other governments took care to deliver appropriate information to the local newspaper from time to time.[16]

The constraints imposed by political power upon the publication of true facts were plainly evident. Censorship laws clearly defined the difference between licit and illicit information; and by interdicting the circulation of the latter, they cast into suspicion the veracity of the former. Writers like Luca Assarino who wrote manuscript newsletters as well as newspapers were explicit about the differences between the two. To justify the higher price of the newsletter, he explained to one correspondent, 'you have to understand that it costs me money and risk.'[17] And readers of an account of the celebrations on the occasion of the coronation of Innocent X could well imagine, as the printer told them, that 'other things could be recorded … but I have only described what is permitted, so that the superiors would allow this work to be printed.'[18]

The newly-invented or newly voluminous sources of political information promised far more than they could ever deliver. They promised to bring reflection upon everyday experience out of the murky realm of oral tradition and myth and into the clear and bright realm of published print. For the first time, printed information seemed to fix the unfixable, to render permanent the ephemeral, to put a hard finish on the ragged edge of early modern time. It seemed to hasten closure of the itinerary of a rumour, to dam the fluid boundaries between various versions of reality and myth within the rigid terms of a single conclusion. News in printed form no longer seemed to be, like the manuscript traditions, in a dialogue with the world outside, part of a context of writings and rewritings, but seemed to propose itself as something in a state of completion.[19] Hard copy seemed to promise hard fact. That, at least, was the expectation, that was the ideal, and that was the intended impression.

How wrong these expectations could be was proved by the result. What the spread of political misinformation in more massive quantities powerfully underscored was the considerable degree of uncertainty at which individuals as well as governments had been accustomed to operating – and would continue to operate. Printed news permitted the comparison of accounts in a way never possible before. Accounts of the same event were in easily enough available abundance to be present at the same time in the same place. The inaccuracies were easy to detect even when the writers themselves did not continuously direct attention to them.

Open party conflict gave a particularly powerful impetus to the proliferation of divergent accounts. And Italy and France, with their frequent rebellions and wars, were by no means the only places where such divergences occurred. Consider the case of England, where a whole generation of readers and writers was reared in the Civil War. This, according to Thomas Fuller, a Church historian writing at the end of the 1650s, could only lead to a fatally damaged credibility, as was proved by the result. All one had to do was to compare writers who wrote before the struggle, when 'there was a general right understanding betwixt all of the nation,' to their later counterparts, who 'are seldom apprehended truly or candidly, save of such of their own persuasion, while others do not ... understand them aright.'[20] And if Thomas Hobbes agreed with this view, Samuel Butler extended it to all historiography. Modern historians, he insisted, far outdid those of classical antiquity only in their partiality, since the ancients, at least, recorded divergent opinions dispassionately by placing them in the mouths of historical characters in the form of staged speeches; whereas the moderns passed off their own tendentious interpretations as facts.[21]

The number of lies, inaccuracies, and half-truths was far greater than anyone could count; and they could be found in the political publishing of every country in Europe. Nor did they go away by the end of the century, if Pierre Bayle still inveighed against their perpetrators from his vantage point in Rotterdam, where newspapers arrived of all sorts. 'Every day they furnish a new comedy,' he exclaimed.[22] When the French armies crossed the Rhine in 1672, newspapers sympathetic to the Dutch spoke of nothing but a few skirmishes in which French prisoners had been taken or deserters had been observed. The Paris *Gazette*, on the other hand, spoke of nothing but the enemy's losses and the tribute to be exacted. When the Germans crossed into French territory in 1694, the Paris *Gazette* concentrated on French success in holding the line and pushing them back. On the contrary, gazettes favourable to the Germans, ignoring all this, gave an exact register of the villages pillaged by the German armies, powder magazines burned, and Frenchmen beaten. During the sieges of Namur in 1692 and 1696, gazettes favourable to the League of Augsburg invented so many imaginary assaults, in which the French lost such an infinite number of men, that continuing the attack ought to have been impossible without a miracle. Far from apologizing for these shortcomings, indeed, the gazette writers seemed to glory in them. 'There is no gazette writer so abashed,' Bayle noted, 'as not to hope for immortality from all the absurd falsehoods he invents in his pipe-dreams.'[23] He conceded that they might fear punishment for publishing unapproved truths. But he added that greed and vanity were equally powerful motives for publishing only what readers wanted to hear. And he classed the gazettes among the libellous and incorrect writings that 'spread throughout history an impenetrable chaos of incertitude.'[24]

Some readers, writers, thinkers, and theorists were less interested in the cultural significance of fraud than in the possible utility of it. And while Paolo

Sarpi, adviser to Venice, encouraged governments to hire historians and propagandists to carry their messages to present and future generations, Virgilio Malvezzi, political theorist and adviser to the grand duke of Tuscany, encouraged the spreading of falsehood.[25] When all political acts were shrouded in secrecy, he argued, curiosity might lead to the revelation of things that could be damaging to the state. Let the prince select the most damaging truth, transform it into a flattering or at least innocuous lie, and allow this to leak out. By placing false rumours in circulation, the government could satisfy curiosity and protect itself from excessive openness at the same time. And in case anyone had any doubts about such a policy, Malvezzi suggested, all they had to do was to consult the example of Scipio, the ancient Roman hero who made people believe that a message he had received from Syphax, the Numidian general, had been an invitation to go into Africa, whereas it had actually been a threat. He thus distracted the multitudes while avoiding a possible cause of unnecessary preoccupation within the army. No modern ruler could avoid pursuing policies of this sort.

Rulers may have found some justification for their manipulations, as writers for their inaccuracies, from the overwhelming pressure of ideology in a troubled age. They were the first to notice that the exigencies of state governments in a time of rising costs, fiscal drain, increasing discontent, and heightened dynastic competition widened the gap between what was promised and what could be accomplished, between words and the things spoken of, between representations of power and effects of power on an international as well as on a local scale. They were well aware of the distance between the ideal and the real both in public and in private life.

A burgeoning literature explained to early seventeenth-century readers why dissimulation was a hallmark of the age. 'Deceit rules the roost,' noted the Spanish cleric Baldassarre Gracián, 'and things are judged by their jackets and many things are other than they seem.'[26] In the midst of this general game of fictions and counter-fictions, the individual had little choice but to play along. Human life, Gracián explained, involved constant warfare against the malice of others, and constant shifts in strategy. 'Sagacity now rises to higher flights on seeing its artifice foreseen, and tries to deceive by truth itself, changes its game in order to change its deceit, and cheats by not cheating, and founds deception on the greatest candor.'[27] Neapolitan lawyer Torquato Accetto, inspired by a society he viewed as being increasingly polarized between powerful and powerless, between rich and poor, between the custodians of truth and their beneficiaries, suggested that where political and social reality could never measure up to the ideals, then 'dissembling' was not only an 'honest' practice among both the great and the humble, it was also a duty.[28]

Among the first to suspect that deception was a condition of politics and not an optional strategy, as Machiavelli and his disciples had maintained in the previous century, was Traiano Boccalini. A governor of several of the subject cities of the Papal State in the time of Paul V, he wrote a series of *Reports from Parnassus*, reflecting upon the ironies of the age. All of politics, he concluded, was an elaborate game of deception: 'The courts of princes are nothing but costume shops,' he suggested, 'where everything on sale is fake, made for the service of falsehood.'[29] And the behaviour of princes toward their subjects was an extension of the same practices. Unwilling or unable to win hearts by policies tending to the public good, they sought vainly to prevent discord by keeping their populations uninformed.

To show modern policies in action, Boccalini imagines that Tacitus, the master of deceitful 'reason of state,' has been invited to apply his insights to the government of the island of Lesbos. No sooner does Tacitus arrive than he puts his own precepts into practice, subtly insinuating discord between the people and the nobility in order to weaken both. Using 'very secret techniques,' he then incites the people to take up arms against the nobles.[30] And after publicly offering himself as a mediator, he exercises this role in such a way as to let the ill feelings smolder. He then gains the support of the people for recruiting a foreign militia to save them from the nobles. At the same time, he cements the loyalty of the militia to himself by allowing it to commit atrocities against both sides. After causing false accusations of treachery to circulate against the nobility, he confiscates the property of some of the most powerful and gives it to the accusers; and he sends others to squander their resources in expensive missions far from Lesbos. Finally, he builds a huge fort under the pretext of foreign invasion but actually arms it against his own subjects and throws dissenters into its dungeons. But since the people of Lesbos retain, during all this time (unlike the inhabitants of so many contemporary polities in Italy, Boccalini wishes to imply), some vestiges of their ancient freedom, they eventually chase him off the island.

Among the same rulers who sought to conceal their own misdeeds, fear of historical truth ran rampant, Boccalini believed. And to illustrate this, he imagines, in another passage of the *Reports*, that Tacitus has been brought up before Apollo, the judge of Parnassus, on charges of having exposed the secrets of political behaviour to the gaze of everyone.[31] Boccalini conveys this concept by means of an extended metaphor referring to the disenchanted analyses of the Roman emperors (and, by extension, all politics) in the *Annals* and *Histories*. Tacitus, he says, has been creating a special type of eyeglasses allowing the wearer not only to see the actions of princes more clearly but also to see through all the artifices used to disguise the real nature of power. And what is worse, the distribution of the eyeglasses has extended far beyond the restricted circle of political adepts, ministers, and princes themselves, to all and sundry. It was well known, the indictment claims, that princes often commit evil actions in order to maintain their authority and represent such actions in the false light of the public good in order to save their reputations. With the new eyeglasses, not only might these reputations be destroyed, but the people, learning the rules of politics, might discover how to wield power for themselves. Then even good princes might be encouraged to give up the problems, frustrations, and perplexities of rule. And monarchy would be no more. In the event, Apollo acquits Tacitus, on the condition that the new eyeglasses will be distributed only on a limited scale. Censorship and dissembling win the day.

With political actors spinning ever more complex webs of deception and dissembling, the possibility of arriving at the bedrock of conviction about politics appeared ever more remote. And among the early seventeenth-century figures who worried about the consequences of this on political information was Agostino Mascardi, writing in Rome in the 1630s. Writers, he observed, often turned to official correspondence or diplomatic documents in order to understand events. Yet the most important information in military and diplomatic affairs, in order to avoid discovery, was communicated by word of mouth, not by writing.[32] Moreover, interested parties jealously protected the documentary sources; and to guard against espionage they often used deliberately convoluted or cryptic language even when they did not resort to cipher. Now, supposing the writer succeeded in acquiring such material and understanding what it said, this still did not guarantee full comprehension of events. Ministers were often mistaken about what went on; and even when they were not, they often modified their reports to correspond to their own interests. Princes, on the other hand, routinely deceived their ministers whenever this suited their purposes. 'Princes proceed in their affairs with such secrecy that penetrating to the heart of them is harder than interpreting the words of the Sphynx.'[33] He concluded by reminding readers that, according to the intellectual categories that had held fast at least up to the last century, history, the genre to which all narratives about events belonged, did not figure among the exact sciences at all, but only among the probable ones. Fact could hardly be separated from opinion; so there was no use demanding of the investigator more than he could deliver. 'The credit one gives to histories is human credit, that is, always joined to doubt,' he reminded readers. 'Those who require infallible certainty based on incontrovertible proof are asking the impossible.'[34] The best that could be expected was that history, far more than any philosophically derived science of civility, could teach practical political prudence by providing a repertoire of relevant historical examples.

In discussing the present state of historiography, even Mascardi dropped his dispassionate facade. The number of unreliable works being produced he found to be a cause of grave concern. 'Anyone who knows how to register credits and debits in a ledger book indiscriminately and temerariously takes up history writing.'[35] Nevertheless, the writing of history, he pointed out, was not merely a leisure time activity. It required 'very long study' and the perfection, through experience, of 'a mature and perfect judgement,' not to mention specific techniques for gathering evidence concerning political behaviour. No one, he said, would be so foolish as to commission a sculpture from a cobbler or a suit of clothes from a baker. Yet something of the kind was happening in historiography. As a result of current fashion, 'an entire population of writers has arisen, who are filling the world with paper and putting printers to work.'[36]

Among the many causes that tipped the scales in the later seventeenth century toward a more radical scepticism than Mascardi and his contemporaries were earlier able to muster, the spread of misinformation and falsehood certainly played an important role. Nor was political information the only field to experience a new wave of scepticism toward the end of the century. There were also science and philosophy.

The questioning of methods and approaches that went on in science and philosophy had powerful collateral effects on the way readers, writers, thinkers, and theorists in this period viewed contemporary accounts of political reality. For one thing, the new experimental and experiential science became in some ways the victim of its own success.[37] Even Galileo's erstwhile enemies, the Jesuits, began to abandon Aristotelianism for a more eclectic and experience-oriented intellectual system by this time.[38] Yet excessive confidence in observation and experiment began to give way to diminished enthusiasm for the empirical attitudes of the Galileian and Baconian schools.

And in order to see a promising new field like microscopy as an example of the new caution about observation, there is no need to belittle its remarkable contributions to the developing sciences of embryology, subtle anatomy, and botany, nor to inflate disagreements between Robert Hooke in England, Jan Swammerdam and Antoni van Leeuwenhoeck in Holland, and Marcello Malpighi in Bologna into sceptical sparring matches.[39] Seized upon in the second half of the seventeenth century among enthusiasts throughout Europe as the tool that would force nature to reveal its innermost parts, just as the outermost ones were coming into view in telescopic astronomy, the new field gradually began to give away to disillusionment and doubt. The closer the observer appeared to get to the tiny structures that were the object of his researches, the more those tiny structures appeared to reveal aspects that could only be half seen or not at all. Imperfections in glassmaking and lens polishing combined with entoptical irregularities to create appearances of the most unbiological sorts. And even when the observations were correct, verbal description seemed as inadequate as graphic representation to convey what the researcher claimed to have seen. Leeuwenhoeck himself cautioned against the multitude of fallacious viewings that were pouring in even to a respected organ like the *Philosophical Transactions* of the Royal Society. He was able to unmask fraudulent researchers who loaded their instruments with devices to produce special effects. But he was unable to dispel the scepticism surrounding his own supposed observation of the microscopic man-shaped beings – the so-called animalicula – forming the active agents in human sperm. And explanations of even the most accurate observations of the invisible structure of things seemed to provide the researcher with only a larger, closer-up version of the same inscrutable appearances, without arriving at truths about the purposes of those structures or how they functioned.

To those who were disillusioned with empiricism, Descartes answered the appeal for a philosophy that might offer epistemological justification for the predominance of reason over sensory perception.[40] And the ideas of Descartes along with the commentaries and critiques by Antoine Arnauld and Nicholas Malebranche began spreading throughout the Continent in the second half of the century.[41] However, in borrowing Descartes' ideas, these thinkers also borrowed Descartes' anti-rhetorical bias. They had no use for methods oriented toward pursuing information about affairs of no enduring moral significance. If certainty was to be obtained via methodical doubt and the systematic unveiling of truths beginning with those already present in the mind, knowledge about politics would have to be relegated to the realm of myth.

However, the sheet-anchor of reason and introspection provided by Descartes was not for everyone. And in England, those who failed to be sustained by the sheet-anchor of empiricism offered in response to Descartes by a defiant tradition proceeding most recently through Robert Boyle, found themselves in dangerous waters indeed. And John Wilmot, the earl of Rochester, spoke for all those with no sufficient answer to the apparent impossibility of gaining secure knowledge about the world, by harking back to the sceptical traditions of Agrippa von Nettesheim at the beginning of the century:

> I'd be a dog, a monkey or a bear
> Or any thing but that vain animal
> Who is so proud of being rational.
> The senses are too gross, and he'll contrive
> A sixth, to contradict the other five.
> And before certain instinct, will prefer
> Reason, which fifty times for one does err.[42]

And at least according to Gilbert Burnet, his biographer, the earl believed in absolutely nothing.[43]

While Rochester doubted everything, the Florentine diplomat and virtuoso Lorenzo Magalotti agreed with the *cogito* principle affirmed by Descartes. But he followed Malebranche in returning to St Augustine for a psychological theory. No thinking substance, Magalotti reasoned, could be so complex as to will and not will at the same time, to divide itself, as he said, into 'Ego' and 'Io,' and to operate instantaneously.[44] Clearly, the correct analysis was that the corrupt human will was in conflict with the original purity of human nature. And Descartes' theory of animals as machines, derived from clear and distinct ideas concerning the nature of the mental substance, was no less improbable than the vortex-filled cosmos he derived from the properties of matter in motion; and neither was any more persuasive than the accepted views he claimed to sweep away by systematic doubt.[45] For Magalotti, all this was yet another proof that the Moderns had vastly exaggerated their superiority over the Ancients. 'I still wonder whether they come any closer to the truth than someone who starts at the number one and keeps counting to infinity.'[46]

In fact, for Magalotti, the absence of certainty about the world around, about contemporary and past affairs, about the nature of the elements, the organization of the cosmos and the cures for the simplest ailments was not just a reminder about the weakness of human reason. In such circumstances, he concluded, the safest harbour for the troubled soul was in the truths of faith.[47]

He took contemporary historiography as an example. Harking back to arguments and developed by Mascardi and so many others, he noted the damage done to the truth by passions and interests. Even the most scrupulous and insightful historian, recounting things he did himself, might have to deceive and dissemble in order to save his own skin. Supposing he wished to tell the truth about events in his immediate vicinity, he was likely to encounter some of the most serious problems of verification. He could not rely on the news. 'I think you know how difficult it is to discover the truth about a solitary battle that is no more than four leagues away from the court in which one writes.'[48] And within the courtly environment where he did his writing, all his influence and all his acquaintances among the powerful might not suffice to help him discover the truth about a conspiracy going on before his very eyes. The actors themselves were often uncertain about their reasons for making decisions. 'I had the fortune,' he explained, 'to be admitted to the secret dealing about a peace treaty, and a war, in our century, whose real reasons are perhaps ... unknown even to this day to those involved and likely to remain so forever.' One could scarcely hope for particularly accurate accounts of such events, even by the protagonists. 'Therefore,' he concluded, 'we must consider, there can be no human history,' either of the past or of the present, 'that is not false in many circumstances.'

All this uncertainty about historical reality was a buttress to faith for Magalotti; not an incitement to scepticism. Because of it, the research of Spinoza and Richard Simon showing the absence of references to biblical events in ancient civic histories was no longer any cause for alarm. Magalotti's reasoning went like this: existing ancient civic histories were obviously full of falsehoods; so divinely inspired history could scarcely avoid conflicting with them. Indeed, because of this very conflict, ecclesiastical history might be true. 'This [conflict] may not be a proof of the divinity [of these accounts]; but it is at least an indication of the possibility of their divinity.' Modern civic histories and news media were even worse. With no better information, belief, he said, echoing Pascal, was the best bet. And there was no need to resort to the rational arguments for faith suggested by Vitus Erbermann, Johann Musaeus, and so many others.[49]

Magalotti was not alone. His Rotterdam-based contemporary Pierre Bayle also turned scepticism about a system of political communication dominated by the passions and the interests into part of a much broader questioning of the usual sources of knowledge.[50] Concentrating his attention on the wars of words between late seventeenth-century Catholics and Protestants, he wondered if the truth about any event described by one or the other side could ever really be known. And when the errors of historical works were compounded by reliance on reports and documents spread about by newspaper writers seeking fast gain by sensationalism and flattery, the unreliability of the result was enough to lead the serious reader to distraction. 'There is no greater mischief,' he remarked, 'than that which can be exercised upon historical monuments.'[51] Consequently, he supposed, many of his contemporaries had stopped believing history at all. 'And their conclusion begins with the newspapers, and extends to the whole range of civil historians, who compile their rhapsodies out of nothing but these miserable sources.'[52] The only mistake of the true sceptics, he believed, was in taking the lack of proof about the existence of worldly things as a cause for atheism rather than an incitement to fall back upon fideism. The truths of faith are probably not, he argued, susceptible to rational understanding at all.[53]

Yet, by the late seventeenth century, media criticism had reached something of an impasse. Nearly everything there was to say about the defects of information had already been said. Nearly every possible explanation for the departures from the truth had already been made. Common sense suggested that defective information did not make life impossible. Let the sceptic simply examine the divergent accounts with a critical eye, wrote Jean Le Clerc, the history theorist. Anyone who, having done that, still routinely doubted everything he read, must be 'a madman.'[54]

Moreover, the same new epistemology that showed the way out of the tunnel of philosophical scepticism also showed the way out of political scepticism. A new notion of truth as the sum of probabilities rather than an absolute fact began to gain ground. The real natures of many things in our experience were now thought to be simply unknowable except by a descriptive account of them, such as by an observer. Let the pursuit of absolute exactitude be limited to the exact sciences, John Locke said; and let us not try to pursue it where it cannot be found. 'It is vain to expect demonstration and certainty in the things not capable of it. ... He that, in the ordinary affairs of life, would admit of nothing but direct plain demonstration would be sure of nothing in this world but of perishing quickly.'[55]

And indeed, by the early eighteenth century, the sceptical crisis seemed to be little more than a bad dream. Even epistemologists like George Berkeley no longer found the radical critique of experience to be a cause for despair. In the field of historiography, the promise of the new methodological advances of Jean Le Clerc and the School of St Maur helped lighten the shadow cast by inaccurate narrations. More widespread knowledge of the nature of the historian's art lowered expectations that had soared too high; and Giambattista Vico insisted that, below the surface of various reports, a knowable past surely existed somewhere in the bedrock of human memory. The point was relevant for any kind of narrative, including newspapers. However doubtful readers might be concerning the information in their midst, experience itself was intact.

But let us return to the question with which we began. In political affairs, could a public sphere exist in a sea of doubt? Gregorio Leti, in the passages quoted earlier, seemed to think so. Indeed, falsehood and fraud were themselves likely to become the subjects of public discussions; and debates about responsibility for such defects cast aspersions on the governments who tainted the news. Then, there was no telling when wagging tongues might release 'the poison of discord' that could 'turn monarchies into republics.' And according to the hired historian Vittorio Siri, the court of public opinion was always in session: 'The universality of men is an inexorable tribunal instituted by nature so that with the fullest liberty of judgement, it may pronounce not only on the actions of princes but on those of private or low condition, to allot to them the blame or the praise they deserve.' Whether those judgements were to be based on accurate information depended, in large part, upon whether it was financially convenient for writers and entrepreneurs to improve their standards. Only one thing was certain: political information was not going to go away.

Notes

1 Secondo Lancellotti, *L'Hoggidì*, vol. 2: *Gli ingegni non inferiori a' passati* (Venice: Guerigli, 1662, orig. ed., 1630), p. 352.
2 Quoted in Ian Atherton, 'The Itch Grown a Disease: Manuscript Transmission of News in the Seventeenth Century,' Joad Raymond, ed., *News, Newspapers and Society in Early Modern Britain* (London, 1999), p. 39.
3 Concerning these problems, interesting perspectives are offered by the papers collected from the conferences at Göttingen, 1990, and Paris, 1993, in, respectively, Hans Erich Bödeker, ed., *Histoires du livre: nouvelles orientations* (Paris, 1995); and Roger Chartier, ed., *Histoires de la lecture: un bilan des recherches* (Paris, 1995).
4 Rome, Biblioteca Apostolica, Stampati Barberini QII 45, *Colonia*, 30 March 1659: 'A Lubecca è stata partorita una creatura con due teste, quattro bracci, e quattro gambe, la quale creatura si morè [*sic*] di lè a pochi giorni. E nella Marcha di Brendenburgo pianse una creaturina nel ventre della madre, che si potè udire benissimo, la cui significazione è nota solo a Dio....' The *Riminio*'s rain of blood is in Nevio Matteini, *Il 'Rimino', una delle prime gazzette d'Italia* (Bologna, 1967), p. 42.
5 These debates have been outlined in excellent studies by Richard H. Popkin, *The History of Skepticism from Erasmus to Spinoza* (Berkeley, 1979); Carlo Borghero, *Le certezze e la storia: Cartesianismo, Pirronismo e conoscenza storica* (Milan, 1983); not to mention, from a very different point of view, Alan Charles Kors, *Atheism in France, 1651–1729, vol. 1: The Orthodox Sources of Disbelief* (Princeton, 1990); and Sergio Zoli, *Europa libertina tra Controriforma e Illuminismo* (Bologna, 1989), updating René Pintard, *Le libertinage érudit dans la premièe moitié du XVIIe siècle*, 2 vols (Paris, 1943).
6 Gregorio Leti, *Dialoghi politici, ovvero la politica che usano in questo tempo i principi e repubbliche italiani per conservare i loro stati e signorie* (Geneva: Chouet, 1666), 1: 255.
7 Here and below, Grabriele Tontoli, *Il Masaniello ovvero discorsi narrativi la sollevazione di Napoli* (Naples: Mollo, 1648), L'autore a chi legge.
8 *Successi hisorici degli acquisti della Serenissima Repubblica di Venezia in Levante* (Venice: Parè, 1688), Preface.
9 A preliminary bibliography for this literature is Sergio Bertelli, *Ribelli, libertini ed ortodossi nella storiografia barocca* (Florence, 1973), chap. 8.
10 Vittorio Siri, *Mercurio*, vol. 15 (Florence: Della Nave, 1682), p. 813.
11 Pier Giovanni Capriata, *Dell'Historie*, vol. 2 (Genoa: Farroni, 1649), Al lettore.
12 Luca Assarino, *Delle guerre e dei successi d'Italia*, vol. 1 (Turin: Zavatta, 1665), p. 1.
13 Maiolino Bisaccioni, *Historia delle guerre civili di questi ultimi tempi* (Venice: Francesco Storti, 1653), p. 87.
14 *Successi istorici della Serenissima Repubblica di Venezia in Levante* (Venice: Giovanni Parè, 1688), p. 8.
15 *Dialoghi politici*, 1: 258.
16 Enrico Jovane, *Il primo giornalismo torinese* (Turin, 1938), p. 61; Ugo Bellocchi, *Storia del giornalismo italiano*, 8 vols (Bologna, 1974–76), 3: 39–43. In addition, Andrew Mousley, 'Self, State and Seventeenth-Century News,' *The Seventeenth Century* 6 (1991), p. 159, and Howard M. Solomon, *Public Welfare, Science and Propaganda in Seventeenth-Century France: The Innovations of Théophraste Renaudot* (Princeton, 1972), p. 149.
17 Achille Neri, 'Curiose avventure di Luca Assarino, genovese, storico, romanziere e giornalista del secolo XVII,' *Giornale ligustico di archeologia, storia e belle arti* 2 (1875): 14.

18 Rome, Archivio di Stato (henceforth ASR), *Cartari-Febei*, 73, fol. 187ff, *Descrizione delle cerimonie fatte dentro e fuori del conclave avanti e dopo la creazione del Sommo Pontefice Innocenzo X* (Rome: Marcioni, 1644).
19 Walter Ong, *Orality and Literacy: The Technologizing of the Word* (London: Routledge, 1982), p. 132.
20 Cited in Daniel R. Woolf, *The Idea of History in Early Stuart England* (Toronto, 1990), p. 248. On the subject, Royce Macgillivray, *Restoration Historians and the English Civil War* (The Hague, 1974).
21 Butler's comments are in *Characters and Passages from Notebooks*, ed. A. R. Waller (Cambridge, 1908), p. 375. For Thomas Hobbes' view of contemporary historians, see Fritz Levy, 'The Background of Hobbes' *Behemoth*,' in Donald R. Kelley and David Harris Sacks, eds, *The Historical Imagination in Early Modern Britain. History, Rhetoric and Fiction, 1500–1800* (Cambridge, 1997), p. 226.
22 *Dictionnaire historique et critique*, 4 vols (Amsterdam: 1740), II: 634. Further examples are in III: 274.
23 *Dictionnaire historique et critique*, II: 8.
24 *Dictionnaire historique et critique*, IV: 582.
25 Sarpi's recommendations are in *Scritti giurisdizionalistici*, ed. Giovanni Gambarin (Bari, 1958), pp. 213–20. Malvezzi's are in *Discorsi sopra Cornelio Tacito. Al Serenissimo Duca Ferdinando II granduca di Toscana* (Venice: Ginami, 1622), discourse 28.
26 *The Art of Worldly Wisdom*, tr. Joseph Jacobs (Boston, 1993), maxim no. 130. Concerning this whole problem in early Modern Europe, there is the exhaustive study by Perez Zagorin, *Ways of Lying: Dissimulation, Persecution and Conformity in Early Modern Europe* (Cambridge, MA, 1990).
27 *The Art of Worldly Wisdom*, no. 13.
28 *Della dissimulazione onesta*, ed. Salvatore S. Nigro (Genoa, 1983 [1st ed. Naples: 1641]), chap. 25.
29 Cited in Alberto Asor Rosa, *La Cultura della Controriforma*, Letteratura italiana Laterza, 26 (Milan, 1974), p. 104. A recent critical appraisal is in Maurizio Viroli, *From Politics to Reason of State. The Acquisition and Transformation of the Language of Politics, 1250–1600* (Cambridge, 1992), pp. 257–67, which now surpasses the previous treatment of Friedrich Meinecke, *Die Idee der Staatsräson in der neueren Geschichte* (Munich and Berlin, 1924), chap. 3. Still useful for biographical information is the entry by Luigi Firpo in *Dizionario biografico degli Italiani* 11 (1969): 10–19.
30 Traiano Boccalini, *Ragguagli di Parnaso*, vol. 1, ed. Giuseppe Rua (Bari, 1910), Century 1, no. 29, p. 91.
31 *Ragguagli di Parnaso*, vol. 2, ed. Giuseppe Rua (Bari, 1910), Century 2, no. 71.
32 Mascardi, *Dell'arte istorica* (Florence: Le Monnier, 1859 [1st. ed. Rome, 1636]), Second Treatise, chap. 2, p. 94. Concerning Mascardi and his context there is also Rodolfo De Mattei, 'Storia e politica in Italia tra il Cinque e il Seicento,' in *Storiografia e storia: studi in onore di Eugenio Dupré Theseider* (Rome, 1974), 2 vols, pp. 876–8.
33 Mascardi, *Dell'arte istorica*, 2nd treatise, chap. 2, p. 92.
34 Mascardi, *Dell'arte istorica*, 2nd treatise, chap. 2, p. 96.
35 Mascardi, *Dell'arte istorica*, 1st treatise, chap. 2, pp. 34–5.
36 Mascardi, *Dell'arte istorica*, 3rd treatise, chap. 1, p. 160.
37 The closest to a philosophical interpretation of these debates is Ugo Baldini, 'La scuola galileiana,' in Gianni Micheli, ed., *Storia d'Italia. Annali 3: Scienza e tecnica nella cultura e nella società dal Rinascimento a oggi* (Turin, 1980), pp. 383–468; in addition, confined to physics, there is Maurizio Torrini, *Dopo Galileo: una polemica scientifica* (Florence, 1979). Michael Segre, *In the Wake of Galileo* (New Brunswick, 1991) somewhat misses the larger intellectual context. A useful survey is *Scienziati del Seicento* (Milan and Naples, 1980), eds Maria Luisa Altieri Biagi and Bruno Basile, La Letteratura Italiana storia e testi, vol. 34, part 2.

38 Gabriele Baroncini, 'L'insegnamento della filosofia naturale nei collegi italiani dei Gesuiti, 1610–1670: un esempio di nuovo aristotelismo,' in Gian Paolo Brizzi, ed., *La 'Ratio Studiorum': modelli culturali e pratiche educative dei Gesuiti in Italia tra Cinque e Seicento* (Rome, 1981), pp. 163–216; Ugo Baldini, *Legem impone subactis: studi su filosofia e scienza dei Gesuiti in Italia, 1540–1632* (Rome, 1992).
39 The following is an interpretation of much information in Catherine Wilson, *The Invisible World. Early Modern Philosophy and the Invention of the Microscope* (Princeton, 1995). A more positivist picture is traced by Marian Fournier, *The Fabric of Life. Microscopy in the Seventeenth Century* (Baltimore, 1996).
40 Gassendi of course offered a sense-oriented alternative. See Margaret Osler, *Divine Will and the Mechanical Philosophy. Gassendi and Descartes on Contingency and Necessity* (Cambridge, 1994), p. 49.
41 A helpful antidote to much writing about Descartes' position is M. Glouberman, *Descartes: The Probable and the Certain* (Amsterdam, 1986). An attempt, not entirely satisfactory, to synthesize the various elements in the Italian case is Claudio Manzoni, *I cartesiani italiani (1660–1760)* (Udine, 1984), revising and updating the previous work of L. Berthè de Besaucèe, *Les cartésiens d'Italie* (Paris, 1920). Probably the first explicit précis of Descartes' position published in Italy was Matteo Giorgi's *Saggio della nuova dottrina di Renato Des-Cartes. Lettera all'Ill.mo Sig. Tommaso Fransone* (Genoa: 1694).
42 'A Satyr Against Reason and Mankind,' *The Complete Poems of John Wilmot, Earl of Rochester*, ed. David M. Vieth (New Haven, 1968), lines 5–11.
43 Gilbert Burnet, 'Life and Death of the Earl of Rochester', in *Lives, Characters and An Address to Posterity* (London, 1833), pp. 210–11.
44 *Lettere familiari* (Venice: Baglioni, 1762), 2 vols. in 1, 1: letter 19. The letters, dated in the 1680s, are analysed by Mario Praz, *Lettere sopra i buccheri con l'aggiunta di lettere contro l'ateismo* (Florence, 1945) and Massimo Baldini, *Magalotti: religione e scienza nel Seicento* (Brescia, 1984). Magalotti's career is analysed in Eric Cochrane, *Florence in the Forgotten Centuries* (Chicago, 1973), book 4.
45 *Lettere familiari*, 1: letter 22.
46 *Lettere familiari*, 1: letter 13.
47 *Lettere familiari*, 2: letter 5.
48 *Lettere familiari*, 1: letter 10, p. 156. The following quotes are from this and the previous page.
49 Compare Susan Rosa, 'Seventeenth-Century Catholic Polemic and the Rise of Cultural Rationalism: An Example from the Empire,' *Journal of the History of Ideas* 57 (1996): 87–107.
50 Bayle's relation to Cartesianism is explored by Ciro Senofonte, *Pierre Bayle: dal Calvinismo all'Illuminismo* (Naples, 1978). The historical theory is outlined by Ruth Whelan, *The Anatomy of Superstition: A Study of the Historical Theory and Practice of Pierre Bayle* (Oxford, 1989). For everything else, the authority is still Elisabeth Labrousse, *Pierre Bayle* (The Hague, 1963–64), 2 vols.
51 *Critique génerale de l'histoire du Calvinisme*, in *Dictionnaire historique et critique* (Amsterdam, 1740), 4 vols, IV, appendix, p. 10.
52 *Critique génerale de l'histoire du Calvinisme*, p. 13.
53 *Dictionnaire historique et critique*, s.v. 'Pyrrho,' also in *Historical and Critical Dictionary*, ed. Richard Popkin (New York, 1965), pp. 194–209.
54 From Jean Le Clerc, 'La verité de la religion chrétienne,' appended to his *De l'incredulité* (Amsterdam, 1696), read in the English translation published in London for John Churchill, 1697. Le Clerc's methodological reflections are in his *Ars critica* (Amsterdam: George Gallet, 1697), 3 vols.
55 *Essay Concerning Human Understanding*, ed. John W. Yolton, (London: Dent, 1961), 2 vols, 2: 233. Concerning this aspect of Locke's philosophy, consider Barbara J. Shapiro, *Probability and Certainty in Seventeenth-Century England* (Princeton, 1983), chap. 2; as well as Steven Shapin, *A Social History of Truth* (Chicago, 1994), chap. 5.

Postscript

Brendan Dooley

Probably the best shorthand account of the effect of the printing press on early modern civilization comes from Fernand Braudel: 'It enlarged and invigorated everything.'[1] Of course, different products of the printing press enlarged and invigorated things in different ways. One commonplace set of products, studied in this book, diffused information about political occurrences to readers in urban areas on a regular basis. These products almost certainly helped bring about important changes in political and social relations. The contributors to this book have shown that their emergence and diffusion occurred everywhere at different rates, with corresponding variations in their impact and long-term effects.

But coming to the subject, so to speak, from within, there is one question that none of our contributors has confronted head-on: namely, why Europe, and indeed, why the seventeenth century? One conclusion seems inescapable. The technological achievement was immense – not only the use of the printing press for turning political information into a material object, but the formation of networks of writers, entrepreneurs, and vendors necessary to turn it into a commodity. And the European experiences we have traced were in many ways unique. Let us now view our results in global terms.

Comparisons across wide geographical areas and chronological periods are always risky, and particularly so in the present context. Taking into account, in each case, all of the variables that defined the complex European information networks we have been analysing would require at least another book. In fact, the essays here have demonstrated that there was more to early modern communications than just the printed word. Presumably even in the parts of the world where printed political communications did not emerge, some form of distribution of what we would regard as political communications was going on – by way of village criers, official messengers, broadsheets, and so on. Some of the essays in this volume touch on the fact that manuscript and oral transmission remained vital and crucial even as the printing press came into its own. One would hope that any complete study of communications in a global perspective would be able to evaluate these forms on their own terms.

Nor can we ignore the direct effect of European communications mechanisms on the rest of the world. Once the new patterns were established, they were there to stay. Something in the world had changed forever and the

European experience became a model for elsewhere. Where there were no autochthonous news publications, European ones were often available. This media colonization of the non-European world may even have smothered independent efforts from time to time, just as the importation of French-language newspapers from Holland during the time of Louis XIV may occasionally have comforted the avoidance of large-scale political publishing in France, and the importation of like publications from England retarded publishing in North America. So there is no way of telling how political information might have developed in a hypothetical world without Europe.

Certainly, technological changes required the proper combination of human resources as well as the proper combination of circumstances. If the European wars of the early seventeenth century, providing endless material for discussion of their enormous political, social, and economic impact, were not a sufficient catalyst to cause journalism to emerge, the presence of a similarly portentous set of events was surely not enough for anywhere else. Likewise, if a well-developed printing industry existed in Europe for at least a century before political information became a recognizable commodity, the existence of such an industry may not have been a sufficient condition for such changes elsewhere, either. The role of ready readers, writers, and entrepreneurs, all concentrated in the same geographical space in relatively large cities and towns, provides perhaps some sort of answer to the first question: that is, why Europe? But again, these conditions were as closely connected there with all the others as they must have been in the areas outside Europe.

In New England, more extensive communication was not demanded for the first hundred years of settlement, for some obvious reasons.[2] In the Puritan villages, economies were still focused on local production, as little in the way of real exchange with the metropolis could be expected over such long distances. Tiny farming populations were still insufficiently diversified and numerous to support local printing. Information concerning events outside that might affect the religious mission of the settlements, such as the Civil War in England, was conveyed by the circulation of the English newspapers, which, as we have seen, were now being produced in amazing profusion. Whatever was necessary to know about events was exchanged from the pulpit and in the meeting-house. Communication between one village and the next, where necessary for survival, was carried on by word of mouth or by the occasional letter.

Toward the end of the seventeenth century, the situation began to change. Previously autarchic village cultures began to be integrated into a larger economic and social community. As the Puritan vision began to decline, a new ethos of economic development began to emerge. Agricultural surpluses permitted more diversification, and as the shipbuilding industry and the carrying trade contributed to turning Boston, Salem, and Charlestown into commercial entrepôts, internal settlements were tied in as producers of tradable goods. Connections to the rest of the Atlantic world, to other parts of North America, the West Indies, and Europe, became more frequent and more profitable. Affluence increased – in Salem alone, among the top 10 per cent of the population, by nearly three-fold. The assumption of more direct Crown control and the Navigation Acts of 1690, integrating all the colonies into a single self-sufficient economic unit centred in London, actually benefited the more prosperous American merchants, both in direct trade with England and in the exchange of goods elsewhere within the English sphere. The advent of a more tolerant religious climate in England provided a congenial context in which this economy could grow. At this stage, all that prevented the emergence of a political information business, arguably, was the temporary setback caused by the fierce intercolonial warfare that went on between 1689 and 1713.[3]

What finally provided the catalyst for an information business in North America was the series of political convulsions that rocked Europe in the first decades of the eighteenth century. When Charles II of Spain died, leaving his kingdom to the strongest contender, the Act of Settlement establishing the new monarchy of William and Mary in England was still under negotiation. And if Louis XIV succeeded in pressing his claims, there seemed no doubt that a Jacobite restoration in Britain would follow, with who knew what consequences for the American merchants. As the Spanish Succession War unfolded, the merchants depended particularly upon the colonial postmasters to provide them with information that they believed could reduce their riches to rags from one day to the next. And when the trickle of news about this conjuncture turned into a flood, it fell to the postmasters to draw up the first newspapers for publication. The first to do so was John Campbell, postmaster of the city of Boston, who opened his *Boston News-Letter* with news of a phantom Jacobite scare in Scotland in late 1703. Similar efforts followed in every colony.[4]

In Spanish America, even more imposing practical obstacles prevented the development of communications for the first one hundred years.[5] Vast distances isolated settlements from one another and from the metropolis. Although Mexico City exerted strong regional communication control in its hemisphere, some 4,000 miles separated it from Madrid; and another 700 miles separated it from Culiacan, the northern outpost – not to mention the much greater distances to Chile and Peru. And these linear distances were made all the more impractica-ble, in the New World, by rough terrain and hostile neighbours. Whatever incentives there might have been to implement improvements in transportation for reasons of commerce were on the whole vitiated by reasons of security, where isolation was thought to provide some sort of bulwark against invasion. And while the force of the king's writ diminished the farther removed a province was, so did the reliability of information about political events either in the colonies or in Europe.

As the colonial economies developed during the course of the seventeenth century, they began to depend more upon exchange between each other than on exchange with Spain and Europe. With the indigenous labour supply in decline, other sectors of the economy besides large-scale planting and mining began to grow.[6] Investors began to pay more attention to the Pacific trade than to the Atlantic, exchanging wheat, cochineal, sugar, pottery, and textiles for oriental goods to be resold in the colonies. Mexico City replaced Seville as the main entrepôt. What information the merchants and local inhabitants needed about other areas came via commercial correspondence. And while the colonists received whatever news they needed from Spain via the *carrera* along the Spanish corridor and special *avisos* ships designed to carry news,[7] it was no wonder that a new gazette published in the 1660s, possibly a reprint of the one in Madrid, fizzled out after a few numbers for lack of interest.[8]

A political information business developed in New Spain when these comfortable arrangements were threatened by the same Spanish Succession War that worried the neighbours to the North. Exactly what might be the consequences of the replacement of the Habsburg government by a potentially far more meddlesome Bourbon one after 1701, no one could tell. Although the Peace of Utrecht guaranteed that the new dynasty would remain independent and distinct from the French branch, few doubted that in some way Spain and its possessions would be made into tributaries of a dynasty with huge current military obligations in Europe. The only condition that prevented journalism from forming now was a virtual halt in the *carrera* and the *avisos* traffic, which cut the colonies off entirely from the metropolis for nearly ten years.[9] In 1720, the *carrera* resumed and *avisos* boats arrived more frequently than ever before, so Juan Ignacio Castorena y Ursúa was able to start up the *Gaceta de Mexico*.[10]

The conditions for journalism seem to have appeared much later in Brazil. A sugar-based agricultural economy, limited sedentary Indian populations, and severe transportation problems in the interior added to decentralization and retarded urbanization. As in New Spain, industries such as the printing press were forbidden to compete with their metropolitan counterparts; but here there was little impetus to question the policy, since imported Portuguese books seemed sufficient to satisfy readers and there seemed little possibility of creating the commercial networks necessary for a domestic industry.[11] All this began to change in the eighteenth century. Thanks to the efforts of Crown minister Marquis de Pombal to encourage new products in new areas – coffee in Pará and cotton in Maranhão – and to introduce free trade with other colonies, growth was rapid and continuous.[12] The tens of thousands of European immigrants who had come during the gold rush of the 1690s could be absorbed into the diversifying economy. Although at first the new interest in the South of Brazil prevented urban growth in the North to some extent, urban centres solidified in both areas throughout the century; and with Rio de Janeiro having come to equal Mexico City in population, Pombal made it the new capital.

Journalism seems to have emerged in response to Napoleon's conquest of Portugal and subsequent events, which sent the colony reeling in an entirely new direction. Prince Regent D. João and his ministers fled to Brazil in January 1808 and forthwith set up a government-in-exile.[13] With the old system of privileged trade between the colony and Portugal suddenly outmoded, the introduction of free trade with other states and the abolition of monopolies were among the government's first acts. Just how Brazilian affairs would proceed in this suddenly widened context was hard to predict, and trade relations with other European countries seemed indispensable for survival. Information about the wars that were transforming Europe day by day was suddenly in demand. The first to begin providing it was Hipólito José, an Inquisition refugee in London, who set up the *Correio Braziliense* within months of the Prince Regent's arrival and distributed it both in Brazil and in Europe. Soon the royal government in Rio saw to the establishment of a local *Gazeta do Rio de Janeiro*, which was followed in Salvador by the independent *Idade d'ouro do Brasil.*

As we travel further west, the bibliography thins out and the time frame lengthens practically beyond the limits of any meaningful comparison. However, the parallels with the European case are too suggestive for us to resist giving a bare sketch here of what we have been able to discover. In China, the catalyst for the emergence of more regular communications of political news was the open door policy and Westernization. Suddenly after the Opium Wars, the vital importance of affairs in Europe and elsewhere came to be recognized in China. At first, this interest was satisfied by the circulation of the existing foreign-language newspapers in the coastal trading cities.[14] Soon the position of Hong Kong as a Chinese city run by the British permitted the formation of new perspectives on the situation of China within world affairs. Here too, the first newspapers were in English. But around 1850, the first attempts were made to tap the Chinese market with a shipping gazette in Chinese, the *Honkong Hsin-wen.* Subsequently, the pioneer Chinese journalist Wu T'ing-Fang formed the first Chinese-language daily, the *Chung-ngoi san-po* (or *Chung-wai hsin-pao*) in 1860, explicitly to inform local Chinese about affairs in the hinterland as well as about international affairs.[15]

In Japan, Matthew Perry's expedition brought about the opening of trade to other nationalities besides the Dutch monopolists and in other ports besides Nagasaki. Already accustomed to viewing their culture in a larger context because of the age-old question of Chinese superiority, the Japanese aristocracy had no difficulty in turning debate about the new treaties into debates about the nature of Japanese civilization and the dangers of Western ways.[16] Japanese journalism almost from the outset served the developing nationalist movement. After the Meji restoration, the independent *Yokohama Mainichi Shimbun* came out as a frankly political organ of the still-hegemonic aristocracy. As each faction of the aristocracy sought to enlist ever wider constituencies in its support, political reform programmes remained almost constantly in the public view, with each faction managing to silence its adversaries only so long as it remained in control.[17] The next twenty-five years saw a widespread intrusion of journalism into the public space.

Further study of the way in which the regular transmission of printed communications about politics emerged in Europe will no doubt shed more light on later developments elsewhere. Our contributors have already suggested a possible answer to the second of our questions about Europe – namely, why the seventeenth century? We are more and more led to surmise that the peculiar interstate situation there from 1600–1648 was decisive. Perhaps parallel situations later on were decisive in other parts of the world. Some evidence seems to suggest that whenever a political or economic conjuncture threatening the equilibrium of local affairs provoked curiosity about events outside, printers, if such there were, inevitably took up the new genre of newspapers in response to the demand. Not surprisingly, the first papers in most places were almost entirely concerned with foreign news. Only as the papers began providing more and more information about foreign affairs did they begin to turn to local ones, with significant consequences for the organization of power in their countries.

The more one looks at the world history of political behaviour, the more one is impressed by the accomplishment of seventeenth-century Europe. Whether by imitation, by exportation, or by spontaneous parallel development, the model of political communication by written gesture has taken precedence over the model of oral and visual representation all over the world. As we move into a new millennium, media of very different sorts may well prevail; we cannot yet be sure with what effects on everyday life.[18] And if some theorists have already suggested that politics, at least as we know it, may well be obsolete, because of changes in the nature of state sovereignty as well as in the way government decisions are now made, we may ask whether the course of events begun in the early modern period and outlined in these chapters is now coming to an end. To find out, we will certainly be watching the news with renewed curiosity.

Notes

1 Fernand Braudel, *Capitalism and Material Life, 1400–1800*, tr. Miriam Kochan (New York, , 1973; orig. ed. Paris, 1967), p. 299.
2 For what follows, Jack P. Greene, *Pursuits of Happiness. The Social Development of Early Modern British Colonies and the Formation of American Culture* (Chapel Hill, 1988), chs. 2–3. In addition, Helmut Lehmann-Haupt, *The Book in America* (New York, 1951).
3 Bernard Bailyn, *The New England Merchants in the Seventeenth Century* (Cambridge, MA, 1955), chap. 5.
4 James Melvin Lee, *History of American Journalism* (Boston, 1917), p. 17. Compare Jack P. Greene, *Pursuits of Happiness*, ch. 8.
5 For what follows, Lyle N. McAlister, *Spain and Portugal in the New World, 1492–1700* (Minneapolis, 1984), chs. 15, 17. In addition, J. H. Elliott, 'Spain and America in the Sixteenth and Seventeenth Centuries,' in Leslie Bethell, ed., *The Cambridge History of Latin America, vol. 1: Colonial Latin America* (Cambridge, 1984), pp. 287–340; Jacques La Farge, 'Literature and Intellectual Life in Spanish America,' *ibid.*, pp. 676–7; John J. TePaske and Herbert S. Klein, 'The Seventeenth-Century Crisis in New Spain: Myth or Reality?,' *Past and Present* 90 (1981): 123–4.
6 Lyle N. McAlister, *Spain and Portugal*, pp. 379–80.
7 Donald E. Worcester and Wendell G. Schaeffer, *The Growth and Culture of Latin America* (Oxford, 1971), pp. 188 ff, 282.
8 Carlos Rizzini, *O livro, o journal e a tipografia no Brasil, 1500–1822* (Rio de Janeiro and São Paolo, 1946), p. 105.
9 Murdo J. Macleod, 'Spain and America: The Atlantic Trade 1492–1720,' in Leslie Bethell, ed., *Cambridge History of Latin America*, 1: 385.
10 Compare Jorge I. Domínguez, *Insurrection or Loyalty. The Breakdown of the Spanish American Empire* (Cambridge, MA, 1980).
11 Donald E. Worcester and Wendell G. Schaeffer, *The Growth and Culture of Latin America*, p. 166.
12 Donald E. Worcester and Wendell G. Schaeffer, *The Growth and Culture of Latin America*, pp. 257 ff.

13 Leslie Bethell, 'Literature and Intellectual Life, Brazil,' in Leslie Bethell, ed., *The Cambridge History of Latin America*, 1: 706–7.

14 H. P. Tseng, 'China prior to 1949,' in John A. Lent, ed., *The Asian Newspapers' Reluctant Revolution* (Ames, Iowa, 1971), pp. 31–42.

15 Linda P. Shin, 'The New Coastal Reformers,' in Paul A. Cohen and John E. Schrecker, eds, *Reform in Nineteenth-Century China* (Cambridge, MA, 1976), p. 266.

16 W. G. Beasley, *The Meji Restoration* (Stanford, 1972).

17 Hisao Komatsubara, 'Japan,' in John A. Lent, ed., *The Asian Newspapers' Reluctant Revolution*, p. 68; Albert A. Altman, 'Towards a Comparative Study of the Emergence of the Press in Japan and China,' in Ian Nish, ed., *Contemporary European Writing on Japan* (Woodchurch, Ashford, Kent, 1988).

18 Consider, for instance, Andreas Schedler, ed., *The End of Politics? Explorations into Modern Antipolitics* (London, 1997), as well as G. J. Mulgan, *Politics in an Antipolitical Age* (Cambridge, 1994).

Index